Mobile Technologies and Socio–Economic Development in Emerging Nations

Fredrick Japhet Mtenzi
Dublin Institute of Technology, Ireland & Aga Khan University, Tanzania

George S. Oreku
Open University of Tanzania (OUT), Tanzania

Dennis M. Lupiana
Institute of Finance Management, Tanzania

Jim James Yonazi
Tanzania Standard (Newspapers) Limited, Tanzania

A volume in the Advances in Wireless Technologies and Telecommunication (AWTT) Book Series

Published in the United States of America by
    IGI Global
    Information Science Reference (an imprint of IGI Global)
    701 E. Chocolate Avenue
    Hershey PA, USA 17033
    Tel: 717-533-8845
    Fax: 717-533-8661
    E-mail: cust@igi-global.com
    Web site: http://www.igi-global.com

Library of Congress Cataloging-in-Publication Data

Names: Mtenzi, Fredrick, editor.
Title: Mobile technologies and socio-economic development in emerging nations
  / Fredrick Japhet Mtenzi, [and three others], editor.
Description: Hershey, PA : Information Science Reference, [2018]
Identifiers: LCCN 2017026834| ISBN 9781522540298 (hardcover) | ISBN
  9781522540304 (ebook)
Subjects: LCSH: Information technology--Economic aspects--Developing
  countries. | Mobile communication systems--Developing countries.
Classification: LCC HC59.72.I55 M63 2018 | DDC 303.48/33091724--dc23 LC record available at
https://lccn.loc.gov/2017026834

This book is published in the IGI Global book series Advances in Wireless Technologies and Telecommunication (AWTT) (ISSN: 2327-3305; eISSN: 2327-3313)

British Cataloguing in Publication Data
A Cataloguing in Publication record for this book is available from the British Library.

For electronic access to this publication, please contact: eresources@igi-global.com.

Advances in Wireless Technologies and Telecommunication (AWTT) Book Series

ISSN:2327-3305
EISSN:2327-3313

Editor-in-Chief: Xiaoge Xu, Xiamen University Malaysia, Malaysia

MISSION

The wireless computing industry is constantly evolving, redesigning the ways in which individuals share information. Wireless technology and telecommunication remain one of the most important technologies in business organizations. The utilization of these technologies has enhanced business efficiency by enabling dynamic resources in all aspects of society.

The **Advances in Wireless Technologies and Telecommunication Book Series** aims to provide researchers and academic communities with quality research on the concepts and developments in the wireless technology fields. Developers, engineers, students, research strategists, and IT managers will find this series useful to gain insight into next generation wireless technologies and telecommunication.

COVERAGE

- Broadcasting
- Wireless Sensor Networks
- Mobile Communications
- Mobile Technology
- Grid Communications
- Telecommunications
- Cellular Networks
- Virtual Network Operations
- Mobile Web Services
- Wireless Technologies

IGI Global is currently accepting manuscripts for publication within this series. To submit a proposal for a volume in this series, please contact our Acquisition Editors at Acquisitions@igi-global.com or visit: http://www.igi-global.com/publish/.

Titles in this Series

For a list of additional titles in this series, please visit:
https://www.igi-global.com/book-series/advances-wireless-technologies-telecommunication/73684

For an entire list of titles in this series, please visit:
https://www.igi-global.com/book-series/advances-wireless-technologies-telecommunication/73684

701 East Chocolate Avenue, Hershey, PA 17033, USA
Tel: 717-533-8845 x100 • Fax: 717-533-8661
E-Mail: cust@igi-global.com • www.igi-global.com

Table of Contents

Detailed Table of Contents

Chapter 1
Mobile Phone Usage in Agricultural Extension in India: The Current and
Future Perspective...1
    Chandan Kumar Panda, Bihar Agricultural University, India

This chapter describes how the rural economy of India is basically agrarian in nature
and agriculture is the life and livelihood of maximum number of rural people. As
per Census 2011 of India there are about 95.8 million cultivators and out of which
about 80 percent of farmers are marginal and small. Information asymmetry,
'Information-haves' and 'information-have-nots', digital divide was once major
paradox of Indian Extension system. Through the mKisan platform, 152 crore SMSs
have sent till date to the Indian farmers in the subjects of weather information, pest
management, market price, quality seed, etc. In addition, the Kisan Call Centre
(KCC) Service, the Buyer Seller Platform, and mobile apps viz. Kisan Suvidha,
IFFCO Kisan Agriculture, Pusa Krishi, Krishi Gyan, Crop Insurance, AgriMarket,
etc., are consistently supporting the farmers. In the future more farmers will be
brought under this mobile-based service.

Chapter 2
Implications of the Proposed Communication Service Tax Bill on the Socio-
Economic Development of Nigeria..22
    Benjamin Enahoro Assay, Delta State Polytechnic Ogwashi-Uku,
    Nigeria

This chapter describes how the decision of the Nigerian government to introduce a
Communication Service Tax Bill to the National Assembly to compel consumers
of certain communication services to pay a 9 percent tax has pitted the government
against major stakeholders in the ICT sector who are concerned about the future of

the industry. While the government wants the legislative process regarding the bill to go on because of the financial gains that will accrue to it monthly, the stakeholders want it jettisoned for fear that it would impact negatively on the ICT sector and the economy, which is currently in recession. This chapter wades through the controversy by presenting the various positions canvassed by stakeholders and points the way ahead for the sector, which is fast becoming the hub of economic activities in Nigeria, to harness its full potentials for the overall benefit of the Nigerian society.

Chapter 3

This chapter describes how mobile technologies have recently emerged as the new wave in Information Technology revolution and are constantly gaining importance and popularity in nearly every avenue of our working and social lives. One area of mobile technology that has become a focus in recent times is the use of mobile devices particularly the mobile phones for an array of financial services. Mobile financial services and their massive adoption and rapid spread in the developing world, has deepened investments in mobile infrastructure and has further contributed to financial inclusion and economic development. Their adoption, in particular, has had a significant impact on consumer financial behaviour. This chapter builds on a rich body of literature available to highlight the impact of mobile financial services on consumer financial behaviour and the implications for financial institutions.

Chapter 4

This chapter describes how the Ebola virus is considered extremely infectious with a series of physical and psychological traumas on the victims. Common clinical signs associated with the disease include a sudden fever, severe headaches, muscle pain, fatigue, diarrhea, vomiting, and unexplained hemorrhages. In Africa, with strained medical facilities and remote localities, prompt identification and diagnosis of the symptoms of Ebola in a suspected patient are important to the control of the epidemic and in curtailing further spread. This chapter presents the development of an Android mobile application called EbolaDiag (Ebola Diagnosis), which is capable of supporting the diagnosis, screening, and healthcare experts working on the frontline in contact tracing and monitoring of the spread of Ebola. Furthermore,

EbolaDiag is suitable for aiding the strained medical facilities in endemic areas. In addressing this gap, the application provided a model for implementing such solutions in pandemic environments. Such a solution becomes more relevant and useful to combat Ebola and several other diseases in similar environments.

Chapter 5

Emmanuel Awuni Kolog, University of Eastern Finland, Finland
Samuel Nana Adekson Tweneboah, University of Oulu, Finland
Samuel Nii Odoi Devine, Presbyterian University College, Ghana
Anthony Kuffour Adusei, Ghana Technology University College, Ghana

This chapter describes how today's technology has provided flexibility for teachers and students to engage in academic discourse irrespective of the location. However, there is an ongoing debate regarding the influence of mobile devices on students' academic engagement and performance. Following this debate, these authors empirically investigate the use of mobile device and its impact on teaching and learning in Ghana. Therefore, students, teachers and Ghana Education Service staff were selected to respond to a questionnaire with a follow up interview. After that, the authors analysed the content of the collected data using mixed research method. The results show that students are disallowed to use mobile devices while in school. However, the participants believe that mobile devices are useful for teaching and learning, especially for mobile learning. In line with the participants' perception of the use of mobile devices in schools, this chapter recommends that the government and other stakeholders of education in Ghana allow students to use mobile devices under restricted and regulated conditions.

Chapter 6

Joseph Kwame Adjei, Ghana Institute of Management and Public Administration, Ghana
Solomon Odei-Appiah, Ghana Institute of Management and Public Administration, Ghana

This chapter describes a recent World Bank report which indicated a sizable percentage of households in developing countries do not have access to formal accounts with financial institutions. The situation has created a major barrier in the quest for a world without poverty due to the exclusion of segments of society from the formal financial system. The phenomenon has resulted in the exclusion of many from traditional financial services, thus the use of other means to conduct informal financial transactions. In Ghana, many households rely on domestic informal forms of remittance to relatives and payments. Such informal mediums of remitting money to and from relatives in Ghana (e.g. via "Bus Driver") received wide patronage irrespective of the associated risks until mobile financial services were introduced. This chapter discussed Mobile Financial Services (MFS) from the perspective of emerging economy and treats the following topics; technology, adoption and the regulatory issues in MFS.

Chapter 7

Sunday Adewale Olaleye, University of Oulu, Finland
Ismaila Temitayo Sanusi, University of Eastern Finland, Finland
Dandison C. Ukpabi, University of Jyväskylä, Finland

This chapter describes how mobile money is an emerging and innovative financial service delivery mechanism. With huge success, recorded mostly in the developing economies, it is scholarly unclear the antecedents of its adoption. Using a survey of 151 respondents comprising both the banked and underbanked in the South-Western part of Nigeria, the authors used the PLS-SEM to test the research hypothesis. The results reveal the enablers of mobile money, which are social influence, performance expectancy, security and effort expectancy, and inhibitors such as system anxiety and cost. Privacy, trust, image and convenience were not found significant in this study. Social influence, performance expectancy and effort expectancy variables adapted from the UTAUT model have considerable influence on mobile money in Nigeria. Study implications and future directions are offered.

Chapter 8

Renatus Michael Mushi, Institute of Finance Management, Tanzania

This chapter describes how the adoption and usage of technologies is influenced by a number of factors. Such factors tend to affect the perception of people to accept or reject a technology in their usage context. Mobile phone technology has gained popularity as a dependable tool in SMEs. In Tanzania, for example, it is used to accomplish activities such as marketing, communication and mobile money transactions. This chapter highlights the key factors which influence the acceptance of mobile phones as they are used by individual peoples in the SMEs. The conceptual model shows that TAM can be extended by factors such as perceived values in explaining the acceptance of mobile phone technology in Tanzanian SMEs.

Chapter 9

For successful data transmission in wireless networks, security features are very much essential to implement. A mobile adhoc network contains a set of autonomous mobile stations that can correspond with each other instead of some adverse situation of wireless environment. Those mobile nodes that are not in the same series can communicate with others through intermediate hops. Security is a challenging mission in mobile adhoc network (MANET) due to many serious issues in the network such as hop-to-hop persistent wireless connectivity, high frequency of variation in topology of the network, and increasing rate of link failure due to higher mobility. So, it is very challenging to develop a secured, dynamic, and efficient routing protocol for such a magnificent network. In this chapter, vulnerability issues of MANET are focused on with a spotlight on prominent MANET protocols. A brief study on technical issues responsible for vulnerability in MANET has been depicted with systematic review on various issues and protocols that provide secured routing in the network.

Activities of prominent terrorist groups like Boko Haram, Al-Shabaab, Ansaru, and Ansar Dine have left thousands of people dead and properties destroyed for a number of decades in some developing nations. The high level of insecurity occasioned by operations of terror groups has impacted negatively on the socio-economic development of these nations. On the other hand, the use of mobile devices, such as cell phones, has gained prominence in developing nations over the past two decades. Putting side-by-side these two facts, namely, that the menace of terrorism among some developing nations is alarming and that the use of mobile devices is common among citizens of developing countries, this chapter develops a mobile application prototype called TerrorWatch. TerrorWatch is equipped with relevant menus, buttons, and interfaces that will guide a user on what to do when confronted with a terrorist attack or threat. The unified modeling language (UML) was deployed to design the architecture of the application, while the object-oriented paradigm served in the implementation.

Chapter 11

Alev Kocak Alan, Gebze Technical University, Turkey

M-commerce is supposed to be a critical issue for initiating consumer relationships due to the opportunities of m-technologies such as combining subsistent advantage of the wireless internet, mobility, and flexibility, especially in emerging nations. But consumers still perceive high risk about m-commerce. Thereby, they prefer to make online transaction with a company they trust. The purpose of the chapter is to underline the substantiality of trust in m-commerce. The chapter presents integrative review of the trust literature; a conceptual model is proposed and tested by SEM with 226 m shopping users. The relative effects of the main of antecedents (relative benefits of mobile shopping, propensity to trust, firm reputation) of trust as well as the extent which personal evaluations exert on trust in m-commerce and satisfaction of m-commerce is the key research question explored in the chapter. The result shows that a significant percentage of the variability in trust and satisfaction of m-commerce can be statistically explained.

Chapter 12

Yakup Akgül, Alanya Alaaddin Keykubat University, Turkey

This chapter explores the present gap in the literature regarding the acceptance of mobile applications by investigating the factors that affect users' behavioral intention to use apps in Turkey. First, structural equation modeling (SEM) was used to determine which variables had significant influence on intention to install. In a second phase, the neural network model was used to rank the relative influence of significant predictors obtained from SEM. The results reveal that habit, performance expectancy, trust, social influence, and hedonic motivation affect the users' behavioral intention to use apps.

Preface

The story of most developing countries is the predominant nature of the informal economy. While a lot of effort have been made to formalize these economies success is far from being achieved. ICT was heralded as a component that will spearhead development and in the process modernize the economy by bringing those in the informal sector to the formal sector, very little progress has been in this as well. For example, these countries have large open markets where monitoring and tax collection is hard with items such as food, clothes, and electronics being sold. The informal sector is believed to be worth billions of shillings/dollars, much of which is untaxed and unaccounted for in the nation's GDP.

In the last few years' use of disruptive technologies such as mobile devices has percolated in all walks of life. Evidence clearly shows that the number of mobile devices has surpassed the world population. Originally, these devices were used for making phone calls only. However, recent developments demonstrate that a lot of value added services have been developed and are being used. These value added services are showing that they are going to be game changers in enabling people who previously were not served by traditional services to be reached with easy. For example, services such as e-financial transactions or e-Government can now reach nearly everyone in the world. Thus, extensive use of mobile devices added services would go a long way in formalizing the informal economy.

Mobile phone payment schemes such as M-Pesa, Tigo Pesa and Airtel Money are some of the mobile applications, which are widely used in Tanzania, Kenya and Uganda. For example, according to the Bank of Tanzania, in the first half of the financial year 2016/17, 20.1 million transactions valued at TZS 988.9 billion took place, which was much higher than 4.4 million transactions valued at TZS 178.1 billion, that took place during similar period of the preceding financial year. The number of mobile phone payment accounts now exceeds traditional bank accounts in most developing countries. This means that mobile phone payment if well regulated can contribute significantly in the developing countries economies.

The advent of mobile phone payment schemes has also stimulated innovation in other value added services. These services range from e-tax collection, e-educational services, e-healthcare, e-agriculture and e-everything. It is clear that further innovation on mobile phone payment schemes will be a fertile ground for more creative ideas in other areas. A few years ago most mobile payment transactions were on traditional airtime top-ups and money transfer options. Today consumers in country like Tanzania have a plethora of mobile money payment options for salaries, bills, utilities, fuel, insurance, bus passes, micro-financing, healthcare, physical goods etc.

One of the newest innovations is an interest-earning mobile money product. Customers receive quarterly interest for having money in their mobile money accounts, a similar concept to gaining interest in a bank account. East Africa countries (Tanzania, Kenya and Uganda) seem to be quickly emerging as a target market for companies to pilot new mobile innovations due to the success of mobile money and favorable market conditions. Examples of these new value added services are covered in the book.

The recognition that mobile payment schemes are here to stay, is supported by frantic development of laws and legislation in a lot of countries. Some countries are promoting the use of mobile payment schemes as vehicle towards a cashless society. What cannot be denied in most countries is the growth in the use of financial services as a result of mobile payment schemes. And the emerging consensus that the mobile money industry will have to be regulated under structures that differ from typical financial services providers. Strange as it may seem, we are witnessing now major players within the financial industry start to work together with players in mobile money the mobile network operators (MNOs). It is expected this partnership will lead to making financial services available to the masses.

All these innovations in the mobile devices space bring their own opportunities and challenges. The security and privacy are going to be even more complex as new integrated services come to light. While there already exists a large body of solutions on security and privacy, for these to be used in mobile devices space they will have to be customized/tweaked. The half-hearted approach to interoperability remains a major impediment within the mobile payment industry. Interoperability is the ability for different information technology systems and services to communicate and exchange data. Without it, consumers suffer from lack of flexibility and accessibility to a wider array of services.

It is expected that in near future mobile payment schemes will be an integral part of the international payment scheme. This will allow international clearing houses to tap into the developing countries wealth potential. Concerns about online fraud which had hindered growth and may be solved by current solutions in security and privacy.

It is therefore in realizing and understanding the immense opportunities and challenges that emerge from mobile devices usage that this book was written. The contributions in this book not only provide solutions to currently existing problems, they provide a framework for a more informed public debate to embrace opportunities and address the challenges in the field. The book acknowledges that for value added services to be successful in the mobile platform then Internet connectivity will be key. Advances in research in artificial intelligence, Data Analytics, Machine Learning, and Internet of Things are covered, especially how they are going to influence future mobile platform solutions.

Acknowledgment

The editors would like to acknowledge the assistance of all the people involved in this project and, more specifically, to the authors and reviewers that took part in the review process. Our sincere gratitude goes to the chapter's authors who contributed their time and expertise to this book. Without the authors' contributions and reviewers' support, this book would not have become a reality.

The editors also acknowledge the invaluable contributions of Dr. Patrick Kihoza - Mzumbe University (MU) – Tanzania; Dr. Oluwapelumi Giwa – North West University Vaal (NWU) Campus - South Africa and Dr. Safaa Al-Mamory - University of Information Technology and Communications - Iraq. The reviewers played a key role on improving quality, coherence, and content presentation of the chapters. Most of the editors also served as referees; we highly appreciate their double task.

Special thanks to our families for being patient with us while executing the project, which reduced the amount of time we spent with them. The auditors also would like to thank their employers for their support. Many thanks to our friends and colleagues for sharing our happiness since starting this project and following with encouragement when it seemed too difficult to be completed.

Chapter 1

Mobile Phone Usage in Agricultural Extension in India:
The Current and Future Perspective

Chandan Kumar Panda
Bihar Agricultural University, India

ABSTRACT

This chapter describes how the rural economy of India is basically agrarian in nature and agriculture is the life and livelihood of maximum number of rural people. As per Census 2011 of India there are about 95.8 million cultivators and out of which about 80 percent of farmers are marginal and small. Information asymmetry, 'Information-haves' and 'information-have-nots', digital divide was once major paradox of Indian Extension system. Through the mKisan platform, 152 crore SMSs have sent till date to the Indian farmers in the subjects of weather information, pest management, market price, quality seed, etc. In addition, the Kisan Call Centre (KCC) Service, the Buyer Seller Platform, and mobile apps viz. Kisan Suvidha, IFFCO Kisan Agriculture, Pusa Krishi, Krishi Gyan, Crop Insurance, AgriMarket, etc., are consistently supporting the farmers. In the future more farmers will be brought under this mobile-based service.

INTRODUCTION

The rural economy of India is basically agrarian in nature and agriculture is the life and livelihood of maximum number of rural people. India is most populous nation of the world after China and its agriculture is characterised by marginal and small farmers. Fates of Indian farmers are squeezing in between vagaries of nature

DOI: 10.4018/978-1-5225-4029-8.ch001

and volatility of market, although addressing the problems of both contexts are information intensive and knowledge intensive. However, in this knowledge economy, farming also become knowledge intensive and precision farming is the future of Indian agriculture. Precision farming is knowledge intensive. Indian has no dearth of agricultural knowledge and technologies with its strong agricultural education system and research. But, major shortfall is noted in linkage in research-extension-farmers. Extension linkage failure resultant is that only 20 per cent in developed agricultural technologies reached to farmers' field. Major ironic on agricultural technologies are that these are pro-literate and big farmers inclined. 'Information-haves' and 'information-have-nots' are very much conspicuous in country side. 'Digital divide' is another noticeable shortfall in agricultural extension and government of India is very much concerned about it; accordingly, 'Digital India' was launched by the Prime Minister of India on 1 July 2015 - with an objective of connecting rural areas with high-speed Internet networks and improving digital literacy. This is one of the breakthroughs for agricultural extension in India.

Agricultural extension is the application of scientific research and new knowledge to agricultural practices through farmer education. Extension is the organized exchange of information and the deliberate transfer of skills. The essence of agricultural extension is to facilitate interplay and nurture synergies within a total information system involving agricultural research, agricultural education and a vast complex of information-providing businesses. Four paradigms of agricultural extension are technology transfer (persuasive + paternalistic), advisory work (persuasive + participatory), human resource development (educational + paternalistic) and facilitation for empowerment (educational + participatory).

From the aforesaid four paradigms, it is well understood that application of these paradigms are information intensive or knowledge intensive. For this cause different extension methods are used viz. individual methods, group methods and mass methods. Now the major challenge is to identify an important mean or combination of means to reach the million of farming community in real time basis to address the problems of climate uncertainties and market volatility. Number of experiments on mobile usage in agricultural extension shown its worthiness; to bridge the gap between 'Information-haves' and 'information-have-nots' and reducing the 'digital divide'. In India agricultural extension services (viz. weather information, crop advisory, market price, buyers and sellers information) is provided to farmers through mobile SMS either through basic mobile, feature mobile, android mobiles. However, potentiality of Android mobile in agricultural extension is more as compare to reaming to mobiles.

Table 1. Major challenges of Indian agriculture and exploring mobile technologies/ ICT for it

Major Challenges of Indian Agriculture	Exploring Mobile Technologies/ICT
Subsistence Farming: Most of the Indian farmers are marginal and small categories and they had limited marketable surplus of their produces.	Marginal and small farmers need timely information for better management of their farm. ICT can play important role this viz. timely weather information, market information, IVR based crop advisory etc.
Burgeoning Population Rate and Squeezing of Arable Land: Population growth is steady, whereas area under cultivation is decreasing. Major challenge is to feed this mammoth population.	ICT based crop husbandry can increase agricultural productivity and production for feeding burgeoning population viz. Digital farming is an important mean for it.
Disguised Unemployment in Farm Sector: Large numbers of rural youth are engaged in farming without major return.	ICT based platform is an less expensively, timely supportive, user friendly means for training of rural youth in virtual mode for more remunerative enterprise involvement in agriculture and allied sectors *viz.* vegetable cultivation, dairying, poultry etc.
Short Fall in Assure Irrigation: Challenge for getting crop by efficient use of each drop of water.	Water resource management is more and more important. Modern agriculture is a large-scale water consumer, which must adjust as well as possible its consumption in adequacy with its needs, while preserving the natural resources and the quality of the productions. Information and Communication Technologies (ICT) offer solutions to make possible a finer approach of the irrigation of the crop by facilitating the work of the farmers. The contributions of ICT to manage irrigation pivots in a farm in the technologies used are ad hoc wireless networks and Web technologies. The farmer can, via the Internet, ensure the monitoring and the remote control of the irrigation equipment, in a more precise way and in conformance with the crop's requirements.
Dependent Upon Monsoon: Indian agriculture is mainly dependent upon monsoon which is uncertain, unreliable and irregular.	Agriculture dependents on weather condition, starting from sowing of seed to harvesting of crops. Uncertain, unreliable and irregular weather have detrimental effect on agriculture, however, timely information on weather condition to the farmers may help them to escape, avoid and manage so many abrupt effect of weather.
Diverse Climatic Condition: India have diverse agro-climatic condition with diverse crops and its varieties.	The pan India agricultural research and research network is unique with developed diverse agricultural technology for varied agro-climatic conditions of the nation. Mobile technology has huge potentiality for supporting the farmers with those technologies.
Predominance of Food Crops: More than two-thirds of the total cropped area is devoted to the cultivation of food crops. However, with the change in cropping pattern, the relative share of food crops came down from 76.7 per cent in 1950-51 to 58.8 per cent in 2002-03.	Government of India has taken a programme in doubling the income of the farmers within 2022. Cash crops, vegetable cultivation, precision farming was grey areas which may make it possible with the judicious use of ICT tools in technology transfer and its adoption.

continued on following page

Table 1. Continued

Major Challenges of Indian Agriculture	Exploring Mobile Technologies/ICT
Rural Youth: India have high percentage of rural youth and their ability and potentiality is not explore for economic growth of the nation.	As per 2011 Census of India, it has 41 per cent youth. It is well established fact that youth cherish technology, efficiency and innovations and accommodate entrepreneurial risks. The ICT-savvy rural youth operated intensive, efficient and profitable farms, producing diverse and branded products for niche markets. The youth transformed the community use and access to ICTs and influenced community economic status. Smart phone technology will revolutionize access to and the use of ICTs, particularly for Facebook, YouTube, Twitter and WhatsApp among the youth. This will enhance the introduction of modern extension and agricultural technologies and will increase extension coverage. The outcome will be improved productivity and profitability of farming activities through higher yields, higher prices and increased farm income, climaxing in more youth engaging in agriculture(Irunga *et al.* 2015).

Information Needs of the Farmers

Bachhav(2012)studied the Information Needs of the Rural Farmers of Maharashtra, India and observed that about 40.00% farmers required daily information for various agriculture work and to them first preferred sources of the information was colleague or fellow farmers followed by newspapers and government officers. Major information needs of the farmers are crop production (Tologbons *et al.*,2008), pest management, disease management (Saravan *et al.*,2009). Elly and Silayo (2013)studied information needs and sources of the rural farmers in Tanzania specifically from Iringa rural district noted that 70 per cent of farmers' information needs is about crop and livestock husbandry, marketing, funding options and value addition. However, there is a significant difference between the information needs for "information on crop and livestock husbandry" as well as information on "value addition". To a great extent, farmers use the old means of communication, the traditional and interpersonal by default due to relevancy in the context and content. The modern means of communication are used to access non-agricultural (other) information. However, Babu *et al.* (2011) noted that the major constraints to information access for the farmers are poor availability, poor reliability, lack of awareness of information sources available among farmers and untimely provision of information. Although, information must be relevant and meaningful to farmers, in addition to being packaged and delivered in a way preferred by them (Diekmann *et al.* 2009). Context-specific information could have higher impacts on the adoption of technologies and increase farm productivity for marginal and small agricultural landholders (Sammadar, 2006).

Rapid growth of mobile telephony and the introduction of mobile-enabled information services provide ways to improve information dissemination to the knowledge intensive agriculture sector and also help to overcome information asymmetry existing among the group of farmers. It also helps, at least partially, to bridge the gap between the availability and delivery of agricultural inputs and agriculture infrastructure (Mital and Mehar, 2012). Ganeshan et al. (2013) noted that a majority of the farmers perceived information on pest and disease control as most important and they also felt that accessing information through mobile phone is easy and convenient; and irrespective of the socio-economic characteristics, farmers were utilizing the mobile multimedia agricultural advisory system. They also concluded that the quality of information, timeliness of information and reliability of information were the three important aspects that have to be considered seriously. A study was conducted by CIMMYT (2011) in India and its resulted showed that farmers are getting benefits by using mobile based information (Table 2).

Telephone Usage Statistics in India

As per Telecom Regulatory Authority of India (TRAI) overall tele-density of India is 83.20 and mobile user base grew 103.5 crore at the end of June,2016. Mobile. Table 3 shows the telephone subscription of India.

Mobile Phone Usage in Agricultural Extension in India

Timely Mobile SMS is always critical inputs for agriculture. Simply a160 words mobile SMS on weather forecasting can help a farmer to take decision on number of cultivation issues *viz.* sowing seed, spraying of pesticide and harvesting of crop.

Table 2. Benefits of mobile based information

States	Percent of Farmers Using Mobile Phone for Agricultural Information	Get Better Connected to Markets	Getting Better Prices	Increasing Yield
Bihar	51	99.2	65.9	21.1
Haryana	65	99.4	79.5	42.9
Punjab	26	77.8	82.5	49.2
Uttar Pradesh	45	69.7	69.7	29.4
West Bengal	17	65.9	48.8	34.1
Total	41	87.2	71.7	34.6

Source: CIMMYT Survey (2011).

Table 3. Teledensity of India

Particulars	Wireless	Wireline	Total (Wireless+Wireline)
Total Telephone Subscribers (Million)	1,127.37	24.40	1,151.78
Net Addition in December, 2016 (Million)	27.86	-0.04	27.82
Monthly Growth Rate	2.53%	-0.16%	2.48%
Urban Telephone Subscribers (Million)	662.60	20.55	683.14
Net Addition in December, 2016 (Million)	24.14	-0.02	24.11
Monthly Growth Rate	3.78%	-0.11%	3.66%
Rural Telephone Subscribers (Million)	464.78	3.86	468.64
Net Addition in December, 2016 (Million	3.72	-0.02	3.71
Monthly Growth Rate	0.81%	-0.45%	0.80%
Overall Tele-density*	88.00	1.90	89.90
Urban Tele-density*	165.04	5.12	170.15
Rural Tele-density*	52.84	0.44	53.27
Share of Urban Subscribers	58.77%	84.19%	59.31%
Share of Rural Subscribers	41.23%	15.81%	40.69%
Broadband Subscribers (Million)	217.95	18.14	236.09

Source: Telecom Regulatory Authority of India New Delhi, 17th February, 2017.(www.trai.gov.in)
  *Based on the population projections from Census data published by the Office of Registrar General & Census Commissioner of India.

A Mobile SMS which is less than one paisa may help a marginal farmer to save thousand rupees. In India mobile is used judiciously for providing the information to all types of farmers. And the mobile usage in agricultural extension in India is extended by both public(Government) and private agencies. Following are the mobile usage in agricultural extension in India.

1. Kisan Call Centre

With the objective of tap the huge potentiality of mobile phone in ICT in Agriculture, Ministry of Agriculture launched the scheme "Kisan Call Centres (KCCs)" on January 21, 2004. Irrespective of the types of mobile phone(basic, feature and android) and landline, a farmer can make call to Kisan Call Centres to the Toll Free number 1800-180-1551 or last four digit(i.e. 1551) from any part of the nation to raise his/her query related to agriculture and allied sectors.. These call Centres are working in 14 different locations covering all the States and UTs. This number is accessible through mobile phones and landlines of all telecom networks including private service providers. Replies to the farmers' queries are given in 22 local languages. Call centre services are available from 6.00 am to 10.00 pm on all seven days of the week at each KCC location. Kisan Call Centre agents known as Farm Tele Advisor(FTAs), are graduates or above (i.e. PG or Doctorate) in Agriculture or allied (Horticulture, Animal Husbandry, Fisheries, Poultry, Bee-keeping, Sericulture, Aquaculture, Agricultural Engineering, Agricultural Marketing, Bio-technology, Home Science etc. and possess excellent communication skills in respective local language. Queries which cannot be answered by Farm Tele Advisor(FTAs) are transferred to higher level experts in a call conferencing mode. These experts are subject matter specialists of State Agriculture Departments, ICAR and State Agricultural Universities.

The Kisan Call Center, consists of three levels namely Level-I (the basic Call Center interface), Level-II (Subject Matter Specialists) and Level-III (the Management Group to ensure ultimate answering and resolution of all the queries of the farmers)

Level-I: The call coming to the call centre is picked up by an operator who after a short welcome message takes down the basic information and the query of the caller. The first level operators preferably would be an agricultural graduate with rural background knowing local language. They should also possess good communication skills. They would be in a position to answer a majority of the questions likely to be asked by the farmers.

Level-II: The level -II consists of Subject Matter Specialists (SMS) who are located at their respective place (Research Stations, ATICs, KVKs, Agricultural colleges), of work. In case the first level operator is not able to answer the question, the operator forwards (in call sharing mode) the call to the concerned Subject Matter Specialist.

Level-III: The level - III consists of a dedicated cell located at the Nodal Office. This would receive the questions that have not been answered at the first and the second levels. Appropriate replies to these questions would be then framed in consultation with the concerned specialists available within or outside the State, by the nodal cell. The replies would be sent to the farmers promptly by post/e-mail/fax/ telephone etc. within 72 hours of receipt of the question.

2. mKisan

mKisan is a SMS portal for farmers. By using this portal experts send farm advisory, weather information *etc.* to the farmers in different local language. Since its launching nearly 50 crore messages or more than 152 crore SMSs and 3.65 lakhs advisories have been sent to farmers throughout the length and breadth of the country. Farmers are supported through USSD (Unstructured Supplementary Service Data), IVRS (Interactive Voice Response System) and Pull SMS without internet service. Semi-

Figure 1. The schematic representation of Kisan Call Centre
Source: http://www.megagriculture.gov.in/PUBLIC/kisan_call_center/schematic_representation.aspx

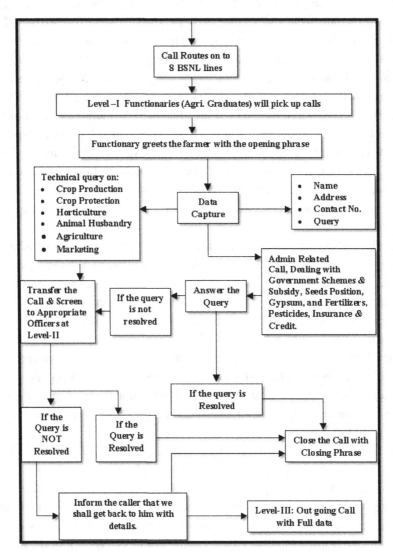

literate and illiterate farmers are also targeted to be reached by voice messages. Officers from block level to Central Ministry level can use this portal for sending SMS to farmers.

Major Objectives of the Portal include are as stated below-

- To make SMS and other mobile based services as a tool of 2 way agricultural extension through Pull SMS or USSD.

8

Figure 2. Homepage of mKisan
Source: http://mkisan.gov.in/. Retrieved on May 18, 2017.

- Making use of huge spread of mobile telephony in the rural areas to cover every farm household in the country to overcome the major impediment in bringing level playing field for small and marginal farmers.
- Centralized system wherein different modes of information flow are channelized and spread to the farmers in their own language.
- Integrated Portal to ensure proper storage in previous advisories/messages and also effective monitoring at various levels.
- Integration of database of farmers from the State Governments, Universities, KVKs web based registration, Kisan Call Centres etc.

3. Indian Meteorological Department (IMD) Agromet Services

This service is for farmers, those registered themselves for getting weather related information. Through this service registered farmers received current weather information and its forecasting. Considering the importance of micro-level weather information, IMD provide information to the farmers in Block level too. Example of a mobile SMS send to the farmers are shown in figure-4. SMS is send both in English and Local Language.

Figure 3. SMS advisory to farmers by IMD

Figure 4. SMS to farmers
Source: http://www.imdagrimet.gov.in/node/3454#retrieved on May 19, 2017.

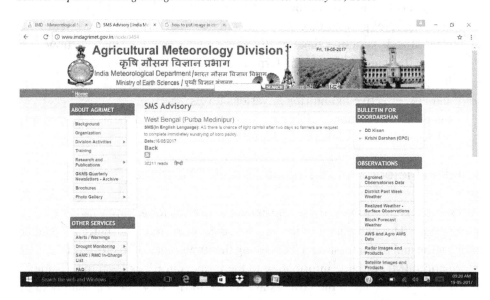

4. Virtual Krishi Vigyan Kendra

Virtual Krishi Vigyan Kendra (http://vkvk.in) is an Indian Council of Agricultural Research initiative to empower India's Krishi Vigyan Kendra's to be able to communicate with their large set of registered farmers via three kinds of medium i.e. voice, SMS and email. This platform supports services like announcing alerts, broadcasting advisories, weather forecasting, farmers asking question to the experts and experts from concerned KVK's replying back to them. Indian Institute of Technology Kanpur (IITK) and Regional Zonal Project Directorate Zone 4 (ZPD) Kanpur together has come up with a solution to empower our existing KVK system called vKVK. Virtual Krishi Vigyan Kendra is a service created specially to help the KVK scientist and farmers to communicate through cell phone like devices. The scientist can send SMS and voice messages to the registered farmers. These messages are classified according to crops and agro climatic zones. The farmers get targeted alert and advisory messages based on the registration information they have provided to their KVK(Bagga,2010).

5. BSNL 'Mandi on Mobile' Service

BSNL in collaboration with Uttar Pradesh(UP) Agricultural Marketing Board (Mandi Parishad) had launched a voice-based 'Mandi on Mobile' service. It will allow farmers to call up a Bharat Sanchar Nigam Limited (BSNL) number and

Figure 5. Login screen of vKVK which depicts interaction between farmer and a KVK expert

Figure 6. Screen after logging in

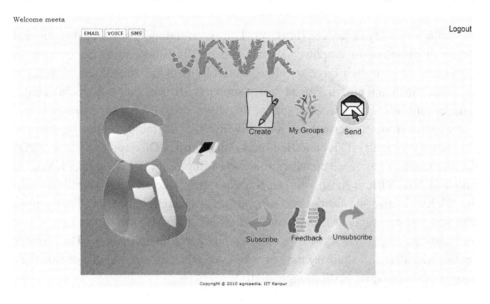

get the rate of commodities, like vegetables, grains, pulses or fruits in any mandi (market) across the state. The 'solely voice-based' service will allow farmers in UP to get to know the latest mandi rates of around 108 commodities by simply dialing a number and by following the simple voice command subsequently. The farmer has to just name the product and the district and he will be told the tehsil (administrative unit)-wise rates. The voice-based service is expected to be beneficial to farmers, especially to those who are illiterate (they will not have to type in various numbers for various commodities).

6. Kissan Kerala

Karshaka Information Systems Services And Networking (KISSAN) is an integrated, multi-modal delivery of agricultural information system for the farming community across Kerala. The basic objective of this project is to provide "Right Information to the Right Person(s) at the Right Time in the Right Place(s) and in the Right Context" dynamically using a combination of advanced technology like Web Technology, Television based mass media programs, Telephone based advisory, Mobile SMS based advisory and broadcast service, dedicated online Agri-video channel provides video on demand service etc, which, involves effective collaboration of experts from key organizations for effective information delivery and knowledge empowerment on demand seamlessly to all farmers across Kerala. The project provides telephone

Figure 7. Kissan Kerala
Source: http://www.kissankerala.net/home.jsp.

based Agri advisory services through a dedicated telephone number (0471-2784136) for the farmers. The farmers can ask any questions to the agricultural scientists and seek expert advice for their crops. As part of this service, the project has developed an extensive crop database across the state to provide location specific advisory services. The SMS based agri – advisory services, enable the farmers to get the information on very fast and it helps to provide location specific information and alert services. The farmers can avail the tele-advisory services from KISSAN throgh this number (0471-2784136). The service will be available between Monday-Friday 10 AM - 5 PM.

7. Rubber Market Price in SMS to Farmers by Rubber Board, India

The Rubber Board of India are supporting the rubber growers and dealers of India by providing daily price of rubber (both national and international) through the mobile SMS. The annual subscription of the SMS service is Rs.345/- (inclusive of service tax) and half year subscription charges is Rs.173/-(inclusive of service tax).

The international prices of rubber are sent to the subscribers at 11 am and domestic prices at 4 pm every day (www.rubberboard.org.in).

8. Intelligent Advisory System for Farmers

This project was started on June 2010 in Manipur and Meghalaya states located in North East Region of India. It was a build an intelligent advisory system, a hybrid system by integrating Expert System (ES) and Case-base Reasoning (CBR) for automatically answering queries related to farming activities. Expertise and scientists were from Department of Agriculture, Government of Manipur; Department of Agriculture, Government of Meghalaya; Central Agriculture University (CAU), Imphal; and Krishi Vigyan Kendra (KVKs) of these states. Technological support or ICT platform were developed by the Centre for Development of Advanced Computing (CDAC), Mumbai. The project covers five major farming activities *viz.* Insect Management, Disease Management, Weed Management, Rice Variety Selection and Fertilizer Management. The main objectives of IASF are (Shabong,2013)-

- Provide improved services to the farming community through the use of ICT.
- Advice and help farmers to solve problems related to their farming activities. Otherwise, they need to contact agricultural experts and private extension workers.
- Providing vital and generic information to farmers so that they get periodic alerts on important/useful tips, ideas, knowhow etc.
- Updates farmers on latest technology in Agriculture sector for improved productivity and quality farming.
- Developing an advisory system which can be extended with any other types of crops in any State of India.
- Improving agricultural extension service by using mobile services so that farmers can send queries about their farming problem from their mobile device.
- To develop an educational materials to be used by students for their practical experience with real case scenario.

9. Interactive Information and Dissemination System (IIDS)

Interactive Information Dissemination System (IIDS) was started with the major objective of *'Information to the farmers as and when they require'*. IIDS is a pull and push based system, there is a mobile interface at front end and web interface at the back end. This is an integrated model largely integration of Toll free IVRS,

Figure 8. Working framework of intelligent advisory system for farmers
Source: *http://iasf-originally.rhcloud.com/ias/jsp/about.jsp . Retrieved on May 20, 2017.*

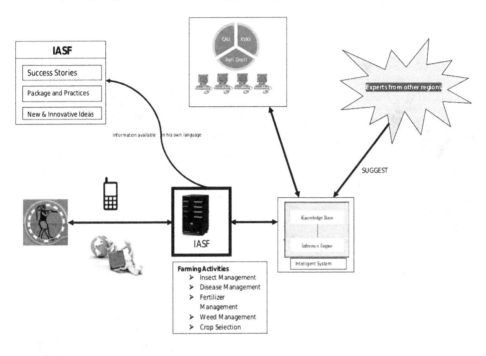

Smart Phone Application and Interactive Portal. The some important features and services for farmers from this system are as cited below-

- Personalized 'Agro Advisory' Based on 'Farm and Farmer Profile'.
- Farm Profile includes Parameters of 'Soil Health Card' & 'Crop History'.
- Advisories in Local Language / Dialects
- Major Advisory Domain- Agriculture, Animal Husbandry and Fisheries
- 'Personal Assistance' to raise 'Multimedia Query'
- 'Live Interaction' with Agri-Scientists
- Facility to 'Refer Critical Problems' to relevant 'Crop Specialist' available virtually
- 'Round the Clock Query Registration Facility' through IVRS and Smart Phones
- 'Anywhere Anytime Access' on Past Advisories
- Facility to 'Push Emergency Message' to Farmers based on 'Location and Crops'
- 'Network Independent' – Accessible from All Networks
- Smart Phone Application

Figure 9. Structural and functional framework of IISD
Source: http://www.medialabasia.in/index.php/research/projects/livelihood.

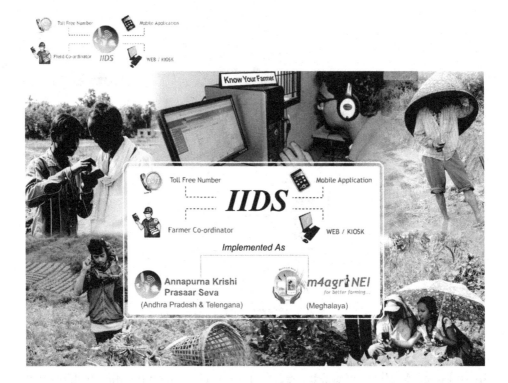

- ○ Standalone Application
- ○ Offline query aggregation capabilities
- ○ Data Synchronization at hotspots (store and forward).
- ○ Offline capability of display of last synchronized data
- ○ Coordinator information system
- ○ Farmer registration and profile

IIDS was launched in the year 2013 through the two Agricultural Universities namely Acharya N. G. Ranga Agricultural University (ANGRAU), Hyderabad as 'Annapurna Krishi Prasaar Seva (AKPS)' and 'm4agriNEI' at Central Agricultural University, Imphal. Under AKPS around 24000 farmers have been registered from 3600+ villages and in M4agriNEI around 11000 farmers have been registered along with their farming database from the 150+ villages of Meghalaya.

10. Kisan Helpline of Bihar Agricultural University(BAU), Sabour

Bihar Agricultural University(BAU), Sabour had started a toll free number (18003456455) since 2012 for the farmers of Bihar to support them in farming in the areas of crop cultivation, animal husbandry, fisheries etc. Scientists of the university directly attend the call of the farmers to resolve farmers farming problem. It works from 10.00 AM to 5.00 PM in all working days.

11. Life-Lines India

It was launched in September,2006 under the founder partnership of British Telecom, Cisco Systems and OneWorld with the motto of 'Knowledge services over your phone'. Life Lines India leverages a mix of internet and telephone technologies - to

Figure 10. Kisan Help Line Service of BAU, Sabour
Source: *http://bausabour.ac.in/KisanHelpline.aspx.*

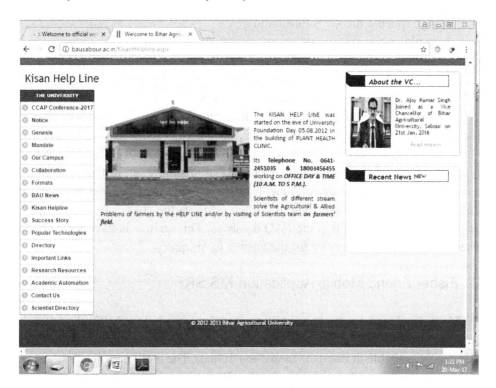

17

provide essential and demand-based information, advice and guidance to remote and rural communities in India - through the medium of "voice, in the local language and within 24 hours." Launched 2006, has completed 10 crop cycles and today reaches more than150,000 farmers in 1000 villages. Key Features of the LifeLines Agriculture service:

- Expert advice on integrated pest management (IPM) methods has helped farmers to improve their input efficiency
- Solutions are made available to farmers within 24 hours
- Information available on more than 50 different fields of agriculture and allied activities covering a complete chain of information from production to consumption, including information on:
- Farm inputs like seeds, fertilizers, pesticides
- Funding schemes
- Government schemes on loans and subsidies
- Banking and insurance
- Market prices
- Region specific market information
- Agriculture news
- Organic farming

Figure 11 shows the schematic diagram which shows how this system work.

The user dials the designated LifeLines number using a landline or mobile phone. The call first reaches the Interactive Voice Response (IVR) System of the service where the user is assisted by a voice menu to register his/her query. The query asked by the user is stored as a voice clip in the LifeLines' database server. Once the query is answered by the expert or available in FAQ database, the LifeLines application alerts the Knowledge Worker. The KW then retrieves the answer from the expert and saves it as a voice clip in the FAQ database. This answer is then played back when the user calls the service for the answer to his query.

12. Fisher Friend Mobile Application-MS SRF

FFMA is developed on an android platform in partnership with Wireless Reach Qualcomm and Tata Consultancy Services by MS Swaminathan Foundation and is currently available in English, Tamil, and Telugu. The mobile application serves to the fish farmers of Tamil Nadu, Andhra Pradesh, and Puducherry. It is single window solution for the holistic shore-to-shore needs of the fishing community, providing vulnerable fishermen immediate access to critical real-time knowledge

Figure 11. LifeLine Agriculture farmers query addressing diagram
Source: http://lifelines-india.net/agriculture/howitworks retrieved on June 4, 2017.

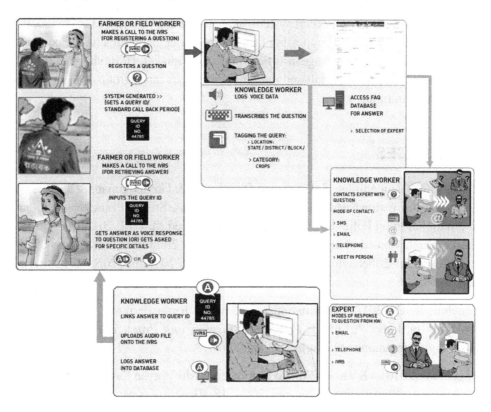

and information services *viz.* weather, potential fishing zones, ocean state forecasts, and market related information. This is an efficient ICT tools for fish farmers decision making.

CONCLUSION

Indian Space Research Organisation had made a breakthrough in Information Communication Technology(ICT) by launching *GSAT-19* and it is being designed for "a game changer communications satellite for India". This will bring revolution in the speed of internet service and in sequel it will give rise to more judicious use of mobile technology in agricultural extension, especially for smart phone or android phone. Information will be cheap, timely and access to any moment for farmers. Mobile usage in agricultural extension will address the present need of India agriculture by involving more number of mobile savvy rural youth in agriculture, creating opportunities of agri-entrepreneurship with more use of ICT in agriculture, real time and dynamic market information through mobile platform, creating artificial intelligence in agricultural expert system, using technology for text to voice mobile message or *vice-versa* and supporting farmers the under changing climate context. However, tailoring mobile usage in agricultural extension, all efforts should be tuned with the consideration of small and marginal farmers as these group of farmers are predominant in India.

REFERENCES

Babu, S. C., Glendenning, C. J., Asenso-Okyere, K., & Govindarajan, S. K. (2011). Farmers' Information Needs and Search Behaviors: Case Study in Tamil Nadu, India. International Food Policy Research Institute. Retrieved May 12, 2017 from http://ageconsearch.umn.edu/bitstream/126226/2/Farmers%20information%20needs%20and%20search%20behaviour%2case%20study%20in%20Tamil%20Nadu%20India.pdf

Bachhav, N. B. (2012). Information Needs of the Rural Farmers: A Study from Maharashtra, India: A Survey. *Library Philosophy and Practice*. Retrieved from http://digitalcommons.unl.edu/libphilprac/866

Bagga, M. (2010). vKVK - A Way to Empower Krishi Vigyan Kendra. *Information Technology in Developing Countries*, *20*(3), 18–21.

Diekmann, F., Loibl, C., & Batte, M. T. (2009). The Economics of Agricultural Information: Factors Affecting Commercial Farmers' Information Strategies in Ohio. *Review of Agricultural Economics*, *31*(4), 853–872. doi:10.1111/j.1467-9353.2009.01470.x

Elly, T., & Silayo, E. E. (2013). Agricultural Information Needs and Sources of the Rural Farmers in Tanzania: A Case of Iringa Rural District. *Library Review*, *62*(8&9), 547–566. doi:10.1108/LR-01-2013-0009

Irungu, K. R. G., Mbugua, D., & Muia, J. (2015). Information and Communication Technologies (ICTs) Attract Youth into Profitable Agriculture in Kenya. *East African Agricultural and Forestry*, *81*(1), 24–33.

Mittal, S., & Mehar, M. (2012). How Mobile Phones Contribute to Growth of Small Farmers? Evidence from India. *Zeitschrift für Ausländische Landwirtschaft*, *51*(3), 227–244.

Sammadar, A. (2006). Traditional and Post-Traditional: A Study of Agricultural Rituals in Relation to Technological Complexity among Rice Producers in Two Zones of West Bengal, India. *Journal of Culture and Agriculture.*, *28*(2), 108–121. doi:10.1525/cag.2006.28.2.108

Saravan, R, & Raja, P. & Tayeng Sheela. (2009). Information Input Pattern and Information Need of Tribal Farmers in Arnuchal Pradesh. *Indian Journal of Extension Education*, *45*(1&2), 51–54.

Tologbonse, D., Fashola, O., & Obadiah, M. (2008). Policy Issues in Meeting Rice Farmers Agricultural Information Needs in Niger State. *Journal of Agricultural Extension*, *12*(2), 84–94.

Chapter 2

Implications of the Proposed Communication Service Tax Bill on the Socio-Economic Development of Nigeria

Benjamin Enahoro Assay
Delta State Polytechnic Ogwashi-Uku, Nigeria

ABSTRACT

This chapter describes how the decision of the Nigerian government to introduce a Communication Service Tax Bill to the National Assembly to compel consumers of certain communication services to pay a 9 percent tax has pitted the government against major stakeholders in the ICT sector who are concerned about the future of the industry. While the government wants the legislative process regarding the bill to go on because of the financial gains that will accrue to it monthly, the stakeholders want it jettisoned for fear that it would impact negatively on the ICT sector and the economy, which is currently in recession. This chapter wades through the controversy by presenting the various positions canvassed by stakeholders and points the way ahead for the sector, which is fast becoming the hub of economic activities in Nigeria, to harness its full potentials for the overall benefit of the Nigerian society.

INTRODUCTION

In an effort to regulate and standardize business practice as well as raise revenue, governments through their agencies have put in place laws to regulate the business environment. The essence of the law is to, among others, regulate the rights and duties of people carrying out business in order to ensure fairness, protect people

DOI: 10.4018/978-1-5225-4029-8.ch002

dealing with business from harm caused by defective services, protect investors, creditors and consumers, and ensure a level playing field for competing business. Law also limits governments from engaging in abusive practices against businesses (Lawrence and Kinder, 1987, Williams, 2007).

Tax is a product of the law. In most organized societies, individuals and corporate organizations pay tax because the law gives impetus to the payment of such taxes (income tax and company tax). The power to impose taxes is generally recognized as a right of governments. Without the money to finance its core responsibilities of ensuring public welfare socially, economically and politically which mostly comes from tax, governments are powerless (Kiable and Nwankwo 2009). However, despite its legality, many individuals and companies still evade and avoid tax for several reasons ranging from insufficiency and complexity of tax legislation, high rate of taxation to a lack of sense of civic responsibility amongst tax payers.

The information and communication technology (ICT) industry is one of the most vibrant sectors in Africa. The mobile telecommunications boom in the continent has been driven by private investment that has brought global communications within the reach of more Africans. Over the past decade, the number of mobile connections in sub-Saharan Africa has increased nearly ten-fold, and over 500 million people in the region are now covered by mobile phone networks. These mobile networks, according to Mats Granryd, director general of GSM Association, are providing subscribers not just with connectivity but a gateway to a range of other essential services in areas such as digital identity, health care and financial services (www. gsma.com/newsroom/press-release/number-of-unique-mobile-subscribers-in-africa-surpasses-half-a-billiion-finds-new-gsma-study/).

Last year (2016), reports had it that 1.13billion (estimated to be 67 percent of Africa's population), now have mobile phones. Besides, about 26.5 percent (297,885,898) of the population is on the Internet, with 50.3billion active on social media platform, facebook (Adepetun, 2017, p. 38). Perhaps the industry's most impressive achievement has been the number of people who now have access to mobile services. The industry figure usually quoted is the penetration rate based on the number of active SIM cards. This reached 722 million at the start of 2015, giving a continental penetration rate of 77 percent, it was forecast to rise to 982 million and 93 percent respectively by 2020. Africa now accounts for 10 percent of the total global subscriber base, with profound implications for African economic and social development.

Nigeria, one of Africa's biggest markets, is a goldmine for telecommunications companies operating in the country despite the much-reported operational deficiencies. Every year, these companies generate revenues that surpass their returns in other African countries. The telecommunications industry is dominated by four major companies – South Africa's MTN Nigeria Communications Limited, indigenous telecommunications outfit Globacom Limited, India-owned Airtel Networks Limited and Emerging Market Telecommunications Services Limited trading as Etisalat and owned by UAE's Mubadala.

As an emerging nation with an estimated population of 170 million people, the demand for telecommunications services in Nigeria has continued to rise. According to the country's telecommunications regulator, the Nigerian Communications Commission (NCC), as of June 2014, active GSM mobile subscriptions in the country were a little over 130 million, representing 98.31 percent of the market share of the telecommunications industry. By June 2015 that figure peaked at 148 million, a jump of 18 million subscribers, which is unprecedented in the annals of global telecommunications industry. As of August 2016, the number of active mobile lines rose to 153 million with a teledensity of more than 109 percent. Internet subscribers stood at 93.5 percent. The ITU/UNESCO report of 2016, credits Nigeria with 20.95 percent internet penetration rate and targets 30 percent broadband penetration for the country in 2018. The investment in the economy (local and foreign) in the past fifteen years stood at $68 billion (www.itnewsnigeria.com.ng/2016/12/nigeria-retains-fastest-growing-telecoms-market-in-recession-ncc/). It is these remarkable achievements that have seen the country claim a position in the top 10 of the fastest growing telecommunications market in the world.

This development and further growth in Nigeria's telecommunications industry, which has been applauded by global key players is currently being threatened by some unfriendly government policies, especially the decision of the Nigerian government to impose a new form of tax – Communication Service Tax (CST) on the people. The bill, which has passed first reading at the National Assembly, if passed into law, will require consumers of voice, data, short message service (SMS), multi-media service (MMS) and pay television services to pay a 9 percent tax on fees paid for the use of these services. The CST bill has not gone down well with Nigerians as it has continued to draw the flak of the people, especially stakeholders in the ICT industry who are mostly concerned about the future of this very promising sector of the economy.

To make matters worse for the sector, the Central Bank of Nigeria (CBN) Governor, Mr. Godwin Emefiele had also suggested that telephone calls above three minutes should be taxed. These plans are coming at a time when some African countries like Ghana, Liberia, Kenya and South Africa have slashed taxes or mulled the plan.

This chapter thus examines the implications of the CST Bill on the socio-economic development of Nigeria. The objectives of the chapter are:

1.   To show how the proposed communication service tax will impact on the ICT sector and other aspects of the Nigerian economy.

2. To draw the attention of government to the need to listen to public outcry and consult widely with major stakeholders in the industry with a view to harmonizing the different positions on the proposed CST Bill before it is passed into law.

3. To establish the fact that there is urgent need for the Nigerian government to explore other ways of raising more revenue from tax other than the proposed CST.

4. To come out with recommendations that will assist government to properly handle the controversy surrounding the proposed CST.

BACKGROUND

Concept of Taxation

The development and growth of any society is dependent on the provision of basic infrastructure. This explains why governments show great concern on how funds can be made available to achieve their set goals for the society. Government needs funds to be able to execute its social obligations to the public. These obligations include but are not limited to the provision of infrastructure and social services.

Meeting the needs of the society calls for huge funds which an individual or community cannot contribute alone. One of the main methods through which funds are acquired for the government is through taxation (Boone and Kurtz, 2006). Citizens are therefore expected to discharge their responsibility by paying taxes to contribute to the development and administration of the society at large.

According to British economist and politician, who was chancellor of the Exchequer from 1945 to 1947, Hugh Dalton, "A tax is a compulsory contribution imposed by a public authority, irrespective of the exact amount of service rendered to the taxpayer in return, and not imposed as penalty for any legal offence" (Sunday, Nelson, Oyebade and Jeremiah, 2017). Most taxes are legislated, meaning that representatives elected by the citizens of a country or region determine what activities to tax, how much to tax, when to collect those taxes, and how to administer the proceeds. Individuals, business, and other entities subject to the tax must remit the tax or face enforcement action (www.investinganswers.com/financial-dictionary/tax-center/taxes-4567).

In order to eliminate any form of arbitrariness in the administration of tax, economist Adam Smith, in his famous book, The Wealth of Nations (1776), wrote about the Canon of Taxation, which he described as the building of a "Good Tax System". Chand (2016) defines cannons of taxation as the "administrative aspects of a tax that relate to the rate, amount, and method of levy and collection of a tax". In the book, Smith only gave four canons. These original four are now known as the 'original or Main Canons of Taxation' (http://www.owlcation.com/social-sciences/ canons-of-Taxation-in-Economics). With the passage of time, and the resultant expansion of governance, modern economists also expanded Smith's principles of taxation hence the birth of modern canons of taxation (www.economicsdiscussion. net/taxes/canons-of-taxation-enuniated-by-adam-smith-discussed/1948). Since a good tax system must be one, which is designed on the basis of an appropriate set of principles, it must strike a balance between the interest of the taxpayer, and that of tax authorities.

The first of the four original rules is the Canon of Equity, which aims at providing economic and social justice to the people. This principle stipulates that every person should pay to the government depending upon his ability to pay. In other words, the rich should pay higher taxes to the government, because without the protection of government authorities they could not have earned and enjoyed their income.

In the second, which is Canon of Certainty, Smith posited that the tax which an individual has to pay should be certain, not arbitrary. The tax payer should know in advance how much tax he has to pay, at what time he has to pay the tax, and in what form the tax is to be paid to the government. Put differently, every tax should satisfy the canon of certainty. At the same, a good tax system also ensures that the government is also certain about the amount that will be collected by way of tax.

The third rule being the Canon of Convenience, talks about the mode and timing of tax payment, which Smith said should be as far as possible, convenient to the taxpayers. This must be so simple because a convenient tax system will encourage people to pay tax and will increase tax revenue.

Canon of Economy, which is the fourth by Smith, states that there should be economy in tax administration. The cost of tax collection should be lower than the amount of tax collected. It may not serve any purpose, if the taxes imposed are widespread but are difficult to administer. Therefore, it would make no sense to impose certain taxes, if they are difficult to administer.

Apart from Smith's original canon of taxation, some writers on public finance (Bastable, 1917 and Tina, 2009) have formulated other important canons/principles of taxation. They are canon of productivity, canon of elasticity, canon of simplicity, and canon of diversity.

The Association of Certified Chartered Accountants (ACCA) while elucidating on the principles that constitute an efficient and just tax system, in 2009, came out with a report titled the '12 tenets of tax'. The report which looked at the wider tax landscape and the new pressures facing governments across the globe, offer the basis for the evaluation of the effectiveness of any tax bill. While some of the tenets contained in the ACCA's policy paper agree with Smith's maxims, others differ with his line of thought due to complexities such as the advances in communications and technology which have led to the concept of tax competition, the level of state expenditure as a proportion of GDP in many countries or the almost universal reliance of governments on withholding of payroll and consumption taxes to collect the bulk of their revenues.

ACCA's 12 tenets of tax is presented below:

A Presumption of Tax Neutrality

Tax distortions can artificially encourage certain kinds of economic behaviours over others. Tax policies should be non-discriminatory unless part of a declared discriminatory policy, such as one which is aimed to discourage undesirable behaviours. There is a wider political question about the extent to which it is appropriate for taxation to be used as an instrument of social policy (e.g. penalizing smoking by heavy duties, or environmental taxes to mitigate climate change). ACCA's view is that this use of tax by elected governments is legitimate but such taxes should then meet the other principles such as being transparent, simple and effective. Governments should be wary of the effect on the complexity of the tax system of too much tinkering to reward certain groups to taxpayers.

There has been criticism that the global financial crisis has been exacerbated (though not caused) by policies in many tax regimes allow companies to deduct interest payments against tax but not returns on equity. As a result both leveraged buy-outs by private equity organizations and the holding of debt rather than equity by institutions has increased, which fuelled the credit boom which preceded the economic downturn. The International Monetary Fund has argued that governments should consider changing their rules which have effectively encouraged companies to seek finance via debt rather than equity and allowed individuals to take out larger mortgages. The IMF has voiced its fear that corporate level tax biases favouring debt finance including in the financial sector are pervasive, often large and hard to justify given the potential impact on financial stability.

While the deeper issues of whether neutrality is best served by taxation of income or consumption may never be amenable to definitive resolution, ACCA argues that governments must seek to remove the distortions in their own national tax systems (which also includes, for example, tax incentives being given for businesses to structure themselves in a certain way) and work together to try to iron out the differences in tax bases which give rise to tax arbitrage. For example, in the European Union, there are still many barriers which frustrate the workings of the single market. The sharing of best practice and knowledge between countries, of the sort envisaged by the G20 in the new era of financial regulation, could certainly be useful in the international tax world. It is important however, that this does not stretch into cartel-like behaviour which would damage the global economy.

Openness and Transparency

Tax payers should understand what they are paying, why they are paying it, and what the benefits of paying will be, paying tax may never be fun, but engagement with a demonstrably fair tax policy will be more palatable. There should be openness on the application of tax policy. So-called 'stealth taxes', such as the quiet reduction of tax exemptions, and the phenomenon of 'fiscal drag', whereby personal tax thresholds are not increased in line with rising prices and incomes, thus bringing more individuals into higher-rate tax bands, cannot be justified. Tax rises should be made openly and subject to debate.

ACCA believes that most countries' tax systems suffer from political positioning in the creation of tax policy rather than taking account of what would be best for the economy. This inevitably leads to poorly thought-out legislation, instability and complications in the system. And due to the complex and specialist nature of taxation we tend not to see sufficient scrutiny of the draft legislation during the democratic processes in many regimes. Too often, consultation processes on tax policy either do not exist or are flawed exercises where Government policy has already been decided and are carried out largely for appearances' sake. On major issues of tax policy, there should be clear consultation where the differing options are specified at the start and properly considered with an audit trail including unambiguous minutes and written responses.

In a policy paper of March 2009 ACCA promoted the use of independent tax policy committees. The proposal was that there should be a body of experts, separate from government-which would be tasked and empowered to formulate and propose tax policy. In addition, it would also have the express remit to seek to simplify tax systems which globally are far too complex. Government, under this model, would set the overall economic framework of the tax environment. It would need to define the public policy objectives (e.g. environmental, social welfare) in terms of public finance demands and fiscal targets that taxation measures were designed to achieve.

It would be of benefit to society, individuals and businesses if there was a clear link from tax takes to its application – i.e. taxpayers could see where the money is being spent. Issues such as 'green taxes' have fallen victim to cynicism as the public has not been convinced that the revenue raised has been spent on activities to help the environment but it simply an additional revenue – raiser cloaked with an environmentally – friendly banner. While we are not convinced that such 'hypothecation' of particular taxes to specific areas of spending is practicable, we do believe that there should be greater clarity in the public finances showing expenditure projections and how these are to be financed.

Simplification

ACCA believes that tax legislation and operations should be as simple and straight forward to understand and to comply with as possible. Complexity in the tax system is in itself a distortion of the economy, diverting productive energies into non-productive administration. Research shows that globally companies spend almost two months per year complying with tax regulations – 15 days for corporate income taxes. 21 days for labour taxes and contribution and 21 days for consumption taxes.

It is essential too that the volume of legislation is kept to a minimum. Much of the increase in tax law and administration in recent years is due to the number of new anti-avoidance measures introduced by tax authorities. Small businesses in particular have no time to engage in esoteric tax planning and are simply trying to cope with the volume of laws. Changes in tax law – particularly those which reverse previous tax breaks or incentives and which businesses have planned on the basis of – should be kept to an absolute minimum.

Certainty

Certainty is another key requirement – and an area where tax systems in many jurisdictions can be criticized in terms of certainty of outcomes or operations. Many tax systems call upon the tax payer to self assess their ability to tax, yet the wording of the legislation may make it impossible for tax payers to accurately establish their liability under the law. The United Kingdom and United States authorities do not explicitly ban certain types of tax planning, which are within the law, but nonetheless take a negative view of them. (In the US these are sometimes referred to as 'abusive transactions'). Companies using these legitimate tax planning techniques may find themselves having to report to the authorities artificial 'blocks' are used by the tax authorities as a way of 'fine – tuning' the legislation where it is unclear where the boundaries and who need certainty. It should always be possible for different taxpayers who look at legislation to come to the same interpretation of the law. And it should not be possible for authorities to challenge long-established practice, which businesses are accustomed to, on an obscure point of law. Tax payers must have certainty over revenue authorities' interpretations. Authorities should establish a proper and efficient clearing mechanism for complex anti-avoidance provisions.

Accountability and Regular Review

Tax systems should have a review principle whereby tax legislation is periodically overhauled and consolidated to bring it up to date and make it easier to follow. Outdated laws should be removed. Incentives operating to promote long term aims, such as investment in green infrastructure, should have been designed to incorporate regular reviews to ensure that the aim of the legislation is being met. There needs to be a positive prompt for justifying the existence of legislation. All anti-avoidance legislation should have sunset clauses attached to it. This will ensure that it is regularly reviewed and the need for it to remain in place is actively considered. Governments and tax authorities should devise clear metrics to gauge whether the tax system is being appropriately and sufficiently reviewed.

Tax Policy Is a Percentage of GDP

ACCA accepts that the current unprecedented economic turmoil may require special measures from governments. Notwithstanding current conditions, we believe that levels of taxation should be clearly stated as a percentage of Gross Domestic Product as far as is practicable. History has shown that too rapid a rise in the taxation burden to a level unsupportable by the economy can do immense harm and governments should monitor the rate of change in tax levels to avoid fiscal shocks in already weakened systems from proving fatal. In countries such as the UK and US, the trend prior to the current economic conditions has been for tax revenues to rise in recent years. In other countries, increasing the tax receipts to GDP ratio by tightening the tax compliance system has been a higher priority for authorities such as the International Monetary Fund.

ACCA does not seek to enter the political debate on the appropriate level of tax and public spending. But substantial tax increases represent a significant burden on businesses and individuals and should be subject to an impact assessment before being introduced. These impact assessments should be used to challenge the need for new regulations and to establish an accurate and updated estimate of costs. Once new measures are put into place there should be a means of measuring and evaluating their impact in terms of their proclaimed public policy objectives. Government should rationalize and set a target or tax levels as a percentage of GDP as part of its economic management and then be held to account via objective measurement and variance analysis.

Efficiency

Tax systems should be efficient for governments in terms of their ability to secure the revenue due and to prevent tax leakage and the development of a black economy. But it should also be efficient for taxpayers in terms of their ability to comply with its requirements. It should not be forgotten that small businesses represent the bulk of economic activity in most countries and regulation can have a disproportionate effect on small firms, as the smaller the business the heavier the compliance cost.

Research has shown that the smallest companies incur five times the administrative burden per employee than larger firms and so every effort must be made to increase efficiency of the system. Some test questions for administrations to consider might include: Can related companies be treated as single entities for VAT and other tax purposes and so be able to make only a single tax thing? Do multi-enquires of the same taxpayer by different parts of the tax authority take place? Are the size of tax returns and the numbers of new or revised forms which need to be completed reasonable and can be the taxpayer have flexibility between completing a paper return or an electronic return?

Governments should embrace new technology where practicable to streamline the administration of the tax system. Tax is part and parcel of economic activity, and as economic activity changes so should taxation. Computerization of banking systems, the virtualization of trade and commerce and the move to technologies such as e-invoicing has profound implications for the measurements and remission of taxes on income and consumption in particular.

Tax Shifting and Hypothecation Have a Role to Play

We have said above that elected governments have the right to use taxation in certain circumstances in pursuance of agreed social policies. ACCA believes one of the most important examples is to change behaviour which can damage the environment. Accountants should play an active part in efforts to reduce global carbon dioxide emissions and the concept of fossil fuels but reducing them for payroll, income or corporate taxes should be promoted. Governments must look to use tax policy as an instrument of positive change by incentivising investment in new cleaner technologies across a wide range of industries. When combined with other tax reductions, green taxes should be seen as a positive step rather than threat to taxpayers. Governments across the world are beginning to take significant steps to creating a low-carbon economy and accountants should help to identify the emerging fiscal incentives which will be a crucial part of that.

Green taxation is one area where it is particularly important that there is international co-ordination, partly because of the global nature of the environmental problem and also to prevent polluting companies moving operations to avoid the taxes. Arbitrage opportunities here would defy the purpose of projecting the environment. It should, however, be recognized that a significant shift in the tax base which places a great deal of reliance on green taxes at currently recognizable rates will probably prove unsustainable in the long term. This is because where such are imposed on emissions and general pollution, a successful system will erode its own tax base.

This is not merely theorizing but a realistic medium-term prospect where the UK government, for instance, intends to reduce CO_2 emissions by 80% by 2050.

Therefore, the way forward may be through a well balanced and broad tax base as well as relying more on regulation to drive down pollution.

Tax Is a Matter of National Sovereignty

The globalization of business means that each country should ensure its tax rates are competitive and its regime user-friendly. Tax is a key factor in ensuring the overall attractiveness of a location to mobile capital (businesses and individuals). Sophisticated taxpayers and investors recognize the importance of considering the underlying tax base of a country and not just the rates of tax. For instance the headline corporate tax rate could be cut but if other aspects of business tax such as capital allowances are consequently abolished then the net effect can be an increase in tax.

It is the quality of the underlying tax system-rather than a simple focus on comparative tax rates-which is of interest to companies. An ACCA study of the tax systems in Hong Kong, Singapore, the US, UK, Australia and Canada in 2008 revealed that accountants believed the first two fared clearly better than the others on key issues such as tax fairness, complexity, transparency and above all, sheer volume of tax laws. Retrospective changes to tax laws and stealth taxes were also criticized and the situation was exacerbated by lack of communication and an aggressive attitude on the part of the tax authorities to taxpayers. If this perception takes hold for long enough with no effective action to ameliorate it, a country's tax system could seriously damage prospects for inward investment and competitiveness. The problem with competition, however, can lie in very low tax rates, where offshore tax havens or flat tax systems can lead to 'beggar my neighbour' approaches, in which inward investment can be lured from one country to another and which may undermine agreed international financial initiatives. They can also have regressive rather than progressive tax outcomes and so entrench wealth inequality.

It is a difficult issue to balance the rights of sovereign nations to set their own tax rates and policies with the danger of low tax regimes causing retaliatory action and trade wars. ACCA supports the principle of nations being free to determine their tax affairs within the context of a global competitive environment. And it is important that powerful, but high-tax countries (for example in 'old Europe') do not use their influence to pressurize neighbouring countries and emerging economies to give up lower-tax regimes in the name of 'harmonization', which can be a means to cover up inefficiencies. The same can be said of G20 pressure on tax havens – while transparency and efforts to prevent tax evasion must be supported, actions motivated by protectionism and dislike of the downward pressure that low-tax jurisdictions engender, cannot be.

Tax Is Subject to the Rule of Law

Taxpayers are under a moral obligation to pay the level of tax set by the law. There is a clear division between tax avoidance (or planning, or mitigation), which is legal, and tax evasion which is not. The former is the legal exploitation of the tax regime to one's advantage, to attempt to reduce the amount of tax that is payable by means that are within the law whilst making a full disclosure of the material information to the tax authorities. In contract, tax evasion works outside the rules by trying to frustrate legal obligations by hiding income through nondisclosure, or improperly taking deductions that one is not qualified for.

But governments increasingly try to blur the distinction between the two by using phrases such as 'unacceptable tax avoidance' which is not helpful to taxpayers or their advisers. Tax law must be clear and certain and it should be remembered that businesses will look to minimize tax impact as a part of their normal commercial activity. Tax is a business cost like any other and company directors typically have a fiduciary duty to run the business in the most cost-effective manner.

As the case above reminds us, it is not unethical to minimize one's taxes. But while most businesses try only to comply with the law, there have been many cases of convoluted tax planning schemes which are designed not for any proper business purpose but to exploit loopholes in the law and avoid its spirit. ACCA does not support this artificial activity, which could be considered the equivalent of the creation of some of the extremely complex financial products, designed to get around banking regulation and which have had such a disastrous effect on banks. Such actions, which may generate short-term financial advantage at the cost of long-term value, cannot be supported.

Respect for Human Rights

Taxpayers have rights as well as responsibilities. They are obliged to pay their tax due, in full and on time, as this is the only way governments can generate the funding to provide the public services everyone depends on, and in this sense tax is part of the social contract of any civilized society. But the huge inequality in resources and power between governments and individual taxpayers places a responsibility on states not to impose their will in the field of taxation in an arbitrary or vexations way. For instance, the incorporation in to UK law since the 2nd October 2000 to the European Human Rights Act has empowered taxpayers to challenge pernicious tax law in cases where it could be argued there is fundamental uncertainty or unjustified additional cost of operating in one particular business vehicle rather than another. A similar approach throughout tax jurisdictions should become the norm.

Avoidance of Double Taxation

An essential principle of tax law must be that income should be subject to tax only once. This applies both to direct tax where an individual or business should suffer tax once and consumption taxes such as VAT where input tax recovery should be available at each stage of the transaction chair and only the end user, in the form of a private individual, ultimately pays the tax.

In the case of direct taxes there needs to be an efficient and effective mechanism available in all countries to give relief to a company which has already paid tax in another jurisdiction before subjecting that same income, in whole or in part, to taxation, in practice, too many countries do not consider it an important enough priority to seek to offer this full relief for tax suffered in another jurisdiction and this aspect of the global fiscal regime is an additional cost burden on multinational businesses.

The 'arm's length' principle whereby tax authorities treat transactions between connected parties by reference to the amount of profit that would have arisen if the same transactions had been executed y unconnected parties is a sensible and long-established convention which should be the basis of international tax affairs. Sales tax regimes are meant to be on the end user only but all too often Governments place restrictions or long delays on full input tax recovery and this again is creating unfair costs on businesses. If full recovery is not facilitated then it is unjust to charge the full VAT rate on the end user and only adds to creating a less efficient business environment.

Given the dynamic nature of modern economics and society, there is the possibility that governments across the world would achieve sustainability in tax collection and administration if they religiously apply the principles of tax enunciated by the foremost accounting body. As ACCA (2009, p. 2) rightly notes "unlike Smith, ACCA does not offer the 12 tenets as universal truths, but believes that if followed by governments these twelve policies would represent the basis of effective tax systems around the world".

Raising more revenue through taxation has form part of a new tax scheme initiatives proposed by World Bank and the International Monetary Fund (IMF) for developing economies. In a statement from IMF, the new initiative to help developing countries strengthen their tax systems was on the back of an analysis, which suggests that many lower-income countries have the potential to increase their tax ratios by at least two to four percent of the Gross Domestic Product without compromising fairness or growth. Besides, enthroning a regime of revenue stream that would ensure raising additional income, without distorting growth, will allow developing countries to fill financing gaps and promote development.

IMF's Managing Director, Christine Lagarde said "A strong revenue base is imperative if developing countries are to be able to finance the spending they need on public services, social support and infrastructure. But experience shows that with well-targeted external technical support and sufficient political will, it can be done". But the World Bank Group President, Jim Yong Kim, noted that financing gaps and promotion of inclusive growth are attainable if everyone pays their fair share of development obligations, even while challenging the status quo. According to him, "we very much want to help developing countries raise more revenues through taxes because this can lead to more children receiving a good education and more families having access to quality health".

The statement noted that the IMF/World Bank initiative has two pillars in response to country demands – deepening the dialogue with developing countries on international issues, aiming to help increase their weight and voice in the international debate on tax rules and cooperation; and developing improved diagnostic tools to help member countries evaluate and strengthen their tax polices. The initiative is riding on the back of the institutions' current tax programmes in over 48 developing countries and the IMF's technical assistance projects in over 120 countries. A key priority for the World Bank and IMF is to bring the voice and interests of developing countries particularly those too small to play a role at the G20 level into the debate on international tax policy issues. The initiative hopes to deepen the institutions' ongoing collaboration with developing countries to identify key international tax policy concerns and potential solutions, both at the country level and in the context of the continuing international dialogue. It concluded that plans are underway for the institutions to strengthen their diagnostic tools, develop new methodologies where needed, to enable member countries to identify priority tax reforms and design the requisite support for their implementation (www.worldbank.org/en/news/press-relese/2015/07/10/world-bank-and-the-imf-launch-joint-initiative-to-support-developing-countries-in-strenghening-tax-systems).

Emerging nations like Nigeria have a lot of benefit if they aggressively pursue tax reforms that would modernize their tax systems. For the desired results to be achieved, the reforms should cut across tax policies, tax laws and tax administration. The tax system in Nigeria has undergone significant changes in recent times. The tax laws are being reviewed with the aim of repealing obsolete provisions and simplifying the main ones. Taxation in Nigeria is within the administrative purview of the three tiers of government, that is, federal, state, and local governments as stated in the constitution, with each having its tax space delineated by the Taxes and Levies (Approved List for Collection).

In pursuing a vibrant tax fiscal policy, the Nigerian government has since 2002 embarked on series of tax reforms at the federal level. Beginning with the Federal

Inland Revenue Service (FIRS) Establishment Act, 2007, the drive has been on institutional reforms and modernization of the Nigerian tax system at the Federal level (Embuka, 2015).

Possible Impact of the CST on Development in Nigeria

Despite the huge revenue the Nigerian Government hopes to generate through the CST, questions are being raised by stakeholders regarding the economic impact of the proposed tax on the ICT sector, individual consumers and the entire economy.

ICT Sector

The controversial Communication Service Tax Bill is anticipated to impact negatively on the ICT sector if passed into law by the National Assembly of Africa's most populous nation. Key areas likely to be affected include the desired broadband penetration across the country, and the progress made so far on social and financial inclusion of the less privileged and unbanked public. Over the years, ICT tools have been deployed to increase access to formal financial services such as having a bank account and using credit and savings facilities of banks in Nigeria, and the result is quite impressive. The benefit of financial inclusion to national development is well documented. Some of these include poverty reduction, decrease in the level of inequality and enhanced private investment (Beck et al., 2007, Allen et., al. 2012). Also, financial inclusion enhances the attraction of remittances, as it eases the transfer of funds from abroad (Demirguc-Kunt et al. 2011). Other gains from financial inclusion include improved household consumption and female empowerment (Ashraf et al. 2010).

Reflecting on the impact the proposed tax would have on the ICT sector, the Alliance for Affordable Internet (A4A1) chaired by Dr. Omobola Johnson, pioneer Minister of Communications Technology in Nigeria, hinted that the new tax being considered by the country's National Assembly would prevent over 50 million Nigerians from being able to afford basic broadband connection. A4A1 noted that if passed into law, the bill would make basic Internet connection unaffordable for an additional 20 million Nigerians. "Broadband penetration stands at just 14 percent right now, imposing the tax may reduce this figure further", it stressed.

The CST is also expected to discourage further investment in the ICT industry, reduce inflow of foreign direction investment into the sector and reduce subscribers' level of data consumption. With an increase in operational costs, and mounting tax burden resulting from multiple taxation the CST would no doubt stifle the growth of the industry.

Consumers

Although the proposed tax would be paid by telecommunication service providers, it is obvious that the consumers will bear the tax burden since the service providers will eventually spread the costs on the services offered.

In a letter to the Finance and Communications ministries and signed by Director Africa, GSMA, Mortimer Hope; Gbenga Adebayo of ALTON; Lanre Adeolu Ogunbanjo of NATCOMS, the bodies stressed that if introduced, such tax will lead to increase in prices for consumers and impact negatively on the adoption of mobile services. The consumers who are already exploited by mobile network operators in the country will further be impoverished by the policy. The chief Executive Officer of Airtel Nigeria, Segun Ogunsanya, attested to this when he said that the planned tax bill would lead to increase in call charges, which would result in less minutes of use on networks.

While reminding the lawmakers of the socio-economic impact that mobile penetration has made in the country, the bodies (GSMA, ALTON, NATCOMS) made reference to a research conducted by the World Bank, which predicted that a 10 percent increase in mobile broadband penetration in low to middle income countries, led to a 1.38 percent increase in GDP growth (Minges 2015). According to them, to connect the yet to be connected Nigerians (who are typically lower income population groups) to the mobile platform, affordability remains a key challenge, just as they posited that further taxation on electronic communication services would nit lower income consumers the most, as they are already struggling due to the adverse economic situation in the country. Affordable access to information and communication technology is critical to the social and economic inclusion of this class of people.

President of ATCON, Olusola Teniola, who led a delegation of members on a courtesy visit to the Senate President, Dr. Bukola Saraki, in Abuja, reiterated that the new tax on ICT services would result in the exclusion of 20 million Nigerians, which represents about 10 percent of the country's population, from accessing telecommunication services. Olusola noted that the survival of the Nigerian economy is tied to attracting more citizens to access Internet and ICT services, stressing that it does not add up if whatever the government does ends up not bringing more people into access. According to him, the reality of Internet access in Nigeria is that it is all about mobile, adding that only 13 percent of Nigerians get broadband access via mobile, while less than one percent gets broadband from fixed services.

Economy

Given the contributions of the ICT sector to the Nigerian economy, one would least expect the government to do anything that will hinder the growth of the industry and by extension the economy of Nigeria since it contributes about 10 percent to the country's GDP. The CST is one tax too many for a sector already over-taxed. Severe over-taxation in the telecommunications industry has been blamed for the slow penetration of services into unserved areas of the country. In the last few years, some service providers have close shop due to the harsh operating environment leaving few to weather the storm. There is every reason to believe that these are not good times for the operators and the economy. Industry watchers are worried that the tax will finally cripple whatever efforts made to keep the sector going in the face of the harsh economic realities in the country. If this happens, there will be loss of jobs and revenue to government and the economy will be negatively affected.

The boom in mobile telecommunications is supposed to be a blessing to Africa. Mobile phones are a vital socio-economic necessity in modern Africa and it is therefore incumbent upon governments to view their proliferation across all societies as a priority. Imposing luxury taxes on mobile consumers is no longer appropriate. Poorer sections of society are hit hardest by the regressive taxes that widen the digital divide. Governments that levy luxury taxes on mobile consumers should urgently review such policies in consultation with the industry and other economic and taxation experts (GSMA 2012).

According to GSMA (2012), by removing luxury taxes on mobile consumers and moving to a more optimal tax structure, millions of Africans will afford connecting to, and communicating through mobile networks for the first time; governments will reap incremental increases in tax payments from the industry and wider economic and social benefits will be enjoyed by all.

MAIN FOCUS OF THE CHAPTER

Issues, Controversies, and Problems

Issues

At the outset of the economic recession in Nigeria, the Federal Government, propelled by dwindling oil revenue and the urgent need to fund budget deficits, proposed to the National Assembly a bill known as 'Communication Service Tax Bill 2015'. The bill was introduced to the Senate and House of Representatives amid citizens growing concern about the quality of service offered by the telecommunication companies operating in the country. While the companies' revenues increase due to growing number of subscribers, problems experienced by users still persist. Dropped calls, failed calls, network interruption, network congestion, failed attempts to load recharge cards, inability to activate the offered service, inability to send or receive SMS, unsolicited messages without an option to opt out and call misdirection to an unintended number, are prevalent, among other difficulties (Adepetun 2017).

A draft of the CST bill seeks to introduce a tax of 9 percent on telecommunication services spanning voice, data usage and other specified services. Communication service providers will be required to charge CST on in-scope services, and remit the CST charged to the Federal Inland Revenue Services, an agency of government responsible for collecting tax revenue at the national level (Ohadike 2016). The FIRS will in turn pay the remitted tax and any interest that might accrue to it to the federation account. Severe and cumulative non-compliance penalties await defaulters including ₦50,000 for failure to file returns on due date and an additional ₦10,000 each day the tax returns are not submitted (Nwakaegho 2016). This tax would be collected on top of the 5 percent Value Added Tax that consumers pay when they purchase devices and communication services, the 12 percent custom import duties paid on ICT devices, and the 20 percent tax levied on Subscriber Identification Module (SIM) cards.

The bill mandates the FIRS, Ministry of Communications and the Nigerian Communications Commission (NCC) to appoint an agent who will put in place electronic and physical monitoring mechanism to monitor, analyze, verify, save all necessary data and information. In addition, the FIRS, the ministry of communications, NCC and such agents must be given access to the network nodes of service providers at an equivalent point in the network where the network providers billing systems are connected (Osuagwu, 2016). However, a service provider who objects to a request for the introduction of an equipment or software to its physical nodes shall within 7 days of the request report in writing stating reasons for the objection to the RIRS and other relevant authorities. If after 14 days the issues are not amicably resolved, the service provider shall within 7 days apply to the high court. Where the high court upholds the request for the introduction of equipment to the service provider's network, the service provider will still be liable to the 5 percent penalty on its annual gross revenue.

However, several stakeholders and advocacy groups in the sector, including the Association of Telecommunication Companies of Nigeria (ATCON), Association of Licensed Telecommunication Operators in Nigeria (ALTON) and PriceWaterhouse Coopers (PWC), a multinational professional services firm, have taken a swipe at the bill describing it as a calculated attempt by government to stifle the growth of the industry. But government says its intentions are genuine and are for the progress of the country.

Controversies

Since the Communication Service Tax Bill 2015 was proposed, there has been a flurry of commentary around it. While the government is insisting that the legislative process regarding the bill must go on because of the revenue it hopes to generate (₦20 billion monthly) through the tax, major stakeholders comprising telecommunication operators in the industry want the bill discarded for the simple reason that it will impact negatively on the sector and the economy of the country.

President, Association of Telecommunication Companies of Nigeria (ATCON), Mr. Teniola Olusola, recently lashed out at the bill saying it would compound the woes of the telecommunication operators whom he described as already being overburden with multiple taxation and other levies. He argued that the necessary thing to do was for the government to discontinue the bill as it would reduce the inflow of foreign direct investment into the sector, reduce subscribers' level of data consumption and affect the sector's contribution to the country's gross domestic product. Engr Gbenga Adebayo, ALTON's President, also join the fray asking the government to withdraw the controversial bill.

PriceWaterhouse Coopers was, however, graphic with its own observations. In its 8-point analysis, the group said that:

1. The Bill seems to mirror the Ghana Communication Service Act. The reference in the Bill to National Health Insurance Levy, which is not applicable in Nigeria, shows the Bill was perhaps developed through a direct 'cut and paste' approach.
2. Although the CST is borne by the users of the electronic communication service, it imposes significant compliance burden and costs on the service providers.
3. The Bill does not provide for penalties for the Government monitoring agents for abuse or data protection violation. Confidentiality of the customers using the infrastructure has to be guaranteed and any consequential claims for damages should be borne by such agents or government officials.
4. The Bill does not clarify whether there will be a charge if the subscriber of the telecommunication or television service is outside Nigeria or foreign interconnect charges billed from Nigeria to foreign telecommunications providers.
5. The 7 days period for service providers to object to a request by the Government to introduce an equipment or software into the subscriber's network may not be sufficient to determine the risk associated with such interference as this may require technical expertise at a significant cost and time.
6. The CST Bill still imposes the payment of 5 percent of annual revenue tax after a court upholds the introduction of the Government monitoring equipment into the network. This will discourage service providers from challenging the

Government where it merely suspects that such introduction may create risks and affect the quality of service enjoyed by subscribers. Interestingly there is no compensation to the service provider where the court rules otherwise.

7.   The use of independent consultants could lead to unprofessional behaviour by consultants/agents who are motivated solely by commission for work done.

8.   Multiple taxation already exists in the information and communication technology industry such as IT tax on profits, Annual Operator Levy on turnover and VAT on consumption of their services. The introduction of the CST therefore increases the tax burden on both service providers and their customers. The consideration of the CST reflects the Federal Government's appetite to increase revenue through taxes.

Apart from voicing their grievances openly, they also expressed their fears in writing. In a letter dated March 30, 2016, the industry groups including the Association of Licensed Telecommunications Operators of Nigeria (ATCON); Association of Telecommunications Companies of Nigeria (ATCON); the National Association of Telecommunications Subscribers (NATCOMS) and the Global System for Mobile Telecommunications Association (GSMA), the body which represents mobile operators worldwide, jointly wrote to the ministers of Finance and Communications, Kemi Adeosun and Adebayo Shittu, stating the dangers the new tax system portend for the industry if it becomes law. In it, they asked government to jettison the move on the ground that it poses a great danger to the industry. In the midst of the agitations that have fuelled the controversy, it is not immediately clear whether government would back down by withdrawing the bill. Nevertheless, the Minister of Communications, Adebayo Shittu, has promised to consult widely and advise President Muhammadu Buhari on the way forward.

Problems

Nigeria is currently experiencing an economic downturn, the most severe in 25 years, that has brought untold hardship on citizens and businesses. In a period like this, there is no doubt, that government all over the world resort to unusual measures to change the negative fiscal template of the economy. Without sufficient funds, there is basically nothing the government can do to improve budget performance and fund development projects. Hence the need for more tax, but mulling different kinds of taxes at a time that food prices have soared, electricity is unstable, infrastructure is failing, cost of living is skyrocketing and the business environment is suffocating gives cause for serious concern.

The information and communication technology sector in Nigeria is already contending with multiple taxes and levies (numbering twenty-six) across all levels of government. The various tiers of government, including local councils and state government agencies, in a bid to shore up revenue and widen the pool of taxpayers, have created enormous challenges for the sector and some of the agencies often threaten to shut down base transceiver stations over alleged refusal of telecommunications companies to comply with a tax regime, which the operators see as grossly excessive. So, introducing another tax would not augur well for the masses and the telecommunications industry.

Solutions

In view of the controversy the 'CST Bill 2015' has provoked and its outright rejection by the key stakeholders in the industry, it is only natural that government gives it second thought and take concrete steps to address all the differing views about the bill in the interest of the growth of the sector and the entire Nigerian economy.

The following solutions are therefore proposed:

1. There is an urgent need for government to harmonize all the existing taxes relating to the telecommunications sector before commencing action on the CST. The number of taxes being paid by telecommunications operators in Nigeria is alarming. No sector can survive under such a huge tax burden.
2. Government should continue to engage the relevant stakeholders in the sector in a robust dialogue that will pave the way for a peaceful resolution of all the contending issues surrounding the CST Bill.
3. Before commencing further action on the bill, the National Assembly should call for public hearing involving telecommunications operators, subscribers, labour unions, organized private sector and other relevant stakeholders to chart the way forward for the industry.

Recommendations

Based on the issues X-rayed in this chapter and the problems presented, the following recommendations have become pertinent:

1. Government should withdraw the bill and re-introduce it later after all the contending issues raised by the advocacy groups and other stakeholders in the ICT sector have been adequately addressed.
2. If government insists on the CST because of the monetary attraction, it should therefore give the bill a human face by slashing the tax to at least 1 percent to lessen the burden on the telecommunications operators and subscribers.

3. Government should take a cue from other African countries where the CST was first introduced, but later mulled due to public outcry.
4. To survive the prevailing economic downturn, government should consider other areas of revenue generation other than the CST because of its multiplier effects on society.

FUTURE RESEARCH DIRECTIONS

Evidently, the ICT sector is playing a major role in the socio-economic development of Nigeria. The sector's contribution over the years is noteworthy and it has received positive reviews globally. Therefore, any policy of government that will unsettle the industry is not welcomed. In as much as government wants to shore up its revenue base, it should not do so at the expense of the industry and the masses who are struggling to survive as a result of the hardship foist on them by the prevailing economic recession in the country.

In line with the focus of the book which has to do with mobile technologies and socio-economic development in emerging nations, it is encouraging to prop up government especially in emerging countries to evolve policies that would promote the growth of the ICT industry rather than stifle it for short term monetary gains. To effectively leverage the ICT sector for the nation's sustainable growth and development, government needs to constantly consult and collaborate with the relevant stakeholders to achieve its set objectives for the industry. The industry can only benefit maximally if government and its agencies tread this path. Government and stakeholders cannot afford to work at cross purposes.

The multi-stakeholder governance model will therefore apply here. Sometimes known as multi-stakeholder initiate (MSI), it is a governance structure that seeks to bring stakeholders together to participate in the dialogue, decision making, and implementation of solutions to common problems or goals. Laurence Stric Kling, U.S. Assistant Secretary for Communications and Information, and NTIA Administrator, posits that the multi-stakeholder process involves the full involvement of all stakeholders, consensus-based decision-making and operating in an open, transparent and accountable manner (Utting 2001).

As government engages the stakeholders in a dialogue, there would be a need to monitor government on how well it is able to use the model to improve its consultation and collaboration strategies to formulate good policies that will stimulate and sustain the growth in the ICT industry. A multistakeholder monitoring involving telecommunication operators, subscribers, labour unions, civil society and organized private sector is desirable to ensure that policies of government are well thought out and articulated before they are unveiled to avoid the type of backlash that heralded the introduction of the CST Bill 2015.

CONCLUSION

Based on the various positions canvassed by stakeholders in the information and communication technology sector, it is evident that the proposed CST Bill would undermine the growth of the industry, if passed into law by the National Assembly.

It is understandable that the government is keen on diversifying its revenue base due to dwindling oil revenue, hence the introduction of the CST Bill. But the private sector players would also like to see an investment friendly tax environment, especially in the light of the prevailing high cost of doing business in the country.

Given the sector's role in digital transformation, improving the level of illiteracy, social and financial inclusion across the country, any success it hoped to achieve through the tax bill could be short-lived especially when considered within the context of its impact on infrastructure investment, broadband penetration, access to ICT services in remote areas, and reduced service usage by existing subscribers.

There is no doubt that the ICT sector is very strategic to sustainable growth and development in emerging societies. The Nigeria's example is a case in point. Emerging nations are therefore encouraged to do everything possible to sustain the tempo of growth in the industry as well as improve on it for the benefit of the larger society.

In view of the critical nature of ICT to the Nigerian economy, it is imperative that the National Assembly commits to making laws that would position the sector for increase performance rather than box it into a tight corner. If properly harnessed for national development, the sector could conveniently provide enduring jobs for the teeming unemployed graduates that roam the streets of Nigeria.

REFERENCES

ACCA. (2009). ACCA's 12 tenets of tax. Retrieved from http://www.accaglobal. com/content/dam/acca/global/pdf/tech-tp-ttt.pdf

Adepetun, A. (2017, January 1). How communication service tax will cripple ICT sector. The Guardian.

Allen, F., Demirgue-Kunt, A., Klapper, L., Soledad, M., & Peria, M. (2012). The foundations of financial inclusion: Understanding ownership and use of formal accounts. *World Bank Policy Research Working Paper*.

Ashraf, N., Aycinena, C., Martinez, A., & Yang, D. (2010). Female empower: Further evidence from a commitment savings product in the Philippines. *World Development*, 28(3), 333–344. doi:10.1016/j.worlddev.2009.05.010

Bastable, C. F. (1917). *Public finance*. London: Macmillan and Company Limited.

Beck, T., Demirgue-Kunt, A., Martinez, A., & Peria, M. (2007). Reaching out: Access to and use of banking services across countries. *Journal of Financial Economics*, 85(1), 234–266. doi:10.1016/j.jfineco.2006.07.002

Boone, L.E. and Kurtz, D.L. (2006). Contemporary business. Boulevard: Thomson South-Western.

Chand, S. (2016). Canons of taxation and equity in taxation explained. Retrieved from https://www.yourarticlelibrary.com/tax/canons-of-taxation-and-equity-in-taxation-explained/26284/

Embuka, A. (2015, March 30). Taxation: The swivel of the economy. DailySun.

GSMA. (2012). Taxation and the growth of mobile services in subSaharan Africa.

Kiable, B. D., & Nwankwo, N. G. (2009). *Curbing tax evasion and avoidance in personal income*. Owerri: Springfield Publishers.

Lawrence, C. S., & Kinder, P. D. (1987). *Law and business*. New Jersey: McGraw-Hill Publishing.

Minges, M. (2015). Exploring the relationship between broadband and economic growth. Background paper prepared for the World Development Report 2016: Digital Dividends. Retrieved from https://www.pubdocs.worlbank.org.en/391452529895999/WDR16-BP-Exploring-the-Relationship-between-Broadband-and-Economic-Growth-minges.pdf

Nwakaegho, T. (2016). Why Nigerians oppose proposed communication service tax bill. *Leadership*, (September).

Ohadike, J. (2016, September 8). Much ado about the proposed CST bill. ThisDay.

Osuagwu, P. (2016). All about new telecom service tax law. Retrieved from http://www.vanguardngr.com/2016/08/new-telecom-service-tax-law

Sunday, E., Nelson, C., Oyebade, W., & Jeremiah, K. (2017, January 1). Tax proliferation as an albatross. The Guardian.

Tina, S. (2009). Basic principles of taxation. Retrieved from http://www.conveyline.com/a/canon-of-Taxation/

Utting, P. (2001). Regulatory business via multistakeholder initiatives: A preliminary assessment paper prepared under the United Nations Research Institute for Social Development (UNRISD) research project "Promoting Corporate Environmental and Social Responsibility in Developing Countries: The Potential and Limits of Voluntary Initiatives.

Williams, H. J. (2007). *Introduction to business*. New York: Harper Collins Publishers.

World Bank. (2015). World Bank and IMF launch joint initiatives to support developing countries in strengthening tax systems. Retrieved from http://www.worldbank.org/en/news/press-release/2015/07/10/world-bank-and-the-imf-lauch-joint-initiative-to-support-developing-countries-in-strengthening-tax-systems

Chapter 3
Mobile Financial Services in Developing Countries:
The Impact on Consumer Financial Behaviour

Gordian Stanslaus Bwemelo
College of Business Education, Tanzania

ABSTRACT

This chapter describes how mobile technologies have recently emerged as the new wave in Information Technology revolution and are constantly gaining importance and popularity in nearly every avenue of our working and social lives. One area of mobile technology that has become a focus in recent times is the use of mobile devices particularly the mobile phones for an array of financial services. Mobile financial services and their massive adoption and rapid spread in the developing world, has deepened investments in mobile infrastructure and has further contributed to financial inclusion and economic development. Their adoption, in particular, has had a significant impact on consumer financial behaviour. This chapter builds on a rich body of literature available to highlight the impact of mobile financial services on consumer financial behaviour and the implications for financial institutions.

INTRODUCTION

Mobile technologies have recently emerged as the new wave in Information Technology (IT) revolution and are constantly gaining importance and popularity in nearly every avenue of our working and social lives. There is vast global interest in the role that mobile technologies can play in social and economic development.

DOI: 10.4018/978-1-5225-4029-8.ch003

Mobile phones, in particular, are now the technology of everyday life and their uses are certainly indispensable. As a convergence technology, mobile phones constitute multi-media devices that can perform multiple communicative functions. People around the world are using their mobile phones for a variety of purposes, such as making calls, sending short text messages, sending and retrieving e-mails, web browsing and retrieving documents.

The adoption and widespread use of mobile phones globally has been experienced as the most significant growth of consumer level technology (Merritt, 2010; Hinson, 2011). By the end of 2015, the total number of mobile phones in use stood at 7.6 billion, representing an estimated 4.6 billion mobile subscribers worldwide (Groupe Speciale Mobile Association [GSMA], 2015). Of the 4.6 billion mobile subscribers, 3.7 billion subscribers were located in low and middle-income economies. In the developing world the number of mobile-broadband subscriptions is increasingly growing: more than 90% of the incremental 1 billion new mobile subscribers forecast by 2020 will come from developing markets (GSMA, 2016).

The ubiquity of mobile phones and other mobile devices in our societies and the continued growth of mobile phone penetration in particular have had a significant social and economic impact. One area of mobile technologies that has become a focus in recent times is the use of mobile devices particularly the mobile phones for an array of financial services including mobile banking and other micropayment solutions. Accordingly, traditional payment providers are now moving aggressively into mobile payment space and also consumers' access to financial services is evolving.

Mobile financial services have established a clear and emerging new channel in the space of banking and payments (Pegueros, 2012). Mobile devices provide a new channel for banking, payments and transfers with greater reach than traditional bricks and mortar locations. Many people are using mobile devices for a range of financial transactions, such as receiving and sending money transfers. The increasing use of mobile technologies to access financial services has the potential to affect consumer finances and consumer behaviour.

This chapter builds on a rich body of literature available to highlight the impact of mobile financial services on consumer financial behaviour and the implications for financial institutions. Specifically, the chapter compares consumers' financial behaviours before and after the advent of mobile financial services.

BACKGROUND

Mobile phones have increasingly become tools that consumers use to interact with their financial institutions, make payments and manage their personal finance. Consumers are using mobile financial services more and more to access accounts, pay bills, pay tuition fees, deposit funds and manage their financial lives (Maree, Piontak, Omwansa, Shinyekwa & Njenga, 2013). Mobile financial services in developing countries help low-income, unbanked; under banked and economically vulnerable consumers achieve their financial goals.

This section provides an overview and the background of mobile financial services and is divided into three main parts. The first part introduces the concepts related to mobile financial services. The second part provides an overview of its trends and status in developing countries, drawing primarily on information from a few selected countries. The next part discusses how mobile financial services have become successful in the developing countries highlighting on factors that made the services successful.

Mobile Financial Services: What Are They?

The term "mobile financial services" (MFS) also known as mobile money services (MMS) refers to financial transaction services through mobile devices such as mobile phones or tablets. Mobile financial services may be provided by mobile network operators (MNOs), as well as by banks and other providers that use the MNOs' network (Kumar, McKay & Rotman, 2010). Ledgerwood, Earne and Nelson (2013) assert that "NMOs provide the ability to use mobile phones for financial services-either directly to consumers or on behalf of other financial service providers, usually through an agent network" (p. 4). The mobile financial services ecosystem encompasses a wide range of financial activities that consumers engage in or access using their mobile devices. MFS as shown in Figure 1 can be divided into three major categories: mobile banking, mobile payments and mobile transfers.

Mobile banking refers to provision of banking and financial services with the help of mobile telecommunication devices (Chandran, 2014). From a user perspective, mobile banking services are only available to people who possess a formal bank account. Like automated teller machine (ATM) services, mobile banking services allow consumers to access account information and perform transactions without

Figure 1. Mobile financial services

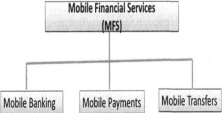

requiring physical access to bank branches. Mobile banking allows consumers to use their mobile phones as another channel for their banking services such as deposits, withdrawals, account transfers, bill payments and balance inquiry. Consumers are able to perform banking transactions from anywhere and anytime. This facility avoids the time spent travelling to a branch and standing in queues. However, there are usually daily mobile banking limits per business day, making it necessary to visit the bank branch.

Mobile payment (also commonly referred to as m-payment) refers to a noncash form of payment service performed via a mobile device (Cheney, 2008). It describes the use of a mobile device, usually a mobile phone to make payments for goods and/ or services. In this case, an electronic account (mobile wallet) linked to the SIM card in the mobile phone is used instead of cash. This electronic account is protected by a personal identification number (PIN), with accounts debited or credited as soon as the transaction takes place. To transact, mobile phone users need to deposit cash into their mobile wallet at the outlet of an agent of a local mobile telecommunications company (Subia & Nicole, 2014).

From a location perspective, mobile payments generally fall into two categories: proximity payment and remote payment. Mobile proximity payment describes the payment initiated from a mobile device at a point of sale (POS), such as a grocery store, gas station or supermarket. This method requires the mobile phone to make contact with a payment terminal (or other hardware) in the immediate vicinity. Near Field Communication (NFC) is the best-known proximity technology. It consists of a small antenna within a smartphone that allows bi-directional communication with NFC readers (contactless POS) to perform contactless payment transactions. Today, the vast majority of new smartphones are equipped with a NFC chip.

Mobile "remote payment," on the other hand, can be performed independently of the mobile phone's location. This method requires payments to be initiated and settled through the mobile cellular phone network in combination with an associated payment network. The necessary software resides online or within an app which enables the user to make online purchases. One of the best-known providers of this type of payment is PayPal. Remote mobile payments include transactions with a remote merchant through a mobile device. For example, payments for airtime top up and utility bills, purchase of ring tones and games can be undertaken without interacting directly with the merchant.

In many developing countries, mobile payments have gained traction because many consumers lack access to other noncash forms of payments such as credit cards or checks (Hayashi, 2012). Thus, mobile payments have been adopted as a convenient way of paying for such services as utility and airtime top up.

Mobile money transfer in this paper refers mainly to a financial service that allows unbanked people to send or receive money to/from any other mobile phone user. The transfer can be domestic or international and can also be called a "peer to peer" (P2P) transfer. When the transfer is international, it is referred to as an international remittance.

Mobile Financial Services Trends in Developing Countries

When it comes to technology-driven financial solutions, developing countries leapfrog ahead of developed countries (Popper, 2015). The best-known fact about mobile financial services is their massive adoption and rapid spread in the developing world. Research from the GSMA (2015) reports that approximately 255 mobile money services deployed in 89 countries globally in 2014 were accessible in more than 60 percent of developing markets.

In the majority of developing countries, mobile money accounts exceed bank accounts (GSMA, 2015). One study for example, found a sharp increase in the number of active mobile money accounts in 2014, where in East Africa one in two connections was linked to a mobile money account (Scharwatt, Katakam, Frydrych, Murphy & Naghavi, 2014). In East Africa alone, it was predicted that an additional 16 million new mobile money accounts would be opened in 2015. At the end of 2013, there were already more registered mobile money accounts than banks accounts in Cameroon, the Democratic Republic of the Congo, Gabon, Kenya, Madagascar, Tanzania, Uganda, Zambia and Zimbabwe. In 2014, Burundi, Guinea, Lesotho, Paraguay, Rwanda, the Republic of the Congo and Swaziland passed this threshold, bringing it to a total of 16 countries (GSMA, 2015).

Mobile financial services have been an invention bringing financial services to millions of previously unbanked and underbanked people around the world, making this industry a key enabler of financial inclusion (GSMA, 2015). The frequently cited region where mobile financial services are most widely spread is Sub Saharan Africa followed by Southeast Asia and Latin America (Runde, 2015).

The Philippines is among the countries where mobile money services have successfully reached a sustainable scale. It was one of the earliest adopters of mobile money services when SMART Communications in partnership with Banco de Oro launched SMART Money in 2001. The service enables customers to send and receive Smart Money domestically and internationally buy airtime, send and receive money domestically and internationally, and pay for goods using a card. In 2004, Globe Telecom launched GCASH, an SMS-based offering, which provides a cashless method for facilitating money remittances, settle loans, disburse salaries or commissions and pay bills, products and services via text message (Lal & Sachdev, 2015).

M-Pesa, first launched in 2007 in Kenya, was one of the first systems to embrace mobile financial services in East Africa and its impact has brought mobile money services to international prominence. Developed by telecom giants Vodafone and Safaricom with the blessing of the Central Bank of Kenya, M-Pesa represents the gold standard for innovative financial services. Using data preloaded on the SIM card, M-Pesa utilizes a SMS based interface to transmit money virtually to other phones. The system allows users to store money on their mobiles and transfer the amount via text message to anyone who owns a mobile phone. The operation is cheap, convenient and safe allowing millions of unbanked and under-banked people to gain financial inclusion.

Kenya has been a leader in the adoption of mobile financial service and M-Pesa is often considered the most successful mobile money service in the developing world. According to Safaricom, M-Pesa has been intricately merged into the daily life of Kenyans, rich and poor, rural and urban. It is rare to find a person in Kenya who is not aware of M-Pesa. Over 18 million Kenyans, equivalent to more than two-thirds of the adult population use the M-Pesa services (di Castri, 2013). Between 2008 and 2011, M-Pesa grew at 88% annually (Deb, & Kubzansky, 2012). In 2014, the service processed over $20 billion in transactions, a figure equal to more than 40% of the nation's GDP. Nearly a decade after its launch, M-Pesa has transformed economic interaction in Kenya. Its success reshaped Kenya's banking and telecom sectors, extended financial inclusion for nearly 20 million Kenyans, and facilitated the creation of thousands of small businesses. M-Pesa has been especially successful in reaching low-income Kenyans: new data indicates that the percentage of people living on less than $1.25 a day who use M-Pesa rose from less than 20 percent in 2008 to 72 percent by 2011.

M-Pesa has become the benchmark for successful mobile money launches and operations such that new mobile financial service operators seek to emulate the success. M-Pesa's success in Kenya has prompted new players to launch similar services in many emerging markets. Today there are a number of successful mobile money services around the world that are similar to or resultant from M-Pesa. A few of the other most successful examples include Tanzania and Ghana which by 2013 had achieved more than 10% of adoption of mobile financial services among their population (Gupta, 2013) (see Figure 2).

Tanzania offers another example of the most advanced mobile money markets in the world representing almost a third of all of East Africa's active mobile money accounts in 2015 (GSMA, 2015). According to GSMA (2015), by 2015 there were four mobile money providers in the country: Vodacom with M-Pesa (42% market share), Tigo Pesa (31%), Airtel with Airtel Money (24%), and Zantel with Ezy Pesa (3%) (see Figure 3). M-Pesa was first introduced in Tanzania in 2008, in 2008 followed by Zain with Zap Money (now Airtel Money), Zantel with Z-Pesa (now EzyPesa) in 2009 and Tigo with Tigo-Pesa in 2010. In 2016, Halotel became the fifth mobile money provider in Tanzania with Halo Pesa.

Figure 2. Adoption of mobile financial services in emerging markets
Gupta, 2013.

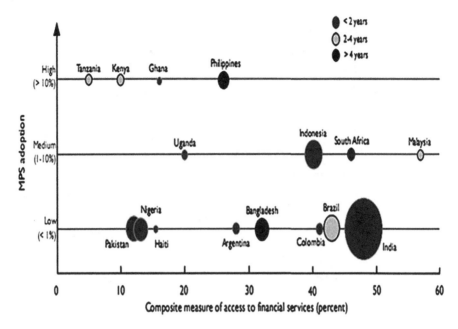

Mobile money has seen impressive growth since its launch in 2008. By the fourth quarter of the year 2016, the number of Tanzanians with mobile money account stood at 18 million (35% of the population) making its penetration rates reach 67%, according to the Tanzania Communications Regulatory Authority (TCRA). Since the launch of mobile money in 2008, over 40m mobile money accounts have been registered making 95m mobile money transactions per month in total, transacting an average of USD1.6b per month

In addition to mobile money services, mobile operators in Tanzania offer other mobile financial services such as financing and micro financing services, and mobile insurance. In 2012, Tigo launched Tanzania's first mobile insurance service, Tigo Bima, offering life and hospitalization cover. Tigo customers, both in Tanzania and Rwanda, were also the first ever to use an international mobile money transfer service with instant currency conversion.

MNOs in Tanzania have managed to interconnect their services with one another making Tanzania emerge as the first country in the world to achieve full interoperability. In December 2014, Tigo connected with Zantel, and in February 2016, Vodacom announced connecting with Airtel and Tigo. International interoperability has also been a reality in Tanzania through the partnerships of mobile money operators with international money transfer services like MoneyGram and Western Union.

Figure 3. Tanzania mobile money accounts and market share by provider
GSMA, 2016.

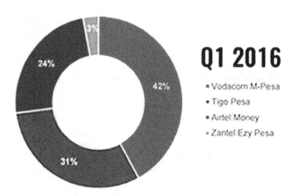

Operator	January	February	March
Airtel Money	4,056,498	4,099,632	3,980,831
Tigo Pesa	5,277,584	5,217,428	5,105,149
M-Pesa	7,469,540	7,180,124	7,030,132
Ezy Pesa	325,736	415,165	419,765
TOTAL	17,129,358	16,912,349	16,535,577

Vodacom Tanzania also allows for operator-to-operator international money transfer interoperability through its partnerships with Safaricom in Kenya.

Ghana is another country whose economy has been reshaped by mobile money services. Telcom Company MTN Ghana was the first company to introduce mobile financial services in Ghana in July 2009. It called it MTN Mobile Money, followed by Tigo with Tigo Cash and Airtel with Airtel Money (Wemakor, 2014).

The mobile financial services industry has created jobs for the mobile money agents, service providers and users including Fintech companies, merchants, retailers, and aggregators (Bank of Ghana, 2017). At the end of December, 2016, the number of mobile money agents stood at 107, 415; with MTN mobile money contributing 54.0 per cent, TIGO Cash 24.9 per cent, Airtel Money 11.0 per cent and Vodafone Cash 10.1 per cent (Bank of Ghana, 2017).

Why Are Mobile Financial Services So Successful in Developing Countries?

Successful implementation of any transformation initiative starts with a question 'what problem can I solve?' This has been apparently the case for the success of mobile money services in developing countries. The circumstance to meet financial needs of low income and financially underserved consumers has been the key success factor of mobile financial services in developing countries. For many people in developing countries, access to financial services at formal financial institutions is very limited, resulting in traditional "bricks and mortar" financial institutions to struggle to provide convenient, safe and affordable financial services to the underserved customers, thereby increasing financial inclusion, particularly in rural areas (Scharwatt et al., 2014). According to Scharwatt et al. (2014), of 2.5 billion people in developing countries who are 'unbanked', approximately one billion of these people have access to a mobile phone, which can provide the basis for extending the reach of financial services such as payments, transfers, insurance, savings, and credit. Hence, mobile phones have a perfect vehicle, given their widespread adoption, even among the low-income earners.

Most of the financially underserved populations live in developing countries. In developing countries, 2.5 billion people are 'unbanked' and have to rely on cash or informal financial services which are typically unsafe, inconvenient and expensive (Scharwatt, Katakam, Frydrych, Murphy & Naghavi, 2014). By 2015, more than 270 mobile-money services were operating in 93 countries, with an estimated 411 million accounts (Rob, 2016). In this context, mobile financial services constitute an opportunity for the financial inclusion of the poor. Based on the current rate of access to mobile phones, the Tanzanian market shows potential for further m-money adoption. According to the first annual FITS survey conducted in 2012, it was found that 56% of households in Tanzania own at least one active SIM card which is required for opening an m-money account.

THE IMPACT OF MOBILE FINANCIAL SERVICES ON CONSUMERS' FINANCIAL BEHAVIOUR

The increasing use of mobile technologies to access financial services over the past few years has been the major development in the consumer financial services market (Consumer Financial Protection Burea [CFBP], 2015). Mobile financial services have not only offered conveniences and security for transfers and payments but also have had a significant impact on people's financial behaviours. Since the mobile financial services took hold in the late 2000's, various consumers' financial practices have changed significantly (GSMA, 2015). Studies of the impact of mobile financial services on the consumers' financial behaviour have just started to emerge. This section highlights the impact of mobile financial services on various behavioural categories such as saving habits, budgeting, interactions with financial institutions, insurance, receiving and sending remittances, spending and purchase behaviour

A number of key findings emerging from various studies indicate that mobile financial services have increased the capacity of low-income earners to save. According to a study conducted by Nandhi (2012) in India, the ability to save has improved for a majority of users through EKO[1] mobile banking by comparison to earlier practices such as keeping cash on hand. With EKO's mobile banking, the majority of low income users in the study (95 per cent) consider EKO mobile money accounts as a preferred alternative over other forms of savings (Nandhi, 2012). Basically, convenience, security of savings, efficiency of transactions, reliability, flexibility, safety, secrecy, promptness of agent servicing were some of the main reasons why EKO mobile banking was considered as a good substitute.

In another study conducted by Sangaré and Guérin (2013) in Mali to assess the potential of mobile banking in favour of financial inclusion in a context where access to formal finance is limited, the impact of mobile banking on users' saving practices was revealed. The mobile wallet allows users to keep aside a surplus of money to deal with unexpected expenses or payments in a context of higher income uncertainty and volatility. 39% of the surveyed population affirms noting a rise in their savings due to the use of a mobile account (Sangaré & Guérin, 2013)

One of the most recent studies was conducted by Wamuyu (2016) to investigate the potential of using mobile money accounts as a money management platform that can help promote a savings culture among poor households in Kenya. The study examined innovative ways in which poor households could use mobile money accounts as a tool for financial inclusion, achieving household financial security, and enhancing family role performance. This was based on the premises that 41% of Kenyans are low income earners and thus they do not save regularly.

The study found that over the years Kenyans, particularly low-income earners; have been saving their money in rotating savings and credit associations of which most of them are informal. In many households, saving was mostly as cash under the mattress. With mobile lock savings accounts, mobile money savings have influenced welfare of many households by providing a chance to save money for a defined purpose and for a specified amount of time hence reducing chances of misusing the money. In many Kenyan families living in slums, most fathers are alcoholic and may not fulfil their family roles. Thus, with a mobile money fixed deposit savings accounts, it is now possible to have fathers locking the money they do not intend to use before going to his drinking location. This allows this parent to have finances to meet his family obligations.

As is the case with savings, mobile devices have increasingly become new tools consumers use for budgeting. Mobile phones have started to be utilized as personal financial management tools. Some people are using mobile devices to manage their finances. It is realized that many mobile banking users use their mobile phones to check account balances or available credit before making a large purchase. Furthermore, some mobile phones not only allow their users to access financial accounts but also to track purchases and expenses. It is known fact that consumers can take advantage of other applications on their mobile phones, such as text alerts, to make smarter financial decisions. For example, the low balance alerts provided by banks are an effective tool for encouraging consumers to engage in better financial behaviours. A good lesson is learnt from the U.S where one-third of mobile banking users indicate that they receive text message alerts from their bank and, out of this group, 66% receive "low-balance alerts". Nearly all report taking some action in response to getting a low-balance text alert from their bank: transferring money into the account with the low-balance (58%), reducing their spending (41%), or depositing additional money into the account (16%) (The Federal Reserve Board, 2013). This suggests that mobile users are less likely to incur overdraft and credit card penalty fees.

Additionally, the emergence of mobile financial services has affected consumers' interaction with their financial institutions (GSMA, 2016). Mobile financial services offer self-service options that enhance the customer experience by making it easier for consumers to interact with their financial institutions regardless of time or location. Today mobile devices have become companions of consumers' mobility such that interaction with mobile phone represents a significant part of the time spent by the mobile phone users. As a result, customers are noticeably spending less time visiting bank branches. Traditionally, customers used to visit physical banking institutions two or three times as frequently as mobile or online banking customers. Nowadays many customers visit physical banking facilities rarely, conducting the majority of their banking transactions such as paying bills, checking balances, or making transfers on their mobile devices. The main reasons that bank clients still visit bank branches are to withdraw cash, deposit money into their bank account, change money into different currencies, make international transfers and for financial consulting. As facilities for mobile payment in retail continue to spread, we can expect to see the number of cash withdrawal visits shrink over time. This interactive nature of mobile banking implies that financial institutions should develop a strategic "digital" or "mobile" plan, and consider mobile as their key infrastructure platform for service delivery.

When it comes to sending or receiving remittances, mobile money is perceived as a gamechanger. In most developing countries a great number of households depend on domestic remittances. An increase in urbanisation in city centres and persistent rural-urban migration means that the need for money transfer services has been quite significant. The impact of mobile money transfer is especially important for poor people in rural areas for whom traditional banks and related financial services are often inaccessible. Until recently, without access to mobile money services, cash could be sent through persons travelling to the destination, such as bus or truck drivers, but such informal mechanism was risky. Other methods of remittances were using visiting family and friends or traveling long distances to remit the funds whenever necessary. Armed robbery, theft and accidents are a few of the challenges with these methods of remittance. Due to its reliability, mobile money is now the main avenue for sending and receiving remittances in many developing countries (Jack & Suri,

2011; Morawczynski, 2009; Mirzoyants, 2013). Rural householdes in developing countries are more likely to receive remittances from their distant relatives and friends through mobile money technology (Kikulwe, 2014). Equally, urban households with relatives in rural areas use mobile money services more frequently.

Another fruitful pathway of how mobile money services affect financial behaviour is through the possibility of using mobile money to create informal insurance. The poor are at risk of multiple communal shocks including natural disasters, conflicts, illness, deaths and theft. To insure against these risks, family, clan and network ties can create informal insurance networks, spreading risk by periodic transfers and monitored by trust relationships amongst members of the network (De Weerdt & Dercon 2006). The mobile money technology allows small and more frequent transfers of money that make for a more flexible management of negative shocks. Thus, informal insurance networks may function more effectively. In turn, more efficient investment decisions can be made, improving the risk and return trade off.

Mobile money technology has also had an impact on the consumers spending behaviours. A handful of studies suggest that the mode of payment affects perceptions of money and spending behaviour (Vandoros, 2013; Raghubir & Srivastava, 2009; Chatterjee & Rose, 2012; Raghubir & Srivastava, 2008). Cobla, Assibey and Asante (2015) conducted a study at the University of Ghana to investigate how the use of the mobile money technology among students affects their spending behaviour. The findings of the study revealed that on a monthly basis, students who use mobile money technology spend nearly 19 Ghana Cedis more than their colleagues who do not use mobile money. Likewise, while studying university students from Jordan, Smadi and Al-jawazneh (2011) noted that students using mobile technology spend more cash in impulse purchase. This is the fact that mobile money facilitates access to funds at any point in time and thus the purchaser would easily make un-planned purchase. This is based on the notion that payments by cash is memorable and painful and that electronic transfers are less so.

CONCLUSION

The overall objective of this chapter was to highlight the impact of mobile financial services on consumer financial behaviour and the implications for financial institutions. The findings from the literature have uncovered some interesting facts about the consumers' financial practices. The chapter reports that mobile financial services have been well established in the majority of developing countries. Mobile financial services have become a core offering for many mobile network operators in developing countries, deepening investments in mobile infrastructure and further contributing to financial inclusion and economic development. Their adoption, in particular, has had a significant impact on various behavioural categories such as saving habits, budgeting, interactions with financial institutions, insurance, receiving and sending remittances, spending and purchase behaviour. Mobile financial services have increased the capacity of low-income users to save. On the other hand, mobile financial services have reduced physical visits and face-to-face interactions with financial institutions. Nowadays, customers are less dependent on bank branches for services such as paying bills, checking balances, or making transfers as these can be carried out easily using online banking from home and are becoming more widely available as mobile services.

In essence, mobile money technology has the potential to lift people in developing countries out of poverty. As mobile financial services continue expanding the opportunities for financial inclusion, they raise the need for financial institutions and MNOs to pursue more synergistic operating models to develop a wider range of financial services that can be extended to more mobile users. Interoperability and more product lines beyond transfers and payments will help to enhance the customer experience by making it easier for consumers and businesses to access more financial services. Further partnerships will increase the volumes of international remittances being conducted via mobile money in while driving down the cost for senders. In addition, more proactive policies are required to ensure that the market can continue to grow and serve local consumers. The obstacles prevailing in some markets should be overcome in order for mobile financial services to reach more people and achieve the scale to which it aspires.

REFERENCES

Bank of Ghana. (2017). *Impact of Mobile Money on the Payment System in Ghana: An Econometric Analysis*. Payment Systems Department.

Chandran, R. (2014). Pros and cons of Mobile banking. *International Journal of Scientific and Research Publications*, *4*(10).

Chatterjee, P., & Rose, R. L. (2012). Do payment mechanisms change the way consumers perceive products? *The Journal of Consumer Research*, *38*(6), 1129–1139. doi:10.1086/661730

Cheney, J. S. (2008). An Examination of Mobile Banking and Mobile Payments: Building Adoption as Experience Goods? Retrieved December 10, 2017 from https://philadelphiafed.org/-/media/consumer-finance-institute/payment-cards-center/publications/discussion-papers/2008/D2008MobileBanking.pdf

Cobla, G.M., Assibey, E.O. & Asante, Y. (2015). Mobile Money Technology and Spending Behaviour of Students at the University of Ghana.

Consumer Financial Protection Bureau (CFPB). (2015). *Mobile financial services; A summary of comments from the public on opportunities, challenges, and risks for the underserved.*

De Weerdt, J., & Dercon, S. (2006). Risk-sharing networks and insurance against illness. *Journal of Development Economics*, *81*(2), 337–357. doi:10.1016/j.jdeveco.2005.06.009

Deb, A., & Kubzansky, M. (2012). *Bridging the Gap: The Business Case for Financial Capability.* A report commissioned and funded by the Citi Foundation. Cambridge, MA: Monitor, March.

di Castri, S. (2013). *Mobile Money: Enabling Regulatory Solutions.* London, United Kingdom: GSMA.

Economides, N., & Jeziorski, P. (2015). Mobile money in Tanzania.

Groupe Speciale Mobile Association (GSMA). (2015). *The Mobile Economy 2015.*

Groupe Speciale Mobile Association (GSMA). (2016). *The Mobile Economy 2016.* Retrieved December 10th, 2017, from https://www.gsma.com/mobileeconomy/archive/GSMA_ME_2016.pdf

Groupe Speciale Mobile Association (GSMA). (2016). The Mobile Economy 2016. https://www.gsma.com/mobileeconomy/archive/GSMA_ME_2015.pdf

Gupta, S. (2013). Te Mobile Banking and Payment Revolution. *European Finance Review*, *3*, 3–6.

Hayashi, F. (2012). *Mobile Payments: What's in It for Consumers?* Federal Reserve Bank of Kansas City.

Hinson, R. E. (2011). Banking the poor: The role of mobiles. *Journal of Financial Services*, *15*(4), 320–333. doi:10.1057/fsm.2010.29

Jack, W., & Suri, T. (2011). *Mobile money: The economics of M-PESA (No. w16721).* National Bureau of Economic Research. doi:10.3386/w16721

Kikulwe, E. M., Fischer, E., & Qaim, M. (2014). Mobile money, smallholder farmers, and household welfare in Kenya. *PLoS One*, *9*(10), e109804. doi:10.1371/journal.pone.0109804 PMID:25286032

Kumar, K., McKay, C., & Rotman, S. (2010). Microfinance and mobile banking: The story so far.

Lal, R., & Sachdev, I. (2015). *Mobile Money Services-Design and Development for Financial Inclusion (Vol. 83)*. Working Paper 15.

J. Ledgerwood, J. Earne, & C. Nelson (Eds.). (2013). *The new microfinance handbook: A financial market system perspective*. World Bank Publications. doi:10.1596/978-0-8213-8927-0

Maree, J., Piontak, R., Omwansa, T., Shinyekwa, I., & Njenga, K. (2013). Developmental uses of mobile phones in Kenya and Uganda.

Merritt, C. (2010). Mobile money transfer services: The next phase in the evolution of person -to-person payments. *Journal*, *5*(2), 143–160.

Mirzoyants, A. (2013). *Mobile Money in Tanzania: Use, Barriers and Opportunities*. Intermedia Financial Inclusion Tracker Surveys Project, February.

Morawczynski, O. (2009). Exploring the usage and impact of "transformational" mobile financial services: The case of M-PESA in Kenya. *Journal of Eastern African Studies: the Journal of the British Institute in Eastern Africa*, *3*(3), 509–525. doi:10.1080/17531050903273768

Nandhi, M. A. (2012). *Effects of mobile banking on the savings practices of low income users–The Indian experience* (working paper 7). Institute for money technology and financial inclusion.

Pegueros, V. (2012). *Security of mobile banking and payments*. SANS Institute Info Sec Reading Room.

Popper, B. (2015). *Can Mobile Banking Revolutionize the lives of the Poor?* Retrieved March 12th, 2017, from www.theverge.com/2015/2/4/.../bill-gates-future-of-banking-and-mobile-money

Raghubir, P., & Srivastava, J. (2008). Monopoly money: The effect of payment coupling and form on spending behavior. *Journal of Experimental Psychology. Applied*, *14*(3), 213–225. doi:10.1037/1076-898X.14.3.213 PMID:18808275

Raghubir, P., & Srivastava, J. (2009). The denomination effect. *The Journal of Consumer Research*, *36*(4), 701–713. doi:10.1086/599222

Runde, D. (2015). M-Pesa and the rise of the global mobile money market. *Forbes*, (August), 12.

Sangaré, M., & Guérin, I. (2013). *Mobile money and financial inclusion in Mali: what has been the impact on saving practices?*

Scharwatt, C., Katakam, A., Frydrych, J., Murphy, A., & Naghavi, N. (2014). *State of the Industry: Mobile Financial Services for the Unbanked.* Retrieved March 12th, 2016, from www.gsma.com/mobilefordevelopment/wp-content/uploads/2015/.../SOTIR_2014.pdf

Smadi, Z. M., & Al-Jawazneh, B. E. (2011). The consumer decision-making styles of mobile phones among the University Level students in Jordan. *International Bulleting of Business Administration.*

Subia, M. P., & Nicole, M. (2014). *Mobile Money Services: "A Bank in Your Pocket" Overview and Opportunities.* ACP Observatory on Migration. Retrieved from http://publications.iom.int/system/files/pdf/mobile_money.pdf

The Federal Reserve Board. (2013). Consumers and Mobile Financial Services.

Vandoros, S. (2013). My five pounds are not as good as yours, so I will spend them. *Experimental Economics*, *16*(4), 546–559. doi:10.1007/s10683-013-9351-2

Wamuyu, P. K. (2016). Promoting savings among low income earners in Kenya through mobile money. In IST-Africa Week Conference.

Wemakor, J. K. (2014, December 19). *The Impact of Mobile Financial Services on Ghana's Economy. How relevant?* Joy Business. Retrieved March 29th, 2017, from http://m.myjoyonline.com/marticles/business/the-impact-of-mobile-financial-services-on-ghanas-economy-how-relevant

KEY TERMS AND DEFINITIONS

Financial Behaviour: Financial management practices such as savings, budgeting, investing, and insurance, credit, cash, and spending and purchase behaviour.

Financial Inclusion: Delivery of delivery of financial services at affordable costs to disadvantaged and low-income groups of society. Financial inclusion initiatives seek to ensure that all households and businesses, regardless of income level, have access to and can effectively use the appropriate financial services they need to improve their lives. Individuals who are financially included are able to make day-to-day transactions, including sending and receiving money; safeguard savings, which can help households manage cash flow spikes, smooth consumption and build working capital; finance their small businesses or microenterprises; plan and pay for recurring expenses, such as school fees; mitigate shocks and manage expenses related to unexpected events such as medical emergencies, a death in the family, theft, or natural disasters; and improve their overall welfare.

Interoperability: A term describing the interconnection that allows transactions to flow across diverse payment systems. With regard to mobile financial services, that would mean transfer of money between mobile money accounts or mobile money and bank accounts, both domestically and internationally. One example of interoperability is the interconnection between m-Pesa and MTN Mobile Money in East Africa. In this case, customers of M-Pesa and MTN Mobile Money are able to transfer money to each other following an agreement between Vodafone Group and MTN Group to interconnect their mobile money services. This interconnection between the two mobile money operators enable convenient and affordable international remittances between M-Pesa customers in Kenya, Tanzania, Democratic Republic of Congo and Mozambique, and MTN Mobile Money customers in Uganda, Rwanda and Zambia.

Mobile Lock Savings Account: A savings account that allows mobile money customers to save for a defined purpose and for a specified period of time. The funds saved on the mobile lock savings account will be kept in the account until the maturity date.

Mobile Technology: Technology that allows tasks to be performed via portable electronic devices particularly the cellular phones. It includes the use of a variety of transmission media such as: radio wave, microwave, infra-red, GPS and Bluetooth to allow for the transfer of data via voice, text, video, 2-dimensional barcodes, etc.

Mobile Wallet: Type of mobile technology that allows businesses and individuals to receive and send money via mobile devices. An individual holds such items as credit and debit cards, medical records and all of the items that a physical wallet would carry on his/her mobile device.

Remittances: Money sent home in form of wire transfer or cash or cheques by relatives or friends working abroad or in urban areas. In developing, where people leave their home to make a new life for themselves in another other country or urban areas, the families left behind may not able to support themselves without some assistance. Support for the families will generally fall on the one (or more) person sent abroad, with the family dependent on remittances being sent back to them.

ENDNOTE

[1]   EKO is a financial service start-up company offering mobile money services in India through partnership with the State Bank of India (SBI). It partners with a network of agents—chemists, grocers, airtime vendors—to provide banking services to people with no access to formal bank accounts.

Chapter 4
Mobile Application for Ebola Virus Disease Diagnosis (EbolaDiag)

Kwetishe Joro Danjuma
Modibbo Adama University of Technology Yola, Nigeria

Solomon Sunday Oyelere
University of Eastern Finland, Finland

Elisha Sunday Oyelere
Obafemi Awolowo University, Nigeria

Teemu H. Laine
Luleå University of Technology, Sweden

ABSTRACT

This chapter describes how the Ebola virus is considered extremely infectious with a series of physical and psychological traumas on the victims. Common clinical signs associated with the disease include a sudden fever, severe headaches, muscle pain, fatigue, diarrhea, vomiting, and unexplained hemorrhages. In Africa, with strained medical facilities and remote localities, prompt identification and diagnosis of the symptoms of Ebola in a suspected patient are important to the control of the epidemic and in curtailing further spread. This chapter presents the development of an Android mobile application called EbolaDiag (Ebola Diagnosis), which is capable of supporting the diagnosis, screening, and healthcare experts working on the frontline in contact tracing and monitoring of the spread of Ebola. Furthermore, EbolaDiag is suitable for aiding the strained medical facilities in endemic areas. In addressing this gap, the application provided a model for implementing such solutions in pandemic environments. Such a solution becomes more relevant and useful to combat Ebola and several other diseases in similar environments.

DOI: 10.4018/978-1-5225-4029-8.ch004

INTRODUCTION

Ebola virus disease (EVD) outbreak in West Africa in 2014, was the largest and most complex Ebola outbreak (Wong & Kobinger, 2015) since it was first discovered in 1976, in terms of geographical spread, number of cases and deaths recorded as well as the proportion of healthcare workers infected (Dahiya & Kakkar, 2016). The epidemic started in Guinea and spread to Sierra Leone, Liberia, Nigeria, Senegal, and Mali (Cenciarelli, et al., 2015; Dhama, Malik, Malik, & Singh, 2015), and was imported into North America, and Europe (Baden, et al., 2014; Roca, Afolabi, Saidu, & Kampmann, 2015).

EVD is a thread-like non-segmented, negative-sense, and single-stranded ribonucleic acid (RNA) virus that belongs to the Filoviridae family (Roca, Afolabi, Saidu, & Kampmann, 2015). Filoviridae is the deadliest pathogens known to both humans and nonhuman primates (NPHs) (Wong & Kobinger, 2015). It is made of the Ebola virus (Zaire ebolavirus), Sudan ebolavirus, Tai-forest ebolavirus (Cote d'Ivoire ebolavirus), Bundibugyo virus and Reston ebolavirus (Beeching, Fenech, & Houlihan, 2014; Kuhn, et al., 2010; MacNeil, et al., 2011).

It causes haemorrhage, uncontrolled virus replication, multiple organs dysfunctions, intravascular coagulation, and shock-like syndrome (Bird, et al., 2016; Feldmann & Geisbert, 2011; Paessler & Walker, 2012). However, prevention and core containment have been established as the most effective response to EVD infection (Krause, et al., 2015). Core containment measure involves effective case management, active surveillance and contact tracing, communication and social mobilization, early detection and timely response (Tom-Aba, et al., 2015).

In order to address these needs, mHealth have demonstrated efficacy in addressing access, coverage, and equity gaps in healthcare management in developing and resource-poor country (Beratarrechea, et al., 2014). The application of mobile phones and the use of innovative health applications in tackling health challenges gave prominence to what is known as mobile health (mHealth) (Bholah & Beharee, 2016). The term was first coined and defined to mean, "emerging mobile communications and network technologies for healthcare" (Istepanian, Laxminarayan, & Pattichis, 2006). During the 2009 mHealth Summit, mHealth was redefined by the Foundation for the National Institutes of Health (FNIH) to mean "the delivery of healthcare services via mobile communicational devices" (Torgan, 2009). It has further been defined by the Global Observatory for e-health of the World Health Organization (WHO) as the "medical and public health practice supported by mobile devices, such as mobile phones, patient monitoring devices, personal digital assistants and other wireless devices" (Kay, Santos, & Takane, 2011).

mHealth holds potentials to transform and alleviate disease management burden on healthcare systems especially in a resource-poor and overstretched healthcare systems.

The Mobile health has the capacity to improve and enhance access to healthcare, engagement and delivery and improves the expected outcome of the healthcare system (Heerden, Tomlinson, & Swartz, 2012). It utilizes short messaging service (SMS), wireless data transmission, voice calling, and smartphone applications to transmit healthcare informatics (Betjeman, Soghoian, & Foran, 2013). Mobile phone enables the rapid collection, transmission, storage and transformation of data with a specific focus on monitoring and evaluation of healthcare systems, and support two-way communication between individuals and large groups, for instance using instant messaging (Leon, Schneider, & Daviaud, 2012).

The mobile phone can benefit the patient and the healthcare providers through the frequent delivery of reminders on disease monitoring and management, education and training using both mobile voice and short message service (SMS) intervention (Krishna, Boren, & Balas, 2009). It further empowers the physician to; (a) respond more promptly to reading test results, (b) reduce errors in medication prescription and hospital discharge, and (c) improve data management and record-keeping practices (Prgomet, Georgiou, & Westbrook, 2009). Outside healthcare, mobile phone extends benefits to employees in reducing unproductive travel time, improving logistics, enabling faster decision-making, and empowering small businesses to communicate effectively across borders (Entner, 2012).

The mobile health (mHealth) have the capacity to connect patients with their doctors and loved ones for timely health monitoring for improved patient engagement and better health outcomes (West, 2013). It can also help provide access to health informatics, lower costs, fast-track remote care while increasing efficiencies by connecting patients to their healthcare providers almost anywhere (West, 2013). The mobile phones and associated mobile health (mHealth) services have demonstrated efficacy in the management of maternal care, chronic disease management, and disease epidemics. It enhances the efficiency and effectiveness of patient tracking and reporting, and extends the most needed healthcare services to resource-poor and underserved areas in the developing countries (West, 2015).

The strong penetration of mobile devices in resource-poor Ebola-affected areas demonstrate great potentials in bringing the Ebola outbreak under control through assessment of anonymized and aggregated mobile call data record used in the mapping of regional population movements. This is important in providing cues on the areas to focus on preventive measures, relief assistance, designing surveillance, and containment strategies (Wesolowski, et al., 2014). This has been demonstrated in controlling malaria and cholera outbreaks in West Africa and Haiti (Tatem, et al., 2014).

Several mobile apps are currently being used to support healthcare workers to collect and transmit crucial data such as case identification, possible contacts, and laboratory data in real-time (Dahiya & Kakkar, 2016). Magpi, a cellphone-based app used by non-profits to trace contacts, identify bodies, report lab results, and track health supplies, making data collection simple and affordable (Magpi, 2017; Appsagainstebola, 2017). An innovative Ebola gaming app was developed to educate health care professionals by providing them reference materials and guidelines for case management as well as personal protection (WelVU, 2017). A Surveillance and Outbreak Response Management System (SORMAS) was developed to support the control of the Ebola virus disease outbreak in West Africa (Fähnrich, et al., 2015). A short message service (SMS)-based system was developed to facilitate active monitoring of person exposed to EVD (Bloomfield & Regan, 2015).

Effective contact tracing and containment were achieved by deploying the same mobile application built on both the Open Data Kits (ODK) and Form Hub technology used during Polio surveys and enumeration of hard to reach areas in Nigeria (Tom-Aba, et al., 2015). Early detection is important for providing appropriate supportive care in preventing the spread of infection and subsequent transmission from human-to-human. On the other hand, uninfected humans may benefit from Ebola testing, by knowing their status, which could help reduce their engagement in risky behaviors. Several apps have demonstrated efficacy in the different aspects of Ebola management, but most Ebola apps are designed for use by healthcare professionals working on the frontline to manage Ebola cases. There is limited evidence to suggest the availability of an Ebola app that focuses on Ebola diagnosis screening for the public to know their Ebola health status. EbolaDiag is designed to allow users take Ebola diagnosis screening to know their Ebola health status. EbolaDiag supports the healthcare professionals working on the frontline to use EbolaDiag contact tracing form for contacts follow-up, identification of cases, case investigation and management. It also provides the public with relevant information and educational materials on Ebola prevention, symptoms, treatment and modes of transmission. In this chapter, we present the development of an Android mobile application called EbolaDiag (Ebola Diagnosis), which is capable of assisting in Ebola diagnosis screening, and case management, whilst providing the right information on early detection, prevention, and transmission of EVD.

LITERATURE REVIEW

Mobile Applications for Ebola Virus Disease (EVD)

During the August-September 2014 Ebola outbreak in Nigeria, (Tom-Aba, et al., 2015) developed an Ebola reporting tool using Open Data Kit (ODK) and Form Technology in combination with Dashboard Technology and ArcGIS Mapping to enhance contact tracing and timely reporting using GPS-enabled Android mobile phone. The app digitized data collection form and focused on contact tracing and follow-up, and timely reporting of suspected cases by sending GPS data of contacts, and integrated laboratory results with feedback to healthcare workers on the frontline.

Node is an Android mobile application originally developed to monitor meningitis amongst University student. In the wake of epidemic outbreaks in West Africa, Node was deployed to complement traditional forms of monitoring and to support the efforts of healthcare workers on the frontline combating the scourge of Ebola virus disease. The app collects passive sensor information using the GPS/WiFi tracking to monitor location patterns, habits and resource need to assist individual find care (Sierra, 2017). In 2015, Rochester researchers received The National Science Foundation (NSF) to conduct a pilot study of Node with healthcare workers in Nigeria.

The US Centers for Disease Control and Prevention (CDC) developed The EpiInfo Viral Hemorrhagic Fever (VHF) to support case management, contact tracing, analysis and reporting services during epidemic outbreaks of EVD, Marburg virus, Lassa virus, Rift Valley Fever, and Crimean-Congo Hemorrhagic Fever (Kanowitz, 2014). The EpiInfo software enables contact tracers to link cases with contacts and track contacts continually over a 14 - 21-day follow-up window and establish contacts information comprising contacts names, sex, ages, locations, status (dead or alive), and case classification (suspected case, confirmed case or otherwise)

Surveillance and Outbreak Response Management System (SORMAS) was developed using In-Memory Database (IMDB), and mobile device management software (SAP Afaria). SORMAS allows real-time, bi-directional information exchange between healthcare workers on the frontline and Emergency Operations Centre (EOC), supervision of contact follow-up, automated feedback and GPS tracking (Fähnrich, et al., 2015). Innovative Technologies for Development Foundation (IT4D) and Cloudware Technologies in consultation with domain experts developed Ebola Prevention Mobile Application. It was designed to detect Ebola-infected area, and deliver relevant preventive measures to citizen's mobile phones. The application is available through the Android Google Play Store and as a short message service (SMS) based application available through the CloudSMS AppStore (Akintoye, 2017).

IntraHealth International and The United Nations Children's Fund (UNICEF) Innovation developed an mHealth integrated SMS-based mobile communication and coordination system known as Mobile Health Worker Electronic Response and Outreach (mHero) for Liberia. The system is built to leverage existing health informatics infrastructures such as IntraHealth's iHRIS, the University of Oslo's DHIS2, and UNICEF's Rapid Pro platform to communicate critical information to healthcare worker (HCW) in real-time using the mobile phones (IntraHealth, 2017). It has been piloted in Liberia and integrated into the Liberia's Ministry of Health and Social Welfare (MOHSW) official investment plan for building a resilient Health System.

The Ebola Care App was built on the Journey Mobile Application platform to support Healthcare workers on the frontline in contact tracing in order to prevent further infection, coordinate with ambulance team for patient data collection, track and care for orphans abandoned after their parents contracted Ebola, observe and evaluate children under quarantine, and coordinate Ebola education across the community (Magid, 2014). The application uses cloud-based data storage to provide timely and accurate access to field data for healthcare decision-makers and non-governmental organizations (NGO's).

The ITU developed the Ebola-Info-Sharing app to facilitate coordination amongst agencies involved in Ebola crisis management. Running on inexpensive Android mobile phones, the app pushes the latest information on Ebola to the citizen's phones and enable agencies to securely signup to store and share useful contacts through an interactive forum (Adepetun, 2017). The app was developed to enhance disease prevention, diagnosis, treatment and monitoring. It is also focused on strengthening healthcare system through improved emergency response, active healthcare practitioners support, surveillance and administration.

Sacks and colleagues developed smartphone-based contact tracing application on CommCare mobile application platform and Tableau business intelligence (BI) software for data visualization and analytics. It is designed to allow for real-time identification of contacts that needs to be visited and strong accountability of contact tracers using tracer's timestamps and collection of GPS points with their surveillance data (Sacks, et al., 2015). The system was piloted in Conakry, Guinea and expanded to 5 other regions. As of April 30, 2015, over 210 contact tracers across the 5 regions have used the system to collectively monitor 9,162 contacts (Sacks, et al., 2015).

EbolaTracks is an automated Short Message Service (SMS) based system for monitoring persons potentially exposed to Ebola virus disease (EVD) involving either travellers returning from EVD-affected countries or contacts of local cases (Bloomfield & Regan, 2015). The system monitors EVD contacts health status by soliciting temperature and symptoms information twice daily through Short Message Service (SMS). OneHealth (OH) disease surveillance uses Android mobile phones running the EpiCollect Application developed and maintained by Imperial College, London (Karimuribo, et al., 2012). The app supports geospatial and clinical data capture, and data transmission from the field to IT servers at remote research hubs for data storage, analysis, feedback, and reporting to improve OneHealth (OH) disease surveillance in South Africa. The app has been piloted across three chosen sites including Ngorongoro, Kagera River basin and Zambezi River basin ecosystem.

eHealth Africa in collaboration with Sierra Leone's Ministry of Health and Sanitation (MoHS), the Center for Disease Control and Prevention (CDC), and World Health Organization (WHO) developed a mobile electronic integrated disease surveillance and response (eIDSR) application (eHealthAfrica, 2017). The app is designed to accurately record and share community-level health information from grassroots to national level. It has demonstrated considerable efficacy in Sierra Leone's disease surveillance and reporting (eHealthAfrica, 2017). Several mobile Ebola apps have shown considerable efficacy in the areas of contact tracing, active surveillance, monitoring and educating health professionals by providing them with reference materials and guidelines, but limited evidence exists for an app that allows an individual to use the mobile phone to answer Ebola screening test to determine their Ebola health status. EbolaDiag is developed to complement this aspect and to support healthcare professionals in contact tracing of suspected, probable or confirmed Ebola victims.

DESIGN AND IMPLEMENTATION OF EbolaDiag

Design of EbolaDiag Object Interactions

The design of EbolaDiag object interaction was carried out using a flowchart (see Figure 1) and Unified Modeling Language (UML) Sequence Markup, which is responsible for the creation of sequence diagram (see Figure 2), and EbolaDiag application user interface landing page (see Figure 3), and EbolaDiag application user interface (see Figure 4).

Figure 1. EbolaDiag object interaction flowchart

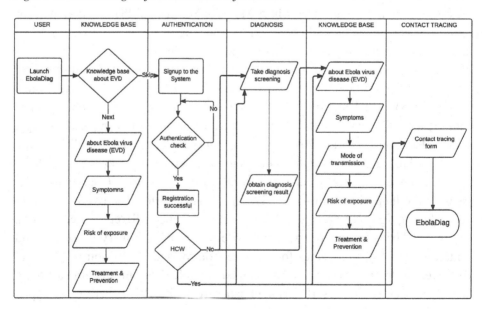

Figure 2. EbolaDiag object interaction sequence diagram

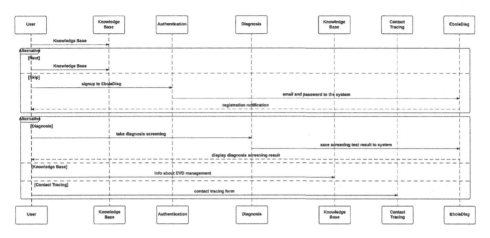

Figure 3. EbolaDiag application user interface landing page

Figure 4. EbolaDiag application user interface

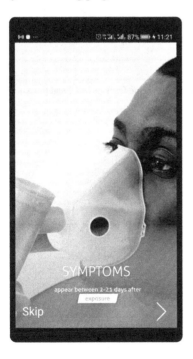

Implementation

The application consists of the Ebola diagnosis module, knowledge base module, and contact-tracing module. The Ebola diagnosis module was implemented using publicly available protocols from the US Centers for Disease Control and Prevention (CDC), and the World Health Organization (WHO, 2014a; CDC, 2014). The Ebola diagnosis screening question was designed to test contacts for Ebola clinical signs and symptoms, and their Ebola exposures and risk history to ascertain the health status of the contact whether an individual or healthcare worker. Based on the answer provided, a contact Ebola health status could be classified either as suspected, confirmed or probable (see Table 1). For instance, EbolaDiag is designed to classify a contact's health status to be suspected if the contact has a sudden onset of high fever (>38°C) and answer "yes" to at least three of the Ebola clinical signs and symptoms screening questions (WHO, 2014a; WHO, 2014b).

Once a contact's health status is defined as either suspected, probable or confirmed, the healthcare workers (HCW) can access the EbolaDiag dashboard, tab

Table 1. Recommended case definition for EVD and Marburg virus

Case	Definition
Suspected	A suspected Ebola patient is any person presenting with acute fever (>38°C) and three or more of the following symptoms: • Headache • Loss of appetite • Fatigue • Difficulty breathing • Nausea • Difficulty swallowing • Vomiting • Hiccups • Diarrhea • Muscle or joint pain • Abdominal pain • Unexplained bleeding Cared for or was cared for by someone who had Ebola, Attended a funeral of someone with Ebola, In the case of a child, breastfed by a confirmed Ebola mother or caretaker OR any unexplained death
Probable	Any person meeting the suspected case definition criteria and has had contact (epidemiological link) with a confirmed case OR any unexplained death
Confirmed	A probable or suspected case whose laboratory test is positive for Ebola virus

Source: WHO, 2014a; WHO, 2014b.

on a particular contact to activate Google map for tracing the location of a contact using the Global Positioning System (GPS). On the same Google map, EbolaDiag enables the healthcare worker to activate contact tracing form for identification of all contacts who must have been exposed to someone with status defined as confirmed or suspected and monitoring them for the incubation period of 21 days (Sacks, et al., 2015). The contact tracing form consists of contact identification and classification, contact listing, contact tracing and follow-up, and discharge of contacts (see Table 2).

The application enables contact tracers or healthcare workers to register contact details upon the first visit by the contact tracer; contact trace and follow-up with contacts daily for the 21-days incubation period to monitor symptoms, and discharge contact (close the contact) from the system upon the completion of the 21-days incubation period monitoring or for reasons such as the contact has been confirmed to have contracted the disease or has moved permanently from the endemic area to another area (Sacks, et al., 2015). The knowledge base module consists of educational information about Ebola virus disease diagnosis, treatment and prevention measures, clinical signs and symptoms, the risk of exposure and Ebola mode of transmission. This module is accessible to both individual and healthcare workers (HCW).

COMPARISON TO OTHER RELATED APPS

The Comparison of EbolaDiag and other related Ebola apps is presented in Table 3.

Table 2. Contact tracing components adopted for EbolaDiag

Components	Components Description
Contact identification & classification	• Identify persons who may have come in contact with EVD infected case • Conduct interviews with suspected contacts to determine if suspected contacts are actual contacts • Locate all possible contacts for further evaluation
Contact listing	List as contacts an anyone considered to have had significant exposure that: • Touched contacts body fluids (blood, vomit, saliva, urine, feces) • Had direct physical contact with the body of the contacts (alive/dead) • Slept or ate in the same household as the patient • Manipulated clothing of or shared linens with case • HCW who sustain injury while attending to a probable or confirmed EVD contact Classify risk status of identified contacts
Contact tracing & follow-up	Contact tracers visit each contact daily During each visit, contact tracers take and record the temperature and observe them for signs of disease
Discharge of contacts	Contact tracers must assess all contacts twice on day 21 Reintegrate contacts back into the community

Source: WHO, 2014a; Wolfe, et al., 2017.

Table 3. Comparative analysis of EbolaDiag to other related apps

S/N	App Name	Platform	Condition	Class	GPS/WiFi	Piloted	User
1	EbolaDiag	Android	Ebola	Educational & Monitoring	Yes	No	Individual & HCW
2	Reporting tool Open Data Kit (ODK) (Tom-Aba, et al., 2015)	ODK, Form Hub, & ArcGIS Mapping	Ebola	Monitoring	Yes	Yes	HCW
3	Node mHealth App (Sierra, 2017)	Android	Meningitis, & Ebola	Monitoring	Yes	Yes	HCW
4	EPiInfo Viral Hemorrhagic Fever (VHF) (Kanowitz, 2014)	EpiInfo	Ebola, Marburg virus, Lassa virus, Rift Valley fever, & Crimean-Congo Hemorrhagic fever	Monitoring	Only during download of the app	Unknown	HCW
5	SORMAS (Fähnrich, et al., 2015)	IMDB & SAP Afaria	Ebola	Monitoring	Yes	No	HCW
6	Ebola Prevention App (Akintoye, 2017)	Android, & CloudSMS	Ebola	Educational	Yes	Yes	HCW
7	mHero (IntraHealth, 2017)	SMS-based with iHRiS, DHIS 2, Rapid Pro, & Open HIE	Ebola	Monitoring	Yes	Yes	HCW
8	Ebola Care App (Magid, 2014)	Journey Mobile Platform	Ebola	Educational & Monitoring	Yes	Yes	HCW
9	Ebola-Info-Sharing App (Adepetun, 2017)	Android	Ebola	Educational	Yes	Unknown	HCW
10	EbolaTracks (Bloomfield & Regan, 2015)	SMS-based	Ebola	Monitoring	Yes	No	HCW
11	OneHealth disease surveillance (Karimuribo, et al., 2012)	EpiCollect	Ebola	Monitoring	Yes	Yes	HCW

CONCLUSION

EbolaDiag is an Android mobile application built to complement the strained medical facility and inaccessible medical care in the disease-ravaged West African States. The app was designed to support the general public take Ebola diagnosis screening test to determine their health status. It provides the healthcare workers or contact tracers with the tools for contact identification and classification, contact listing, and contact tracing and daily monitoring. The knowledge base module offers educational information that seeks to educate the public and health workers on early detection, prevention, transmission and containment of the epidemic in minimizing secondary transmission.

Diagnosis feature focuses on early detection of symptoms onset to provide appropriate supportive care in preventing the spread of infection and transmission. It affords uninfected humans the opportunity to benefit from Ebola testing, by knowing their status, which could help to reduce their engagement in risky behaviors. Contact tracing feature allows for the tracking of patients with identified onset of symptoms in contacts and or new contacts. Effective contact tracing, monitoring and rapid isolation of potentially infectious contacts account for one of the major reason Nigeria avoided a far worse epidemic outbreak in 2014 (Fasina, et al., 2014). Due to the proliferation of inexpensive Android mobile phone, EbolaDiag has been developed to run on Android mobile phone in an endemic area. EbolaDiag is a demonstration of proof of concept, as EbolaDiag has not been piloted in any endemic region with sudden outbreak of Ebola virus disease.

REFERENCES

Adepetun, A. (2017, May 11). ITU launches 'Ebola-Info-Sharing' mobile application. *T.guardian.ng*. Retrieved from https://t.guardian.ng/business-services/business/itu-launches-ebola-info-sharing-mobile-application/

Akintoye, A. (2017, May 10). *The mobile app that detects ebola presence in an area and helps prevents Ebola Virus Disease*. Retrieved from TheNigerianVoice.com: https://www.thenigerianvoice.com/news/157520/1/the-mobile-app-that-detects-ebola-presence-in-an-area-and-helps-prevents-ebola-virus-disease.html

Appsagainstebola. (2017, May 30). *Apps against Ebola*. Retrieved from appsagainstebola.org: www.appsagainstebola.org

Baden, L. R., Kanapathipillai, R., Campion, E. W., Morrissey, S., Rubin, E. J., & Drazen, J. M. (2014). 10). Ebola — An Ongoing Crisis. *The New England Journal of Medicine, 371*(15), 1458–1459. doi:10.1056/NEJMe1411378 PMID:25237780

Beeching, N. J., Fenech, M., & Houlihan, C. F. (2014). Ebola virus disease. *BMJ (Clinical Research Ed.), 349*, g7348. PMID:25497512

Beratarrechea, A., Lee, A. G., Willner, J. M., Jahangir, E., Ciapponi, A., & Rubinstein, A. (2014). The impact of mobile health interventions on chronic disease outcomes in developing countries: A systematic review. *Telemedicine Journal and e-Health*, *20*(1), 75–82. doi:10.1089/tmj.2012.0328 PMID:24205809

Betjeman, T. J., Soghoian, S. E., & Foran, M. P. (2013). mHealth in Sub-Saharan Africa. *International Journal of Telemedicine and Applications*, (6): 482324. PMID:24369460

Bholah, L. A., & Beharee, K. (2016). Mobile health applications for Mauritius and Africa. In *Proceedings of the IEEE International Conference on Emerging Technologies and Innovative Business Practices for the Transformation of Societies (EmergiTech)*, Balaclava, Mauritius (pp. 300-302). IEEE.

Bird, B. H., Spengler, J. R., Chakrabarti, A. K., Khristova, M. L., Sealy, T. K., Coleman-McCray, J. D., ... Spiropoulou, C. F. (2016). Humanized mouse model of ebola virus disease mimics the immune responses in human disease. *The Journal of Infectious Diseases*, *213*(5), 703–711. doi:10.1093/infdis/jiv538 PMID:26582961

Bloomfield, L., & Regan, A. (2015). EbolaTracks: An automated SMS system for monitoring persons potentially exposed to Ebola virus disease. *Eurosurveillance*, *20*(1), 20999. PMID:25613652

Booker, E. (2017, May 30). Magpi Mobile Data Tool Aids Ebola Fight. *InformationWeek*. Retrieved from http://www.informationweek.com/healthcare/mobile-and-wireless/magpi-mobile-data-tool-aids-ebola-fight/d/d-id/1317577

Cenciarelli, O., Pietropaoli, S., Malizia, A., Carestia, M., D'Amico, F., Sassolini, A., ... Gaudio, P. (2015). Ebola Virus Disease 2013-2014 Outbreak in West Africa: An Analysis of the Epidemic Spread and Response. *International Journal of Microbiology*, *2015*, 1–12. doi:10.1155/2015/769121 PMID:25852754

World Health Organization Regional Office for Africa Brazzaville. (2014a). *Contact tracing during an outbreak of Ebola virus disease.*

Dahiya, N., & Kakkar, A. K. (2016). Mobile health: Applications in tackling the Ebola challenge. *Journal of Family Medicine and Primary Care*, *5*(1), 192. doi:10.4103/2249-4863.184667 PMID:27453876

Dhama, K., Malik, Y. S., Malik, S. V., & Singh, R. K. (2015). Ebola from emergence to epidemic: The virus and the disease, global preparedness and perspectives. *Journal of Infection in Developing Countries*, *9*(5), 44–445. doi:10.3855/jidc.6197 PMID:25989163 eHealthAfrica. (2017, May 18). eHealth Africa Transforms Disease Surveillance and Response in Sierra Leone. Retrieved from https://www.ehealthafrica.org/latest/2017/3/30/ehealth-africa-transforms-disease-surveillance-and-response-in-sierra-leone

Entner, R. (2012). The wireless industry: The essential engine of us economic growth. *Recon Analytics, 30*, 33.

Fähnrich, C., Denecke, K., Adeoye, O. O., Benzler, J., Claus, H., Kirchner, G., ... Krause, G. (2015). Surveillance and Outbreak Response Management System (SORMAS) to support the control of the Ebola virus disease outbreak in West Africa. *Eurosurveillance, 20*(12), 21071. doi:10.2807/1560-7917.ES2015.20.12.21071 PMID:25846493

Fasina, F. O., Shittu, A., Lazarus, D., Tomori, O., Simonsen, L., Viboud, C., & Chowell, G. (2014). Transmission dynamics and control of Ebola virus disease outbreak in Nigeria, July to September 2014. *Eurosurveillance, 19*(40), 20920. doi:10.2807/1560-7917.ES2014.19.40.20920 PMID:25323076

Feldmann, H., & Geisbert, T. W. (2011). Ebola haemorrhagic fever. *Lancet, 377*(9768), 849–862. doi:10.1016/S0140-6736(10)60667-8 PMID:21084112

Heerden, A. v., Tomlinson, M., & Swartz, L. (2012). Bulletin of the World Health Organization. *Point of care in your pocket: a research agenda for the field of m-health, 90*(5), 393-394.

IntraHealth. (2017, May 11). IntraHealth Receives Grand Challenge Award for Ebola Response. Retrieved from https://www.intrahealth.org/news/intrahealth-receives-grand-challenge-award-for-ebola-response

Istepanian, R. S., Laxminarayan, S., & Pattichis, C. S. (2006). M-Health: Emerging Mobile Health Systems. (R. S. Istepanian, S. Laxminarayan, & C. S. Pattichis, Eds.) NY: Springer Science+ Business Media, Incorporated. doi:10.1007/b137697

Kanowitz, S. (2014, August 11). Tracking Ebola with CDC's app. *GCN Technology*. Retrieved from https://gcn.com/articles/2014/08/11/ebola-virus-tracking-app.aspx?m=1

Karimuribo, E. D., Sayalel, K., Beda, E., Short, N., Wambura, P., Mboera, L. G., ... Rweyemamu, M. M. (2012). Towards One Health disease surveillance: The Southern African Centre for Infectious Disease Surveillance approach. *The Onderstepoort Journal of Veterinary Research, 79*(2), 1–7. doi:10.4102/ojvr.v79i2.454 PMID:23327374

Kay, M., Santos, J., & Takane, M. (2011). mHealth: New horizons for health through mobile technologies. *World Health Organization,* (3), 66-71.

Krause, P. R., Bryant, P. R., Clark, T., Dempsey, W., Henchal, E., Michael, N. L., . . . Gruber, M. F. (2015). Immunology of protection from Ebola virus infection. *Science translational medicine, 7*(286).

Kuhn, J. H., Becker, S., Ebihara, H., Geisbert, T. W., Johnson, K. M., Kawaoka, Y., . . . Jahrling, P. B. (2010). Proposal for a revised taxonomy of the family Filoviridae: classification, names of taxa and viruses, and virus abbreviations. *Archives of virology, 155(12),* 2083-2103.

Leon, N., Schneider, H., & Daviaud, E. (2012). Applying a framework for assessing the health system challenges to scaling up mHealth in South Africa. *BMC Medical Informatics and Decision Making, 12*(1), 123. doi:10.1186/1472-6947-12-123 PMID:23126370

MacNeil, A., Farnon, E. C., Morgan, O. W., Gould, P., Boehmer, T. K., Blaney, D. D., . . . Rollin, P. E. (2011). Filovirus Outbreak Detection and Surveillance: Lessons From Bundibugyo. *J. Infect. Dis., 204*(Suppl. 3), S761-S767.

Magid, L. (2014, October 30). An Android App That Could Help Fight Ebola. *Forbes*. Retrieved from https://www.forbes.com/sites/larrymagid/2014/10/30/an-android-app-that-could-help-fight-ebola/#3fedfa6c7fc4

Paessler, S., & Walker, D. H. (2012). Pathogenesis of the Viral Hemorrhagic Fevers. *Annual Review of Pathology: Mechanisms of Disease, 8*(1), 411–440. doi:10.1146/annurev-pathol-020712-164041 PMID:23121052

Prgomet, M., Georgiou, A., & Westbrook, J. I. (2009). The impact of mobile handheld technology on hospital physicians' work practices and patient care: A systematic review. *Journal of the American Medical Informatics Association, 16*(6), 792–801. doi:10.1197/jamia.M3215 PMID:19717793

Roca, A., Afolabi, M. O., Saidu, Y., & Kampmann, B. (2015). Ebola: A holistic approach is required to achieve effective management and control. *The Journal of Allergy and Clinical Immunology, 135*(4), 856–867. doi:10.1016/j.jaci.2015.02.015 PMID:25843598

Sacks, J. A., Zehe, E., Redick, C., Bah, A., Cowger, K., Camara, M., ... Liu, A. (2015). Introduction of mobile health tools to support Ebola surveillance and contact tracing in Guinea. *Global Health, Science and Practice, 3*(4), 646–659. doi:10.9745/GHSP-D-15-00207 PMID:26681710

Sierra, L. (2017, May 10). New smartphone app would track spread of Ebola. *Rochester.edu NewsCenter*. Retrieved from http://www.rochester.edu/newscenter/rochester-researchers-receive-nsf-grant-for-pilot-study-of-smartphone-technology-for-monitoring-of-ebola-103622/

Tatem, A. J., Huang, Z., Narib, C., Kumar, U., Kandula, D., Pindolia, D. K., ... Lourenço, C. (2014). Integrating rapid risk mapping and mobile phone call record data for strategic malaria elimination planning. *Malaria Journal, 13*(1), 52. doi:10.1186/1475-2875-13-52 PMID:24512144

Taylor, R., Kotian, P., Warren, T., Panchal, R., Bavari, S., Julander, J., ... Sheridan, W. P. (2016). BCX4430 — A broad-spectrum antiviral adenosine nucleoside analog under development for the treatment of Ebola virus disease. *Journal of Infection and Public Health, 9*(3), 220–226. doi:10.1016/j.jiph.2016.04.002 PMID:27095300

Tom-Aba, D., Olaleye, A., Olayinka, A. T., Nguku, P., Waziri, N., Adewuyi, P., ... Shuaib, F. (2015). Innovative technological approach to ebola virus disease outbreak response in Nigeria Using the open data kit and form hub technology. *PLoS One, 10*(6), e0131000. doi:10.1371/journal.pone.0131000 PMID:26115402

Torgan, C. (2009). *The mHealth Summit: Local & Global Converge - Kinetics*. Washington, D.C: Foundation for the National Institutes of Health.

Welvu. (2017, May 30). *Ebola Provider and Patient Education App – Free Download*. Retrieved from http://www.welvu.com/

Wesolowski, A., Buckee, C. O., Bengtsson, L., Wetter, E., Lu, X., & Tatem, A. J. (2014). Commentary: Containing the Ebola outbreak–the potential and challenge of mobile network data. *PLOS currents outbreaks*.

West, D. M. (2013). Improving health care through mobile medical devices and sensors. *Brookings Institution Policy Report, 10*, 1–13.

West, D. M. (2015). *Using mobile technology to improve maternal health and fight Ebola: A case study of mobile innovation in Nigeria*. CFTI.

Wolfe, C. M., Hamblion, E. L., Schulte, J., Williams, P., Koryon, A., Enders, J., ... Fallah, M. (2017). Ebola virus disease contact tracing activities, lessons learned and best practices during the Duport Road outbreak in Monrovia, Liberia, November 2015. *PLoS Neglected Tropical Diseases, 11*(6), e0005597. doi:10.1371/journal.pntd.0005597 PMID:28575034

Wong, G., & Kobinger, G. P. (2015). Backs against the Wall: Novel and Existing Strategies Used during the 2014-2015 Ebola Virus Outbreak. *Clinical Microbiology Reviews*, *28*(3), 593–601. doi:10.1128/CMR.00014-15 PMID:25972518

World Health Organization. (2014). *Case definition recommendations for Ebola or Marburg Virus Diseases*.

Chapter 5
Investigating the Use of Mobile Devices in Schools:
A Case of the Ghanaian Senior High Schools

Emmanuel Awuni Kolog
University of Eastern Finland, Finland

Samuel Nana Adekson Tweneboah
University of Oulu, Finland

Samuel Nii Odoi Devine
Presbyterian University College, Ghana

Anthony Kuffour Adusei
Ghana Technology University College, Ghana

ABSTRACT

This chapter describes how today's technology has provided flexibility for teachers and students to engage in academic discourse irrespective of the location. However, there is an ongoing debate regarding the influence of mobile devices on students' academic engagement and performance. Following this debate, these authors empirically investigate the use of mobile device and its impact on teaching and learning in Ghana. Therefore, students, teachers and Ghana Education Service staff were selected to respond to a questionnaire with a follow up interview. After that, the authors analysed the content of the collected data using mixed research method. The results show that students are disallowed to use mobile devices while in school. However, the participants believe that mobile devices are useful for teaching and learning, especially for mobile learning. In line with the participants' perception of the use of mobile devices in schools, this chapter recommends that the government and other stakeholders of education in Ghana allow students to use mobile devices under restricted and regulated conditions.

DOI: 10.4018/978-1-5225-4029-8.ch005

INTRODUCTION

Today's technology has provided flexibilities for teachers and students to engage in academic discourse irrespective of the location (Darling-Hammond et al., 2014). While in Africa some countries have accepted to allow students to use mobile devices in schools for learning, others are reluctant to allow students to use mobile devices while residing in their school premises. This is because many scholars and stakeholders of education hold different perspectives on the issue of allowing students to use mobile devices in schools. For several years, this has been the subject of debate without much empirical studies to ascertain the rationale of this decision, as to whether the decision of disallowing the use of mobile devices by students is merited. The ongoing debate on this subject is centred on whether the use of mobile device usage in school influences students' academic engagement and performance. Following this debate, these authors empirically investigate the use of mobile devices in the senior high schools (SHSs) of Ghana.

The senior high schools in Ghana are predominantly a boarding school system where students are housed in a restricted environment over a period of time until they pass out as graduates. The authors of this chapter are aware that students who are found with mobile devices in schools are punished. This, in effect, is a challenge towards the adoption of mobile learning in the senior high school sector. The situation, as it is, is divergent to Ghana's 2003 policy on Information and communication technology (ICT) for Accelerated Development and Ministry of Education's ICT in Education Policy (2008) which are both geared towards integrating ICTs into teaching and learning in schools. By observation, the policies are well intended and suggest the use of ubiquitous technologies such as personal computers and mobile phones in the curriculum, given that mobile devices are well adopted in most parts of the world to provide flexibilities in teaching and learning through mobile learning platforms. For instance, Squire and Jan (2007) used game-based approach in a classroom setting to illustrate how mobile technologies afford learners' unique ability to construct scientific arguments in the wild. Generally, mobile devices are useful for easy communication and searching for information, and this can be used to enhance classroom learning (Sung et al., 2016). To the best of our knowledge, there is no empirical research that has been conducted to ascertain the reason for disallowing students to use mobile devices while at school, though Grimus and Ebner (2016) investigated how mobile devices could trigger creativity and initiate shifts in the senior high schools in Ghana.

In Ghana, the SHS education is categorised into two systems: boarding and day school. The 'boarding' school system is residential where students are provided with accommodation for a stipulated period of time to conduct their studies. Teachers and other non-teaching staff are mostly resident in the school premises, where the staff ensures that rules and regulations of the school are enforced and obeyed. The 'day' school system is non-residential, hence students commute to and from the school on daily basis. Since the 'day' students are not resident on school campus, certain rules and regulations are not applied to them (Kolog et al., 2014). For instance, the "day" students are not restricted to stay in the confines of the school premises.

Over the years, the Ghanaian educational system has seen some improvement with attempts being made to integrate ICT in the teaching and learning process. Notable areas of concern regarding the integration of ICT in education are mainly for workload management, school administrative activities and teaching and learning processes. This integration process is fraught with numerous challenges, and as such, slows down the integration process (Kolog, 2017). For instance, the high cost of ICT tools/software is a major challenge for the schools to ensure smooth integration of ICT in the school activities. To achieve this aim, the Government of Ghana and other stakeholders of education need to assist the schools to overcome the challenges of ICT integration.

While the authors of this chapter acknowledged that technology has its negative impact on students towards their academic engagement and performance, the relevance of mobile devices should not be overlooked, especially in the context of teaching and learning. Traxler (2007) believes that mobile devices are becoming more sophisticated with potentially advance capabilities for flexibilities in teaching and learning. This chapter is geared towards investigating the use of mobile devices in the senior high schools of Ghana. In addition, the key reason for disallowing students from using mobile devices in the senior high schools of Ghana is investigated. The authors of this chapter examine the perception of students, teachers and the staff of the Ghana Education Service (GES) regarding the impact of mobile devices in mobile learning.

Research Questions

To achieve the set objectives, as elaborated in the last paragraph of Section 1, these authors are aiming to find answers to the following research questions (RQ):

RQ1: Why are students in the Ghanaian senior high schools not allowed to use mobile devices in school?

RQ2: Are there any policy framework that regulates the banning of students from using mobile devices in schools?

RQ3: What is the perceived impact of the use of mobile devices on teaching and learning by the Ghana Education Service staff, teachers and students?

RQ4: What is the perception students and teachers towards the use of mobile devices in mobile learning?

BACKGROUND

In this section, we provide the framing background of the study by discussing some related works in the area. With this in mind, mobile learning, mobile device and their role in education are discussed.

Use of Mobile Device in Schools

Considering the current trend in education through the past few years, mobile learning (*M-Learning*) is seeking to gradually replacing electronic learning (e-Learning). E-learning involves the use of multimedia technologies normally on desktop and laptop computers, whereas mobile learning incorporates such multimedia technologies on portable mobile devices such as Personal Digital Assistants (PDAs). Interestingly, many researchers situate mobile learning as a form of learning that falls under the umbrella of e-learning which utilizes wireless and mobile device technology as the main tools for facilitating learning (Korucu & Alkan, 2011; Laouis & Eteokleous, 2005; Mostakhdemin-Hosseini & Tuimala, 2005; Oyelere et al., 2016). Asabere (2013) views mobile learning as the focus for the future in education, especially in the developing countries such as Ghana. This agrees with the notion that mobile learning is key to promoting lifelong learning to enable learners to strategically position themselves to succeed in this ever increasingly competitive global terrain (Staples, 2000; Muyinda, 2007).

Literature has revealed that several descriptions and definitions have been ascribed to the concept of mobile learning with focus being either on the technology to support learning activity and/or the context in which learning is carried out. Some researchers consider mobile learning as encompassing the facilitation of interactions between the learner and teacher through the provision or delivery of information whilst getting the required responses (Muyinda, 2007; Grimus & Ebner, 2014). In this study, we consider Kurkela's (2011) definition to mobile learning. Kurkela (2011) describes mobile learning as the possibility of making learning activities take place in multiple locations, across multiple times and accessing learning content with various items of equipment, such as smartphones or tablets. Perhaps, a clearer explanation of mobile learning is summed up by Traxler (2007), thus, accessing information and knowledge anywhere and anytime from devices that learners are used to "carrying everywhere with them" and that they regard as "friendly and personal". This implies that mobile learning enables learning, formal or informal (Grimus & Ebner, 2016), to occur "anytime, anyplace, anywhere" and on "any device" (Asabere, 2013; Annan et al., 2014). In Keegan's view, such devices that can be "friendly and personal" include what "a lady can put in her purse or handbag or what a gentleman can put in his pocket or bag" (Keegan, 2005). Thus, a key terminology associated with the definition of mobile learning is portability. From the learning theorists' point of view, mobile learning supports a social constructivist's view of learning due to the fact that it enhances students' ability to learn and apply course content in context with other students (Alexander, 2004; Bryant, 2006; Cobcroft et al., 2006). This study looks at mobile learning from the view point of being an education and training conducted by means of portable computing devices, such as smartphones or tablet computers.

In 2009, Koole described a model for framing mobile learning, exploring three distinct aspects: device, learner and social. The functionalities or effectiveness of each of these three components are crucial for a successful mobile learning. Apart from the State sponsored mobile devices, mobile devices such as smartphones and tablets are currently affordable and it is easier for one to lay hands on them. From the social perspective, various studies have reported different subtleties in the use of mobile devices (Zhu et al., 2012; O'Neill et al., 2013) and that a particular society is 'classified' based on its use of mobile devices. The use of mobile devices is now a social norm; there is no 'stigmatization' towards the use of mobile devices. The availability of such mobile devices coupled with the social status associated with the use of mobile device arouses the interest of learners to explore more in their classrooms (Sung, Chang & Liu, 2016). Considering the proposed mobile learning model by Koole (2009) and the subsequent explanations given, the Ghanaian educational setting can be said to be 'ready' to receive the implementation of mobile learning in the SHSs.

The general benefits to which teaching and learning derive from mobile devices is embedded in their portability. Hence, mobile devices are critical, strategic and novel educational tools for modern day teaching and learning. This agrees with the observation by Asabere (2013) as he viewed mobile learning as potentially viable tool for teaching and learning in developing countries like Ghana. Although little can be said about its usage in the SHSs in Ghana, Alexander (2004) believes that mobile learning complements the conventional way of teaching and learning in schools. Some benefits of using mobile learning include improved adaptive learning, learning independently of location and time, progress tracking and up-to-date content. Typical example is a mobile learning tool "*Edmodo*"[1]: a social media microblogging learning environment (Oyelere et al., 2016). Oyelere et al., (2016) concluded that teachers and students appreciate the use of Edmodo in their teaching and learning activities. This and many other mobile learning platforms are available online for free, accessible to both teachers and students, to promote teaching and learning in schools. Suitably, mobile devices provide students with the opportunity to access such platforms, as they seek to enhance their knowledge at their own convenience and pace, promoting lifelong learning. That notwithstanding, Keengwe & Bhargava (2014) believe that the implementation of mobile learning can be more effective when the social and cultural contexts are taken into consideration, especially in developing countries. In addition, the use of mobile learning tends to favour certain age groups. For instance, adolescents and young people are able to interact and use mobile learning than other age groups (Walsh et al., 2011). Typically, most students in the SHSs in Ghana are adolescents whose age brackets fall within 14-18 years. Hence, the use of mobile learning in SHSs might be a great stride towards the development of these adolescents. The subsequent section looks at the role mobile devices play in mobile learning.

The Role of Mobile Device in Mobile Learning

The phrase, *mobile device*, is a handheld tablet or other device that is made for portability, and is therefore both compact and lightweight (Sharehu & Achor, 2015). These devices are designed with extreme portability and are capable of performing and being used for many things including teaching and learning. Mobile devices are used to facilitate mobile learning hence its relevance in education is indispensable. Despite the wider applications of mobile devices in mobile learning, certain aspects of teaching and learning process tend to make gains in the use of mobile devices in mobile learning.

With the use of mobile devices, communications are easily facilitated. For example, a teacher might tend to form a social media group with their students, where assignments, project works, reminders, reading materials and other useful information that students need to successfully complete their training can be put in such groups. This affords the teacher the opportunity to interact individually with each student and assess their progress of learning. On the part of the students, they could use such platforms to make clarifications, and in turn deepen their understanding of certain concepts by interacting with their peers (collaborative learning) on such platforms or individually contacting specific students through such platforms (Gikas & Grant, 2013). In the same vein, teachers can communicate the progress of each student to their parents or guardians, thereby making suggestions to improve the academic life of their children. Inevitably, this will provide feedback for teachers, students and parents. Other digital devices such as the desktop computers are capable of providing feedback and correspondence between the teacher, students and parents, however, mobile devices, due to their portability, make it easier to achieve these at any time and at anywhere. Consequently, the teacher-student, student-student and teacher-parent relationships could be improved.

The use of mobile devices in education bridges the gap between formal and informal education (Gikas & Grant, 2013). For the purpose of this study, in the formal educational setting, teachers decide the type of mobile device that is to be used. In contrast, since mobile learning occurs at any time, anywhere and at any place, students tend to use their mobile devices even without a 'formal' educational setting. Learning, thus, becomes spontaneous and unstructured. If students want to deepen their understanding about a concept that has been taught in the classroom, they are able to do so at their private time with their mobile devices once connected to the internet. Hence, students will be able to use mobile devices either in the formal or informal educational settings. In effect, the efficacy of teaching and learning process will be complemented and cemented by these mobile devices.

Considerable research on the use of mobile devices in schools has been conducted, especially in the context of the developed economies. Chen-Hsiun (2013) asserts that many researchers are currently using mobile devices to work on developing instructional designs, theories and strategies that will enhance teaching and learning process. The future to enhancing the effectiveness of teaching and learning might as well rest on mobile devices, and as such it is important for both teachers and students to 'update' themselves for the future. A study conducted by Evans (2008) concluded that students prefer to learn anywhere at any time. This highlights the relevance and focus of mobile learning, which seeks to encourage and enhance learning through novel methods with the aid of mobile devices. The relevance in the use of mobile devices in education cannot be overlooked though the researchers' experience indicates that students are disallowed to use mobile devices in Ghanaian high schools. Considerable studies have been conducted in the area of mobile learning, mainly focusing on the usage and the role mobile learning plays in teaching and learning. Table 1 shows some related works on mobile learning in Ghana. As shown in the table, these authors provide some works in the area of mobile learning in Ghana, touching on the main objectives and the key findings reported.

Effects of Mobile Devices in Schools

Despite the numerous advantages of mobile devices in teaching and learning, as discussed in the previous section, mobile devices cannot be devoid of limitations and setbacks when using them for teaching and learning purposes. Such limitations should be considered if one intends to achieve effective learning. This section delves into discussing some effects of mobile device usage in the senior high schools of Ghana, particularly for teaching and learning.

Health issues are a major concern regarding the use of mobile devices in schools. For instance, constant reading via tablets and smartphones poses threat to the eye. Students may tend to spend more time with their mobile devices, and thus prevent them from having enough rest and eventually affecting their health. Related to the health issues are the psychological adverse effects that mobile devices bring to users. This includes over dependence on and addiction to mobile devices. Shuib et al. (2015) are of the view that a strong addiction to mobile devices may lead

Table 1. Related studies in mobile learning in Ghana

Author(s) and Year	Main Objective	Key Finding
Grimus & Ebner (2016)	Explores the capacity of mobile devices for learning science, technology, engineering and mathematics (STEM) at Senior High schools by engaging teachers and students through 3 workshops and series of collaborative activities.	Identified that through cooperative strategies on teacher-student interaction, mobile devices can play an active role in promoting creativity both at the content development and learning stages which has the potential of enhancing the study of STEM-based courses.
Bass-Filmmons & Kinuthia (2015)	Content analysis of how YouTube videos are used to promote teachers' development through participatory approaches to problem-solving and assessing their acceptance of mobile learning.	Mobile learning projects focusing on access to open education resources are becoming accessible through mobile devices for teacher development.
Annan, Ofori-Dwumfuo & Falch (2014)	Conducts a one-year mobile learning pilot project to experiment the use of mobile technology for teaching and learning using the AD-CONNECT mobile learning tool.	Study affirmed the notion of mobile learning technology as a tool viable for improving the quality of education delivery and enhancing teacher-student interaction.
Grimus & Ebner (2014)	Investigation on how mobile devices can trigger creativity and initiate shifts in education-practice at a Senior High School in Ghana.	Teacher-student collaboration was identified as stimulation for content development and tackling cross-disciplinary learning activities.
Asabere (2013)	Analysis of major mobile learning implementation challenges in developing countries and the perceived benefits associated to its adoption focusing on Ghana.	Identifies mobile learning as the future for developing countries but requires a holistic policy formulation strategy encompassing all stakeholders and ICT vendors, with cloud computing playing a key role in facilitating large scale proliferation.
Grimus, Ebner & Holzinger (2012)	The study looks at exploring opportunities of mobile learning with mobile phones in Ghana, thereby enhancing the provision of education in developing economies.	The rapid proliferation of mobile phones has the potential of providing novel approaches to addressing the systematic educational challenges in Ghana, based on holistic implementation model.

to complications such as emotional stress, damaged relationships and attention deficit disorders. Currently, mobile device users suffer from a phenomenon called cognitive salience or behavioural salience, where mobile device users keep thinking and checking their devices, even though they are not using them (Ye et al., 2012, Marinagi et al., 2013). In addition, the use of mobile devices may cause interruptions during instructional hours. A classic example is when a teacher has only prepared to use a mobile device and during class delivery, such mobile devices fail to work. Another scenario is when a mobile device 'rings' during instructional hours or when learners fail to pay attention to teachers and rather concentrate on their mobile devices. In such instances, students exhibiting such tendencies often have divided attention. Moreover, the societal status associated with the use of more 'sophisticated' and 'expensive' mobile devices may bring an unhealthy competition among the students. It is feared that, when such competitions arise, other unaccepted vices such as pilfering of another student's mobile device or money in order to obtain such mobile devices may occur.

One cannot talk about the issues relating to the use of mobile devices in learning without recognising the issue of 'safety' and 'privacy'. This is true since the SHS students are mostly teenagers. Shuib et al., (2015) admit that a mobile learning device that uses Global Positioning System (GPS) and accesses users' location can easily disclose user location through undocumented features or exploitation of software. Similar to the disclosure of a user's location is that mobile devices may store the learner profile and progress across networks or cloud-based networks. When learners' profiles and progress are stored, malicious parties such as Trojan horses, malwares can easily intercept and misuse. This breeds confidentiality and privacy issues. To overcome the challenges associated with security and privacy, it is important that mobile learning apps strictly forbid apps from storing and broadcasting user locations over networks and GPS position should be used in context for the learning applications.

Another setback related to the use of mobile devices is teachers' apathy. The role of teachers in the implementation of mobile learning cannot be overemphasised. However, when teachers are not 'comfortable' with the use of mobile devices and lack the necessary requisite skills needed to implement mobile learning, mobile learning cannot be seen to be effective in such learning environments. Hence, there is the need for teachers to acquaint and upgrade themselves towards the implementation of mobile learning in their classrooms. These upgrading may require some financial commitments of the teachers as well as the school authorities. In a school, whose finances are limited, they would opt to use their limited finances on other areas of the school rather than on upgrading teachers' skills in mobile learning. In addition, there would be lacklustre attitude from the school authorities in purchasing these mobile devices. Consequently, the implementation of mobile learning in such schools would be hampered.

RESEARCH METHOD

This section takes into account the method on which the study was conducted. This comprises the participants' selection, context and the data collection procedure. The method on which the collected data was analysed is also elaborated in this section.

Context and Data Collection

This study is limited to the context of the senior high school (SHS) education in Ghana. Therefore, data was collected from randomly selected students, teaching staff and Ghana Education Service (GES) staff through a survey. The rational for the selection of these diverse participants is rooted in the fact that the participants are directly involved in the implementation and enforcement of Government policies, via the Ministry of Education (Mereku et al., 2009). Figure 1 represents the context view of the flow of government directives from the Ministry of Education (MoE) through GES to the various schools (primary, junior and senior high schools). From the figure, it is indicated that the tertiary level, which comprises the polytechnics, universities, among others receives directives directly from the MoE.

In Ghana, the SHSs are diverse in terms of the gender of the students. While some schools are single-sex (boys or girls only), others are mixed-sex (both boys and girls). With this in mind, three SHSs from Ghana were selected for this study, drawing one each from the boys only, girls only and a mixed-sex schools. The selected schools are Adisadel College (boys), Holy Child SHS (girls) and University Practice SHS (mixed). The reason for this approach is to understand the perspective of participants from diverse school systems. After that, questionnaires were developed and administered to the selected participants to respond. The questionnaire was developed comprising both open and close-ended questions. The open-ended part of the questions allowed the participants to respond subjectively. A 5-point Likert scale was used for the close-ended part of the questions, where 5 - strongly agree, 4 – agree, 3 – Neutral, 2 – disagree and 1 – strongly disagree. The initial number of questionnaires administered to the students, teaching staff and GES staff were 300, 30 and 10 respectively. Although, we were not expecting all the selected participants to respond to the questionnaires, 277 students, 24 teaching staff and 8 GES staff responded and returned their questionnaires. Also, a follow up interview was conducted with the GES staff to buttress the intended findings from the questionnaire.

Figure 1. Context view of the directional flows of command in the education of Ghana

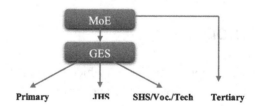

Method of Data Analysis

The method for analysing the collected data is mixed research method. With this method, the authors aim to give credence to both the qualitative and quantitative research approaches. The open-ended part of the data was thematically analysed. In the light of the quantitative method, both descriptive and inferential statistics were employed. By the descriptive statistics, the authors computed for the measures of central tendencies, particularly the mean ($\vec{x}$) and standard deviations (SD) of the various constructs that were contained in the questionnaires. Further, some selected constructs were computed using inferential statistics, particularly linear regression, to make predictions of the participants' perception towards the impact and relevance of mobile devices in teaching and learning.

RESULTS AND DISCUSSION

In this section, the authors present the findings of the study arising from the data analysis. Discussions of the results based on the analysed data are also reported in this section. The results are reported and supported with literature.

Participants Demography

This section discusses the demographic information of the participants. This takes into account the selected students, teaching staff and the GES staff who participated in the data collection. Of the 277 students who responded to the questionnaires, 143 of the students representing 52% were male while the remaining 134 students representing 48% were female. Figure 2 illustrates the gender representation of the participants in the survey. Of the total number of students (277), 19 (7%) of the students were at age 14, 88 (32%) of the students were 15 years old, 127 (46%) of the students were at the age of 16 years and the remaining 43 (16%) students were beyond the age of 16 years.

Students' residential status (day or boarding) was considered a relevant information for this study. The reason is that these authors perceived diverse views from the two classes of students regarding the use of mobile devices in teaching and learning. Thus, 37 students representing 13% were non-resident (day), 238 representing 86% of the students were campus resident (boarding) and the remaining 2 representing 1% of the students did not indicate their residential status. At the time of the data collection, the year three students, thus final year students, were almost preparing to wrap-up their final exams, hence the data was only collected from the year one and two students. Therefore, of the 277 students, 141 (51%) of the year one students responded to the questionnaires while the remaining 136 (49%) of the students were all from the year two.

The total number of the teaching staff who responded to the questionnaires were 24. Of the 24 teaching staff, exclusive teachers were 15 (63%), form masters who combine with teaching duties were 6 (25%), house masters who also combine with teaching duties were 2 (8%) and the remaining 1 (4%) was the head teacher of a school. Notable teaching subjects (course) found to be taught by the teaching staff were English Language, Accounting, Government, Clothing and Textiles, Food and Nutrition, Mathematics, Graphic Design, and Physical Education. In terms of gender, 17 (79%) of the teaching staff were male while the remaining 7 (29%) were female. Of the 24 teaching staff, 7 of the them had their ages between the range of 20-29 years, 13 had their ages between the ranges of 30-39 years, 3 had their ages between the range of 40-49 years and one had his age between the range of 50-60 years. Given the context and objectives of this study, the authors found that most of the teaching staff (70%) are resident in their various school campuses with their families. They live in the same premises with students where teachers are able to act as the parents of the students.

Of the 8 participants from the GES, 5 representing 63% were male while 3 representing 27% were female. With respect to the roles or positions they hold in the GES, 2 of them were account officers, one was a mathematics and science district coordinator, 2 were planning and statistics officers, 2 were national service personnel and the remaining one was IPPD coordinator (Individual Plan for Professional Development). From the content of the data, the authors understood that 2 of the GES staff had been in the services for only 0-1 year, 1 for 1-5 years, 2 for 6 – 10 years, 1 for 11-20 years and 2 of them, beyond 20 years of service.

Figure 2. Gender representation of the participants

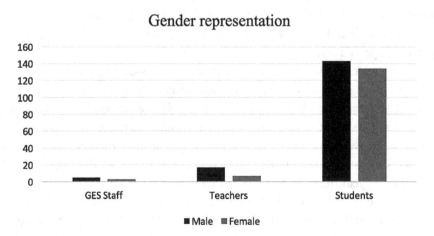

Mobile Device Ownership and Usage

In this subsection, these authors investigated the perception of the various representatives of the participants based on the ownership and use of mobile devices in schools. This delves into whether there is a policy framework regulating the use of mobile devices in the Ghanaian senior high schools (SHSs). This section however provides answers to RQ1 (*Why are students in the Ghanaian Senior high schools not allowed to use mobile devices in school?*), RQ2 (*Are there any policy framework that regulates the banning of students from using mobile devices in schools?*) and RQ3 (*What is the perceived impact of mobile device on teaching and learning by GES, teachers and students?*)

Ghana Education Service Staff

The questions contained in the questionnaire for the Ghana Education Service staff were mainly open-ended. The reason stems from the fact that senior high schools receive directives directly from the GES for implementing in the senior high schools (see Figure 1). With this in mind, the authors of this chapter deemed it necessary to source subjective views of the GES staff in this study. The authors, in this chapter, are unofficially aware that students are not allowed to use mobile devices in schools while conducting their studies. For this reason and part of the objectives of this chapter, the authors aimed to inquire whether there is a policy framework or directive banning the use of mobile devices in schools.

From the content of the collected data, all the 8 (100%) GES staff agreed that they are aware of a ban on the use of mobile devices in the SHSs. This situation implies that students are not allowed to use their mobile devices for academic purposes while residing in the school campuses (boarding). The GES staff further claimed that the ban has been monitored and regulated by their outfit, thus, the schools have not erred on enforcing the government directives. Owing to this claim, these authors enquired from the participants if there is any policy document or directive to that effect. Of the 8 GES staff, only 1 (12.5%) of them is not aware that a policy documents/directives have been given out to the heads of the SHSs to enforce. The remaining 7 (87.5%) GES staff were aware that a directive has been forwarded to the various schools for implementation. Nevertheless, the participant who was not aware of the directive did not deny that mobile devices are banned from use in the SHSs. Given that mobile devices are banned from use in schools, as these authors have ascertained, the participants (GES staff) gave reasons for the ban. According to the participants, GES believes that the use of mobile devices in school will be: 1) a distraction to students' academic engagement, citing that students would be using the devices at odd times (late in the night instead of resting), 2) using only for entertainment purposes instead of academic work, 3) using to watch movies such as pornographic materials, using it for social media chats among others.

As the study had revealed, while the participants agreed to the aforementioned reasons, 75% of them believe that strict measures could be put in place for students to use mobile devices in schools. This will, in a long run, help in the implementation of mobile learning as the Government of Ghana had advocated in the 2004 policy framework on accelerated ICT development in education (NERIC, 2007). On further probe, these authors deduced that GES has mandated some of their staff members to monitor and enforce their policies, thereby ensuring the compliance of the directives by the schools. While the participants believe that the directives were given from the above (Government), 6 (75%) of the participants agreed that mobile devices should be allowed in schools with clearly defined policies on the limit of its use in the schools. 25% of GES staff were of the view that the ban on the use of mobile devices is not necessary, but remarked that students should be allowed to use the devices *"under strict supervision"* by developing policies to regulate their use in schools. For instance, they cited that students should not be allowed to use the device in normal class hours because it may distract their attention. Those who believe that students should be allowed to use mobile devices attributed the reason to the fact that students' academic performance would improve. This is because the use of mobile devices will give students the opportunities to trawl for online information, such as seeking guides for academic development.

Teaching Staff

Teachers are, as part of the GES directives, mandated to ensure that the ban on the use of mobile devices in schools is enforced. However, all the 24 teaching staff who participated in the survey believe that owning a mobile device is useful ($\vec{x} = 4.04$, SD = 1.97) considering the fast advances in information technology in this knowledge economy. Despite the fact that students are not allowed to use mobile devices in schools, research has been conducted about the impact of mobile learning on students' academic performance and engagement in the senior high schools of Ghana (Grimus & Ebner, 2014; Muntaka, 2014).

Based on the GES directives on the ban of mobile devices in schools, students who are caught with the possession of mobile devices in the school premises are warned ($\vec{x} = 1.67$, SD = .702) and punished ($\vec{x} = 4.00$, SD = 1.10) as well. The punishment is dependent on the situation and the circumstances under which the mobile device is found with students. After that, the device is ceased but majority of the teachers could not tell whether the confiscated devices are returned to the students ($\vec{x} = 3.29$, SD = 1.57). Some of the teachers disagreed that students get their mobile devices back at the end of the term ($\vec{x} = 2.48$, SD = 1.53). As we probed further, the teachers explained that returning of the ceased mobile devices is completely dependent on the teacher who is said to have confiscated the device. It is for this reason that majority of the teachers could not tell if the confiscated devices are returned to students at the end of the term. The authors perceived that some students may have been allowed to use mobile devices in schools on special permission, the teachers disagreed ($\vec{x} = 2.00$, SD = 1.22), and insisted that mobile device usage should not be allowed for only some students on special reasons. Nevertheless, teachers agreed that mobile devices should rather be allowed for all students under strict or regulated conditions ($\vec{x} = 4.04$, SD = 1.97) for promotion of effective teaching and learning.

Given the exuberance of students at their teenage the authors predicted, based on the data collected from the teachers, that students would not be overwhelmed by using mobile devices only for entertainment if they are allowed to use under restricted and regulated conditions ($b = .29$, $t\,(23) = 1.479$, $p < .154$). Also, majority of the teachers do not believe that if students are allowed to use mobile devices in schools it will contribute to their deviant behaviours, such as truancy and watching of pornography materials ($b = .44$, $t\,(23) = 1.64$, $p < .879$). On further probe, the authors found that students may use mobile devices for their private activities but this will not significantly affect their academic performance. Majority of the teachers believe that some students still sneak mobile devices into school but only use in secrecy. This prompted some of the teachers to comment that, once in a while, a general search is conducted in the student halls of residence to retrieve mobile devices under the possession of the students. This is to buttress the point that the students who own mobile devices use them in secrecy in the school premises. Although, teachers have agreed that mobile devices should be allowed under tight restriction and supervision, they believe that confiscating the devices are not the best. Table 2 presents the mean ($\vec{x}$) and standard deviation (SD) of the responses of the teachers regarding the use of mobile devices in the SHS.

Students

Similar to the views of the Ghana Education Service and the teaching staff, all the students (277) who responded to the questionnaires agreed that their schools do not allow them to use mobile devices while residing on the school premises. 228 (82%) of the students responded affirmatively for owning a mobile device while the remaining 49 students do not have in their possession any mobile devices. In view of this, students attributed the reason for the possession of their mobile devices as a useful tool to communicate with their parents, information search and for social media chats. In effect, students believe that owning mobile device in school is very useful and can improve their academic development ($\vec{x} = 5$, SD = .78). Of the 228

Table 2. The use of mobile devices in the senior high schools

	Questions	Mean	SD
1.	Owning a mobile device is very necessary in our lives today.	4.04	1.97
2	Mobile devices are allowed and encouraged to be used by students in schools for personal use.	1.46	1.00
3	Mobile devices are allowed and encouraged to be used by students in my school with special permission.	2.00	1.22
4	Students are only warned when they are caught with mobile device	1.67	0.70
5	Students are punished when they are caught with mobile device	4.00	1.10
6.	Mobile devices found with students are ceased and not returned.	3.29	1.57
7	Mobile devices found with students are ceased and returned after the term ends.	2.48	1.53

students who use mobile devices, 55.7% (127) are male and 44.3% (101) female. Most students had their mobile devices provided for them by their parents, with fathers being the highest providers 48.7% (111) and 32.5% (74) are mothers. It is an undeniable fact that parents are aware of the ban on the use of mobile devices in schools yet they allow their children to carry them. This could explain why parents believe mobile devices facilitate the learning abilities of their ward irrespective of the challenges it poses.

Students disagreed that mobile devices are allowed to be used by students in schools ($\bar{x} = 1.78$, SD = 1.05) and this prompted the majority of the students to call for their schools to allow them to use mobile devices to support their learning ($\bar{x} = 2.94$, SD = 1.51). This is because students believe that the advantages of using mobile devices in schools outweigh that of its disadvantages. The majority (81.9%) of the students who owned mobile devices, nevertheless, conceded that they use mobile devices stealthily on their various school campuses. With this, as shown in Table 3, the study found that students are aware that they will not only be warned ($\bar{x} = 2.27$, SD = 1.26) but punished ($\bar{x} = 3.73$, SD = 1.42) if they are caught in the school with any mobile device. In effect, we found from the students that the ceased mobile phones are sometimes not returned to them ($\bar{x} = 3.43$, SD = 1.41), and other times they are returned but only after the term (semester) has ended ($\bar{x} = 2.94$, SD = 1.52). This goes to support the findings from the teachers who made the same revelations.

A total of 63.9% of the students perceived the use of mobile devices, if not restricted, as a distraction to their academic development. In this way, 43.4% of the students believe the use of mobile devices would not contribute to poor academic performance whilst 25.6% rather believe that allowing the use of mobile would lead to poor academic performance. In agreement to the use of mobile devices

Table 3. Ownership and perception of the use of mobile devices in schools

	Questions	Mean	SD
1.	Owning a mobile device is very necessary in our lives today.	4.55	0.78
2	Mobile devices are allowed to be used by students in schools	1.78	1.05
3	Mobile devices should be allowed and encouraged to be used by students in schools under strict supervision.	2.94	1.51
4.	Students are only warned when they are caught with any mobile device.	2.27	1.26
5.	Students are punished when they are caught with any mobile device	3.73	1.42
6.	Mobile devices found on students are ceased and not returned again.	3.43	1.41
7	Mobile devices found on students are ceased and returned to students after the term ends	2.94	1.52

contributing to deviant behaviours of students if the use is not restricted, 54.9% of the students are strongly in support whilst 28.2% disagreed. However, 84.8% of the students also agreed to the notion that mobile devices can help to improve teaching and learning tremendously if the usage is restricted and regulated in the schools.

Perception Towards Using Mobile Device in Learning

Mobile learning has long been studied where several mobile learning platforms have been developed for both contextual and global use. Mobile learning can, undoubtedly, be facilitated by mobile devices and mobile learning software such as Edmodo, massive open online course (MOOC), among others. In this section, the authors delve into the perception that teachers and students hold about the use of mobile devices in mobile learning. This provides an answer to the RQ4 (*What is the perception students and teachers towards the use of mobile devices in mobile learning?*).

Teachers' Perception of Mobile Device in Mobile Learning

From Table 4, the teachers believe that allowing students to use mobile devices in schools will improve teaching and learning ($\vec{x} = 3.88$, SD = 1.17). In line with this finding, Lan & Huang (2012) believe that using mobile devices for educational purposes is becoming a common expectation of learners, for the purpose of knowledge and information search. As the Ghanaian education is modelled similar to the British educational system, Conole *et al.* (2006), in a study conducted in the United Kingdom, found that students choose mobile device technology based on the extent to which it improves their learning. Rossing *et al.* (2012) have concluded that mobile devices allow students to adapt course content to fit their learning style and pace. This is however in contrary to the case of Ghana where students do not have the opportunity to use mobile devices in the senior high schools.

Although, it has been established earlier in this chapter that mobile devices are not allowed in schools, teachers are able to use mobile devices, such as tablets in their teaching activities. Nonetheless, some teachers have passionately integrated mobile devices into their teaching activities; others have not integrated the use of mobile devices in their teachings. With this view, Isaacs (2012) believes that teachers, who have not integrated mobile devices, such as tablets, in their teaching lack the needed knowledge, skills and attitude to integrate such devices into teaching. In addition, Rodrigo (2011) attributed teachers' unwillingness to integrate mobile devices to "the rapid improvement of new mobile products and the advanced functions and numerous applications and accessories available these days", and that teachers are not able to catch up with the complexities of the emerging technologies. In this study, some of the teachers disagreed that they use mobile devices to teach their subjects in schools ($\vec{x} = 2.23$, SD = 1.28). The reason for the disagreement could be attributed to the challenges of mobile learning implementation in Ghana, such as the ban on the use of mobile devices in schools, poor or no internet connections, poor and no electricity and the cost of acquiring mobile learning platforms. Mereku et al. (2009) found that "Pedagogical integration of ICTs from 2009-2011 in 10 Ghanaian schools indicates that there is a gap between the policy directives and actual practices in schools." Though the authors could not find any literature backing this claim from 2011 to date, the authors believe that the situation is still a challenge in the sector. Mereku *et al.* (2009) outlined that "The emphasis of the official curricula is on the development of students' skills in operating ICTs but not necessarily using the technology as a means of learning subjects other than ICTs." Since teachers can freely use mobile devices and its related ICT tools for teaching, these authors recommend the GES to provide some in-service training for teachers on intermittent basis.

These authors found no statistically significant association between the use of mobile devices in teaching and the poor academic performance of students ($b = -0.26$, t (23) = -.221, $p < .827$). This goes to highlight that if students are equally allowed to use mobile devices teaching and learning would be flexible, and this will have a corresponding improvement in the academic performance of students ($\vec{x} = 3.58$, SD = 1.37). On further probe, teachers believe that this can be successfully accomplished if the devices are allowed under strict and regulated conditions. Teachers agreed that if students are allowed to use mobile devices, it will enable them to complete their teaching syllabus in timely fashion ($\vec{x} = 3.96$, SD = 1.23). Although, the teachers relish that legitimately allowing mobile devices to be used by students will help in the teaching and learning, this study has revealed a strong correlation between allowing students to use mobile devices and mobile learning implementation in the schools ($r =. 582$). This justifies that mobile device plays an important role in mobile learning, and that allowing mobile devices to be used by students will facilitate the use of mobile learning environments.

As teachers have agreed that they use mobile devices, such as tablets in teaching, these authors were concerned with the use of the hardcopy books and educational materials in teaching and learning. The idea is to ascertain whether text books and other educational materials are still relevant to teaching and learning. While teachers hailed the relevance of using mobile devices for downloading educational materials, they also agreed that textbooks and other hardcopy educational materials should still be used in order to complement the use of mobile devices ($\vec{x} = 4.17$, SD = .46). Given that both GES staff and the teaching staff know the relevance of mobile devices in terms of mobile learning, 50% of the teaching staff predicted that the schools will welcome students to use mobile devices in mobile learning should the policy be changed to skew towards its usage. However, the remaining 50% did not see the willingness of schools embracing such policy with ease. This could be attributed to the challenges associated with mobile learning implementation as stated in the background of this chapter. From the perspective of the teachers, only 30% of the teachers believe that integrating mobile learning by allowing the use of mobile devices would be bedevilled with challenges. The remaining 70% believe that since teachers use mobile phones and other devices already, there would not be serious challenges associated with the implementation of mobile learning by allowing students to use mobile devices in schools. Figure 3 summarises the key findings of the teachers' perception of the use of mobile devices in mobile learning.

Figure 3. Graphical representation of teachers' perception regarding the use of Mobile Device (MD) in the senior high schools

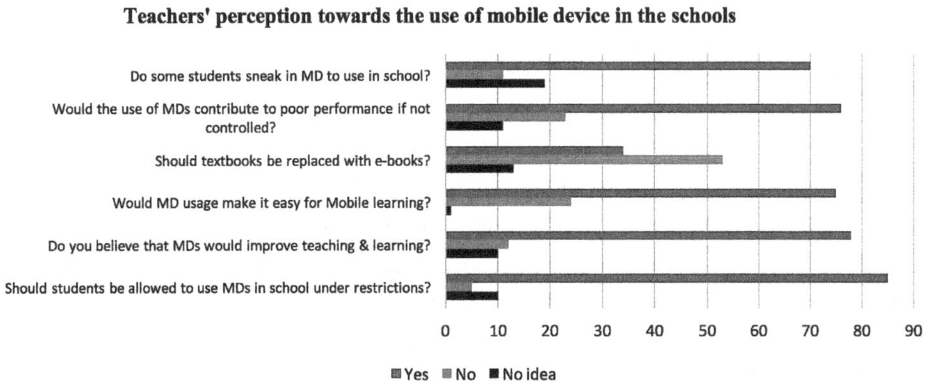

Teachers' perception towards the use of mobile device in the schools

Table 4. Teachers' perception of the use of mobile device in teaching and learning

	Questions	Mean	SD
1.	Mobile devices can help in improving teaching and learning	3.88	1.17
2.	Mobile devices are often use in my subject area for teaching and learning	3.00	1.35
3.	I use mobile devices frequently in my classes for teaching and learning.	2.23	1.28
4.	Use of mobile devices will make teaching and learning easier for both teachers and students	3.58	1.37
5	Mobile devices should replace text books and other educational materials for students	2.04	.95
6.	Mobile devices should be used side by side with text books and other educational materials for students.	4.17	.46
7.	Use of mobile devices in teaching and learning will assist teachers and students in covering and/or completing syllabus.	3.96	1.23
8.	Integrating mobile devices usage into teaching and learning in my school would be accepted by both teachers and students.	3.33	1.09
9.	Management of my school will be willing to accept and adopt mobile device integration into my teaching and learning.	3.00	1.22

Students' Perception of Mobile Device in Mobile Learning

Just like the perception of the teachers, the students also hold the perception that mobile devices are a capable tool for facilitating teaching and learning through mobile learning ($\bar{x}$ = 4.48, SD = .88). Students were quick to add that school work (exercises) and assignments could be accessed digitally on their mobile devices while away from school or even in the school premises. Students agreed that when mobile devices are allowed freely at all times some students will abuse the use and perhaps cause distraction. By computing for the regression, the study revealed a statistically significant association between allowing mobile devices in schools at restricted and regulated times and the academic performance of students (b = .529, $t(273) = 8.34, p < .000$). This implies that allowing students to use mobile devices in schools would improve their academic performance but only under restrictions.

Research indicates that the use of mobile devices in school is diverse in terms of its application. For instance, aside using mobile devices for teaching and learning, students are able to get connected with their counsellors while away from the school premises (Kolog & Montero, 2017). Many students nowadays prefer to contact their school counsellors anonymously instead of the traditional face-to-face method. Many students decline to access face-to-face counselling simply because of trust issues (Kolog *et al.*, 2016; Kolog & Montero, 2017). Hence, students would be able to seek counselling anonymously through the use of mobile devices (Kolog *et al.*,

2015). In view of this, students want their schools to provide them with mobile devices ($\vec{x}$ = 3.71, SD = 1.19), and 78.5% agreed with the idea of the school prescribing and purchasing the type of mobile device with its specifications as well ($\vec{x}$ = 3.8, SD = 1.18). Mobile learning platform could be developed to allow students to seek counselling, even from their teachers.

It is worth noting that 81.2% of students believe that teaching and learning with better understanding of subjects can be attained through the use of mobile devices. This can be considered as technical tools for making and/or enhancing teaching and learning easier and effective ($\vec{x}$ = 3.99, SD = 1.14). In consonance with this, 56.3% of students supported the idea of printed textbooks be replaced with electronic textbooks for teaching and learning ($\vec{x}$ = 3.58, SD = 1.27) which can be supported with the use of mobile device. Nonetheless, 68.2% believe using printed and electronic textbooks side by side is much better. As a result, a greater number of students shared the view that using mobile devices is a modern tool that schools should adopt in teaching and learning ($\vec{x}$ = 4.22, SD = 1.04).

Notably, 61% of the students do not see any mobile devices being legitimately used by students anywhere in the Ghanaian senior high schools for learning purposes. This affirms that schools in Ghana do not allow students to use these emerging assistive teaching and learning (pedagogies/educational) tools. Contrary to popular belief, about 67.8% of students think or know that teachers use mobile devices in teaching and demonstration in class with 32.5% disagreeing. Even though schools in Ghana are currently not accepting the idea of using mobile devices for teaching and learning, 73% of Ghanaian students believe that it is possible and feasible to integrate such technologies into teaching and learning. A greater percentage of the students (75.4%) shared their views, that this would go a long way to improve interaction between students and teachers for better understanding of their subject areas ($\vec{x}$ = 3.99, SD= 1.14). This supports the notion that the majority of the students believe it is possible and indeed practical to implement or use mobile devices in teaching and learning, as only 24% of the students do not see it to be possible.

In the nutshell, students believe that mobile devices can facilitate mobile learning, and as a result, bridges the gap between them (students) and their teachers. In line with this, Elfeky & Masadeh (2016) studied the impact of mobile learning on students' academic and conversational skills in Egypt. In the study, fifty (50) students were involved. The results of their study showed that mobile learning had significant effect on both students' academic achievement and conversational skills. Based on their findings, Elfeky & Masadeh (2016) recommended for higher education in Egypt to adapt the use of Mobile Learning in their classes. In this case, mobile devices are to be allowed for use by students. Figure 4 illustrates the findings of the students' perception on the use of mobile devices for mobile learning.

Figure 4. Graphical representation of students' perception regarding the use of Mobile Device (MD) in the senior high schools

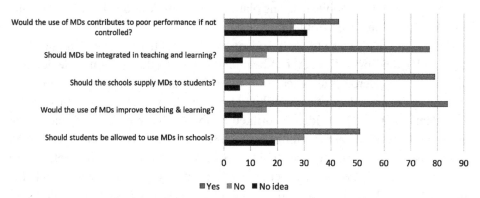

Key perception of students towards the use of mobile device in schools

Table 5. Students' and perception of the use of mobile device in teaching and learning

	Questions	Mean	SD
1	Mobile devices are useful for teaching and learning	4.48	.884
2	Mobile devices can help improve teaching and learning	4.30	.934
3	Mobile devices are modern tools that schools that should be adopted for teaching and learning in schools.	4.22	1.04
4	Mobile devices should be acquired and given to students to assist them in teaching and learning activities.	3.71	1.19
5	Mobile devices should be allowed to be used at restricted times such as prep, library times and during computer class	4.07	1.21
6	Mobile devices with electronic forms of textbooks should replace printed textbooks for teaching and learning.	3.58	1.27
7	Mobile device usage in teaching and learning will improve interaction between teachers and students for better understanding of subjects in the schools in Ghana.	3.99	1.14
8	Mobile device usage for teaching and learning is not possible nor practical in any school in Ghana.	2.41	1.36
9	Mobile devices must carefully be chosen, bought and given by the school to students.	4.00	1.25

CONCLUSION

In this book chapter, these authors have investigated how mobile devices are being used in the senior high schools in Ghana. This considered an investigation into the reason for disallowing students to use mobile devices in the senior high schools of

Ghana. Questionnaires, containing both open- and close-ended questions were used to collect data from the staff of Ghana Education Service, selected students and teaching staff of three different senior high schools in Ghana. After analysing the content of the data, this study revealed and affirmed the banning of mobile devices in the senior high schools in Ghana. This study further revealed that the Ghana Education service has policy frameworks that regulate the banning of the mobile devices. The reason for banning of the mobile devices in the schools, according to the Ghana Education Service directives, is attributed to the fact that students could easily be distracted by them (mobile devices), and in turn, affect their academic performance and engagement.

In addition, these authors found that some students sneak in mobile devices to their various school campuses for personal use. While in this study, the participants agreed with the reasons for the ban, they believe that allowing students to use mobile devices in school under restricted and regulated conditions would facilitate teaching and learning. Based on the findings of this study, these authors recommend for the Ghana Education Service to allow students to use mobile devices in schools under restriction and well-developed regulations. This is because these authors believe that the advantages of allowing students to use mobile device in schools outweigh that of the disadvantages. In future, these authors intend to investigate, empirically, the possible implementation challenges of Mobile learning in schools in case mobile devices are allowed to be used by students in schools.

REFERENCES

Alexander, A. (2004). Going Nomadic: Mobile learning in higher education. *EDUCAUSE Review*, *39*(5), 29–35.

Annan, N. K., Ofori-Dwumfuo, G. O., & Falch, M. (2014). Mobile Learning Platform: a case study of introducing m-learning in Tertiary Education. *GSTF Journal on Computing*, *2*(1).

Asabere, N. Y. (2013). Benefits and Challenges of Mobile Learning Implementation: Story of Developing Nations. *International Journal of Computers and Applications*, *73*(1).

Bass-Fimmons, E., & Kinuthia, W. (2015). Mobile Learning in Ghana: A Content Analysis of YouTube Videos promoting Teacher Development Opportunities within Higher Education. Retrieved from http://transform2015.net/live/Resources/Papers/Mobile%20Learning.pdf

Bryant, T. (2006). Social software in academia. *EDUCAUSE Quarterly*, *29*(2), 61.

Chen-Hsiun, C. (2013). Instructional design models of mobile learning. *EXCEL International Journal of Multidisciplinary Management Studies*, *3*, 4.

Cobcroft, R. S., Towers, S. J., Smith, J. E., & Bruns, A. (2006). Mobile learning in review: Opportunities and challenges for learners, teachers, and institutions.

Conole, G., Latt, M. d., Dillion, T., & Darby, J. (2006). JISC LXP Student experiences of technologies. *Draft final report*.

Darling-Hammond, L., Zielezinski, M. B., & Goldman, S. (2014). *Using technology to support at-risk students' learning*. Stanford Center for Opportunity Policy in Education.

Elfeky, A. I. M., & Masadeh, T. S. Y. (2016). The Effect of Mobile Learning on Students' Achievement and Conversational Skills. *International Journal of Higher Education*, *5*(3), 20. doi:10.5430/ijhe.v5n3p20

Evans, C. (2008). The effectiveness of m-learning in the form of podcast revision lectures in higher education. *Computers & Education*, *50*(2), 491–498. doi:10.1016/j.compedu.2007.09.016

Gikas, J., & Grant, M. M. (2013). Mobile computing devices in higher education: Student perspectives on learning with cellphones, smartphones & social media. *The Internet and Higher Education*, *19*, 18–26. doi:10.1016/j.iheduc.2013.06.002

Grimus, M., & Ebner, M. (2014). Learning and Teaching with Mobile Devices an Approach in Secondary Education in Ghana. *In proceedings of International Conference on Mobile Learning 2014, 10.* Madrid-Spain.

Grimus, M., & Ebner, M. (2016). *Mobile Learning and STEM First Experiences in a Senior High School in Ghana: Case Studies in Practice* (H. T. Crompton, Ed.). Routledge.

Grimus, M., Ebner, M., & Holzinger, A. (2012). Mobile Learning as a Chance to Enhance Education in Developing Countries-on the Example of Ghana. *In mLearn 2012 Conference Proceedings*, 340-345.

Isaacs, S. (2012). Turning on Mobile Learning in Africa and the Middle East, Illustrative Initiatives and Policy Implications, by the United Nations Educational, Scientific and Cultural Organization 7. UNESCO 2012, France: Place de Fontenoy, 75352 Paris 07 SP.

Keegan, D. (2005). The incorporation of mobile learning into mainstream education and training. In *World Conference on Mobile Learning* (p. p. 11). Cape Town.

Keengwe, J., & Bhargava, M. (2014). Mobile learning and Integration of mobile technologies in education. *Education and Information Technologies, 19*(4), 737–746. doi:10.1007/s10639-013-9250-3

Kolog, E. A. (2017). Contextualising the Application of Human Language Technologies for Counselling. PhD Dissertation in Forestry and Natural sciences, University of Eastern Finland publication. Vol. 218.

Kolog, E. A., & Montero, C. S. (2017). Towards automated e-counselling system based on counsellors emotion perception. *Education and Information Technologies*, 1-23. doi:10.1007/s10639-017-9643-9

Kolog, E. A., Montero, S. C., & Sutinen, E. (2016). Annotation Agreement of Emotions in Text: The Influence of Counselors' Emotional State on their Emotion Perception. In *Proceeding of International Conference on Advanced Learning Technologies (ICALT)* (pp. 357-359). IEEE. doi:10.1109/ICALT.2016.21

Kolog, E. A., Sutinen, E., & Vanhalakka-Ruoho, M. (2014). E-counselling implementation: Students' Life stories and counselling technologies in perspective. *International Journal of Education and Development Using Information and Communication Technology, 10*(3), 32–48.

Kolog, E. A., Sutinen, E., Vanhalakka-Ruoho, M., Sohunen, J., & Anohah, E. (2015). Using Unified Theory of Acceptance and Use of Technology Model to Predict Students' Behavioral Intention to Adopt and Use E - Counseling in Ghana. *International Journal of Modern Education and Computer Science, 7*(11), 1–11. doi:10.5815/ijmecs.2015.11.01

Koole, M. L. (2009). A model for framing mobile learning. *Mobile learning: Transforming the delivery of education and training, 1*(2), 25-47.

Korucu, A. T., & Alkan, A. (2011). Differences between m-learning (mobile learning) and e-learning, basic terminology and usage of m-learning in education. *Procedia: Social and Behavioral Sciences, 15*, 1925–1930. doi:10.1016/j.sbspro.2011.04.029

Kukulska-Hulme, A. (2007). Mobile usability in educational contexts: What have we learnt? *The International Review of Research in Open and Distributed Learning, 8*(2). doi:10.19173/irrodl.v8i2.356

Kurkela, L. J. (2011). Systemic approach to learning paradigms and the use of social media in higher education. *IJET, 6*, 14–20.

Lan, Y.-F., & Huang, S.-M. (2012). Using mobile learning to improve the reflection: A case study of traffic violation. *Journal of Educational Technology & Society*, *15*(2), 179–193.

Laouris, Y., & Eteokleous, N. (2005). We need an educationally relevant definition of mobile learning. In *Proceedings of the 4th World Conference on Mobile Learning* (pp. 290-294).

Marinagi, C., Belsis, P., & Skourlas, C. (2013). New directions for pervasive computing in logistics. *Procedia: Social and Behavioral Sciences*, *73*, 495–502. doi:10.1016/j.sbspro.2013.02.082

Mereku, D. K., Yidana, I., Hordzi, W., Tete-Mensah, I., Tete-Mensah, W., & Williams, J. B. (2009). *Pan African Research Agenda on the Pedagogical Integration of ICTs: Ghana Report*. Retrieved 5th Otober, 2017, from http://www.ernwaca.org/panaf/pdf/phase-1/Ghana-PanAf_Report.pdf

Ministry of Education. (2008). *ICT in education policy" Republic of Ghana*. Retrieved 23 April, 2017, from http://www.moe.gov.gh/assets/media/docs/ICTinEducationpolicy_NOV2008.pdf

Mostakhdemin-Hosseini, A., & Tuimala, J. (2005). Mobile learning framework. In *Proceedings IADIS International Conference Mobile Learning 2005*, (pp. 203-207).

Muntaka, M. N. (2014). *Exploring mobile phone usage and potentials for enhancing higher education Ghana, West Africa*. Retrieved from https://etda.libraries.psu.edu/files/final_submissions/9560

Muyinda, P. B. (2007). MLearning: Pedagogical, technical and organisational hypes and realities. *Campus-Wide Information Systems*, *24*(2), 97–104. doi:10.1108/10650740710742709

NERIC. (2007). *Education Reform 2007 at a glance*. Retrieved 23 May 2017 from http://planipolis.iiep.unesco.org/upload/Ghana/Ghana_education_reform_2007.pdf

O'Neill, E. C. O., & Lewis, D. (2013). Situation-based testing for pervasive computing environments. *Pervasive and Mobile Computing*, *9*(1), 76–97. doi:10.1016/j.pmcj.2011.12.002

Oyelere, S. S., Paliktzoglou, V., & Suhonen, J. (2016). M-learning in Nigerian higher education: an experimental study with Edmodo. *International Journal of social media and interactive learning environments, 4*(1), 43-62.

Rodrigo, R. (2011). Mobile teaching versus mobile learning. *EDUCAUSE Quarterly 101 Magazine, 34*(2).

Rossing, J., Miller, W., Cecil, A., & Stamper, S. (2012). ILearning: The future of higher education? Student's perceptions on learning with mobile tablets. *The Journal of Scholarship of Teaching and Learning, 12*(2), 1–26. Retrieved 2 April 2017 from http://josotl.indiana.edu/ article/view/2023/1985

Sharehu, A. L., & Achor, E. E. (2015). Readiness of Teachers and Pupils for Use of Mobile Devices as Support for Effective Pedagogy in Nigeria: Could Location be a Major Determinant? *Online Journal of Distance Learning Administration, XVIII*(3).

Sharples, M. (2000). The design of personal mobile technologies for lifelong learning. *Computers & Education, 34*(3-4), 177–193. doi:10.1016/S0360-1315(99)00044-5

Shuib, L., Shamshirband, S., & Ismail, M. H. (2015). A review of mobile pervasive learning: Applications and issues. *Computers in Human Behavior, 46*, 239–244. doi:10.1016/j.chb.2015.01.002

Squire, K. D., & Jan, M. (2007). Mad City Mystery: Developing scientific argumentation skills with a place-based augmented reality game on handheld computers. *Journal of Science Education and Technology, 16*(1), 5–29. doi:10.1007/s10956-006-9037-z

Sung, Y. T., Chang, K. E., & Liu, T. C. (2016). The effects of integrating mobile devices with teaching and learning on students' learning performance: A meta-analysis and research synthesis. *Computers & Education, 94*, 252–275. doi:10.1016/j.compedu.2015.11.008

Traxler, J. (2007). Discussing and evaluating mobile learning: the moving finger writes and having write. *The international Review of research in open and distance learning Defining, 8*(2).

Walsh, S. P., White, K. M., Cox, S., & Young, R. M. (2011). Keeping in constant touch: The predictors of young Australians' mobile phone involvement. *Computers in Human Behavior, 27*(1), 333–342. doi:10.1016/j.chb.2010.08.011

Wheeler, S. (2000). The Role of the Teacher in the use of ICT. In *Proceedings of National Czech Teachers Conference*. Czech Republic: University of Western Bohemia.

Ye, J., Dobson, S., & McKeever, S. (2012). Situation identification techniques in pervasive computing: A review. *Pervasive and Mobile Computing, 8*(1), 36–66. doi:10.1016/j.pmcj.2011.01.004

Zhu, F., Carpenter, S., & Kulkarni, A. (2012). Understanding identity exposure in pervasive computing (Marinagi, Belsis, & Skourlas, 2013) environments. *Pervasive and Mobile Computing*, *8*(5), 777–794. doi:10.1016/j.pmcj.2011.06.007

KEY TERMS AND DEFINITIONS

Ghana Education Service: The Ghana Government institution that is responsible for the coordination and implementation of the education policy on pre-tertiary education. The Ghana education service receives government directives from the Ministry of Education.

ICT: ICT covers all technical means used to handle information and aid communication. This includes both computer and network hardware, as well as their software.

Linear Regression: A statistical approach for modeling the relationship between independent and dependent variables in statistical data analysis.

Ministry of Education: The ministry is mandated to provide relevant education to all Ghanaians. The Ministry is committed to put in place an education system focused on promoting creativity and problem-solving through the development of academics, technical and vocational programmes that will improve the acquisition of skills and assure job-market readiness.

Mobile Device: A portable computing device such as a smartphone or tablet computer.

Mobile Learning: Training conducted by means of portable computing devices such as smartphones or tablet computers.

ENDNOTE

[1]   https://www.edmodo.com/

Chapter 6
Mobile Financial Services in Emerging Countries:
Technology, Adoption, and Regulatory Issues

Joseph Kwame Adjei
Ghana Institute of Management and Public Administration, Ghana

Solomon Odei-Appiah
Ghana Institute of Management and Public Administration, Ghana

ABSTRACT

This chapter describes a recent World Bank report which indicated a sizable percentage of households in developing countries do not have access to formal accounts with financial institutions. The situation has created a major barrier in the quest for a world without poverty due to the exclusion of segments of society from the formal financial system. The phenomenon has resulted in the exclusion of many from traditional financial services, thus the use of other means to conduct informal financial transactions. In Ghana, many households rely on domestic informal forms of remittance to relatives and payments. Such informal mediums of remitting money to and from relatives in Ghana (e.g. via "Bus Driver") received wide patronage irrespective of the associated risks until mobile financial services were introduced. This chapter discussed Mobile Financial Services (MFS) from the perspective of emerging economy and treats the following topics; technology, adoption and the regulatory issues in MFS.

DOI: 10.4018/978-1-5225-4029-8.ch006

INTRODUCTION

In this chapter, Mobile Financial Services (MFS) is discussed from the perspective of emerging economies. Topics discussed are the technology, adoption and the regulatory issues of MFS. In the concluding section of this chapter we proffer solutions that ensure adoption of MFS is deepened.

OVERVIEW OF MOBILE FINANCIAL SERVICES

According to World Bank report in 2012, over 50 per cent of households in developing countries do not have formal accounts with financial institutions (Donovan, 2012). The report also observed that a major barrier in the quest for a world without poverty is exclusion of segments of society from the formal financial system (Donovan, 2012). The phenomenon has resulted in the exclusion of many from traditional financial services, thus the use of other means to conduct informal financial transactions. In Ghana, many households rely on domestic informal forms of remittance to relatives and payments (Tobbin, 2010). Such informal medium of remitting money to and from relatives in Ghana (e.g. via "Bus Driver") received wide patronage irrespective of the associated risks until mobile financial services were introduced.

Mobile financial services (MFS) refers to financial services and transactions delivered through mobile devices (IFC, 2011; Donovan (2012). MFS has been defined to encompass the broad range of financial services which include payments, insurance and banking (Donovan, 2012). Tobbin (2010, p. 1) sought to define MFS as to include "all the various initiatives (long-distance remittance, micro-payments, and informal air-time battening schemes) aimed at bringing financial services to the unbanked using mobile technology". Hence, MFS has been described as a generic term consisting of the use of mobile devices in the conduct of diverse financial services including; mobile money, mobile insurance, mobile credits, mobile payments, mobile savings and mobile banking. Interestingly, there are overlapping descriptions of MFS and its allied terminology in literature. MFS architecture usually includes software applications that are loaded unto the Subscriber Identification Module (SIM) cards of mobile devices for onward deployment on mobile networks. MFS transactions usually does not require the use of sophisticated mobile devices, and MFS technology provides transacting parties a means to verify the identity of parties making the mobile devices, principal in MFS. According to (Tobbin, 2010), MFSs usually target the poor and unbanked in society (Tobbin, 2010).

In this method, the sender approaches a bus driver at a lorry station and after pleading and negotiating with the driver to take a little incentive, he accepts and sends the remittance to the family within hours. Another informal method is using visiting family and friends, and also whenever necessary, travelling long distances to remit the funds. Some of the challenges associated with these informal ways of remittance are thefts, armed robbery and accidents (Tobbin, 2010).

MOBILE FINANCIAL SERVICES ECOSYSTEM

Tobbin (2010) made the observation that the ecosystem of mobile financial services comprises mobile network operators (MNOs), merchants and agents, financial institutions, mobile application and services, service vendors, consumers and regulators. The MNOs supply the core infrastructure and capabilities to the ecosystem. Such services include; core infrastructure, mobile device applications and distribution channel for the sale of prepaid credits and subscriptions (Tobbin, 2011). The MNOs' ability to reach customers from all income levels and provide them with customer services including agents; earns them the qualification of being a major key player in the ecosystem (Jenkins, 2008). The nature of their involvement means MNOs must adopt strategies that restrain them from dominating the ecosystem.

The financial institutions or banks in the ecosystem are responsible for payment systems and mechanisms for storing value while the regulators in the system provide balance between innovation, efficiency, value creation and financial inclusion by imposing regulations and enforcing their compliance too (Balasubramanian & Drake, 2015). The agents (which are non-bank entities like retailers) from the distribution channels serve as the customers' primary contact who handle the registration of customers and on behalf of the MNOs conduct cash-in and cash-out services (Tobbin, 2011). These agents who are often small shop owners and naturally become the MNOs' branches earn a little commission for rendering these mobile financial services (Balasubramanian & Drake, 2015). Per transaction, these are usually small amounts but the expectation is that it would be added up to a good amount based on the volume of transactions (Tobbin, 2011). As agents act as the bridge between physical cash and e-money, the success of MFS platforms critically depends on a healthy network of these agents because the convenience in their performance of such transactions is crucial to ensuring customer confidence and satisfaction (Balasubramanian & Drake, 2015; Donovan, 2012).

Opportunities are brought into the MFS ecosystems by the customers in the form of their diverse needs since they are the final recipients of the service (Tobbin, 2011). When potential MFS customers become aware of the service for the first time, they form expectations as to how the service could be useful to them (Davidson & McCarty, 2011). The degree by which these expectations are met or confirmed impacts on the satisfaction of the customer (Bhattacherjee, 2001a). "It is therefore imperative that customer needs are met by mobile financial services and that they have good experience with the services" (Tobbin, 2011).

Mobile Network Operators (MNOs), traditional banking institutions, as well as third party service providers can deliver MFS (Tobbin, 2013). There are many models that have been described for MFS applications. The most common ones include operator-centric, bank-driven, and the collaboration models, given that these industries have control over a mass customer base.

In each country, the MFS ecosystem develops in different ways, and between different service providers and mobile network operators as technology advances (Yakub et al., 2013). In the operator-centric model, the MNO offers the technology, operates the transaction and compensates the system and thereby reaps the benefits of its customer base and the already established billing relationships (Yakub et al., 2013). With the bank-centric model, the relationship between the customers and their bank continues with the bank providing the same services but in a more convenient way, which is by using the mobile phone (Yakub et al., 2013). Payments will be processed over mobile networks and the bank will have to partner with mobile operators and agree on an attractive revenue-sharing system (Yakub et al., 2013). In the collaboration model, banks, mobile operators and other stake-holders including

Figure 1. The mobile financial services ecosystem

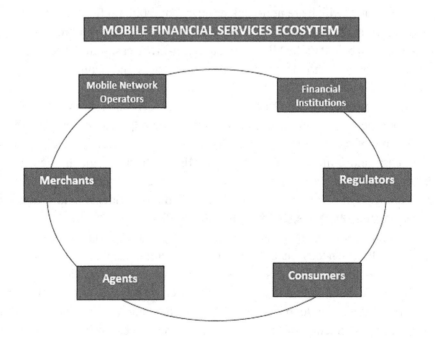

a trusted third party, collaborate to manage the deployment of mobile applications (Yakub et al., 2013). According to Tobbin (2013), the best business model is the operators-centric one, where the MNO is the major player when it comes to providing financial services to those unbanked, and this study is limited to this model.

The MFS concept revolves round the mobile phone but that technology alone is just not enough, given that there is also the requirement of an infrastructure for making payments consisting of a network which connects agents and merchants to provide points of contact where users can perform their cash in and cash out transactions (Donovan, 2012). Because MFS straddles between two industries - financial and telecommunications – it is made up of diverse sets of actors in its ecosystem. The convergence of these industries creates the need for two sets of regulators to ensure consumers' protection through competition and enhancement of service delivery (Tobbin, 2013). Moreover, the harmony between the requirements of the two regulators has to be ensured in order to create a conducive environment to develop the services.

The MFS network is made up of a number of interconnected systems. The system is a client-server one and the application of the client resides on the SIM card by which the phone number of the subscriber is identified and connected to the server of the MNO (Tobbin, 2013). Whenever it is initiated, the application on the client's SIM card connects to the network of the MNO and based on the protocol of the SIM, the application communicates with the server. Before any of the services could be used by a consumer, most MFS transactions usually require the first step of a registration process which is done only once. The registration involves a customer visiting an agent and filling an application form after which the customer's ID (could be national ID, drivers' license, etc.) is verified by the agent, then temporarily, the customer is registered onto the MNO's server using the agent's phone. Thus, on the server, a mobile wallet account is created and this is confirmed by sending an SMS message to the customer who then enters a chosen PIN which will become their main token for authentication in all subsequent transactions.

The cash-in process is the next step after registration and this has to do with the user purchasing e-money onto the mobile wallet. This is done by the agent being visited by the customer to pay an equivalent cash amount for the e-money. A transfer of the e-money is then made to the customer from the agent's special SIM phone via the MNO's server. After this, the transfer between the two accounts has to be affected and this is done by the agent sending an encrypted SMS request from their phones to the server. The customer is then sent an encrypted SMS as a confirmation of the transaction. The stored e-money at this stage can be used to conduct other transactions while it also remains accessible for use within the system.

Mobile Financial Services Agents

Agents of MFS (which are non-bank entities like retailers) from the distribution channels serve as the customers' primary contact who handle the registration of customers and on behalf of the MNOs conduct cash-in and cash-out services (Tobbin, 2011). They naturally become the MNOs' branches and earn a little commission for rendering these services to customers (Balasubramanian & Drake, 2015). According to Bandura (2001) one of the core features that characterizes human agency is the quality of functioning. The quality of service from the functions of an MFS agent relates to literature that focuses on service quality (Balasubramanian & Drake, 2015). Service quality in the IS literature is described as the quality of support from the IS department and its support personnel received by system users (Peter et al., 2013). While Delone & McClean describe it in the e-commerce context as the support that service centers, hotlines and help desks provide to users or customers, they also acknowledge that the e-commerce context has no specific well-established measure for service quality and that responsiveness and technical competence should be included in any reliable measure of service quality. In their study, Balasubramanian & Drake, (2015) measured agent quality in two dimensions namely; pricing transparency (which relates to the credibility of the agent) and agent expertise (which relates to agent competence). In the current study, the measurement of the construct of good agent quality includes the competence, trustworthiness, availability at post and cash/e-money account balance of MFS agents.

HOW MOBILE FINANCIAL SERVICES WORK

Mobile Financial Services Categories

Accessing financial services and making financial transactions using the mobile phone is generally referred to as Mobile Financial Services (MFS). Included in this are services which are transactional and non-transactional like when a user views financial information on his/her mobile phone. MFS may be used interchangeably with mobile money but so far as this study is concerned however, the term is a generic one which refers to the use of the mobile phone for conducting any type of financial service. The types of these services which are components of MFS include mobile money (M-money), mobile payments (M-payments), mobile banking (M-banking), mobile insurance (M-insurance), mobile credits (M-credits) and mobile savings (M-savings).

Mobile Money

It is the use of a mobile phone in transferring and receiving money and making payments as well (Penicaud &Katakam, 2013). In order for a service to be classified as mobile money, it must offer one or more of these services: person to person (P2P), customer to business (C2B), business to business (B2B) business to government (B2G) and government to customer (G2C) transfers as well as international remittance, merchant payment, bulk payment and bill payment (Penicaud & Katakam, 2013).

To make mobile money service accessible to the unbanked and the underbanked, it has to be heavily supported by a network of locations where transactions can take place, and these locations are outside bank branches. A mobile money account doesn't have to be a normal bank account. Customers therefore need not be previously banked before they can use the service. A mobile phone is linked to a cash pool that has been pre-funded and so would be able to pay for goods and services in a similar way to what m-banking offered but without necessarily accessing full banking service. The M-money Service can be available on basic mobile devices to provide an interface through which both customers and agents can initiate transactions.

Of all the financial services, M-money is one of the most patronized globally. According to the GSMA report (2013), 219 M-money services were in operation in 84 countries as against 179 found in 75 countries by close of 2012. Moreover, 52% of these live services are found in the sub-Saharan Africa region, and also 113 new services at the end of 2013 have been identified to be planning to launch (GSMA, 2013).

Customers can store value in their mobile wallet accounts and access them by the use of the mobile phone. M-money services rely heavily on mobile wallets. Once customers have value in their mobile wallet (whether by converting cash into electronic value or having it transferred from another account), they can directly perform transactions (either transfers or payments) with their phone on their own without the need of an agent (Donovan, 2012). GSMA, (2013) reports that as at June 2013 registered M-money accounts globally numbered 203 million.

Mobile Insurance

Penicaud & Katakam, (2013, p 49) defines insurance as "an arrangement by which a company or the state undertakes to provide a guarantee of compensation for specified loss, damage, illness, or death in return for payment of a specified premium." Low-income people are not catered for by traditional insurance regardless of them residing in developed or developing countries (Penicaud & Katakam, 2013). This is mainly because in insurance, the cost to sell, underwrite, collect premium payments and administer a claim is not proportional to the value of the policy in question. In other words, a low-valued policy does not decrease the operational cost. Therefore, an opportunity may exist for mobile technology to be leveraged for the provision of cost effective insurance.

Insurance that aims to cover lives and protect assets of people and household with low income is referred to as micro insurance (Tellez, 2012; Churchill, 2012). M-insurance can therefore be defined as any product of micro insurance by which the mobile channel is used as a leverage whether a mobile money platform exists or not to offer insurance services which include claims payment and policy administration (Leach, 2011). The use of the mobile phone in insurance is a strong driver for M-insurance, in that, it lowers the cost of collections, especially where mobile money has already been offered by the Mobile Network Operator. It also improves persistency of premium payment through SMS reminders whiles it empowers the consumer in managing their insurance cost effectively and accessibly (Leach, 2011). Through the networks (both physical and virtual) provided by MNOs, a significant number of clients in low–premium environments could potentially be reached by insurers at low cost (Tellez, 2012). Using the mobile communicating channel, insurers can promote their service and also handle policy administration over the air whiles customers can self-enroll and submit their claims as well in the same manner (Tellez, 2012). Mobile money or airtime can be used to pay premiums and pay-outs can also be disbursed by insurers into customers' mobile wallets, or better still, both payments could be made over the counter (Tellez, 2012).

There are 84 live M-insurance services, 16 of which were launched in 2013 with an additional 8 planning to launch in the next 12 months (Penicaud & Katakam, 2013). In terms of number of policies initiated, M-insurance has been most popular in the sub-Saharan Africa and South Asian regions. It is estimated that globally 500 million people have M-insurance, up from 78 million in 2008 (Churchill, 2014). Major M-insurance product offerings include life cover, health insurance, accident coverage and agricultural insurance. Seventy-six per cent of the service provides life cover whiles the other 24% provides the rest (Penicaud & Katakam, 2013).

Collection of premiums from customers can be optional to insurers because to consumers who make certain levels of expenditure like top-ups, M-insurance could be offered as a reward for loyalty (Tellez, 2012). That is turning to MNOs instead to cover for customers' cost of insurance. This model is referred to as "freemium" whereby "customers are given free insurance in exchange for loyalty to the MNO and given the option to upgrade to a more robust paid policy with additional features or coverage" (Penicaud & Katakam, 2013, p. 53).

Although the potential for M-insurance to expand beyond its existing stage of development is significant, there are also existing range of challenges. A major one is marketing and distribution. Relatively, acquiring customers for M-insurance is quite sophisticated, therefore providers need to use a sales force through whom necessary education could be provided for customers in trying to sign them on (Penicaud & Katakam, 2013). There is the need for ensuring that marketing materials are suitable and understandable to customers. Marketers of the product should have adequate training in order for those who buy the product to be adequately informed (Leach, 2011).

Mobile Credit

One of the most significant constraints to escaping poverty is perceived to be a lack of access to affordable credit (Donovan, 2012). In the absence of formal financial services, the poor resort to the informal credit service which usually come with exorbitant interest charges. Personal interaction is required for effective debtor monitoring in order to maintain low rates of defaults and this eventually results in high transaction costs. Mobile technology can provide avenues for people to access loan products with no paper work or bank queuing involved. The mobile money service can be used for loan disbursement and repayments.

On one M-money deployment, a lot of mobile credit services can be run concurrently (GSMA, 2013). For example, Kenya's Safaricom offers the M-Shwari service whiles a third-party provider also offers the Musoni service. These services therefore are not restricted to the M-money domain or deployment; third-party providers also have the opportunity to come aboard. The potential of the mobile credit industry is recognizable; however, it will need the mobile money deployment infrastructure to rely on in order to succeed in reaching unbanked communities (Katakam, 2014). To date, the most successful mobile credit services as a result are found in countries that M-money services have already caught up with a large proportion of the population (example Kenya, Zimbabwe, Pakistan) (Katakam, 2014).

There are 17 live mobile credit services with 2 launched in 2013, and 8 are reported to be planning to launch within the next 12 months (GSMA, 2013). Algorithms that use airtime purchase and call history data is used for credit scoring for customers in order to improve the provision of mobile credit services by providers to a greater number of individuals (Katakam, 2014). Most mobile credit services are still in their early stages of development. Although early successes that have been seen are encouraging, the evolution of this product will take time since it requires the rails laid down by mobile money deployments (Penicaud & Katakam, 2013).

Mobile Savings

There are many adults in developing countries who have no bank accounts, hence if any money is saved at all, it is probably under a mattress or under a lock without accruing any interest (Katakam, 2014; Demombynes & Thegeya, 2012). Mobile savings service is an innovative way of encouraging the culture of saving without requiring minimum account balances and other traditional bank charges. There are individuals who will actually perform a cash–in transaction in order to store the value in their mobile wallet till a digital transaction or cash-out is needed to be performed (GSMA, 2013).

Mobile savings can be distinguished into two types: basic mobile saving and bank-integrated mobile saving (Demombynes & Thegeya, 2012). Basic mobile saving involves the use of a standard mobile money system (like MPESA) to store funds but do not earn interest. The bank integrated one on the other hand involves accessing an account through which financial services could be offered through a mobile phone (for example M-KeESAO). This service is not limited to basically storing and transferring money, because for example that account may offer interest and also allows loans and insurance to be accessed.

Customers of mobile savings can also have distinct savings accounts different from that of mobile money, and other relevant functionalities needed for saving are also provided by these accounts (GSMA, 2013). There are 22 live mobile savings services, 9 launched in 2013 and plans were advanced to launch additional 7 in 12 months' time (GSMA, 2013). Also, with no bias, mobile savings services are available in every region but it is fewer as compared to mobile insurance because the latter does not necessarily rely on the infrastructure of mobile money.

Although almost half of all mobile savings service providers do not pay interest, customers still choose to save. This demonstrates that there is a customer demand for mobile savings. As a result, providers of mobile money services are continuously considering a move to savings from the usual payments because if customers could comfortably maintain huge e-money account balances then they are likely to increase the rate at which they transfer money (Mas, 2011).

Mobile Banking

Mobile banking (M-banking) can be defined as the use of the mobile phone to perform any banking transaction (Baba & Mohammed, 2007). According to Suoranta (2003), it refers to applying mobile commerce in a fashion that will enable bank customers to virtually perform transactions at any convenient time and place. To Tiwari & Buse (2007), M-banking is the provision of banking and related financial services such as savings, funds transfer, stock market transactions and others on mobile devices. Customers registered for M-banking could check the balance of their accounts, perform transactions with their credit cards and also access information about the latest transaction performed.

With M-banking, a user can basically operate a bank account using one's mobile phone. With a registered mobile phone linked to a bank account, the customer using his or her mobile phone can perform basic operations including topping up airtime, transferring money, paying bills, and also making special requests to the bank. With only 20 percent of African households which have bank accounts, majority of that population do not have access to banking services (Dovi, 2008). In Africa, people's limited access to financial services generally can be attributed to infrastructural deficiency, financial illiteracy and inaccessibility or physical–geographical isolation. All these contribute to a very high cost in the provision of banking services (Ondiege, 2010). For example, for each of the countries; Tanzania, Uganda and Ethiopia, there is less than one bank branch for every hundred thousand people as compared to a hundred branches for the same number of people in Spain (Dovi, 2008). Due to high costs of transactions, even the minority of Africans who have bank accounts have got to deal with high charges for moving their money around. Such a gap provided by the financial services market is what is giving the opportunity to mobile banking to develop, in order to enable an increasing section of the population on the continent to for the first-time access financial services (Ondiege, 2010).

More than 60 percent of Africa's total population are in the rural areas and have no access to banking services (Ondiege, 2010). And banks are recognizing the potential of mobile banking to reach millions of these prospective customers. For instance, in Kenya, Safaricom and Barclays bank went into partnership in October 2010 to allow account holders of Barclays to make deposits and withdrawals to and from their M-PESA mobile wallets and this is the eighth of such partnerships with M-PESA after those of Kenya Commercial Bank, Family Bank and others (Ondiege, 2010). Also, in other countries, there have been similar partnerships with Vodafone partnering with Vodacom, Roshan, and Nedbank in Tanzania, Afghanistan and South Africa respectively and in South Africa alone, 13 million customers are the target.

With such partnerships, mobile banking services have been extended to remote areas where there are physical absence of traditional banks. And so now subscribers can have the opportunity of opening their accounts, checking balances, transferring money, bills payment and catering for some basic daily needs (Ondiege, 2010).

Mobile Payments

Mobile payment refers to a mobile device like the mobile phone playing an instrumental role in making payments between two parties for the purchase of products or services (ISACA, 2011). A wide variety of digital or hard goods and services can be paid for by a consumer with the use of the mobile phone instead of paying in cash with credit cards or check.

There are different kinds of mobile payments. According to Gencer (2011), mobile payments include person-to-person (P2P) indicating domestic or international remittance payment between people; consumer-to-business (C2B) indicates customers' payments to merchants; business-to-business (B2B) payments are between businesses to help reduce cash upon inventory delivery in the supply chain; and business/government-to-consumer (B/G2C) indicating payments to employees or citizens in the form of salaries, benefits, pension disbursements, etc.

ADOPTION AND USE OF MOBILE FINANCIAL SERVICES

Although the number of MFS developments have experienced explosive growth, active usage of the services have not witnessed the same amount of growth (Davidson & McCarty, 2011). Of the 203 million registered accounts in June 2013 globally, 29.9 per cent were active in June 2013. In other words, the last ninety days saw only 61 million of the total registered accounts being used to perform one or more transactions (37 million active users in a 30 day basis) (Penicaud & Katakam, 2013).

Across the industry, one challenge that has been persistent is low customer activity rates due to significant challenges operators encounter. Davidson & McCarty, (2011) posit that some of these challenges include customers being aware of the MFS but do not understand how it could be beneficial to them. Also, during the registration process, customers get bogged down and they never try the product. Moreover, apart from trust issues with providers' brand and network, customers also lack understanding of the mechanics involved in performing transactions. This makes them apprehensive to try something which is so novel.

To increase customer activity therefore, operators have been thinking of ways to add value to every single interaction by a customer so that the average revenue per user (ARPU) of the service will be increased. Penicaud & Katakam (2013, p 20) believe that "perhaps the most important interaction is the point of registration where a customer learns about the service, identifies how it might fill a specific need, and also draws first impressions." It is therefore not out of place to believe that if a customer goes through the registration process and afterwards perceives that experience to be a positive one, it might encourage him/her to transact even on the same day and this could propel him/her into becoming a regular or active user. This is so when considering a customer who after registration walks away without performing any transaction, perhaps due to a bad experience. This customer perhaps after a few months is likely to forget how to access the service and forget as well even his/her PIN. This suddenly creates a barrier to usage and 30 percent of these customers are lost and they never transact (Penicaud & Katakam, 2013).

Factors of Post-Adoption Behaviour

Limayem and colleagues, (2007) describe information Systems (IS) continuance or IS continuous usage as behavioural patterns which reflect continual or continued use of a particular IS. At the individual level, this behaviour can be described as an IS usage stage which has gone beyond conscious behaviour and has now become a part of a usual routine activity (Bhattacherjee, 2009). An initial adoption decision is a one-time event but same cannot be said about IS continuance because the latter is an outcome of a series of decisions taken by an individual to continue the use of a particular IS and these decisions follow an initial adoption decision (Limayem et al., 2007).

Enablers

The theoretical foundations for the antecedents in post-adoption use of IS traditionally include but not limited to the Theory of Reasoned Action, the Technology Acceptance Model, IS Continuance Model, Symbolic Adoption Theory, Psychological Empowerment Theory, and Self-Efficacy Theory (Tennant, 2014). The categories of the antecedents in such models include user / individual characteristics (for example attitude, satisfaction, user competence), perceptions of the system (for example satisfaction, perceived ease of use, perceived usefulness, compatibility), control factors (for example facilitating conditions), and level of use (for example routinization) (Tennant, 2014).

Although theories like TAM and TRA are fundamental in explaining intention or regular use, these theories lack in explaining actual use or deeper types of use and are therefore insufficient in addressing use that increases productivity (Grgecic & Rosenkranz, 2010). According to Hsieh & Wang (2007), therefore, there is the need to work further on factors that are better suited in the post-adoption context. In addition, Jasperson and colleagues (2005) posit that factors which have not been adequately explored in previous research are likely to have influence on post-adoption use. Calls have therefore been made by researchers for further work on advancing the understanding of factors that enable post-adoption use, such as individual characteristics and differences like experience, expertise, attitude towards each potential use of the system, efficiency, motivation, etc. (Hsieh & Wang, 2007).

Inhibiters

Cenfetelli & Schwarz (2011) assert that research on inhibiting factors in the IS use domain is scanty, and there is an implicit assumption that the inhibitors of use are the opposite of the facilitators. However, based on the negative potency principle, it is argued that given two opposing events, one negative and the other positive but of the same magnitude, subjectively the negative event is superior in potency and importance than the positive one (Rozin & Royzman, 2001). Therefore, to assume that the effect of a negative element is the reverse of a positive element is not necessarily accurate (Choi et al., 2009). Rozin & Royzman, (2001) further argue that the negative aspect of a negative event grows more rapidly than the positive aspect of a positive event. As a result, negative factors can have strong adverse effects on one's actions over time (Tennant, 2014).

Findings in IS research indicate that the presence of an inhibiting factor is likely to have an adverse effect on use. Such investigated inhibitors include lack of knowledge, lack of IT support, user resistance, information inhibitors and system inhibitors (Tennant, 2014). Consequently, in a study to investigate barriers perceived to be hindering adoption and use of mobile banking by Ghanaian consumers, Iddris (2013), identified (the lack of) knowledge about using the service to be topping the list of barriers. This will obviously affect the users' perceived ease of use of the system. It is therefore essential not to solely focus on enablers and exclude other relevant factors that influence continual use.

REGULATORY FRAMEWORK

Many business people almost instinctively react negatively to the word "regulation". However, regulation is essential to create and maintain an enabling environment for the growth of every business including mobile financial services (MFS).

Figure 2. MFS key regulatory concerns

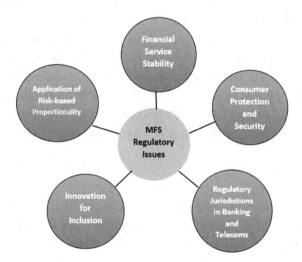

While attempting to increase the outreach of financial services, there are some issues that are key concerns of financial regulators (DFID, 2006). These include whether consumers are adequately protected. The most important ingredient for MFS growth is trust among consumers. Therefore, there is the need for appropriate consumer protection against fraud, loss of privacy and loss of service in order to establish trust and public confidence.

Jenkins (2008) posits that "public confidence is predicated on the stability of the financial system." As such another major concern of regulators is how MFS affect the stability of the country's financial system (DFID, 2006). Financial inclusion aside financial stability is another concern of the regulator. Billions of people currently live without access to formal financial services as described earlier. At the expense of their full financial potentials and their physical security as well, they live entirely in cash-based economies. The regulator is responsible for guiding and facilitating innovation and competition among service providers since these are what financial inclusion requires.

Innovation for inclusion on the one hand and the need for stability on the other hand requires that regulators strike a delicate balance that is constantly evolving (Jenkins, 2008). However, it is particularly difficult in the MFS ecosystem to strike a balance between stability and innovation. This is because MFS involves multiple regulatory domains from banking and telecommunications as a result "there is a significant risk of coordination failure in policy-making around mobile financial services" (Lyman et al., 2008). It is therefore not surprising that many leaders in the industry perceive the regulatory environment as presently not particularly enabling. What is recommended therefore is 'incrementality' where regulators "take a relaxed, mature approach and let the channels emerge. Then add regulations as risks manifest" (Peachy, 2008). Another need is proportionality (Jenkins, 2008) so that "regulators need to weigh the potential gain against the potential damage, and then take a pragmatic, risk-based approach to KYC and other relevant regulations" (Dostov, 2008).

IMPACT OF MOBILE FINANCIAL SERVICES

The basic qualities of MFS can help the unbanked overcome barriers and reap the benefits of financial services. There are five unique advantages that telecommunication companies (telcos) have over traditional banks (BCG, 2011). Traditionally these telcos have focus on all customers, not just the most profitable among them, and they already have a secure device—the mobile phone—in customers' hands. The telcos unlike the banks have already established relationships with these customers and gained their trust as well, in addition to the added benefits of a large distribution network (BCG, 2011).

Mobile Financial Services could transform financial inclusion by extending financial services to the poor. They enhance the convenience of individual customers and save time as well because in order to make a transaction, the customer does not need to be physically present at the bank premises to interact with it. This even leads to the reduction of their cost in accessing and using the services of the bank. In most cases one factor that makes MFS succeed is the fact that considerably it is cheaper as compared to other alternatives to the use of cash (Donovan, 2012). Mckay & Pickens in their 2010 study found that averagely, MFS and other types of branchless banking were 19 per cent less expensive as compared to other services offered alternatively. By lowering cost and increasing efficiency, MFS is expected to improve productivity and provide customers with a better administration of their funds.

MFS do not only contribute to enhancing the market image of the financial and banking institutions. Since they are accessible worldwide they increase the extent to which the institution's products penetrate the market and also provides the opportunity for new products to be advertised to the growing number of users. Aside all these benefits, there is even a stronger effect from MFS because the system can be used as a launch pad from which other innovative services like payment of bills which avoid long queues can arise (Donovan, 2012). Another benefit is that money transfers are made to some individuals as compensation or reliefs when they are adversely affected by some conditions like drought, flood, etc. For instance, there was an initiative funded by the World Bank in the Democratic Republic of Congo where through the use of mobile phones, ex-combatants in the country were paid some compensations as a result of drought (Donovan, 2012).

Furthermore, MFS can be used to transform a lot of lives in places where there is no financial infrastructure. In 1991 due to the civil war in Somalia, the central government as well as the central bank collapsed. The financial system and also the country's entire banking system were destroyed (Sayid et al., 2012). Even though after 18 years the offices of the central Bank were reopened in Mogadishu and Baidoa, it seemed inactive and powerless and looked like it needed a long time before it could regain control over the economy as well as the country's monetary policies (Sayid et al., 2012). It took MFS companies which arose to put some life back in the financial system by providing some basic financial and banking services. Due to its speed, affordability, the growing trust from the public etc., MFS became the major financial system in the country (Sayid et al., 2012).

CONCLUSION

In a nutshell, some of the economic benefits that can be derived from MFS are "increase in domestic capital formation, the drawing of credit into the banking system, and the time and cost savings MFS brings to individuals and companies, and all these impacts serve to form the larger economic effects which include growth in domestic gross product (GDP), entrepreneurship, and jobs" (BCG, 2011, pp. 8-9). Also, social benefits that MFS can provide include supplementing of incomes through remittances, provision of a safer means of storing income when the times are good and means of accessing insurance (BCG, 2011). Larger social benefits that these impacts lead to include an increase in financial inclusion, the poor becomes more resilient to financial shocks, and in case of a shock, keeping children in school becomes easier (BCG, 2011).

REFERENCES

Adjei, J.K. & Odei-Appiah, S. (2008, May 14). Interview of Victor Dostov, Paycash. Personal communication () .

B. C. G. (2011). *The Boston Consulting Group*. The Socio-Economic Impact of Mobile.

Balasubramanian, S., Peterson, R. A., & Jarvenpaa, S. L. (2002). Exploring the implications of m-commerce for markets and marketing. *Journal of the Academy of Marketing Science*, *30*(4), 348–361. doi:10.1177/009207002236910

Balasubramanian & Drake. (2015). Service Quality, Inventory and Competition among Mobile Money Agents (manuscript no. MSOM-15-289). Manufacturing & Service Operations Management.

Bandura, A. (2001). Social Cognitive Theory: An Agentic Perspective. *Annual Review of Psychology*, *52*(1), 1–26. doi:10.1146/annurev.psych.52.1.1 PMID:11148297

Bhattacherjee, A. (2001a). Understanding Information Systems Continuance: An Expectation- Confirmation Model. *Management Information Systems Quarterly*, *25*(3), 351–370. doi:10.2307/3250921

Bhattacherjee, A. (2009, February 12). An empirical analysis of the antecedents of electronic commerce DFID. Douglas Alexander sets out how branchless banking can help the poorest people. Retrieved September 26, 2009, from http://www.dfid.gov.uk/Media-Room/Speeches-andarticles/2009/Douglas-Alexander-sets-out-how-branchless-banking-can-help-the-poorest-people/

Churchill, C. (2014). "Microinsurance: Much progress, but challenges remain" (available at http://www.ilo.org/global/about-the-ilo/newsroom/comment-analysis/WCMS_237793/lang--en/index.htm) Last visited 12-1-15.

Davidson, N., & McCarty, M. Y. (2011). "Driving Customer Usage of Mobile Money for the Unbanked.

Demombynes, G. & Thegeya, A. (2012). "Kenya's Mobile Revolution and the Promise of Mobile Savings." The World Bank Africa Region Poverty Reduction and Economic Management Unit March 2012

Donovan, K. (2012). Mobile money for financial inclusion. In T. Kelly & C. Rossotto (Eds.), *Information and Communication for Development* (pp. 61–74). Washington, DC: World Bank.

Dovi, E. (2008). Boosting Domestic Savings in Africa.

G. S. M. A. (2013). Global Mobile Money Deployment Tracker." Retrieved from http://www.wirelessintelligence.com/mobile-money

Gencer, M. (2011). *The Mobile Money Movement: Catalyst to Jumpstart Emerging Markets*. Innovations Publication Winter.

Hsieh, J., & Wang, W. (2007). Explaining employees' Extended Use of complex information systems. *European Journal of Information Systems*, *16*(3), 216–227. Retrieved from http://www.ifc.org/wps/wcm/connect/93fdb8004a1b4f46909bfddd29332b51/Tool+4.7e.+. doi:10.1057/palgrave.ejis.3000663

IFC (International Finance Corporation). (2011). Mobile Money Study 2011. Retrieved from http://www.ifc.org/ifcext/globalfm.nsf/Content/Mobile+Money+Study+2011

ISACA. (2011). Mobile Payments. Retrieved 21-1-15 from http://www.isaca.org/Groups/Professional-English/pci-compliance/GroupDocuments/MobilePaymentsWP.pdf

Jasperson, J. S., Carter, P. E., & Zmud, R. W. (2005). A comprehensive conceptualization of post-adoption behaviors associated with information technology enabled work systems. *Management Information Systems Quarterly*, *29*(3), 525–558. doi:10.2307/25148694

Jenkins, B. (2008). *Developing Mobile Money Ecosystems*. Washington, DC: IFC and the Harvard Kennedy School.

Katakam, A. (2014). "The State of Mobile Credit and Savings – how has mobile technology expanded credit and savings services?" GSMA Retrieved 15-1-15 from http://www.gsma.com/mobilefordevelopment/the-state-of-mobile-credit-and-savings-how-has-mobile-technology-expanded-credit-and-savings-services

Kim, S. S., & Malhotra, N. K. (2005). A longitudinal model of continued IS use: An integrative view of four mechanisms underlying postadoption phenomena. Management science, 51(5), 741-755. doi:10.1287/mnsc.1040.0326

Leach, J. (2011). M-Insurance: The Next Wave of Mobile Financial Services? Retrieved 11-1-15 from http://www.microensure.com/news.asp?id=47&start=5

Limayem, M., Hirt, S. G., & Cheung, C. M. K. (2007). How habit limits the predictive power of intention: the case of information systems continuance. *Management Information Systems Quarterly*, *31*(4), 705–737. doi:10.2307/25148817

Lyman, T. R., Mark, P., & Porteous, D. (2008). Regulating Transformational Branchless Banking: Mobile Phones and Other Technology to Increase Access to Finance." CGAP Focus Note No. 43. Washington, DC: CGAP. Retrieved June 18, 2008 from http://www.cgap.org/p/site/c/template.rc/1.9.2583

Mas, I. (2011). Enabling different paths to the development of Mobile Money ecosystems. Mobile Money for the Unbanked, Annual Report 2011. Retrieved 17-1-15 from http://ssrn.com/abstract=1843623

McKay, C., & Pickens, M. (2010). *Branchless Banking 2010: Who's Served? At What Price? What's Next?* Washington, DC: Consultative Group to Assist the Poor.

Ondiege, P. (2010). Mobile Banking in Africa: Taking the Bank to the People. *AfDB Africa Economic Brief*, *1*(8).

Peachy, Dc. (2008). Wholesale & Prudential Policy Division, Financial Services Authority. In *Presentation at GSMA Mobile Money Summit*, Cairo, May 15.

Pénicaud, C., & Katakam, A. (2013). State of the industry 2013: mobile financial services for the unbanked. GSMA. Retrieved from http://www.gsma.com/mobilefordevelopment/wp-content/uploads/2014/02/SOTIR_2013.pdf

Petter, S., DeLone, W., & McLean, E. R. (2013). Information systems success: The quest for the independent variables. *Journal of Management Information Systems*, *29*(4), 7–62. doi:10.2753/MIS0742-1222290401

Rozin, P., & Royzman, E. B. (2001). Negativity bias, negativity dominance, and contagion. *Personality and Social Psychology Review*, *5*(4), 296–320. doi:10.1207/S15327957PSPR0504_2

Sayid, O., Heights, D., Echchabi, A., Pusu, J. S., Sciences, M., & Pusu, J. S. (2012). Investigating service continuance. *Decision Support Systems*, *32*(2), 201–214.

GSMA. (n.d.). Services for the Unbanked (tech. rep.). Retrieved from http://www. gsma.com/mobilefordevelopment/wp-content/uploads/2015/03/SOTIR_2014.pdf

Tellez, C. (2012). Emerging Practices in Mobile Microinsurance.

Tennant, V. (2014). Understanding Changes in Post-adoption Use of Information Systems (IS): A generalized Darwinism Perspective [Thesis Doctor of Philosophy]. Accounting and Information Systems in the University of Canterbury.

Tiwari, R., & Buse, S. (2007). *The Mobile Commerce Prospects: A Strategic Analysis of Opportunities in the Banking Sector*. Hamburg, Germany: Hamburg University Press.

Tobbin, P. (2011). Understanding Mobile Money Ecosystem: Roles, Structure and Strategies. In *Proceedings of the 2011 Tenth International Conference on Mobile Business (ICMB)* (pp. 185-194). IEEE. doi:10.1109/ICMB.2011.19

Tobbin, P. E. (2010). Modeling Adoption of Mobile Money Transfer: A Consumer Behaviour Analysis. In *Proceedings of the 2nd International conference on M4D Mobile Communication Technology for Development M4D 2010* (pp. 280–293).

Tobbin, P. E. (2013). Examining the Adoption and Use of Mobile Data Services: A Consumer Behavior Analysis [Thesis Doctor of Philosophy]

UN.org. (n.d.). To invest more, countries must tap assets now outside the banks. Retrieved from www.un.org/ecosocdev/geninfo/afrec

Yakub, J. O., Bello, H. T., & Adenuga, I. A. (2013). Mobile Money Services in Nigeria: An inquiry of existing Models. *International Journal of Economics and Management Sciences*, *2*(9), 94–105.

Chapter 7
Assessment of Mobile Money Enablers in Nigeria

Sunday Adewale Olaleye
University of Oulu, Finland

Ismaila Temitayo Sanusi
University of Eastern Finland, Finland

Dandison C. Ukpabi
University of Jyväskylä, Finland

ABSTRACT

This chapter describes how mobile money is an emerging and innovative financial service delivery mechanism. With huge success, recorded mostly in the developing economies, it is scholarly unclear the antecedents of its adoption. Using a survey of 151 respondents comprising both the banked and underbanked in the South-Western part of Nigeria, the authors used the PLS-SEM to test the research hypothesis. The results reveal the enablers of mobile money, which are social influence, performance expectancy, security and effort expectancy, and inhibitors such as system anxiety and cost. Privacy, trust, image and convenience were not found significant in this study. Social influence, performance expectancy and effort expectancy variables adapted from the UTAUT model have considerable influence on mobile money in Nigeria. Study implications and future directions are offered.

DOI: 10.4018/978-1-5225-4029-8.ch007

INTRODUCTION

Mobile banking is thriving but the rural dwellers that account for more than half of the population of Nigeria are lagging in benefitting maximally in this technological advancement. Nigerian banking sector has shifted its attention from traditional banking to internet banking to add more values to the services it offers. Despite the complementary innovation in the banking sector, a vast range of customers has still left behind especially the rural areas due to the infrastructural deficit (Asongu, 2015). Mobile Money can be used to top up the phone, pay for groceries, transfer funds to other subscribers and helps to carry cash in a digital wallet instead of carrying a physical cash that is vulnerable to robbery (Greenacre, 2013). Despite the benefits of mobile money, it is not yet to practice all these functionalities in Nigeria.

The benefits and the challenges of mobile money are growing together. Regardless of its benefits, mobile money had failed to catch up quickly in the rural areas of Nigeria where relatively few people have bank access. It is also difficult to ascertain whether the success stories of mobile money in one part of Africa can be replicated in another part with the same result. As the users' knowledge, adoption, use and continuous use is progressive in Nigeria, some existing scholars have considered the rise of mobile money in the context of Australia regulation (Greenacre, 2013). There has been a focus on mobile money market development with a study on migration from giant robots to mobile money platforms, integrating trust into the technology acceptance model with a focus on poor citizens of India. Mobile money has been studied in the context of the promises and pitfalls (Bhattacharya, 2015; Chauhan, 2015; Osei-Assibey, 2015; Kusimba, Yang and Chawla, 2015; Osazevbaru and Yomere, 2015; Alao and Sorinola, 2015; Blumenstock, Callen, Ghani and Koepke, 2015), mobile money remittances and household welfare (Munyegera and Matsumoto, 2016), comparison of two countries on politics of mobile money (Suárez, 2016) and mobile money in non-profit sector (Yunus, Khan, Tasnuba, Husain and Misiti, 2016).

Mobile money is an emerging technology without a universal business model. It is a developing technology in Africa with an ecosystem of banking sectors, mobile network operators, merchants, retailers, and consumers. Though the goal of every business is to reduce running costs and improve business performance, mobile money emergence is not without its own challenges. Presently, there is a vacuum in interoperability of mobile money operators, lack of unified method of operations, lack of trust, insufficient user's experience, limitation of smartphones users in the rural areas, low literacy level in the rural areas, erratic mobile network, limits on the amounts that mobile money user can transfer per day and regulatory issues (Greenacre, 2013; Ondiege, 2015). These are the standing challenges that are contending against the enabling factors of mobile money penetration and advancement. Though the practitioners are working towards finding solutions to these challenges, there is a need for scholars to fathom the enabling and inhibiting factors of mobile money to ensure its diffusion.

The overall goal of this research project is to assess, analyze and evaluate mobile money in Nigeria. The specific objective is to find out the enablers of mobile money in Nigerian rural and urban areas and the inhibiting factors of mobile money penetration and advancement. The study will examine in detail the benefits of mobile money to its stakeholders through its enabling factors and how to seek caution from its inhibitors. This study will use positivist approach to examine the hypothetical relationships within the conceptual model. The study adapted the predication of Pantano and Priporas (2016) as they suggested a quantitative method for mobile retailing study for insight. The sections of this study will be in the following order. Part two evinces the background of mobile money globally and the brief overview of mobile money. Part three explore the relevant literature while part four showcase the methodology and the data analysis for the mobile money study. Part five discusses the findings, managerial implications and future direction of mobile money.

BACKGROUND

Lawack (2012) defines mobile money as "…a digital repository of electronic money developed and implemented on mobile devices, allowing peer-to-peer transactions (P2P) between mobile devices (M2M) from users of the same service." Mobile money has revolutionized money transfer and payment systems (Kirui, Okello and Nyikal, 2012). Thus, with access to a mobile phone, payment could be made such as school fees, utilities, transport fares and even professional charges such as legal and medical bills. This has largely minimized the hardships occasioned by lack of access to banking platforms faced by rural dwellers in the emerging markets. Globally, there are about 150 mobile money services offering subscribers range of money transfer options. The origin of mobile money has been traced to Safaricom, a mobile operator who launched the M-PESA platform in Kenya in 2007 and currently has about 15 million active subscribers making 3 million transactions a day totaling 700 million dollars per month (Brookings Institutions, 2013). The success of M-PESA has resonated in the emerging markets with different mobile money services across different countries. In the developing countries where banking services are mainly available in the cities and urban areas, the emergence of mobile money has improved livelihood. As a matter of fact, urban migrants could easily send money to dependents in the countryside without resorting to traveling or postal charges.

The success of mobile money globally has been attributed to enablers such as mobile phones, network access, government regulation and interoperability. The workability of the innovation thrives on the mobile phones. Consequently, the success of the innovation in the emerging markets is attributed to the deregulation of the telecommunication industry in such markets thereby making access to mobile phones easier and accessible. As a matter of fact, the person sending the money must have access to a mobile phone just like the person receiving the money. Additionally, market size is a contributory factor to the success of the mobile money innovation, as the two countries where the innovation has recorded huge success are Kenya and Indonesia with a population of 48 million and 242 million respectively. Government regulation/central bank support is also a factor for the success of the innovation. Strong state support has been cited as a critical antecedent for the success of the Indonesia model of mobile money (EY, 2017). According to the report, the government provided the policy guidelines that specified terms for outsourcing mobile payments to retail agents. With this, many people bought into the service based on a clearer understanding of the *modus operandi* of the innovation. The policy guidelines also helped to imbue trust into the system by clarifying areas that were considered as legal loopholes in its operation. Finally, interoperability, that is, the attribute of a system to work synergistically with other systems without restriction, is also lauded for the success of the Indonesia model. The Indonesian three mobile operators agreed to an interoperable mobile interface thereby enabling subscribers to send money irrespective of the network.

The socio-economic impact of the mobile money innovation is profound. First, it has opened employment opportunities for many unemployed. The success of M-PESA in Kenya has created 40,000 agents who also employ additional people with different capacities for the day-to-day operation of their business (Oyebode, 2014). Other countries where the innovation succeeded, for instance, Indonesia has also provided employment opportunities for the jobless. Second, mobile money has improved the standard of living of the people by having access to finance as at when needed. Access to finance has been a major contributor to poverty in developing countries. Thus, with the introduction of mobile money, a husband for instance, who works in the city can easily transmit cash to his family in the countryside to meet up with their present financial needs. Mobile money has also contributed to the ease of doing business and reduction of traffic and road crashes. Indisputably, developing countries are noted for poor and chaotic traffic systems. Sometimes, these traffic challenges arise because of an urgent need to meet up with issues such as to send money and make payments. With the introduction of mobile money, one can easily transmit payment without necessarily being on the road, thus, reducing the amount of vehicular traffic on the road at any given time.

However, as novel as the mobile money innovation with its profound impact on the economy, it has woefully failed in many countries. After an extensive review of 196 peer-reviewed and practitioner papers published between 2001-2011 on the subject, Diniz, de Albuquerque and Cernev (2011) summarised that failure of the mobile money innovation in many countries is attributed to the following: first, lack of business model. The hype in the adoption of the innovation because of its success in Kenya led to a chaotic and fuzzy operation deficient of a clear-cut business model. Therefore, many people were lethargic to embrace the service. Second, technological security/user interface limitation posed a serious challenge to its smooth operation. For instance, many feared that their phones would be hacked or cloned and the personal identification number (PIN) through which users gain access to the platform would be abused. Thus, trust, being the cornerstone of exchange relationship was lacking. Third, lack of infrastructure/poor network especially in the developing countries where solid telecommunications infrastructure is a new phenomenon. Many of the developing countries leapfrogged to mobile telephony without experiencing the robust infrastructure that enabled the wired telephone lines. Some country-sides are yet to be connected and those living in such areas are completely cut off from the mobile money revolution. Fourth, deficient regulatory framework and lack of co-operation among service providers also hampered its success in many countries. Some governments did not provide the regulatory guidelines necessary for its success, as a result, there were many legal loopholes in its operation. This mainly contributed to the cold feet some service providers developed and because of interoperability challenges, money transfer was only limited within those in the same network. Finally, illiteracy has also been blamed for its failure in some countries. Some people in the developing countries though possess mobile phones but only use such for its functional purpose of making and receiving calls. Mobile money thrives on mobile apps that needs to be downloaded with basic instructions and inability to read and understand those instructions hampered its usage.

Assessment of Mobile Money in Nigeria

According to the CNBC Africa (2016), Nigeria is the leading country in Africa with the highest diffusion of smartphone and internet penetration. Consequently, many areas are benefitting from digitization. Scholarly evidence exists on the use of internet in Nigerian secondary schools (Adomi and Kpangban, 2010) and universities (Oye, Iahad and Rabin, 2011) with significant impact on the performance of Nigerian students in both national and international academic competitions. Curiously, the impact of ICT on consumers' banking services is comparatively lower. Mobile money emergence is an answer to the quest of the unbanked and the underbanked Nigerians. The banking industry in Nigeria has gone through several structural reforms; however, the most dramatic was the recapitalization of the capital base of the banks in 2004 from 2 Billion Nigerian Naira to 25 Billion Nigerian Naira (Barros and Caporale, 2012). After the consolidation, the number of banks shrank from 89 to 75 with the capital base moving from 3209 Billion Nigeria Naira to 6555 Nigeria Naira. Additionally, Barros and Caporale (2012) report that the number of bank branches grew from 3,382 to 4,500. The post-consolidation Nigerian banks became stronger and customer-driven. In a bid to attract more customers, efforts were made to diversify their channels of reaching to customers. Considering the huge number of the underbanked, the regulatory authorities came up with the policy of mobile money consisting the bank-led and non-bank led-models (Yakub, Bello, Adenuga, 2013). The bank-led model is made up of a licensed deposit money bank in a consortium of other registered business who come together to deliver mobile money services while non-bank-led model consists registered businesses independent of banks who operate mobile money services in Nigeria. As at 2015, Giginyu (2015) reports that there were 21 licensed mobile money operators comprising 15 non-bank operators and 6 bank operators. Furthermore, the expansion drive of the Central Bank of Nigeria to reach as many Nigerians as possible has also led to 8 additional operators who are currently under pilot schemes and are awaiting registration. However, security and lack of basic infrastructure such as stable power supply are critical setbacks to the rapid acceptance of the initiative.

CONCEPTUAL FRAMEWORK AND HYPOTHESES

Closely related to mobile money is mobile banking. Scholars have extensively studied mobile banking in the context of adoption, usage, and continuous usage, as such, different theories, models and frameworks have been used in these studies (Shaikh and Karjaluoto, 2015). With the understanding that mobile money is an emerging concept in the electronic finance literature, our study shall adopt some prominent theories and models in examining mobile money adoption in an emerging market context. Thus, the unified theory of acceptance and use of technology (UTAUT), Trust-technology acceptance and some relevant models will be integrated into this study.

System Anxiety

Many of those who are newly introduced to a piece of information system usually feel anxious about using it, however, that anxious feeling ebbs as they continue to use it. System anxiety is defined as "the apprehension or fear that results when an individual is faced with the possibility of using an IS" (Hackbarth, Grover, and

Figure 1. Integrated conceptual framework of mobile money

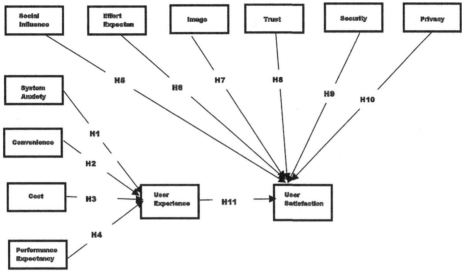

Mun, 2003, p.223). System anxiety varies across demographics with adults and women demonstrating more anxiety than the young and male users (Malaquias and Hwang, 2016). Hackbarth, Grover, and Mun, (2003) reported that system experience is a stronger approach to decreasing system anxiety and increasing ease of use. Earlier, Brown and Coney (1994) contended that self-rated skills, typing ability, and computer attitudes were the factors that induced computer use anxiety among medical practitioners. In the mobile shopping context, Lu and Yu-Jen (2009) argue that anxiety is a key negative determinant of using mobile phones. In the same study, it was reported that the user's self-perception of mobile skillfulness significantly influences anxiety, enjoyment, and usefulness. Finally, in the mobile banking study in Brazil, (Malaquias and Hwang, 2016) reported that effective communication with users outlining its importance can reduce anxiety in the use of mobile banking services. Thus, this study argues that mobile money as an innovation is bound to generate anxiety among users and negatively influence user experience.

H1: System anxiety of mobile money platform will negatively influence user experience.

Convenience

Using a piece of technology poses some difficulties to early users. As a matter of fact, convenience is an important construct in the information systems literature.

A proper understanding of the concept of convenience should incorporate sub-elements such as time, place, acquisition, use and execution dimensions (Yoon and Kim, 2007). In a study of mobile commerce adoption, Wu and Wang (2005) found that convenience and time saving is a critical motivation for consumers to engage in mobile commerce. Additionally, Luo, Li, Zhang, and Shim (2010) posit that the growth and popularity of mobile banking is a result of the convenience users enjoy, thus saving them time and effort. Users can simply conduct banking transactions at the convenience of their homes or offices without necessarily travelling to the banks. Similarly, when users perceive that using mobile money will increase their convenience in banking transactions, its adoption will be high. This leads to the following hypothesis:

H2: Convenient mobile money platform will positively influence user experience.

Cost

Marketing literature usually conceptualizes the monetary cost or price of a product with the quality of that product or service to determine its value to consumers (Venkatesh, Thong and Xu, 2012). Generally, it is perceived, the more expensive products are of higher quality than the less expensive ones. As a result, firms usually adopt different pricing strategies which usually appeal to different classes of customers. In the information technology literature, cost, sometimes modelled as price, it is usually evaluated based on the monetary value the user places on the piece of the technology. Thus, when the cost is perceived as high, it is expected to have more value and quality than a piece of technology that is less costly. In mobile commerce adoption, the cost is a significant factor which was found to have a negative effect on behavioural intention to adopt the technology (Wu and Wang, 2005). Similarly, it is likely a significant factor in adopting mobile money, implying that users will develop a negative response to its adoption when the cost of its usage is considered high. Thus, the following hypothesis is proposed:

H3: The cost of using mobile money services will negatively influence user experience.

The Unified Theory of Acceptance and Use of Technology (UTAUT)

The UTAUT theory unified prior existing information technology adoption models and not only identifying the individual-level factors that underpin technology adoption but also uniquely underscores the antecedents that either constrain or support the influence of these factors (Venkatesh and Zhang, 2010). It postulates that performance expectancy, effort expectancy, social influence and facilitating conditions are the triggers of technology adoption. Furthermore, the theory adds that education, age, and income could also moderate how these factors influence individuals. Though not as popular as the original technology acceptance model (TAM), the application of UTAUT in different countries and contexts has assumed a significant proportion. For instance, it was applied in a study of e-government services in Kuwait (AlAwadhi and Morris, 2008), health information technology in Thailand (Kijsanayotin, Pannarunothai and Speedie 2009) and most importantly, studies on mobile information systems (Min, Ji, and Qu, 2008; Zhou, Lu and Wang, 2010; Yu, 2012). While there are other important constructs in the UTAUT theory, a critical review of relevant literature in mobile banking underpins the extensive use of performance expectancy, effort expectancy, and social influence. Accordingly, our study will be limited to these three. Therefore, Carlsson et al. (2006) found that performance expectancy and effort expectancy were the main determinants of mobile services usage in Finland. Interestingly, however, Zhou, Lu and Wang (2010) contend that mobile banking adoption in China was significantly influenced by performance expectancy, social influence and facilitating conditions, as effort expectancy exerted insignificant influence. Furthermore, by integrating the UTAUT, the Task Technology Fit model (TTF) and Initial Trust Model (ITM), Portuguese mobile banking users reported that initial trust in mobile banking is formed when users identify performance gains from the platform. Thus, to optimize trust in the mobile banking platform, practitioners should ensure that users derive performance gains from the services of the mobile banking platform. However, another study found that as important as these variables are in mobile banking adoption, the individual's behavioural intention is the most significant determinant in mobile banking adoption (Yu, 2012). Thus, the following hypotheses are proposed:

H4: Performance expectancy of mobile money will positively influence user experience.

H5: Social influence will positively influence user satisfaction of mobile money.

H6: Effort Expectancy will positively influence user satisfaction of mobile money.

Image

Service provider's image has long been identified as having a strong influence on intention and continuous patronage (Jin, Lee, and Lee, 2015). To this end, firms try to deliver consistent quality products and services to maintain a good image with its customers. As a matter of fact, the image of a firm is not determined by the firm's communications efforts through advertising and new media platforms, but through the experience of customers during service encounters. In the mobile money context, since financial services are adopted with caution, users may wish to determine the corporate image of the service provider before they adopt the service. Thus, those who have performed well through good services conjure the positive image and are more patronized than those relatively unpopular. Additionally, customer determination of the service quality which is a yardstick for performance is underpinned by speed, interactivity, security, and promptness to answer queries. The study thus argues that image is a significant factor in determining users' perception of satisfaction with mobile banking services. Thus, the following hypothesis is proposed:

H7: Image of mobile money operator will positively influence user satisfaction.

Trust-Technology Acceptance Model

Trust is a critical factor in an exchange relationship. As a matter of fact, the ubiquitous diffusion of information systems underscores the importance of trust in their adoption. As a multi-faceted construct that applies to different disciplines, trust has been defined based on disciplinary trajectories. Thus, Luo, Li, Zhang and Shim (2010) identified three dimensions of trust in relation to new information technology adoption: disposition to trust, structural assurance, and trust belief. They defined disposition to trust as "a general inclination in which people show faith or belief in humanity and adopt a trusting stance toward others" (p.224). Trust in financial systems-related information technology is important because users usually form security perceptions on the IT and when that perception is confirmed as secure, the trust will be developed towards it (Carlos, José, and José, 2009). In terms of mobile banking, initial trust, security, and privacy are very crucial in their adoption. Accordingly, Kim, Shin and Lee (2009) argue that trust-inducing forces: structural assurances, perceived benefits, personal propensity and firm reputation underlie the extent of mobile banking. Interestingly, firm reputation was not found to attract people, but more attractive forces were the perception of initial trust and relative benefits to the users. Within the trust framework, users trust is likely to increase if they perceive that security and privacy in the mobile banking platform are guaranteed. Thus, the following hypotheses are proposed:

H8: Trusted mobile money platform will positively influence user satisfaction of mobile money.

H9: Security of mobile money platform will positively influence user satisfaction of mobile money.

H10: Privacy confidence of mobile money platform will positively influence user satisfaction.

User Experience

User experience as a concept draws from both psychology, sociology, management and information systems (Olaleye, Sanusi, and Oyelere, 2017), thus, very difficult to proffer a concise definition. However, it has generally viewed as the perception an individual form from using or anticipated the use of a product, service or an information system (Law, 2011). It is a critical determinant of the adoption, use and continuous use of a piece of information technology. Those who are knowledgeable about the piece of the technology encounter less difficulty in its use. Conversely, new users usually encounter more difficult times using a piece of technology. Accordingly, Karahanna, Straub, and Chervany (1999) argue that at the initial adoption phase of a technology, subjective norm and affect play a key role in user experience, however, their influence wanes over time as the user gains more experience on the technology. In terms of mobile banking, Oliveira, Faria, Thomas, and Popovič (2014) posit user experience will be optimized if banks and relevant bodies highlight the benefits of its adoption. Thus, the following hypothesis is proposed:

H11: User experience of mobile money will positively influence user satisfaction.

User Satisfaction

Satisfaction is an important construct in both marketing and information systems literature because it leads to patronage or continuous usage of a piece of information systems. As a result, marketing practitioners make all necessary provisions to reduce unpleasant experiences that may arise in the consumption process. Equally, information systems are to provide utmost and pleasant experiences to the user. Thus, once a user is satisfied, he/she is likely to continue with the usage of the system. However, satisfaction varies across time and contexts. According to Mahmood, Burn, Gemoets, and Jacquez (2000), user's background, user experience, gender and degree of involvement all play a significant impact on the level of satisfaction which is derived from a piece of information technology. Additionally, in a study of mobile banking adoption among Korean users, Lee and Chung, (2009) contend that interface design quality has no effect on customer satisfaction, but customer satisfaction is affected by system and information quality.

RESEARCH METHODOLOGY AND SAMPLE

To accentuate objective measurements, the study employs quantitative methods to explain mobile money phenomenon in Nigeria. Ten independent variables were used to predict two dependent variables and later commingle the two models. The first model considered mobile money user experience and adopted system anxiety, convenience, cost and performance expectancy as the predictors while the second model dwells on mobile money satisfaction and used social influence, effort expectancy, image, trust, security and privacy to predict mobile money user's satisfaction. To get a deeper insight into mobile money, user experience was used as an antecedent of mobile money satisfaction. The target of this study is the unbanked and underbanked that constitute the resident of urban and the rural dwellers acclaimed to be mobile money users in Nigeria. The study adopts measurement from the extant studies (see Table 1 for details) and employ 7-Point Likert Scales with a minimum of scale 1 as strongly disagree and a maximum of scale 7 as strongly agree. Apart from the Likert Scales, the study examines the in-depth demographic profile of the mobile money users.

The survey for the study was administered between 06.02.2017 to 09.03.2017 in the South West part of Nigeria and the questionnaire was designed to capture the knowledge, experience and the satisfaction of the mobile money users. 250 copies of the questionnaire were administered offline and retrieved 163 copies back with a response rate of 60.4% which is above average. 12 questionnaires were excluded during the data cleaning process due to their inconsistency. The participants of the mobile money study (n=151) consist of 81 (54%) male, 70 (46%) female, single 81 (54%), married 70 (46%), Yoruba 118 (78%), Igbo 16 (10%) Hausa 10 (7%) other tribes 7 (5%), bachelor's degree 85 (56%), high school/diploma 45 (30%), master's degree 17 (11%), doctoral degree 3 (2%), no formal education 1 (1%), students 85 (56%) public sector 18 (12%) teaching, 14 (9%) private sector, 14 (9%) self-employed 13 (9%) researchers 3 (2%) armed forces 2 (1%) other occupations 2 (1%), Less than ₦100000 109 (72%), ₦100000-₦200000 26 (17%), ₦200001-₦300000 9 (6%), ₦300001-₦400000 5 (3%).

Data Analysis and Results

To analyze the mobile money data, the study employed three steps consecutively. The data were examined to take care of outliers, unengaged responses, and missing data to pave the way for confirmatory factor analysis (CFA). The study runs partial least square-structural equation modelling (PLS-SEM) for convergent validity to ensure correlation between the study items and its parent factor and discriminant validity to examine if any of the study items correlate highly with another variable other than its parent factor. The study used SPSS 24 for reliability test of Cronbach alpha and varimax rotation for Exploratory Maximum Likelihood factor analysis to explore the dimension of the constructs. The study retained the items that load higher than 4.0 and excluded the items with low loadings (Sundaram 2016). The higher factor loading has a better explanatory power than the factor loadings that

Table 1. Overview of items measure

Constructs and Measurement Items

System Anxiety
It scares me to think that I could cause to destroy a large amount of information by hitting the wrong key during mobile money transfer.
I hesitate to use mobile money platform for fear of making mistakes that I cannot correct.
M-money is somewhat intimidating to me.
I am scared of losing a lot of information by using mobile money system.

Convenience
M-money makes money transfer easy
M-money makes transactions convenient
I believe m-money reduces turnaround time to transfer money
M-money system reduces stress for me

Cost
M-money system enables the transfer of money at low cost
Using mobile money services is cost burden to me
The mobile device setup for using mobile money charges me a lot of money
The cost of using mobile money is higher than using other banking channels

Performance Expectancy
Using mobile money would save my time
I can use mobile money in anyplace
I would find mobile money useful
Mobile money is a useful technology for me.

Social Influence
People who are important to me think that I should use mobile money
People who are familiar with me think that I should use mobile money
People who influence my behavior think that I should use mobile money
Most people surrounding me use mobile money

Effort Expectancy
Learning to use mobile money is easy for me
Becoming skillful at using mobile money devices is easy for me
Interaction with mobile money platform is easy for me
Mobile money system would be flexible for me to utilize.

Image
If I use mobile money system I will have more prestige than those who do not.
If I use mobile money system I will have a high profile.
Mobile money will be a status symbol for me.
Mobile money will enhance my self-importance.

Trust
M-money is a trustworthy service
I can count on m-money to protect my money
I can count on m-money to transfer my money safely
The m-money can be relied on to keep its promises

Security
I feel comfortable that mobile money technological structures adequately protect me from problems.
I feel comfortable that encryption and other technological advances of mobile money systems make it safe for me to do transaction on the Internet.
Mobile money systems provide a safe environment to transfer money.
Secured mobile money platform allay me fear of cyber theft

Privacy
I am concerned that using mobile money collects too much personal information about me.
I am concerned about threats to my personal privacy when using the m-money.
I believe that mobile money vendor will protect my information from unauthorized person.
I believe that mobile money vendor will not sell my information

User Experience
I believe m-money is easy to use
I believe m-money is simple and understandable for performing transactions
I believe that the use of m-money is trouble-free
I believe mobile money system is fast to use for transactions

User Satisfaction
I have a favorable experience using m-money
I believe that the use of m-money is beneficial
I like the idea of transferring money through m-money platform
I am satisfied with mobile money features.

The items of User Experience (UE), User Satisfaction (US) and Convenience (CON) were adopted from the existing TAM studies (Davis, 1989; Wu, 2011; Igbaria *et al.*, 1997; Venkatesh *et al.*, 2003; Venkatesh and Davis, 2000; López-Nicolás *et al.*, 2008, Chauhan, 2015). Items pertaining to trust (TR) were adapted from Fogel and Nehmad (2009) and Chauhan (2015), Image (IM) adapted from Fain and Roberts (1997), Kuisma et al. (2007) and Laukkanen and Kiviniemi, (2010). Cost (CT) and Effort Expectancy (EE), Performance Expectancy (PE), Social influence (SI) adopted from Luarn and Lin [2005], Venkatesh and Zhang [2010], Foon and Fah [2011], Sripalawat, Thongmak, and Ngramyarn [2011], Security (SR) adopted from Arun, Brown, and Tang (2009), and Privacy (PR) was adopted from Awad, Farag, and Krishnan (2006).

*Note: Items of the constructs adopted from the corresponding authors

*Exchange rate: ₦1 = $0.0028

Figure 2. Integrated conceptual framework of mobile money

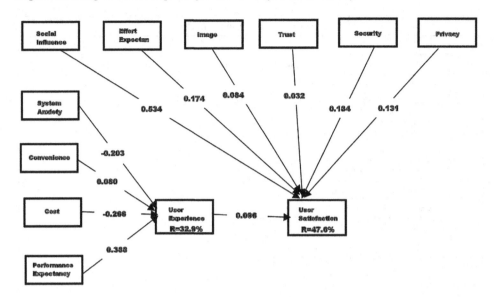

below 0.30 (See Table 2). SmartPLS statistics software is gaining popularity in different research domain most especially in marketing and the behavioural sciences (Lu, Kwan, Thomas, and Cedzynski 2011). SmartPLS was considered fit for this study because of its robustness to handle data small sample size and sensitive model (Ringle, Sarstedt, and Straub 2012). Table 2 shows the result of the data analysis and the factor loadings with a minimum of 0.46 and maximum of 0.97. The composite reliability (CR) and average variance extracted (AVE) meet the threshold

Table 2. Overall CFA for the measurement model

Constructs and Measurement Items	Standardized Loadings	Mean	SD	CA	CR	AVE
System Anxiety						
SA1	0.84	3.45	2.02	0.79	0.67	0.51
SA3	0.56	3.37	1.67	0.78		
Convenience						
CON3	0.93	5.40	1.43	0.78	0.75	0.61
CON4	0.59	4.52	1.59	0.77		
COST						
CT1	0.93	5.53	1.40	0.78	0.68	0.54
CT4	0.47	3.89	1.63	0.78		

continued on following page

Table 2. Continued

Constructs and Measurement Items	Standardized Loadings	Mean	SD	CA	CR	AVE
Performance Expectancy						
PE1	0.70	5.23	1.48	0.77	0.78	0.64
PE4	0.89	5.30	1.53	0.77		
Image						
IMG3	0.53	2.60	1.55	0.78	0.71	0.57
IMG4	0.93	3.07	1.70	0.78		
Social Influence						
SI1	0.96	5.02	1.33	0.78	0.76	0.62
SI2	0.57	5.58	1.14	0.78		
Effort Expectancy						
EE1	0.72	4.29	1.80	0.78	0.85	0.59
EE2	0.91	4.81	1.56	0.78		
EE3	0.70	4.65	1.84	0.78		
EE4	0.75	4.70	1.67	0.78		
Trust						
TR1	0.70	5.38	1.45	0.78	0.88	0.65
TR2	0.71	4.95	1.73	0.78		
TR3	0.91	4.90	1.50	0.77		
TR4	0.89	4.75	1.44	0.77		
Security						
SR1	0.81	4.91	1.46	0.78	0.83	0.56
SR2	0.65	5.17	1.40	0.78		
SR3	0.85	4.46	1.66	0.77		
SR4	0.64	5.09	1.43	0.78		
Privacy						
PR3	0.82	5.17	1.44	0.78	0.70	0.54
PR4	0.64	4.41	1.66	0.78		
User Experience						
UE2	0.88	4.77	1.75	0.77	0.75	0.61
UE3	0.66	5.23	1.70	0.78		
User Satisfaction						
US3	0.46	5.74	1.19	0.78	0.71	0.57
US4	0.97	4.98	1.45	0.77		

of 0.7 and 0.5 but CR for cost was marginal. The Cronbach's alpha for the items all reached the threshold of 0.7. Table 5 reveals the latent variables correlations. Table 4 exhibits the path coefficients of the constructs. System anxiety of mobile money platform will negatively influence user experience, that is, SA → UE β = .20 and t = 2.77, the path SA → UE is significant at (p<0.01) and the cost of using mobile money services will negatively influence the user's experience COST →

Table 3. Latent variable correlations

	CON	COST	EE	IMG	PE	PR	SA	SI	SR	TR	UE	US
CON	1											
COST	0,1752	1										
EE	0,3228	0,0865	1									
IMG	0,0794	0,0391	0,1408	1								
PE	0,647	0,138	0,2726	0,0655	1							
PR	0,1378	0,0728	0,1517	0,035	0,1923	1						
SA	0,0259	0,049	0,0337	0,138	0,0217	-0,0883	1					
SI	0,0841	-0,1218	0,0713	0,158	0,2178	0,15	0,0622	1				
SR	0,0244	0,117	0,076	0,043	0,2083	0,0087	0,0039	0,0399	1			
TR	0,0103	0,0944	0,2167	0,077	0,0922	0,1868	-0,1176	-0,0731	0,2086	1		
UE	0,3762	0,3037	0,1533	0,0934	0,4758	-0,0478	0,2249	0,0424	0,1022	0,0941	1	
US	0,2004	0,0356	0,2793	0,2166	0,5286	0,2428	-0,0671	0,588	0,2401	0,1091	0,169	1

Table 4. Standardized path coefficients and corresponding hypothesis results

Hypothesis	Path	Sample Mean (M)	Standard Deviation (STDEV)	Standard Error (STERR)	Beta	T-Test	Hypothesis Confirmed
H1	SA → UE	-0.204	0.073	0.073	0.20	2.77	Yes
H2	CON → UE	0.094	0.109	0.109	0.08	0.73	No
H3	COST → UE	-0.226	0.064	0.064	0.23	3.54	Yes
H4	PE → UE	0.386	0.105	0.105	0.38	3.71	Yes
H5	SI → US	0.526	0.078	0.078	0.54	6.81	Yes
H6	EE → US	0.179	0.074	0.074	0.18	2.34	Yes
H7	IMG → US	0.086	0.061	0.061	0.09	1.37	No
H8	TR → US	0.036	0.078	0.078	0.03	0.42	No
H9	SR → US	0.193	0.062	0.062	0.18	2.98	Yes
H10	PR → US	0.130	0.073	0.073	0.14	1.78	No
H11	UE → US	0.091	0.067	0.067	0.09	1.44	No

Figure 3. Descriptive statistics

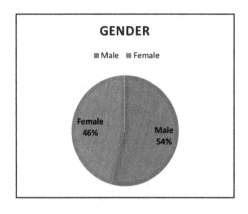

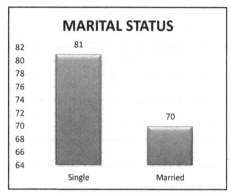

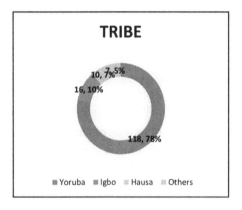

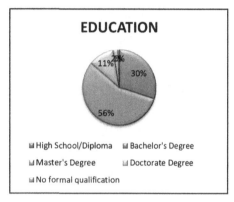

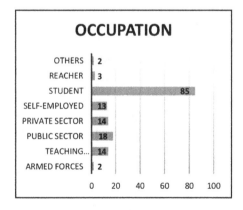

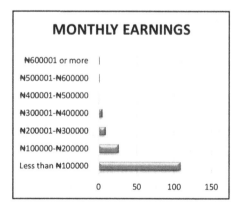

UE $\beta = 0.23$ and t $= 3.54$ at (p<0.0005). Performance expectancy of mobile money will positively influence the user's experience PE $\rightarrow$ UE $\beta = .38$ and t $= 3.71$ at (p<0.0003) and social influence will positively influence the user's satisfaction of mobile money SI $\rightarrow$ US $\beta = 0.54$ and t $= 6.81$ at (p<0.05). Effort expectancy will positively influence the user's satisfaction of mobile money EE $\rightarrow$ US $\beta = 0.18$ and t $= 2.34$ at (p<0.02) and security of mobile money platform will positively influence the user's satisfaction of mobile money SR $\rightarrow$ US $\beta = 0.18$ and t $= 2.98$ at (p<0.003). Perception of performance expectancy (3.71) is the highest predictor of user experience while cost (3.54) intermediate and system anxiety (2.77) is the lowest predictor of user experience. On the other hand, social influence is the highest predictor of user satisfaction of mobile money (6.81) and effort expectancy is the lowest predictor of user satisfaction (2.34). Mobile money user satisfaction records the highest variance and explains (R^2=47.6%) while user experience of the mobile money user explains (R^2=32.9%). 52.4% and 67.1% variance of the mobile money model could not be explained.

DISCUSSION AND IMPLICATION

The main objective of this study is to find out the enablers of mobile money in Nigeria rural and urban areas and the inhibiting factors of mobile money penetration and advancement. The study was limited to three constructs from UTAUT theory namely performance expectancy, effort expectancy and social influence as literature review reveals its extensive use and shows mobile banking adoption is influenced by the three constructs (Carlsson et al., 2006; Zhou, Lu, and Wang, 2010). Other constructs were incorporated into the study such as convenience, cost, image, privacy, system anxiety, security, trust, user experience and user satisfaction to increase perceptiveness of the enablers and inhibitors of mobile money in Nigeria. This study has filled a vacuum in the extant studies in developing countries by using integrated models by incorporating UTAUT (performance expectancy, effort expectancy, and social influence), convenience, cost, image, privacy, system anxiety, security, trust, user experience with user satisfaction intent. The result reveals that out of the eleven hypotheses tested six were accepted and five rejected.

The results reveal the enablers of mobile money which are the social influence, performance expectancy, security and effort expectancy, and inhibitors such as system anxiety and cost. Privacy, trust, image, and convenience were not found significant in this study. Social influence, performance expectancy and effort expectancy variables adapted from the UTAUT model have considerable influence on mobile money in Nigeria as their influence has been established in previous studies (Venkatesh, et al., 2003; Carlsson et al., 2006; Zhou, Lu, and Wang, 2010). This research provides several contributions. First, social influence had a positive association with user satisfaction and the highest predictor of user satisfaction. This is an indication that the influence of other people like family members or friends motivates the satisfaction of mobile money users. Second, performance expectancy positively impacts user experience and emphasis on the outcome is that the rate at which an individual believes that using the system will help him or her to attain gains in performance or will be more useful than existing form influences user experience. Third, cost influences user experience, this reveals cost as a significant factor in mobile money adoption, implying that users will develop a negative response to its adoption when the cost of its usage is considered high and as well adopt it when the cost is considered low. Again, security affects user satisfaction which suggests that security concerns bothering on cyber theft, unsafe environment for the transaction or technological structure of mobile money influence the satisfaction of users. Furthermore, system anxiety influences user experience, that is, the negative effect that may stir up phobia during intention to use or in the process of interacting with computers of any kind will affect the experience of using mobile money. Effort expectancy finally impacts user satisfaction, and it reveals the dependence of Effort expectancy on user satisfaction. This depicts that the user of mobile money will be satisfied with the usage of the system if the system is easy to use.

Managerially, this study has two implications. As evident in the study that social influence is found to be the most influential predictor of user satisfaction, it is, therefore, the understanding of the possibilities of third parties to influence the decision of adopting mobile money. In this respect, banks could develop marketing campaigns illustrating the benefits of mobile banking compared to other ways of using the financial services (Laukkanen, Sinkkonen, Kivijärvi and Laukkanen, 2007). The output of the study informs the mobile money stakeholders that security policy awareness and functional policy is profitable to bring about user satisfaction of the system. This will encourage the users to use mobile money without the fear of security concerns while intending to do a transaction or during transactions. The result of this study gives a technical solution to mobile money providers in Nigeria. The mobile money providers need to galvanize their existing mobile money platform and come up with a user experience (UX) design that will increase mobile money user's satisfaction. The UX design should be simple to use and free from technical jargons likely to confuse the mobile money users. Inculcating gratification elements such as social media that will pave the way for socialization and interaction will increase social influence in a communal setting of Nigeria. Introduction of Public Key Infrastructure (PKI) for encryption and decryption will alleviate insecurity of the mobile money users.

LIMITATIONS AND FUTURE RESEARCH

Although this study provides some insights, it is not without limitations. The study shows the difference among the tribes which the respondents belong to in percentage, and this constitutes a limitation to this study. The Yoruba tribe has 78% and other tribes in the country represent 22%. This result shows that the perception of the tribes is not congruent. It will be interesting if the future research could investigate enablers of mobile money and the inhibiting factors of mobile money in Nigeria rural and urban areas based on various tribes as the country houses over 256 tribes. The research should also extend to segment profiling and consider more members of the society as against student's dominant in the sample. The future study can probably consider using gender, age, experience and voluntariness of use as moderating variable regarding user experience and satisfaction as Carlsson et al. (2006) emphasized the mediators. Future researchers should evaluate the introduction of mobile money considering the underbanked and unbanked using mixed method. The combination of the quantitative and qualitative methodology will enrich the study and get deep insight from rural dwellers and urban of the unbanked and underbanked.

REFERENCES

Adomi, E. E., & Kpangban, E. (2010). Application of ICTs in Nigerian secondary schools. *Library Philosophy and Practice*, 345.

CNBC Africa. (2016). Africa Rising Smartphone Penetration Hits 30% in Nigeria. Retrieved November 6, 2017 from https://www.cnbcafrica.com/news/western-africa/2016/07/13/africa-rising_smartphone-penetration-hits-30-in-nigeria/

Alao, A. A., & Sorinola, O. O. (2015). Cashless policy and customers' satisfaction: A study of commercial banks in Ogun State, Nigeria. *Research Journal of Finance and Accounting*, 6(2), 37–47.

AlAwadhi, S., & Morris, A. (2008). The Use of the UTAUT Model in the Adoption of E-government Services in Kuwait. In *Proceeding of 41st Hawaii International Conference on System Sciences*, Hawaii (pp. 219-219). doi:10.1109/HICSS.2008.452

Asongu, S. (2015). The impact of mobile phone penetration on African inequality. *International Journal of Social Economics*, 42(8), 706–716. doi:10.1108/IJSE-11-2012-0228

Awad, N. F., & Krishnan, M. S. (2006). The personalization privacy paradox: An empirical evaluation of information transparency and the willingness to be profiled online for personalization. *Management Information Systems Quarterly*, *30*(1), 13–28. doi:10.2307/25148715

Barros, C. P., & Caporale, G. M. (2012). Banking consolidation in Nigeria, 2000–2010. *Journal of African Business*, *13*(3), 244–252. doi:10.1080/15228916.2012.727756

Bayero, M. A. (2015). Effects of Cashless Economy Policy on financial inclusion in Nigeria: An exploratory study. *Procedia: Social and Behavioral Sciences*, *172*, 49–56. doi:10.1016/j.sbspro.2015.01.334

Bhattacharya, K. (2015). From Giant Robots to Mobile Money Platforms: The Rise of ICT Services in Developing Countries. *IEEE Internet Computing*, *19*(5), 82–85. doi:10.1109/MIC.2015.99

Blumenstock, J. E., Callen, M., Ghani, T., & Koepke, L. (2015, May). Promises and pitfalls of mobile money in Afghanistan: evidence from a randomized control trial. In *Proceedings of the Seventh International Conference on Information and Communication Technologies and Development* (p. 15). ACM. doi:10.1145/2737856.2738031

Brookings Institution. (2013). Retrieved 20 February 2017 from https://www.youtube.com/watch?v=yE-jFQnu5Jg

Brown, S. H., & Coney, R. D. (1994). Changes in physicians' computer anxiety and attitudes related to clinical information system use. *Journal of the American Medical Informatics Association*, *1*(5), 381–394. doi:10.1136/jamia.1994.95153426 PMID:7850562

Carlos Roca, J., José García, J., & José de la Vega, J. (2009). The importance of perceived trust, security and privacy in online trading systems. *Information Management & Computer Security*, *17*(2), 96–113. doi:10.1108/09685220910963983

Carlsson, C., Carlsson, J., Hyvonen, K., Puhakainen, J., & Walden, P. (2006, January). Adoption of mobile devices/services—searching for answers with the UTAUT. In *Proceedings of the 39th Annual Hawaii International Conference on System Sciences HICSS '06* (Vol. 6, p. 132a). IEEE.

Chauhan, S. (2015). Acceptance of mobile money by poor citizens of India: Integrating trust into the technology acceptance model. *Info*, *17*(3), 58–68. doi:10.1108/info-02-2015-0018

Chauhan, S. (2015). Acceptance of mobile money by poor citizens of India: Integrating trust into the technology acceptance model. *Info, 17*(3), 58–68. doi:10.1108/info-02-2015-0018

Davis, F. D. (1989). Perceived usefulness, perceived ease of use, and user acceptance of information technology. *Management Information Systems Quarterly, 13*(3), 319–340. doi:10.2307/249008

Diniz, E. H., de Albuquerque, J. P., & Cernev, A. K. (2011). Mobile Money and Payment: a literature review based on academic and practitioner-oriented publications (2001-2011).

EYGM. (2014). Mobile money – the next wave of growth. Optimizing operator approaches in a fast-changing landscape. Retrieved 21 February 2017 from http://www.ey.com/Publication/vwLUAssets/EY_-_Mobile_money_-_the_next_wave_of_growth_in_telecoms/$FILE/EY-mobile-money-the-next-wave.pdf

Fain, D., & Roberts, M. L. (1997). Technology vs consumer behavior: The battle for the financial services customer. *Journal of Direct Marketing, 11*(1), 44–54. doi:10.1002/(SICI)1522-7138(199724)11:1<44::AID-DIR5>3.0.CO;2-Z

Fogel, J., & Nehmad, E. (2009). Internet social network communities: Risk taking, trust, and privacy concerns. *Computers in Human Behavior, 25*(1), 153–160. doi:10.1016/j.chb.2008.08.006

Foon, Y. S., & Fah, B. C. Y. (2011). Internet banking adoption in Kuala Lumpur: An application of UTAUT model. *International Journal of Business and Management, 6*(4), 161–167.

Giginyu, I. B. (2015). CBN Grants Licenses to 21 Mobile Money Operators. Retrieved 6 November, 2017 from https://www.dailytrust.com.ng/news/business/cbn-grants-licences-to-21-mobile-money-operators/121506.html

Greenacre, J. (2013). The rise of mobile money: Regulatory issues for Australia. *JASSA,* (1), 24.

Hackbarth, G., Grover, V., & Mun, Y. Y. (2003). Computer playfulness and anxiety: Positive and negative mediators of the system experience effect on perceived ease of use. *Information & Management, 40*(3), 221–232. doi:10.1016/S0378-7206(02)00006-X

Igbaria, M., Zinatelli, N., Cragg, P., & Cavaye, A. L. (1997). Personal computing acceptance factors in small firms: A structural equation model. *Management Information Systems Quarterly, 21*(3), 279–305. doi:10.2307/249498

Jin, N. P., Lee, S., & Lee, H. (2015). The effect of experience quality on perceived value, satisfaction, image and behavioral intention of water park patrons: New versus repeat visitors. *International Journal of Tourism Research*, *17*(1), 82–95. doi:10.1002/jtr.1968

Karahanna, E., Straub, D. W., & Chervany, N. L. (1999). Information technology adoption across time: A cross-sectional comparison of pre-adoption and post-adoption beliefs. *Management Information Systems Quarterly*, *23*(2), 183–213. doi:10.2307/249751

Kijsanayotin, B., Pannarunothai, S., & Speedie, S. M. (2009). Factors influencing health information technology adoption in Thailand's community health centers: Applying the UTAUT model. *International Journal of Medical Informatics*, *78*(6), 404–416. doi:10.1016/j.ijmedinf.2008.12.005 PMID:19196548

Kim, G., Shin, B., & Lee, H. G. (2009). Understanding dynamics between initial trust and usage intentions of mobile banking. *Information Systems Journal*, *19*(3), 283–311. doi:10.1111/j.1365-2575.2007.00269.x

Kirui, O. K., Okello, J. J., & Nyikal, R. A. (2012). Awareness of Mobile Phone-Based Money Transfer Services in Agriculture by Smallholder Farmers in Kenya. *International Journal of ICT Research and Development in Africa*, *3*(1), 1–13. doi:10.4018/jictrda.2012010101

Kuisma, T., Laukkanen, T., & Hiltunen, M. (2007). Mapping the reasons for resistance to internet banking: A means-end approach. *International Journal of Information Management*, *27*(2), 75–85. doi:10.1016/j.ijinfomgt.2006.08.006

Kusimba, S. B., Yang, Y., & Chawla, N. V. (2015). Family networks of mobile money in Kenya. *Information Technologies & International Development*, *11*(3).

Laukkanen, T., & Kiviniemi, V. (2010). The role of information in mobile banking resistance. *International Journal of Bank Marketing*, *28*(5), 372–388. doi:10.1108/02652321011064890

Laukkanen, T., Sinkkonen, S., Kivijärvi, M., & Laukkanen, P. (2007). Innovation resistance among mature consumers. *Journal of Consumer Marketing*, *24*(7), 419–427. doi:10.1108/07363760710834834

Law, E. L. C. (2011, June). The measurability and predictability of user experience. In *Proceedings of the 3rd ACM SIGCHI symposium on Engineering interactive computing systems* (pp. 1-10). ACM. doi:10.1145/1996461.1996485

Lawack, V. A. (2012). Mobile money, financial inclusion and financial integrity: The South African case. *Wash. JL Tech. & Arts*, *8*, 317.

Lee, K. C., & Chung, N. (2009). Understanding factors affecting trust in and satisfaction with mobile banking in Korea: A modified DeLone and McLean's model perspective. *Interacting with Computers*, *21*(5), 385–392. doi:10.1016/j.intcom.2009.06.004

López-Nicolás, C., Molina-Castillo, F. J., & Bouwman, H. (2008). An assessment of advanced mobile services acceptance: Contributions from TAM and diffusion theory models. *Information & Management*, *45*(6), 359–364. doi:10.1016/j.im.2008.05.001

Lu, H. P., & Yu-Jen Su, P. (2009). Factors affecting purchase intention on mobile shopping web sites. *Internet Research*, *19*(4), 442–458. doi:10.1108/10662240910981399

Lu, I. R., Kwan, E., Thomas, D. R., & Cedzynski, M. (2011). Two new methods for estimating structural equation models: An illustration and a comparison with two established methods. *International Journal of Research in Marketing*, *28*(3), 258–268. doi:10.1016/j.ijresmar.2011.03.006

Luarn, P., & Lin, H. H. (2005). Toward an understanding of the behavioral intention to use mobile banking. *Computers in Human Behavior*, *21*(6), 873–891. doi:10.1016/j.chb.2004.03.003

Luo, X., Li, H., Zhang, J., & Shim, J. P. (2010). Examining multi-dimensional trust and multi-faceted risk in initial acceptance of emerging technologies: An empirical study of mobile banking services. *Decision Support Systems*, *49*(2), 222–234. doi:10.1016/j.dss.2010.02.008

Mahmood, M. A., Burn, J. M., Gemoets, L. A., & Jacquez, C. (2000). Variables affecting information technology end-user satisfaction: A meta-analysis of the empirical literature. *International Journal of Human-Computer Studies*, *52*(4), 751–771. doi:10.1006/ijhc.1999.0353

Malaquias, R. F., & Hwang, Y. (2016). An empirical study on trust in mobile banking: A developing country perspective. *Computers in Human Behavior*, *54*, 453–461. doi:10.1016/j.chb.2015.08.039

Min, Q., Ji, S., & Qu, G. (2008). Mobile commerce user acceptance study in China: A revised UTAUT model. *Tsinghua Science and Technology*, *13*(3), 257–264. doi:10.1016/S1007-0214(08)70042-7

Munyegera, G. K., & Matsumoto, T. (2016). Mobile money, remittances, and household welfare: Panel evidence from rural Uganda. *World Development, 79*, 127–137. doi:10.1016/j.worlddev.2015.11.006

Olaleye, S. A., Sanusi, I. T., & Oyelere, S. S. (2017, September). Users Experience of Mobile Money in Nigeria. In *Proceedings of the 13th AFRICON Conference in AFRICON '17*, Cape Town. IEEE. doi:10.1109/AFRCON.2017.8095606

Oliveira, T., Faria, M., Thomas, M. A., & Popovič, A. (2014). Extending the understanding of mobile banking adoption: When UTAUT meets TTF and ITM. *International Journal of Information Management, 34*(5), 689–703. doi:10.1016/j.ijinfomgt.2014.06.004

Ondiege, P. (2015). Regulatory Impact on Mobile Money and Financial Inclusion in African Countries-Kenya, Nigeria, Tanzania and Uganda. Center for Global Development (CGD).

Osazevbaru, H. O., & Yomere, G. O. (2015). Benefits and Challenges of Nigeria's Cash-Less Policy. *Kuwait Chapter of the Arabian Journal of Business and Management Review, 4*(9), 1–10. doi:10.12816/0018986

Osei-Assibey, E. (2015). What drives behavioral intention of mobile money adoption? The case of ancient susu saving operations in Ghana. *International Journal of Social Economics, 42*(11), 962–979. doi:10.1108/IJSE-09-2013-0198

Oye, N. D., Iahad, N. A., & Rabin, Z. A. (2011). A model of ICT acceptance and use for teachers in higher education institutions. *International Journal of Computer Science & Communication Networks, 1*(1), 22–40.

Oyebode, A. (2014). M-Pesa and Beyod – Why Mobile Money Worked in Kenya and Struggles in other Markets. Retrieved 27 May 2017 from https://vc4a.com/blog/2014/01/15/m-pesa-and-beyond-why-mobile-money-worked-in-kenya-and-struggles-in-other-markets/

Pantano, E., & Priporas, C. V. (2016). The effect of mobile retailing on consumers' purchasing experiences: A dynamic perspective. *Computers in Human Behavior, 61*, 548–555. doi:10.1016/j.chb.2016.03.071

Rai, A., Brown, P., & Tang, X. (2009). Organizational Assimilation of Electronic Procurement Innovations. *Journal of Management Information Systems, 26*(1), 257–296. doi:10.2753/MIS0742-1222260110

Ringle, C. M., Sarstedt, M., & Straub, D. (2012). A critical look at the use of PLS-SEM in MIS Quarterly. *Management Information Systems Quarterly, 36*(1), iii–xiv.

Shaikh, A. A., & Karjaluoto, H. (2015). Mobile banking adoption: A literature review. *Telematics and Informatics, 32*(1), 129–142. doi:10.1016/j.tele.2014.05.003

Sripalawat, J., Thongmak, M., & Ngramyarn, A. (2011). M-banking in metropolitan Bangkok and a comparison with other countries. *Journal of Computer Information Systems, 51*(3), 67–76.

Suárez, S. L. (2016). Poor people' s money: The politics of mobile money in Mexico and Kenya. *Telecommunications Policy, 40*(10), 945–955. doi:10.1016/j.telpol.2016.03.001

Sundaram, A. (2016). A Painstaking Exploration on the Influence of Perceived Benefits towards Training on Training and Development in Indian IT/ITES Industry. *Journal of Internet Banking and Commerce, 21*(2), 1.

Venkatesh, V., & Davis, F. D. (2000). A theoretical extension of the technology acceptance model: Four longitudinal field studies. *Management Science, 46*(2), 186–204. doi:10.1287/mnsc.46.2.186.11926

Venkatesh, V., Morris, M. G., Davis, G. B., & Davis, F. D. (2003). User acceptance of information technology: Toward a unified view. *Management Information Systems Quarterly, 27*(3), 425–478. doi:10.2307/30036540

Venkatesh, V., Thong, J. Y., & Xu, X. (2012). Consumer acceptance and use of information technology: Extending the unified theory of acceptance and use of technology. *Management Information Systems Quarterly, 36*(1), 157–178.

Venkatesh, V., & Zhang, X. (2010). Unified theory of acceptance and use of technology: US vs. China. *Journal of Global Information Technology Management, 13*(1), 5–27. doi:10.1080/1097198X.2010.10856507

Wu, J. H., & Wang, S. C. (2005). What drives mobile commerce?: An empirical evaluation of the revised technology acceptance model. *Information & Management, 42*(5), 719–729. doi:10.1016/j.im.2004.07.001

Wu, W. W. (2011). Developing an explorative model for SaaS adoption. *Expert Systems with Applications, 38*(2), 15057–15064. doi:10.1016/j.eswa.2011.05.039

Yakub, J. O., Bello, H. T., & Adenuga, I. A. (2013). Mobile money services in Nigeria: An inquiry of existing models. *International Journal of Economics and Management Sciences, 2*(9), 94–105.

Yoon, C., & Kim, S. (2007). Convenience and TAM in a ubiquitous computing environment: The case of wireless LAN. *Electronic Commerce Research and Applications*, *6*(1), 102–112. doi:10.1016/j.elerap.2006.06.009

Yu, C. S. (2012). Factors affecting individuals to adopt mobile banking: Empirical evidence from the UTAUT model. *Journal of Electronic Commerce Research*, *13*(2), 104.

Yunus, F. M., Khan, S., Tasnuba, T., Husain, P. A., & Misiti, A. J. (2016). Are we ready to adopt mobile money in non-profit sector? *Journal of Innovation and Entrepreneurship*, *5*(1), 32. doi:10.1186/s13731-016-0060-x

Zhou, T., Lu, Y., & Wang, B. (2010). Integrating TTF and UTAUT to explain mobile banking user adoption. *Computers in Human Behavior*, *26*(4), 760–767. doi:10.1016/j.chb.2010.01.013

Chapter 8
Exploring the Factors Influencing Acceptance of Mobile Phone:
A Perspective of SMEs

Renatus Michael Mushi
Institute of Finance Management, Tanzania

ABSTRACT

This chapter describes how the adoption and usage of technologies is influenced by a number of factors. Such factors tend to affect the perception of people to accept or reject a technology in their usage context. Mobile phone technology has gained popularity as a dependable tool in SMEs. In Tanzania, for example, it is used to accomplish activities such as marketing, communication and mobile money transactions. This chapter highlights the key factors which influence the acceptance of mobile phones as they are used by individual peoples in the SMEs. The conceptual model shows that TAM can be extended by factors such as perceived values in explaining the acceptance of mobile phone technology in Tanzanian SMEs.

INTRODUCTION

Mobile phone has been dependable technological innovation to the society of developing countries in business perspectives. This because it has been relatively cheap to acquire, easy to use and there are usage opportunities on the developed apps and availability of infrastructure which is maintained and operated by operators. This tend to fuel the technological leapfrogging where majority of individuals and

DOI: 10.4018/978-1-5225-4029-8.ch008

small businesses jumps directly from 'not using technology' to 'using mobile hones' to perform their business obligations while skipping the use of desktop computing technology.

Small and Medium Enterprises (SMEs) have taken a huge percentage in Tanzania. Like in many other developing countries, SMEs is a place where majority of unemployed, low educated, less exposed, retired, retrenched and low-income people are found. In Tanzania, for example, more than 90% of SMEs have less than 5 employees. Across the streets of Tanzania, a broad range of SMEs such as restaurants, bars, taxis, townbuses (daladalas), retail shops, etc., who do not have financial powers to own desktop computers, taking aside the fact that they are likely in need of mobile phones as their best alternative due to their nature of activities.

Despite of the popularity and applicability of its usage in the SMEs level, important factors which influence its uptake are not well exposed. In practical, involving work performance with the use of mobile phones is exposed to many factors which influence the usage process. The issues which are involved on using personal mobile phones for work purposes, knowledge requirement, voluntariness on using technology, intentions and others need to explicitly be discussed. The addressed concerns will provide suggestions on how the usage can be optimised for the benefit of the SMEs under study.

This chapter presents discusses the factors which can be practical in the Tanzanian context and other similar regions. The contents of this chapter will be beneficial to stakeholders involved in acceptance of technologies, SMEs managers and employees as well as mobile network operators. The rest of this article is organised as follows:

Technology Adoption

The word adoption is closely related to acceptance in many researches of in information systems. The Concise Oxford Dictionary defines acceptance as "...consent to receive or undertake something..." (Oxford, 2009, p.7). It also defines adoption as "...the act of taking up and treating as one's own. This shows that adoption is more than just agreeing to a new idea or method. This happens in the case when there are several choices to make because it is about choosing a new innovation, taking it up, and owning it into specific perspective..." Rogers (1995), when proposing the Diffusion of Innovation (DOI) model, define adoption as the process of communicating innovation in order to attain the acceptance of intended potential adopters. On the other hand, Hernandez, Jimenez and Martin (2009) when analysing the key website features required for e-business activities, consider adoption as the decision to use something and acceptance as post-adoption perception. Technology adoption can also be defined as an outcome of result of the users' comparison of the uncertain costs and benefits of using the new technology (Hall and Khan, 2003). This means, a detailed balancing between the intentions of designers and the expectation of users should be considered in the process of ICT adoption. Adoption occurs when intended users accept and opt to use innovations as their best choice in their business activities.

While adoption and acceptance have some similarities, there are still some differences between the two terms. Renaud, K & Van Biljon, J (2008) differentiates acceptance from adoption in the context of *attitude* towards a technology involved while adding that there exist various factors which influences this situation. On insisting their concept, they insisted that, user who has purchased a new technology item has not yet adopted it adding that there are other stages beyond simple purchasing and this is where acceptance takes part. In this case, if the user buys an item and then does not accept it, the full adoption has not occurred.

While several studies have discussed the adoption aspects in the desktop computerized systems, mobile phones are much less studied. The factors which influence users of mobile phones in accepting or rejecting it have not well being explored.

Mobile Phone Technology

The introduction and the adoption of mobile technology changes the ways of doing businesses to a huge extent. The demonstration is seen in different sectors upon adoption of different mobile technologies. For example, the usage of mobile commerce applications has caused transformation of the way that business and governments deliver their services (Wang et al., 2010). The main driver towards the use of mobile technologies are due to the availability of Wi-Fi-enabled portable devices which tends to convince businesses and governments to prepare themselves for transition from electronic services to mobile services (Shaikh and Karjaluoto, 2015).

Mobile technologies allow the usage of smartphones tablet PCs and other handheld devices for different purposes. The main uses of mobile technologies are seen in the form such as mobile banking (including mobile payments), mobile commerce (including mobile shopping), mobile services (including the mobile Internet) etc. (Shaikh and Karjaluoto, 2015; van Biljon and Kotzé, 2007). Mobile technology require supports for connectivity such as Wireless Application Protocol (WAP), Bluetooth, 3G, and General Packet Radio Service (GPRS) as well as good mobile information appliances such as mobile phones, PDA, and laptop computers (Sheng et al., 2005). The extension of computing and the internet into the wireless medium through mobile technology allow users to access information and applications at anytime, anywhere while providing greater flexibility in terms of communication, collaboration, and information sharing (Sheng et al., 2005).

Small and Medium Enterprises (SMEs)

The existing literature includes various definitions of SMEs. Most of definitions of concepts are available from literatures of business commerce, development and economics (Mutula & Van Brakel, 2006). Despite of these multiple sources, the common definition adopted by the Organization for Economic Co-operation and Development (OECD) countries is based only on employment figures and pointing out that SME have less than 500 employees (OECD, 2004). In Britain, SMEs are the enterprises which have annual turnover of €2 million or less with fewer than 200 paid employees while in Australia, SMEs are defined as enterprises having between five and 199 employees (Migiro, 2006). However, the European Union define a micro-business as the company which have less than 10 employees and annual turnover and balance sheet total not exceeding 2 million euros while small businesses have fewer than 50 employees while the annual turnover doesn't exceed 10 million euros and balance sheet total is beyond 10 million euros and medium business have less than 250 employees, turnover does not exceed 50 million euros and the annual balance sheet total is beyond 43 million euros (Avram and Kühne, 2008). The World Bank (WB) defines micro scale company as the one having less than 50 employees, small scale company is having 50 employees and medium scale company having 50-200 employees (Kiriş and Kiriş, 2008). On the other hand, in Indonesia, SME is an enterprise which has five to 99 employees (Migiro, 2006). For the context of Africa, South African's SME Act defines SMEs as the companies having 100-200 employees or having a turnover of five million Rand (USD 833,000) (Mutula, M and Van Brakel, P, 2006). However, In Egypt, the ministry of trade defines SMEs by combining three criteria which are the number of workers, fixed assets and annual turnover (Rizk, 2004).

The Tanzania Small Industries Development Organisation (SIDO) uses the same definition as seen in the Table 1 but also highlights that in the event of an enterprise falling under more than one category, the level of investment will be the deciding factor (SIDO, 2002).

The Tanzania Revenue Authority (TRA) has different definitions for small businesses. They term a small business as the one whose annual taxable turnover

Table 1. The description of definition of Small, medium and large enterprise

Type of Enterprise	Micro	Small	Medium	Large
No. of Employees	0-4	5-49	50-99	100 and above
Working Capital	<2,800 USD	2800-111,100 USD	111,100-444,400USD	>444,400USD

Adopted from (SME Policy, 2013).

is less than TZS 40 Million (USD 22,500). On the other hand, the Tanzania SMEs policy includes micro enterprises in the group of SMEs. In this study, SMEs are defined as the businesses which comprise of one up to 99 employees and with a capital starting from zero up to 800 million (444,000 USD). In this research, SMEs can be defined as businesses which comprises of one up to 99 employees and with a capital starting from zero up to 800 million (444,000 USD). We assume that with this definition, there will be a reasonable and common understanding across the aspects the stakeholders and existing Tanzania ICT policies regarding SMEs.

RESEARCH METHODOLOGY

The unique features of SMEs and dual uses of mobile phones are the main motivations to contextualise this research. In order to get more insightful information, interviews were conducted with different stakeholders in the Tanzanian SMEs and to get their opinions. In that regards, results of questions which are asked in this part plays role mostly in the development of conceptual framework.

The interview questions were grouped according to the respondents. That is, managers were having their own sets of questions and ordinary employees have theirs too. This separation was performed because the two groups differ in the superiority of the roles they play in the SMEs which might influence their perceptions in the aspects such as voluntariness and technology usage supports. The combination of interview results and literature reviews constitutes the arguments for identifying the potential factors and setting up of the hypotheses of this study.

Factors Affecting Adoption of Mobile Phone Technology in SMEs

The development of the conceptual framework follows the Technology Acceptance Model (TAM) which explains the factors that facilitate integration of technologies into an organisation and discover why users accept or reject a technology (Davis, 1989). Development of TAM was based on adopting the concepts of the theory of reasoned action (TRA) (Fishbein and Ajzen, 1975) which is a more generalised theory to be used to explain specific contexts (Lindsay et al., 2011). In social psychology, TRA has been used to explain the why people performs a particular behaviour in situations of 'reasoned action' through identifications of causal relationships which exists between beliefs, attitude s, intentions and behaviour (Kwon and Chidambaram, 2000; Pedersen, 2005). Since then, TAM has been used to identify factors contributing towards acceptance of technologies. TAM theorises that when users are given a piece of technology, there are several factors which influence their decisions on how and when they will use such technology (Davis, 1989; Yueh et al., 2015).

TAM explains the acceptance of technology by two key perceived attributes or measures: perceived usefulness (PU) and perceived ease of use (PEU). According to Davis (1989), PU is whether the technology will enhance the user's job performance whereas PEU relates to whether using the system will be free from effort. The integrity of the original TAM has been tested through a number of empirical research, which extends the model to different settings, providing consistency and good re-test reliability, confirming the its validity (Lindsay et al., 2011; Venkatesh and Davis, 2000a). In this regard, TAM is arguably the best model to provide a framework of exploring the issues which motivates the adoption of mobile phone technology in Tanzania tourism SMEs.

A number of other studies PU of the technology and PEU do directly influence the BI of users in attempts to adopt a new technology (Kim et al., 2008; Tassabehji et al., 2008; van Biljon and Kotzé, 2007). Also, most of empirical research have shown that PEU is the antecedent of PU due to the fact that, through PU, PEU indirectly tends to influence the intention to adopt technology and finally its usage (Gallego et al., 2008; Peng et al., 2012; van Biljon and Kotzé, 2007). Therefore, the following hypothesis should be true:

H1a: Perceived ease of use (PEU) of mobile phones in SMEs will positively influence the employees' perceived usefulness (PU).

H1b: Perceived ease of use (PEU) of mobile phones in SMEs will positively influence the employee' behaviour intention (BI).

H1c: Perceived usefulness (PU) of mobile phones in SMEs will positively influence the employee' behaviour intention (BI).

H1d: Employees behavioural Intention (BI) of using mobile phones on Tanzania tourism SMEs will influence its actual usage (U).

Factors Affecting Perceived Usefulness (PU)

Venkatesh and Davis (2000a) proposed extensions in the original TAM to include the key determinants of PU constructs. The added constructs are social influence and cognitive instrumentation processes. Within the social influence category include subjective norm, voluntariness, image and experience whereas in cognitive instrumental processes category, job relevance, output quality and result demonstrability.

Subjective norm acknowledges the influence of peers on whether they should or shouldn't perform the behaviour in question; voluntariness accounts the effect of mandatory and non-mandatory usage on usage intentions (Venkatesh, 2000).

The original idea of voluntariness was explained by Kelman (1958) in terms of Compliance. According to Kelman, compliance occurs when an individual adopts an induced behaviour not because he/she believe in its usage, but with the expectation of getting a reward or avoiding punishment. Compliance tends to occur if the power of the influencing agent is based on the means of control through surveillance by the influencing agent (Kelman 1958). Therefore, in working roles, employees are complying with working conditions as stipulated in their job requirements. When the usage of technology is mandated, the users have no other option other than obeying its usage. In this case, the intention to use technology is changed to the mandated usage (Brown et al., 2002).

This study went to assess the extent of voluntariness of employees on using mobile technology in SMEs by asking managers and employees their opinions. The findings show that the usage of mobile phones in performing their activities within SMEs is mandatory. That is, in any possible circumstances where mobile phone is needed, it must be used. For example, a manager in one sports and recreation centre in Dar es salaam asserts that:

Mobile phone usage is not an excuse for not performing any working task. – MD

Therefore, managers assume that as long as the employee has mobile phone, all tasks associated with its usage must be performed. On the other hand, employees feel that they are obliged to use their phones whenever their tasks need them to. For example one employee in a bar claims that:

When my boss calls me and I don't pick up the phone without convincing reasons, I will be fired. – EB

The more explanation is due to the key definition of mandated usage of technology where it is also referred to …

… as one in which users are required to use a specific technology or system in order to keep and perform their jobs. (Brown et al., 2002)

This means, as long as employee in the SMEs need to use mobile phones to perform activities such as making calls, sending and receiving text SMS, sharing information with customers through social media etc. they are performing a mandated usage. Therefore, In this case, the usage of mobile phones in the work environment for the Tanzania tourism SMEs is not voluntary in nature. Carlson et al (1999) asserts that in organisational context, mobile phones can be used to accomplish business needs such as dealing with business on the road, making appointments, changing time schedules or attend the urgent needs of clients. In this regard, the influence of subjective norm on using mobile phones in Tanzania SMEs is affected by compliance. Therefore, this study hypothesises that:

H2a: Subjective Norm (SN) will positively influence Perceived Usefulness (PU) of mobile phones technology in Tanzania tourism SMEs.

H2b: Subjective Norm (SN) will positively influence behavioural Intention (BI) to use mobile phone technology in Tanzania Tourism SMEs.

H5a: The voluntariness (VOL) will moderate the effect of subjective norm on the Perceived Usefulness (PU) of mobile phone technology in the Tanzania tourism SMEs.

H5b: The voluntariness (VOL) will moderate the effect of subjective norm on the Behavioural intention of using mobile phone technology in the Tanzania tourism SMEs.

On the other hand, image refers to the degree to which a technology may affect the status of an individual (Venkatesh, 2000). According to Kelman (1958b), image is achieved through identification process in which the power of an influencing agent is based on attractiveness where individuals performs an action under the conditions of salience with their relationship to the agent. On the other hand, Moore and Benbasat (1991) in their study on diffusions of innovations defines image as:

… a degree to which use of an innovation is perceived to enhance one's status in one's social system. (Moore and Benbasat, 1991)

According to Warshaw (1980), subjective norm can also be in the form of Internalization, which refers to incorporation of beliefs of people who are important (referents) into one's belief structure. This means that, the employees will provide their insights based on their working experiences on their opinions.

Also, TAM theorises that subjective norm will positively influence image because when important members in a person's social group at work happen to believe that he/she should perform a behaviour then performing will tend to elevate his/her standing within the group (Venkatesh and Davis, 2000a). Theoretically, the improvement of image tends to increase the social status within the group which in turn provides basis for greater productivity which leads to improvement of job performance in the form of PU (Venkatesh and Davis, 2000).

Previous studies show that Tanzanian SMEs do not have well defined plans for their activities (Mashenene, 2015; URT, 2013; Venkatakrishnan, 2014). The plans would have been used to dictate key aspects in the enterprise including the company direction as well as resource demand and utilisation (Henry et al., 1998). Most of

SMEs cares mostly about the immediate profits which are realised in short time basis. For example, the analysis of interview with owners and employee in Tanzania tourism SMEs have shown that despite the great role played by mobile phones, the owners do not have clear plan on how to utilise it to its fullest in their businesses. This shows that they do not have goals which they need to achieve through the usage of technology despite the existing opportunities.

Despite the fact that this study focuses on SMEs, the key users of mobile phones are individuals. Moreover, since they use their mobile devices for jobs and personal purposes, they stay with them all the time. Therefore, the more they get better image through having mobile phones, the more influence to their overall usefulness is expected to occur. Therefore, this study hypothesises that:

H2c: The Image (IMG) on the use of mobile phones will positively influence the perceived usefulness (PU) by the employee of Tanzania tourism SMEs.

The experience is a moderating effect of subjective norm as time of using system elapses. In this case, the subjective norm will have influence only when users have enough experience if using the technology (Venkatesh and Davis, 2000a) . However, according to Hartwick and Barki (1994), the effect of experience becomes realistic only in the first three months because after the elapse of this time, the technology will be 'vague and ill-formed' to the users hence making experience to be less relevant on the study.

The interview findings with the employee working in SMEs which perform tourism-related activities in Tanzania show that most of them have used mobile phones to perform their personal activities too. Besides, most of them have started to know how to use the mobile phone equipment for significant long time before they started to use them for working purposes. This shows that they have prior experience in using mobile phone technology. Therefore, experience is will not be considered as a moderating effect on the influence of social influence and image towards PU and BI in the model.

In addition, social influences were found to influence image (Venkatesh and Davis, 2000a). This happens when the pressure from the society influence individuals to get insights of whether their personalities have been elevated due to the use of mobile phones. In this regard, this study hypothesises that:

H1e: The Subjective Norm (SN) will positively influence Image (IMG) towards using mobile phones in Tanzania Tourism SMEs.

Apart from social influences processes, the cognitive instrumentation processes explained in TAM Job relevance, output quality and results demonstrability and perceived ease of use (as seen in Table 2) also influences PU. The theoretical background relies on Vallacher and Kaufman (1996) by postulating that people cognitively tend to regulate their behaviours when aiming to achieve high-level goals. Davis and Vankatesh (2000a) incorporated the behaviour theories such as work motivation theory (Katzell and Thompson, 1990), the action theory from psychology (Ewart, 1991) and task-contingent decision theory (Van de Ven and Delbecq, 1974) to design task-specific plans which are cognitive mechanisms by which acts are selected, combined and sequenced in order to achieve goals. The studies on the behaviour theories tends to converge on view that behaviour is driven by mental representation that links higher-level goals to the specific actions are influential to achieving those goals (Venkatesh and Davis, 2000). All of these elements help to explain the PU construct of the original TAM, and can be used to design of organisational interventions that promote usage of new systems (Lindsay et al., 2011). In fact, these processes are based on the technological attributes which are likely to influence users to use a technology.

Mobile phones are used by individuals to perform both work and personal obligations. In traditional computing contexts, both users and computing device are stationery and the use of the device takes place at the same place and familiar location which in turn leads to the perception that most of usage of traditional computing technology are for the benefits of the company (van Biljon and Kotzé, 2007). In contrast, mobile devices changes physical, social and cultural contexts in the way users interact with the system (Ruuska-Kalliokulju et al., 2001). The ability to use mobile devices any time allow employee to perform multiple activities

Table 2. Determinants of perceived usefulness

Determinants	Definition
Perceived Ease of Use	The extent to which a person believes that using an IT will be free of effort (Davis, 1989)
Subjective Norm	The extent to which an individual perceives that most people who are important to him think he should or should not use the system (Fishbein and Ajzen, 1975; Venkatesh and Davis, 2000)
Image	The degree to which an individual perceives that use of a technology will enhance his or her status in his or her social system (Moore and Benbasat, 1991)
Output Quality	The degree to which an individual believes that the system performs his or her job tasks well (Venkatesh and Davis, 2000).
Result Demonstrability	The degree to which an individual believes that the results of using a system are tangible, observable, and communicable (Moore and Benbasat, 1991)
Job Relevance	The degree to which an individual believes that the target system is applicable to his or her job (Venkatesh, 2000).

poses challenge on setting out which roles and challenges are associated with job environment and which are for personal uses. Failure for most of SMEs to have specialised roles show that they employ generalists hence ending up having neither unclear job roles nor job descriptions.

In addition, the nature of usage of mobile phone technology usage is different from traditional computer systems. Desktop computers can store huge amount of data and support a number of business-related functions such as inventory management, asset management, spreadsheets etc. which can clearly be explained in the form of job relevance, output quality and result demonstrability constructs while mobile phone technology does not support well-defined task like desktop computers. Instead, they act as a supporting tool of already existed fundamental tasks which have human influence in them. Therefore, using these constructs to explain mobile the usage of phone technology in the context of this study would result to ambiguities in the research instruments and may confuse the respondents.

Despite its inappropriateness acting as a valid construct of TAM, the study of Kim (2008) have shown that Individuals have different perceptions of outcomes from using mobile wireless technologies (MWT) due to the difference in the nature of their jobs. Kim (2008) asserts that the elaboration likelihood model (ELM) (Bhattacherjee and Sanford, 2004) posits external information as a primary reason that individuals reinvestigated their beliefs and attitudes. The ELM framework was used to examine the moderating effects of job relevance on PU and attitude and found that potential users will be influenced to make decisions on usefulness after that gets informed (Bhattacherjee and Sanford, 2004). Therefore, in order to test the involvement of job relevance in using mobile phone technology, the following hypothesis is included:

H4c: Job Relevance (JR) will moderate the effect of PU on BI to use mobile phones in Tanzania tourism SMEs.

In output quality construct, TAM posits that individuals tends to assess how well the system performs tasks (Venkatesh and Davis, 2000a). Mobile phones do not store and process data as it happens in desktop computers. They therefore don't have realistic outputs which are expected out of SMEs processes. However, due to the fact that mobile phones provide a number of lightweight services, the corresponding option is to measure the service quality instead of output quality (Leea et al., 2002). Leea et al (2002) replaced output quality with service quality of mobile internet services in the context of personal uses and found that it influences the perceived usefulness. Therefore, this study hypothesises that:

H4a: Perceived Service Quality (PSQ) will positively influence Perceived Usefulness (PU) of mobile phone technology in Tanzania tourism SMEs.

Result demonstrability represent the extent to which the results are tangible as a result of using a technology (Venkatesh and Davis 2000a). It is, therefore, assumed that the clearer the results will positively influence usefulness of a computer system. However, since computers are normally located and used for office purposes, mobile phones are not. Mobile phones are performing light activities which are normally for personal use. Therefore, this construct is discarded in the development of conceptual framework.

According to the interview results, the nature of usage of mobile phones in Tanzania tourism SMEs help employee in performing their activities in a number of ways. The traditional ways of communications, sending and receiving money, broadcasting information have been improved through innovative usage of mobile phones. In this regard, their workflow has been improved or re-defined by fitting mobile phones usage in them. The concept of improvement work practices through the use of technology have previously been realised by Furukawa et al (2007). In such study, the use of online systems by physicians resulted to the improvement of their work practices and so the revenues (Furukawa et al., 2007). Similarly, Workflow practices were found to positively influence behaviour intention to use mobile phones for maternal healthcare practice in Uganda (Byomire and Maiga, 2015). Therefore, this study hypothesises that:

H4b: The Perceived Workflow Practices (PWP) will positively influence Behavioural Intention (BI) to use Mobile phone technology in Tanzania Tourism SMEs.

The use of mobile phone is faced with a number of challenges and limitations in performing the duties of employees. This is due to the fact that the technology depends on the support from mobile network operators, set-up of mobile devices as well as user profiles. These values will represent the things which employees and managers of SMEs care about most concerning their usage of mobile phone technology. According to Keeney (1992), values are the desires that one wants to achieve. In a case of a study conducted in a multinational company, the intentions of employee to use mobile phones were found to be influenced by the values (Tassabehji et al., 2008b). Other attempt was made by a study of Byomire and Maiga (2015) in explaining mobile phone adoption in the healthcare sector. Although they found that the perceived values of mobile phones in have positive influence on the behavioural intention to use it. However, they define value differently as this study. In their study, perceived value was referred to as a judgment or a valuation by the customer of the comparison between the benefits or utility obtained from a product, service or relationship, and the perceived sacrifices or costs. Such definition does not necessarily define the needs or desires which users of mobile phones needs from a certain context. Therefore, this study hypothesises that:

H2d: Perceived Values (PV) of mobile phones in Tanzania Tourism SMEs will positively influence Behaviour Intention to (BI).

Factors Affecting Perceived Ease of Use (PEU)

Apart the factors which explain the perceived usefulness, others were found to influence perceived ease of use (PEU) through 'anchoring and adjustment' of behaviour theory (Davis et al., 1986). "anchoring" denotes that, in the absence of understanding about a specific system, individuals are expected to "anchor" their system-specific PEU of a new system to their general beliefs regarding computers and computer use (Leea et al., 2002; Lindsay et al., 2011; Venkatesh, 2000). But, once individuals starts to get experience with the system, they starts to "adjust" their system-specific PEU to reflect their interaction with the system (Leea et al., 2002). Since Tanzania people have been in use of mobile phones for long time, they are assumed to have experience. Therefore, both anchors and adjustment constructs are expected to be included in the conceptual framework of this study. The factors which influence the PEU are summarised in Table 3.

Computer self-efficacy refer to the individual beliefs on their ability to use a system, perceptions of external control relate to the belief that the management is always there for providing support, computer playfulness refer to the intrinsic motivation

Table 3. Determinants of perceived ease of use

Determinant	Definition
Computer Self-Efficacy	The extent to which a person believes that he or she has the ability to perform a specific task/job using the computer (Compeau and Higgins, 1995)
Perception of External Control	The degree to which a person believes that there are supportive organizational and technical resources to use the system (Venkatesh et al., 2003).
Computer Anxiety	The degree of "an individual's apprehension, or even fear, when she/he is faced with the possibility of using computers…" (Venkatesh, 2000)
Computer Playfulness	"… the degree of cognitive spontaneity in microcomputer interactions…" (Webster and Martocchio, 1992)
Perceived Enjoyment	The extent to which "the activity of using a specific system is perceived to be enjoyable in its own right, aside from any performance consequences resulting from system use" (Venkatesh, 2000)
Objective Usability	A "comparison of systems based on the actual level (rather than perceptions) of effort required to completing specific tasks" (Venkatesh, 2000)

relate to the motivations dealing with the use of new technology (Venkatesh, 2000). However, Venkatesh (2000) asserts that the judgements of users on these anchors towards perceived ease of use are adjusted accordingly as users gets experience in using technology where computer anxiety and computer playfulness less relevant while self-efficacy and perception of external control will continue to be strong. Similarly, once the individual gets experience on the system, adjustments: perceived enjoyment and objective usability starts to be strong determinants of perceived ease of use (Venkatesh, 2000).

The analysis of interviews conducted with the employees in the Tanzanian SMEs show that they have been using mobile phones for long time before they were employed for the first time. Therefore, the users targeted by this study who have enough experience of using mobile technology. Even though the mobile phones are becoming more complex and keeps on performing more and more functionalities with time, it is not difficult to study mobile phones compared to desktop computers. Therefore, the factors which will be included in this study are only those which are relevant with experienced situations. Therefore, possible constructs which are likely to be significant to influence the perceived ease of use of mobile phone technology in Tanzania tourism SMEs are computer self-efficacy, perceived external control, perceived enjoyment and objective usability.

This study takes computer self-efficacy in the form of mobile phone self-efficacy. In this case, this study defines mobile phone self-efficacy a degree to which an individual believes that he or she has the ability to perform a specific task/job using the mobile phone. The assumptions based on this construct are that there is a possibility that, for whatever reasons, individuals think that they cannot use mobile phones to perform their tasks. This becomes significant in the applications which require knowledge apart from requirements of performing basic calls and text SMS. The interviews findings show one of the owners in a car rental SME in Tanzania who highlights that some of the employees face difficulty in using some of the functionalities of mobile phones while mentioning an example of internet based services.

Self-efficacy is a concept originated from the Bandura's social cognitive theory (Bandura, 1977). Self-efficacy is defined as a belief of an individual in their own abilities to organise and execute the actions necessary to manage certain situations in their activities (Prieto et al., 2015). According to Chen et al. (2009), self-efficacy involve predicting the result (whether the action will lead to a result) and efficacy (whether he or she can successfully execute procedures to achieve the result. In respect to this study, mobile phone self-efficacy refers to the employee's belief that they have required abilities to perform several SMEs activities by using mobile phones. Mobile phone self-efficacy was found to positively influence teacher's acceptance of mobile phones in pre-school learning (Prieto et al., 2015). Also, Smart phone self-efficacy was found to have direct effect on perceived ease of use in the logistics industry (Chen et al., 2009).

The analysis of interviews with the employee in the Tanzania tourism SMEs show that they do mostly use mobile phones to performs job/task such as communications, marketing, performing bank mobile money services and sharing of information with customers and peers. Some of these activities need self-confidence of users to accomplish them, otherwise, they will perceive them complex and eventually, the tasks will not be performed. In this regard, this construct will be included into the conceptual framework to get more understanding out of it. This study hypothesises that:

H3a: The Perceived mobile phone self-efficacy (MSE) will positively influence the employee perceived ease of use (PEU) of mobile phone technology.

The next construct is perceived external control. This construct refers to the degree to which an employee believes that organisational and technical resources exist to support the use of the system. Lee et al. (2005) found that there is a strong correlation between the perceived high levels of organisational support with the greater job satisfaction to the workers. Funding, for example is very important for employee and individuals to adopt and use new technologies. Kim et al (2008) asserts that the company willingness to fund for technology use enhances the individual adoption of mobile wireless technology.

Mobile phones are somehow expensive to buy and the operational costs, especially, in terms of top ups is another notable expense. Even though employees are using their phones in private purposes, the SMEs should be aware that they benefit from the same as well. The assistance which is applicable to the use of mobile phones could range from buying for employee or supporting them financially. The analysis of interview with the employee of Tanzania tourism SMEs show that they have important work-related obligations which need internet data bundles to accomplish. For example, sharing of pictures through social media, accessing email accounts etc. need extra support from management for them to perceive the easiest way of technology use. In that regard, it is important to include this construct in the conceptual framework for evaluation purpose. This study hypothesises that:

H3b: The perceived organisation support (POS) in SMEs will positively influence employee perceived ease of use (PEU) of mobile phone technology.

Perceived enjoyment is this context can refer to extent to which the activity of using a mobile phone is perceived to be enjoyable in its own right which is not related to the performance consequence on its use (Kim et al., 2008). Mobile phones contain a lot of fancy functionalities such as games and social media sites which have taken attention of most of people. Since this construct has not specified whether the enjoyment are from which functionalities, then mobile phones are one of those devices which people like to use. Also, studies show that people can be influenced to adopt mobile phones not only because it can help perform business activities, but also as a result of source of enjoyment (Karaiskos et al., 2012; Kwon and Chidambaram, 2000). Therefore, the enjoyment can be one of the potential factors which influence employee perception that mobile phones are easy to use. Therefore this study hypothesises that:

H3c: The increase in perceived enjoyment (PE) in using mobile phone technology will positively influence its employee perceived ease of use (PEU) in Tanzania tourism SMEs.

Another factor which influences PEU is objective usability. This is a "... comparison of systems based on the actual level of effort required to completing specific tasks..." (Venkatesh, 2000). This implies that there should be clear tasks which are assigned to a system in question of which the efforts of performing them are compared. Specifically, Venkatesh (2000) tested its influence to the PEU in the context of desktop computers, which can actually be used to perform a lot of tasks. However, mobile phones have commonly been used to perform simple functionalities but with specific purposes (innovative uses). In this regard, it is difficult to single out the tasks which would definitely be used to study the opinions through the data collection instruments. Besides, there have not been any clear studies in the context of adoption of mobile phones which have tested objective usability construct, which indicate a number of doubts about its relevance to this study. Therefore, objective usability will be dropped in this study.

Impact of Personal Privacy

Privacy has been discussed as among the key security measure in previous studies such as Rumanyika, J (2015)'s study on security risks in using mobile banking in Tanzania and the study in which data privacy was found to be among the key bottlenecks. However, while such previous studies were looking at privacy in terms of security-wise, this study discuss privacy in terms of violation of an employee's time (Tassabehji et al., 2008). The 33 focus group sessions study conducted by Jarvenpaa and Lang (2005) covering China, Finland and USA in examining the user experience in using mobile technology in working places reported paradoxes which shapes user experiences and behaviours.

Unlike desktop or even laptop computers, the mobile phone is typically always with its user, rarely separates from its owner, and it is in use, or ready for use, all the time. (Jarvenpaa and Lang, 2005)

The view of prominent philosophies of technology asserts that technology has destroyed distance by destroying closeness such that it tends to create a situation where everybody is at the same time close and far, independent of geographical distance (Arnold, 2003). This technological paradox has been observed and found that they are heavily exhibited by mobile phone usage (Arnold, 2003; Jarvenpaa and Lang, 2005). Jarvenpaa and Lang (2005) found that despite the fact that mobile technology had made some improvements to their lives in terms of convenience, flexibility, connectedness, and new freedoms of choice, there were some conflict situations they had encountered in terms of circumstances that prompt users to take actions whose consequences clash with their original intentions or expectations. Moreover, Tussabehji et al. (2008) found that personal privacy has positive relationship with the mandated use of mobile phone technology. From the individual user's side, mobile phone technology result in "less personal time" and "the inability to separate and keep distance from work which results to a collapse in the desirable boundaries between work and leisure (Arnold, 2003; Jarvenpaa and Lang, 2005) and an expected state of constant availability, resulting in a negative impact on employees' wellbeing and interpersonal relationships (Sarker and Wells, 2003).

Kwon and Chidambaram (2008) asserts that users of mobile phones are likely to feel pressure and disturbances when they use them in work-related purposes. Eventually, the relationship between privacy sensitivity of individuals with the benefits of mobile phone technology becomes realistic. Ng-Kruelle et al. (2002) highlights the concept of cost balancing by arguing that the private information which are disclosed in such exchanges establishes a significant but hidden aspect of the cost of using mobile commerce applications.

The benefit offered by each "convenience" is, in general, associated with a loss of privacy. (Ng-Kruelle et al., 2002)

Based on the usage of mobile phones in the Tanzanian SMEs, this study proposes the following hypothesises:

H4a: Perceived impact of personal privacy (PIPP) in using mobile phone technology will positively influence its perceived usefulness (PU) in Tanzania tourism SMEs.

H4b: Perceived impact of personal privacy (PIPP) in using mobile phone technology will positively influence its behavioural intention (BI) in Tanzania tourism SMEs.

Proposed Conceptual Model

Based on the justifications from previous studies and information from interviews in the usage context of mobile phones in the Tanzanian tourism SMEs, hypothesises were developed. A pictorial representation of the relationships between such hypothesises is as seen in Table 3. This conceptual framework is therefore constructed by considering the contextual characteristics of the environment towards which it will be tested into. Therefore, this conceptual model should be evaluated before it is qualified to represent a generalised population of context. It should also be noted that with exception of the perceived values, all the rest of the constructs have already been tested in other contexts.

Figure 1. The Conceptual Model of Mobile Phone Technology acceptance in SMEs
Source: Author.

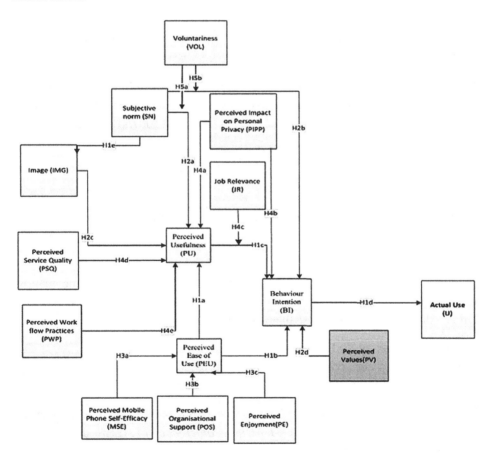

CONCLUSION

This book chapter discussed the adoption perspectives of mobile phones in the SMEs. Specifically, key factors which influence individual's intention to use mobile phones in their working roles were explored. The methodology used to explore the factors were the use of literature reviews and interviews conducted to the staff of SMEs. The discussions were used to generate the hypotheses that show how each of the factors influences each other. The final output is a conceptual model which can then be tested in any context to validate it. The future study will be to validate this model in terms of reliability of the factors and statistical significance of the hypotheses through a survey.

REFERENCES

Arnold, M. (2003). On the phenomenology of technology: The "Janus-faces" of mobile phones. *Information and Organization, 13*(4), 231–256. doi:10.1016/S1471-7727(03)00013-7

Avram, D. O., & Kühne, S. (2008). Implementing responsible business behavior from a strategic management perspective: Developing a framework for Austrian SMEs. *Journal of Business Ethics, 82*(2), 463–475. doi:10.1007/s10551-008-9897-7

Bandura, A. (1977). Self-efficacy: Toward a unifying theory of behavioral change. *Psychological Review, 84*(2), 191–215. doi:10.1037/0033-295X.84.2.191 PMID:847061

Barki, H., & Hartwick, J. (1994). Measuring user participation, user involvement, and user attitude. *Management Information Systems Quarterly, 18*(1), 59–82. doi:10.2307/249610

Bhattacherjee, A., & Sanford, C. (2004). Persuasion strategies for information technology usage: An elaboration likelihood model. Retrieved from http://mis.temple.edu/research/documents/BhattacherjeeITUsage.pdf

Brown, S. A., Massey, A. P., Montoya-Weiss, M. M., & Burkman, J. R. (2002). Do I really have to? User acceptance of mandated technology. *European Journal of Information Systems, 11*(4), 283–295. doi:10.1057/palgrave.ejis.3000438

Byomire, G., & Maiga, G. (2015). A model for mobile phone adoption in maternal healthcare. In Proceedings of the *IST-Africa Conference '15*. IEEE. doi:10.1109/ISTAFRICA.2015.7190562

Carlson, P. J., Kahn, B. K., & Rowe, F. (1999). Organizational impacts of new communication technology: A comparison of cellular phone adoption in France and the United States. *Journal of Global Information Management, 7*(3), 19–29. doi:10.4018/jgim.1999070102

Chen, J. V., Yen, D. C., & Chen, K. (2009). The acceptance and diffusion of the innovative smart phone use: A case study of a delivery service company in logistics. *Information & Management, 46*(4), 241–248. doi:10.1016/j.im.2009.03.001

Compeau, D. R., & Higgins, C. A. (1995). Computer self-efficacy: Development of a measure and initial test. *Management Information Systems Quarterly, 19*(2), 189–211. doi:10.2307/249688

Davis, F. D. (1989). Perceived usefulness, perceived ease of use, and user acceptance of information technology. *Management Information Systems Quarterly, 13*(3), 319–340. doi:10.2307/249008

Davis, H. L., Hoch, S. J., & Ragsdale, E. E. (1986). An anchoring and adjustment model of spousal predictions. *The Journal of Consumer Research, 13*(1), 25–37. doi:10.1086/209045

Ewart, C. K. (1991). Social action theory for a public health psychology. *The American Psychologist, 46*(9), 931–946. doi:10.1037/0003-066X.46.9.931 PMID:1958012

Fishbein, M., & Ajzen, I. (1975). Belief, attitude, intention and behavior: An introduction to theory and research.

Furukawa, M. F., Ketcham, J. D., & Rimsza, M. E. (2007). Physician practice revenues and use of information technology in patient care. *Medical Care, 45*(2), 168–176. doi:10.1097/01.mlr.0000241089.98461.e5 PMID:17224780

Gallego, M. D., Luna, P., & Bueno, S. (2008). User acceptance model of open source software. *Computers in Human Behavior, 24*(5), 2199–2216. doi:10.1016/j.chb.2007.10.006

Hall, B. H., & Khan, B. (2003). *Adoption of new technology.* National Bureau of Economic Research. doi:10.3386/w9730

Henry, M., James, B. Q., & Sumantra, G. (1998). *The strategy process* (pp. 76–78). Hertfordshire, UK: Prentice Hall Europe.

Hernández, B., Jiménez, J., & Martín, M. J. (2009). Key website factors in e-business strategy. *International Journal of Information Management, 29*(5), 362–371. doi:10.1016/j.ijinfomgt.2008.12.006

Jarvenpaa, S. L., & Lang, K. R. (2005). Managing the Paradoxes of Mobile Technology. *Information Systems Management, 22*.

Karaiskos, D. C., Drossos, D. A., Tsiaousis, A. S., Giaglis, G. M., & Fouskas, K. G. (2012). Affective and social determinants of mobile data services adoption. *Behaviour & Information Technology, 31*(3), 209–219. doi:10.1080/0144929X.2011.563792

Katzell, R. A., & Thompson, D. E. (1990). Work motivation: Theory and practice. *The American Psychologist, 45*(2), 144–153. doi:10.1037/0003-066X.45.2.144

Kelman, H. C. (1958). Compliance, identification, and internalization: Three processes of attitude change. *The Journal of Conflict Resolution, 2*(1), 51–60. doi:10.1177/002200275800200106

Kim, S. H. (2008). Moderating effects of job relevance and experience on mobile wireless technology acceptance: Adoption of a smartphone by individuals. *Information & Management, 45*(6), 387–393. doi:10.1016/j.im.2008.05.002

Kim, T. G., Lee, J. H., & Law, R. (2008). An empirical examination of the acceptance behaviour of hotel front office systems: An extended technology acceptance model. *Tourism Management, 29*(3), 500–513. doi:10.1016/j.tourman.2007.05.016

Kiriş, C. Ş.-H. K., & Kiriş, P. T.-H. M. 2008. Can SMEs in developing countries resist crisis? An analysis on Turkish and Albanian cases. In *Proceedings of the First International Conference on Balkans Studies (ICBS 2008)* (p. 208).

Kwon, H. S., & Chidambaram, L. 2000. A test of the technology acceptance model: The case of cellular telephone adoption. In Proceedings of the 33rd Annual Hawaii International Conference on System Sciences. IEEE.

Lee, H. Y., Lee, Y.-K., & Kwon, D. (2005). The intention to use computerized reservation systems: The moderating effects of organizational support and supplier incentive. *Journal of Business Research, 58*(11), 1552–1561. doi:10.1016/j.jbusres.2004.07.008

Leea, W.J., Kimb, T.U., Chungc, J.-Y. (2002). User acceptance of the mobile Internet.

Lindsay, R., Jackson, T. W., & Cooke, L. (2011). Adapted technology acceptance model for mobile policing. *Journal of Systems and Information Technology, 13*(4), 389–407. doi:10.1108/13287261111183988

Mashenene, R. (2015). The Dynamics of Mobile Phone Technologies and the Performance of Micro and Small Enterprises in Tanzania.

Mawona, A., & Mpogole, H. (2013). ICT and Financial Inclusion: Adoption of Mobile Phone Banking Among Small Business Owners in Iringa, Tanzania.

Migiro, S.O. (2006). Diffusion of ICTs and E-commerce adoption in manufacturing SMEs in Kenya : research article.

Moore, G. C., & Benbasat, I. (1991a). Development of an instrument to measure the perceptions of adopting an information technology innovation. *Information Systems Research*, *2*(3), 192–222. doi:10.1287/isre.2.3.192

Mutula, M. S., & Van Brakel, P. P. (2006). E-readiness of SMEs in the ICT sector in Botswana with respect to information access. *The Electronic Library*, *24*(3), 402–417. doi:10.1108/02640470610671240

Ng-Kruelle, G., Swatman, P. A., Rebne, D. S., & Hampe, J. F. (2002). The price of convenience: Privacy and mobile commerce. *Quarterly Journal of Electronic Commerce*, *3*, 273–286.

OECD. (2004). Measuring the information economy.

Pedersen, P. E. (2005). Adoption of mobile Internet services: An exploratory study of mobile commerce early adopters. *Journal of Organizational Computing and Electronic Commerce*, *15*(3), 203–222. doi:10.1207/s15327744joce1503_2

Peng, R., Xiong, L., & Yang, Z. (2012). Exploring Tourist Adoption of Tourism Mobile Payment: An Empirical Analysis.

SME Policy. (2013). Tanzania SMEs Policy Review After 10 years.

Prieto, J. C. S., Migueláñez, S. O., & García-Peñalvo, F. J. (2015). Mobile acceptance among pre-service teachers: a descriptive study using a TAM-based model. In *Proceedings of the 3rd International Conference on Technological Ecosystems for Enhancing Multiculturality* (pp. 131–137). ACM. doi:10.1145/2808580.2808601

Rizk, N. (2004). E-readiness assessment of small and medium enterprises in Egypt: A micro study.

Rumanyika, J. D. (2015). Obstacles towards adoption of mobile banking in Tanzania. *RE:view*.

Ruuska-Kalliokulju, S., Schneider-Hufschmidt, M., Väänänen-Vainio-Mattila, K., & Von Noman, B. (2001). Shaping the Future of Mobile Devices. *SIGCHI Bulletin*, *33*, 16–21.

Sarker, S., & Wells, J. D. (2003). Understanding mobile handheld device use and adoption. *Communications of the ACM*, *46*(12), 35–40. doi:10.1145/953460.953484

Shaikh, A. A., & Karjaluoto, H. (2015). Making the most of information technology & systems usage: A literature review, framework and future research agenda. *Computers in Human Behavior*, *49*, 541–566. doi:10.1016/j.chb.2015.03.059

Sheng, H., Nah, F. F.-H., & Siau, K. (2005). Strategic implications of mobile technology: A case study using value-focused thinking. *The Journal of Strategic Information Systems*, *14*(3), 269–290. doi:10.1016/j.jsis.2005.07.004

SIDO. (2002). Small industries development organisation in Tanzania.

Tassabehji, R., Wallace, J., & Srivastava, A. (2008). Corporate Acceptance of M-Technology in the Service Sector: A Case Study. Proceedings of AMCIS 2008.

URT. (2013). *Tanzania SME Development Policy 2003: "ten years after.* Implementation Review.

Vallacher, R.R., & Kaufman, J. (1996). Dynamics of action identification: Volatility and structure in the mental representation of behavior.

van Biljon, J., & Kotzé, P. (2007). Modelling the Factors That Influence Mobile Phone Adoption, In *Proceedings of the 2007 Annual Research Conference of the South African Institute of Computer Scientists and Information Technologists on IT Research in Developing Countries, SAICSIT '07 (*pp. 152-161). New York, NY: ACM. doi:10.1145/1292491.1292509

Van Biljon, J., & Renaud, K. (2008). Predicting technology acceptance and adoption by the elderly : a qualitative study.

Van de Ven, A. H., & Delbecq, A. L. (1974). A task contingent model of work-unit structure. *Administrative Science Quarterly*, *19*(2), 183–197. doi:10.2307/2393888

Venkatakrishnan, V. (2014). Mobile phones and micro and small enterprises (mse) performance and transformation in Dodoma, Tanzania. In *Proceedings of the REPOA's 19th Annual Research Workshop*. Retrieved 3.14.16 from www.repoa. or.tz/documents/S1G2014.doc

Venkatesh, V. (2000). Determinants of perceived ease of use: Integrating control, intrinsic motivation, and emotion into the technology figure acceptance model. *Information Systems Research*, *11*(4), 342–365. doi:10.1287/isre.11.4.342.11872

Venkatesh, V., & Davis, F. D. (2000a). A theoretical extension of the technology acceptance model: Four longitudinal field studies. *Management Science*, *46*(2), 186–204. doi:10.1287/mnsc.46.2.186.11926

Venkatesh, V., Morris, M. G., Davis, G. B., & Davis, F. D. (2003). User acceptance of information technology: Toward a unified view. *Management Information Systems Quarterly*, *27*(3), 425–478. doi:10.2307/30036540

Wang, Y.-M., Wang, Y.-S., & Yang, Y.-F. (2010). Understanding the determinants of RFID adoption in the manufacturing industry. *Technological Forecasting and Social Change*, *77*(5), 803–815. doi:10.1016/j.techfore.2010.03.006

Warshaw, P. R. (1980). A new model for predicting behavioral intentions: An alternative to Fishbein. *JMR, Journal of Marketing Research*, *17*(2), 153–172. doi:10.2307/3150927

Webster, J., & Martocchio, J. J. (1992). Microcomputer playfulness: Development of a measure with workplace implications. *Management Information Systems Quarterly*, *16*(2), 201–226. doi:10.2307/249576

Yueh, H.-P., Lu, M.-H., & Lin, W. (2015). Employees' acceptance of mobile technology in a workplace: An empirical study using SEM and fsQCA. *Journal of Business Research*.

Chapter 9
Security Issues in Mobile Devices and Mobile Adhoc Networks

Mamata Rath
C. V. Raman College of Engineering, India

George S. Oreku
Open University of Tanzania (OUT), Tanzania

ABSTRACT

For successful data transmission in wireless networks, security features are very much essential to implement. A mobile adhoc network contains a set of autonomous mobile stations that can correspond with each other instead of some adverse situation of wireless environment. Those mobile nodes that are not in the same series can communicate with others through intermediate hops. Security is a challenging mission in mobile adhoc network (MANET) due to many serious issues in the network such as hop-to-hop persistent wireless connectivity, high frequency of variation in topology of the network, and increasing rate of link failure due to higher mobility. So, it is very challenging to develop a secured, dynamic, and efficient routing protocol for such a magnificent network. In this chapter, vulnerability issues of MANET are focused on with a spotlight on prominent MANET protocols. A brief study on technical issues responsible for vulnerability in MANET has been depicted with systematic review on various issues and protocols that provide secured routing in the network.

DOI: 10.4018/978-1-5225-4029-8.ch009

INTRODUCTION

There are many essential features of MANET which makes it well known and very special. But susceptibility still emerges because of the inbuilt features of self-arrangement and frequent re-configuration. There are some reasons mentioned below that causes vulnerability in MANET.

Lack of Restriction

There is no such constraint for nodes to combine, join, detach and go in or outside of the network. Along these lines, the absence of security measures makes the MANET inclined to the attacks. The MANET is open to attacks (Razak et al, 2014) because of absence of firewall and network gateway.

- **Dynamic Change in Topology:** Due to high mobility of the nodes, the topology of MANET changes very frequently (Joshi, 2011). Since, nodes are changing & joining the mobile network, It is impractical to record the freed in a dynamic network. Some of these nodes can be scoundrel and can be put to danger as these nodes do not have a place with the trusted zone.
- **Absence of Central Authority:** There is no central administrator in MANET that controls the working of activities in MANET . During the hop to hop data transmission, this issue sometimes brings about breakdown and failure in transmitted data. Thus, nodes don't contribute in any security operations (Ghoreishi et al, 2014). An inadequacy of this type cause can hamper the general operations of the nodes association and disjoints.
- **Restricted Power Supply:** Nodes in a MANET rely on their battery power for any activities such as packet forwarding, processing, sending, receiving etc. But the limited power supply is not sufficient because the power drains away with use of it during functioning of the nodes.
- **Inconsistent Scalability:** Everything well thought-out in wired network scale is predefined when outlined and not change such all through the usage, however scale is changing each time in case of compliance in MANET. There is no network to anticipate number of nodes in MANET, due to which the congestion (Rashidi et al, 2009) occurs in routers and secured congestion control (Kumaran et al, 2010) mechanism need to be employed. This infers that network needs scale all over at every one time in network.

In this section important work has been presented which are carried out by eminent persons with their proposed protocols with security features executed by them.

Table 1. Details of security mechanisms studied

Literature	Year	Basic Security Mechanism
V. Sheesha Bhargavi et.al.	2016	Improvement of the security of files shared across MANET
Vishnu Sharma et.al.	2016	Attacks on the network layer of the protocol stack. Has been prevented
Shilpi burman Sharma et.al.	2015	Security issues in MANET has been analyzed
Seyed-Mohsen Ghoreishi et.al.	2014	Rushing attack prevention has been carried out
Praveen Joshi	2010	Security threats in Network layer are analyzed
Jan Von Mulert et.al.	2012	Focuses on networks that use AODV and SAODV protocols for security
Rashid Sheik et.al.	2010	Identification mechanism is needed between nodes using identification and credentials and this leads to privacy attack
Athuly MS et.al.	2012	Secure transmission of audio over the network
Md. Qayyum et.al.	2011	Security issues of data query processing and location monitoring has been discussed
Edl Echchaachoui et.al.	2014	Data security as a key issue in MANET has been emphasized

CHALLENGES AND ATTACKS

It is a very challenging issue to prevent attacks in a MANET. General types of attacks and challenges found in MANET Routing Protocols are described in this section. Mobile ad-hc networks are more challenging in comparison to other wire based networks due to their dynamic nature of network re-configuration. The challenged overpowering on MANET routing protocols are featured as passive attack cannot disturb the behaviour of the protocol, but reveal the creative data by tuning into movement of the nodes. In general concept, the passive attacks get important routing knowledge by sniffing regarding the network (Lv et al, 2015). These type of network attacks are habitually difficult to set up and in this method, checking against such attacks is difficult. It was observed that it is not practical to compute the exact location of a station in a network. But however, one may be able to get the knowledge about the network topology using these type of attacks. Another class of active attack encompasses groups of nodes (Ghoreishi et al, 2014) and makes an effort to halt the functioning of the protocol and tries to get confirmation. In this way they try to hack the information from network stations. The target is done in an magnanimous way to draw in all groups to the attacker to weaken the network. Such attacks could be set and the nodes may be perceived (Mishra et al, 2003).

Attacks on MANETs

Commonly recognizable attacks in a MANET are eavesdropping, DoS, Dropping,Blackhole ets which are discussed in this section.

1. **Eavesdropping Attacks:** These attacks are normally exposure attacks that are done by outside and interior stations who are not much involved in network activity. The basic purpose of the The attacker's target of Eavesdropping is to separate show messages and procure some accommodating information about the network that is important all through the communication.
2. **Denial of Service (DoS):** In DoS attacks, attackers endeavour to attack at the availability of organizations of the entire Mobile Ad hoc network. The attackers use the battery exhaustion routines and the radio adhering to perform Dos attacks to the Mobile Ad hoc network.
3. **Dropping Attacks:** In Mobile Ad hoc network nodes those are malicious nodes intentionally drops all the packets that are not headed for them. In dropping attack, malicious nodes expect to disturb the affiliation, while self absorbed nodes plan to protect their benefits. It diminishes the network execution by bringing on data packs to be transmitted yet again; new routes to the destination are to be found.

OBJECTIVE OF SECURITY IN MOBILE DEVICES AND MANET

Objective of security is to develop a secured network system. The following security goals with their standardization have to be developed in the network.

Availability

A node always provides services it is designed for. It concentrates crucially on Denial-of-Service attacks. Some selfish nodes make some network services unavailable

Integrity

It refers to the process of guaranteeing the identity of the messenger. There are challenges such as malicious attacks and accidental altering. The difference between the two is intent i.e., in malicious attack, the attacker intentionally changes information whereas in accidental altering, alteration is accidentally done by a benign node.

Confidentiality

Sometimes, some information ought to be accessible only to few, who has been authorized to access it. Others, who are unauthorized, should not be get a hold of this confidential information.

Authenticity

Authenticity checks if a node is an impersonator or not (Mulert et al, 2012). It is imperative that the identities of the participants are secured by encrypting their respective codes. The adversary could impersonate a benign node and can gain access to confidential resources or even distribute some harmful messages.

Non-Repudiation

Non-repudiation ensures that the sender and the receiver of a message cannot deny sending or receiving such a message. The instance of being compromised is established without ambiguity. For e.g. if a node recognizes that the message it has received is erroneous or genuine. The node can then use the incorrect message as a proof to notify other nodes that the nodes should have been compromised.

Authentication

A confide credential to be issued by the appropriate authority which will be mandatory to assign access rights to users at different levels. It usually uses an authorization process.

COMPARATIVE ANALYSIS OF SECURITY BASED PROTOCOLS

This section performs comparative analysis of MANET based Routing Protocols based on security parameters such as power and delay management techniques, security at multimedia data transmission, prevention of link failures, and prevention of cyber attack. Table 3 shows various OLSR protocols based on their security approaches.

A trust based security protocol TBS (Rajaram et al, 2010) has been designed with an improved security feature at the MAC layer. Many improved AODV protocol (Wuiankun Et al, 2011) and (Li et al, 2010) has been proposed named MAODV (Choudhury et al, 2015) based on the receive reply method specifically designed to prevent the black hole attack. In a secured DSR algorithm called SDSR (Bhargavi et al, 2016) has been proposed for better network security during routing. In the

Table 2. Security mechanism implemented in protocols with security goals

Proposed By	Basic Mechanism
Praveen Joshi	Security threats in Network layer has been analyzed for confidentiality
Jan Von Mulert et.al.	Focuses on networks that use AODV and Secured AODV protocols in MANET
Rashid Sheik et.al.	Identification mechanism suggested between nodes using identification and credentials which leads to privacy problems.
Athuly MS et.al.	Secure transmission of audio over the network has been tested for integrity
Md. Qayyum et.al.	Security issues of data query processing and location monitoring for authenticity
E. Echchaachoui et.al.	Data security as a key matter with non-repudiation
V. Sheesha Bhargavi et.al.	Improvement of the security of files shared across MANET with authentiocation
Vishnu Sharma et.al.	Prevention of attacks on the network layer of the protocol stack
Shilpi burman Sharma et.al.	Security issues in MANET with basic security goals
Seyed-Mohsen Ghoreishi et.al.	Rushing attack is prevented with keeping confidentiality intact.
Chinmaya Ghosh et.al.	It tests the scenarios of security models using simulator ns2.
Slavica V. Bostjancic Rakas et.al.	Here a functional model of Policy Based Management (PBM) is proposed which deals with four entities i.e. QoS, network resources, configuration and security.
Nawneet Raj et.al.	Identifying the security issues in wireless networks like MANET
Subodh Kumar Gupta et.al.	It uses binary conversion technique in addressing mode for security purpose.

Table 3. Proposed OLSR protocols with advantages and disadvantages

Name of the Protocol	Advantages	Disadvantages
OLSR-SDK (Secure Data Key)	It provides high level security and improved traffic performance.	It does not improve Packet Delivery Ratio.
RA-OLSR (Radio Aware)	It provides high level security.	It has significant impact on traffic performance.
COD-OLSR()	It does not generate a significant additional traffic load.	It cannot counteract severe attacks.
Secure traffic routing OLSR	It encounters link – spoofing attacks.	It has major effect on routing performance and it does not reject violent attacks.
Trust to secure OLSR	It has good routing performance in a highly attacked environment.	It does not provide high – level security against complex attacks.

following section three prominent security based protocols those discussed above have been simulated for their performance for the network parameters such as packet delivery ratio (PDR), transmission delay and power consumption.NS2 software was used for simulation with the following network parameters.

Table 4 shows the network simulation parameters considered during the simulation process for simulating the protocols considered for comparison of energy efficient and security based protocols.

Figure 1 displays the graphical result of comparison of packet delivery ratio (PDR) . TBS Protocol with an improved MAC Layer technique shows better PDR when compared with MAODV and SDSR approach.

Figure 2 shows the comparison of average end to end delay between the discussed protocols. TBS exhibits minimum delay when compared with other approaches.

Similarly Figure 3 shows the comparison of power consumption between the three prominent protocols and TBS consumes minimum power due to power efficient technique used by it.

In this section an attempt has been taken to present an analysis and survey on routing issues in MANET and important protocols proposed by researchers with their routing significance and security mechanism, other novel contributions and their performance results for security based routing protocols in a very energetic Mobile Ad hoc network environment. First, the features of the secured protocols (Mulert, Weich, KG, 2012) have been discussed and then we have enlightened the challenges that emerge due to different types of attacks in MANET (Mishra and Nadkarni, 2003). Taking the fundamental concept of Mobile routing, this section highlights on the unfocussed areas of routing (Rath et al, 2016) with novel contributions which provides ample opportunity for new researchers to work further in the area of MANET routing.

Table 4. Simulation parameters used

Simulation Parameters	Data/Value
Channel Type	Wireless Channel
MAC Protocol	802.11
Traffic Type	CBR
Packet Size	512 Bytes
No. of Mobile Nodes	120
Simulation Time	600 seconds
Simulation area	2000 x 2000 m
Protocols Name	MAODV,SDSR,TBS
Model for Node Movement	Random way point
Data rate	11 mbps
Application Type	Video Transmission (Real Time)
Bandwidth	2Mb/s for both
Simulator	Ns2.35

Figure 1. Comparison of packet delivery ratio

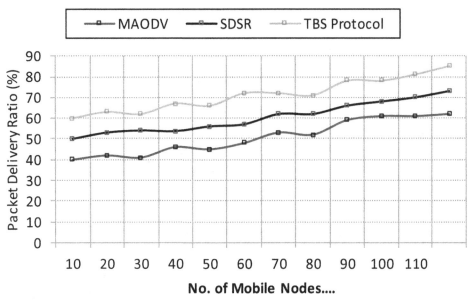

For a more accurate representation see the electronic version.

Figure 2. Comparison of average delay

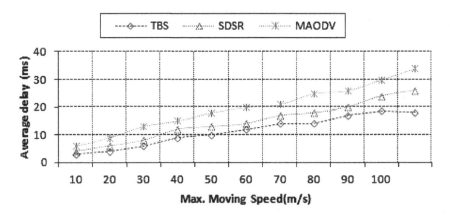

NETWORK SECURITY WITH IOT DEVICES

This section describes significant and advanced issues those arises due to vulnerability in MANET when they are used with IoT (Internet of Things) system. This section also puts light on the security issues of big data management using IoT systems, existing techniques for big data and personal data security including authentication

Figure 3. Comparison of average power consumption

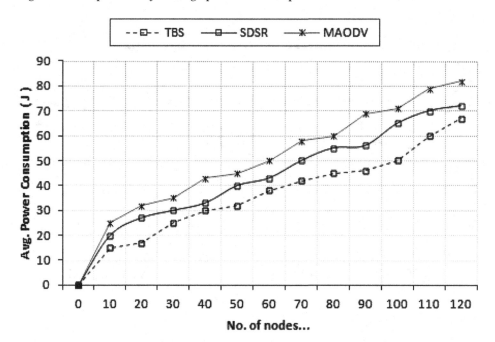

and secured communication in IoT. This chapter also include a succinct discussion of techniques available to handle confidentiality issues in IoT systems. The chapter It is predicted that 50 billion devices will all be connected to the Internet. One of the biggest challenges will be having enough trained and skilled workforce to help implement and scale IoT. Cisco is addressing this challenge by working with industry partners to build education and training curriculums. These courses address several verticals and markets like manufacturing, utilities, transportation, mining, and oil & gas where the IP network is prevalent now. These e-Learning offerings will help you learn the basic skills needed to become an active participant in the evolution of the Internet and prepare you for real-world implementations.

Security Issues in Health Monitoring Systems

There are many application areas of Internet of Things (IoTs) in our day to day life in which there is a high necessity of security and privacy measures of those applications. In those applications, a variety of IoT devices are used such as IoT devices for home and appliances, lighting and heating, safety monitoring devices such as video cameras and sensors etc. In health monitoring systems, devices for fitness such as wearables FitBit Pulse, blood pressure and blood sugar monitoring equipment etc. In transportation, smart solutions for better transportation using IoT devices have been developed with use of traffic signals and smart parking facility. In Industrial sector, different activities are checked using IoT devices such as controlling the flow of materials, checking of oil and gas flow interruptions and electricity usage control by monitoring devices. But, in all these applications security and privacy have equal importance and are the challenging issues for IoT systems.

Security Issues in Application Programming Interface

As the sensor nodes in wireless networks produce high volume of data, therefore, storage and their security also plays a big challenging task with Big Data related issues with in such IoT based devices. As per current research on Application Programming Interface, approximately 200 exabytes in 2014 and an estimation of 1.6 zetta bytes in 2020 is supposed to be processed, 90% of these data are currently processed locally and the processing rate increases day by day. In the same time the risk of critical data theft, data and device manipulation, falsification of sensitive data as well as IP theft, manipulation and malfunction of server and networks also can not be avoided. There is a great impact of data consolidation and data analytics in network configuration i.e. CISCO, HPE and others. Next, in application platform areas based on clouds and firewalls at the network boundaries are more prone from external attacks. Companies are paying high cost for secured management of their business data, transaction information, and personal data of customers in banks and in MNCs are also maintained by software security systems. There are definite policies for data privacy which need to be strongly covered with secured envelops in IoT devices so as to restrict the process of unauthorized access to the IoT systems (Hua et al, 2011). Exact requirement from the customer side must be provided for customizing data security package about who is going to use the data and how it is to be utilized. Similarly there is also a need of adhering suitable practice to preserve the reputation of the organization with regular monitoring and controlling the security modules and timely updating them. Therefore, it is required to consider the security and privacy measure of big data.

ROBOTIC NETWORKS IN MANET

This section deals with MANET based protocols used in Robotics and the vulnerability found in this area with how these robust protocols are able to solve the security issues. Comparative analysis based on throughput, network life time, bandwidth consumption, number of attempts to attack, failure and success rate.

Nanotechnologies promise new possibilities for sustaining connectivity issues in Mobile robots in a Robotic Mobile Adhoc Networks. In Multi-robot systems with disaster scenario, military applications, for search and rescue operations and natural misfortunes this issue is even more critical. Timely communication and forwarding control messages in a Mobile Adhoc Network which is suitable for these drastic situations from one robot to another is a crucial factor in all these solicitations and it is a challenging issue in MANET due to the auto-reconfiguration nature of the network which is not based on any fixed infrastructure and there is frequent variation in its topology due to highly moving mobile nodes. This paper presents an organized analysis of connectivity issues of mobile robots in Robotic MANET and their performance enhancement using Nanotechnology. Secondly, getting inspired from the study of challenges and possible research directions, this paper also proposes an energetic MANET based ROBOTIC protocol that suits better in robotic management especially to prolong the inter-robotic communication period. MANETs are specialized networks that operate without any infrastructure and allow mobile users to remain connected. These are useful networks to extend the communication in disaster situations. A major challenging issue in both Mobile Adhoc Network and Robotics is to control and accomplish proper communication with each other and the operators. Figure 4 shows the overall structure of a Mobile Adhoc Network. There are some specific purpose multi-robot systems which form MANET during search and rescue operations, whose performance are improved by human beings to complement individual expertise.

Figure 4. Structure of a MANET (Luis et.al, 2011)

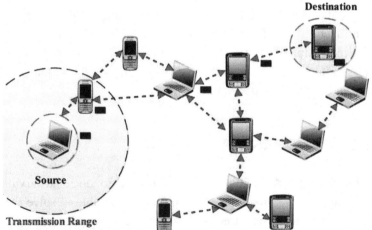

In many applications like natural disasters or in battle fields the infrastructure may not be there or if there then it has got damaged, so it requires formation of a number of mobile robots to create a MANET (Figure 4) for short period of time. Design and implementation of an efficient communication protocol is very much essential in Mobile Robot Systems. Figure 5 shows a multi-robot system.

SECURITY ISSUES IN ROBOTIC NETWORKS

There are many security issues related to proper communication among mobile robots in MANETs which are described by many researchers time to time. Along with proper communication capacity, the MANET should provide position data and information to support the localization property of the robots and humans which are of great importance to properly control the human along with robots to special targets (Kumaran et al, 2010). The GPS system can provide the position data for outdoor applications. For such type of applications, every node of an adhoc network must have knowledge of its location autonomously.

Mobile Adhoc Network design is suitable to be used in large burning industrial warehouses. This network supports the assisting group of the robots as well as the fire fighters with a communication infrastructure as positional data. The issue of connection preserving for longer period has been discussed by eminent researchers. The most proposed solutions are to strictly preserve connectivity while performing specific tasks

ROBOTIC, NANOTECHNOLOGY, AND SECURITY ISSUES

Nano robots establishes a "SMART" structure with capacity to activate, actuate, to sense the channel, to send signal, intelligence processing and manipulation of swarm

Figure 5. Multi-robot system (webuser.unicas.it, 2015)

Figure 6. A Robotic MANET showing agent, mobile antenna, and base station (webuser.unicas.it, 2015)

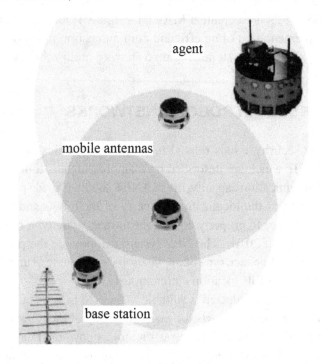

behavior at an extreme nano scale. There are some bio nano robots which are inspired by harnessing properties of peptides, DNA with the design and functionalities of such objects. Nano robots recommend solution for biomedicine problems.

The main part of a Multi-Robot System as shown in Figure 7 constitutes infrared module of inter-robot inter- communication technology and acts as localization system. This device provides each robot, its local network information such as network connectivity and local position estimation of adjoining robots. Multi-robot formation control processes must be able to track the connectivity topography of the network. The most communal sensor models accept that the distance among the robots is known. There are many security issues related to robotic management which are presented here.

SECURED GROUP COMMUNICATION AMONG MOBILE ROBOTS IN MANET

Communication in a group of mobile robots requires very dynamic protocol design which can operate without any central architecture and should be able to

Figure 7. Autonomous multi-robot system (www.cs.cmu.edu, 2015)

handle variant topology in a MANET (Rashidi et al, 2009). Multicasting offers a better way of sending some data to multiple recipients. In (Rashidi et al, 2009) a routing algorithm has been proposed to improve the network performance using nanotechnology, called NAODV. In this protocol the AODV concept (Li et al, 2010) is integrated with Nanotechnology that uses Nano computer to collect information from the surrounding environment and communicate this information to the Nano stations. This information is useful for info stations to take intelligent decision and actions. By the use of TN (Transmitter Nano) and RN (Receiver Nano) messages the protocol send and receives the messages from its neighbor nodes. Objective of Nano-AODV if enhancement of the network performance and higher throughput in comparison to normal AODV protocol (Kumar, Kumar and Kumar, 2010). During disaster situation, the mobile robots can move fast to the concerned place and help as a guide of fire fighters to search and find the target locations and avoids the dangerous objects (Kumaran et al, 2010) They can internally communicate with each other and also with the fire fighters. Mobile Adhoc Networks are useful in multi-robot system. An important application of a multi-robot system is USAR(Urban Search and Rescue). Mobile Adhoc Network can be communicated with the Mobile Robots which acts as forwarding node and this combination provides a better infrast6ructure for communication.

Figure 8 describes a MANET scenario in Military field during was where it is very much essential to form an adhoc network for communication between major war vehicles and provision of updated sensitive information. Mobile Robots can be implemented in these fields to operate fast and efficiently.

Figure 8. Secured MANET in a military application (www.military.ethernet.com, 2015)

Controlling of Real Swarm Robot's Communication

Robot Management is a demanding area for research specifically in MANETs. It depends on the successful logical execution of robots in a group. Multi robot operation can be improved effectively by improving the efficiency of individual robots. Robots always better react through a cooperative manner. They are always concerned about their local information pertaining to locality, bandwidth, energy and relative distance between other robots in group.

Secured Multi-Robot System With Distributed Control

There is a need of multi-robot co-ordination so that work efficiency of the system is developed, so that the application can be completed successfully. Multi-robot cooperation is an important matter for suitable communication.

SECURED CONNECTIVITY IN ROBOTICS

In Robotics the basic problem lies in connectivity of robotic devices with each other for long period of time. Lot of research work has been carried out to prolong the period of connectivity preservation and many advanced research proposals have been presented by eminent researchers in this field. Few of them are discussed here. A large number of member robots in ROBOT Swarm take active part in SART (Search and Rescue Team) during very critical and dangerous situations where immediate communication among mobile robots is essential for information transfer (Araujo et al, 2014). In this type of condition, it is also very difficult to arrange an external energy provider which will energise the robots instantly as heavy energy is consumed during the data communication and forwarding the packets of information. Paper (Semnova et al, 2015) discusses key challenges and network architecture of mobile robotic networks. Mobile robotic teams require robust communication in order to coordinate effectively, which is a challenge given the dynamic, unpredictable nature of mobile ad hoc networks (MANET). These networks are subject to rapidly varying link qualities as robots move through their environment. Improving the robustness of these point-to-point links leads to greater overall network performance, which in turn allows the robots to perform their mission more effectively (Marcotte et al, 2016). In multi-robot applications strong wireless connectivity is very much essential to perform the real life events. A single access point that controls and monitors all the network activities is good enough to manage a network but still there is need of multi-hop communication to get rid of limitations of highly mobile robots. In Tardioli et al. (2014), a wireless protocol specifically designed for communication in distributed robotics systems has been proposed which is capable of managing highly mobile robots with performing better in end-to-end delivery delay. Paper (Srovnal et al, 2009) describes modern topics and future scopes in wireless communication for mobile robotic and industrial devices in the real time (Rath et al, 2015) situation. It explains the benefits of using parallel processing with varying network topologies with focus on ultra low power communication chips based on a specific frequency range. A brief description about the work contributed by researchers on above discussed issues are presented in Tabular form in this section in Table 5.

Table 5. Details of connectivity issues

Basic Issue	Literature	Year
Control of real swarm robots communication	Tutuko, *et al*	2014
Performance of MANET Routing Protocols	Hanieh, *et al*	2014
Multi-Robot Formation	Zhang *et al*	2009
Service co-operation of Robot swarn	Li *et, al*	2009
Connectivity preservation	Cor nejo *et, al*	2009
Multi-robot system in disaster scenario	Ulf *et al*	2008
Reliable co-operative system	Kim, *et al*	2008
Probability of Wireless Connectivity	Manoja, *et al*	2008
Group communication in Robotic MANETs	Das, *et al*	2005
Requirement of Advanced Robotic Controller	Willium, *et al*	2004

Mobile Robot Sensor Networks supports mission critical applications where there is communication between sensor nodes play vital role during the real time applications. It requires long lasting network connectivity (Mi et al, 2015) with application level co-ordination among sensors. The main challenge in this type of networks comes to picture when failure of some critical sensor results in decomposition of the entire network into disjoint segments.

SECURY IN REAL TIME APPLICATIONS

It is a challenging issue in MANET to efficiently handle the real time information over the network successfully.General challenges faced by real time applications are video streaming for multimedia data, bandwidth availability, dedicated connectivity issue, mobility of stations, downloading problem and availability of resources.In this section we have studied basic protocols which are specially designed for real time load transmission and after analysis their strategies we have re-simulated them under the specified parameters as follows and then we have compared them in terms of packet delivery ratio, delay and power consumption rate.

RT-WMP has been proposed as a real-time protocol in MANET that ensures timely delivery of data in MANET (Tardioli et al, 2015) Cross layer communication has been used in this proposal that uses a improved MAC scheme for control of routing considering the link quality among the nodes that participate in routing. In a multi-hop communication, this protocol also facilitates real time transmission in small swarm robots.

A Real time security protocol in MANET has been proposed which is called MCT (Multi Cast Tree) (Kumar and Ravichandran, 2013), that finds a solution for smooth transmission of multimedia streams. This protocol provides better connectivity and avoids the channel disturbance up to a greater level. It uses a balanced method of selecting nodes during routing so that all the nodes are burdened with equal load without any loss of data. Another interesting approach called MRMF (MANET Real-Time Frequency Management) has been proposed in (Boksiner et al, 2013) to address the increasing demand of spectrum access. It uses centralized control to monitor the confliction of network connectivity with background electromagnetic waves in the wireless environment. This approach automates the re-use of frequency among nodes in MANET. Use of this approach also enables Dynamic Spectrum Access (DSA) among MANET radios which do not have such facility.

COMPARATIVE ANALYSIS AND SIMULATION RESULTS

Table 6 shows the simulation parameters considered during simulation of the above three protocols. Network Simulator simulation software was used for simulation of our comparison.

Figure 9 shows the comparative analysis of secured routing protocols in MANET. From the result we can observe that the packet delivery ratio in all the secured

Table 6. Simulation parameters

Simulation Parameters	Data/Value
No. of Nodes	30, 60 and 90
Simulation Time	600 seconds (10 mins)
Simulation area	1100 x 1200 m
Protocols Name	RTWMP,MRFM,MCT
Model for Node Movement	Random way point
Data rate	11 mbps
Application Type 1	Realtime
Bandwidth	2Mb/s for both
Simulator	Ns 2.35

Figure 9. Comparative analysis of PDR

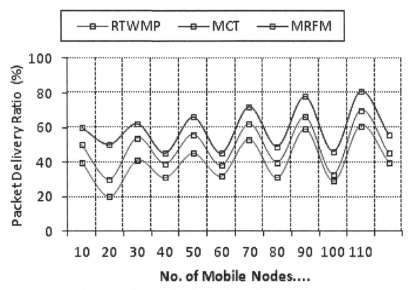

For a more accurate representation see the electronic version.

protocols are more or less affected due to complex logic for secured routing. Figure 10 shows the comparative analysis of end to end delay in network which concludes that the three prominent protocols are able to send back the packets in real time situation efficiently with minor variation of delay. Figure 11 depicts the average power consumption among the mobile nodes in the representative protocols considered in this chapter.

Due to intelligent logic implemented in protocols during mobile routing, they consume little more energy which violates from protocol to protocol. This analysis concludes that we can use more secured logic during implementation of protocols in mobile devices and wireless networks which may affect the packet delivery ration, power consumption and average end to end delay up to a very minor extent to avoid vulnerability in the network.

CONCLUSION

This chapter focuses on the primary vulnerability issues in wireless network with Mobile Adhoc Network as a special case study. Study and analysis part of this chapter highlights on security issues at different levels of routing and how those issues has

Figure 10. Comparative analysis of average delay

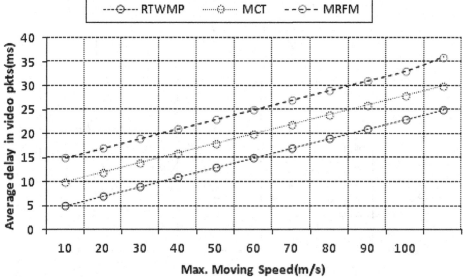

For a more accurate representation see the electronic version.

Figure 11. Comparative analysis of average power consumption

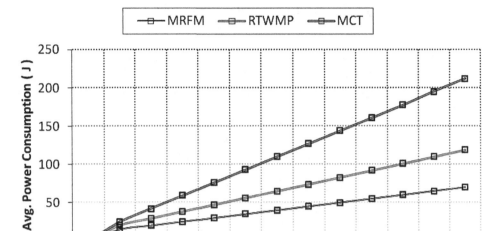

For a more accurate representation see the electronic version.

been handled by incorporating intelligent prevention strategies. Other than the general and conventional security issues in MANET, this chapter provides more stress on security at the junction point of MANET and IoT, security in ROBOTIC MANET in real time applications. Therefore, this chapter generates a lot of research interest and encourages researchers to extend their research in this magnificent area of security.

REFERENCES

Araujo, Santos, & Rocha. (2014). Implementation of a routing protocol for ad hoc networks in search and rescue robotics. *2014 IFIP Wireless Days (WD)*, 1-7.

Bhargavi, V. S., Seetha, M., & Viswanadharaju, S. (2016). A hybrid secure routing scheme for MANETS. *2016 International Conference on Emerging Trends in Engineering, Technology and Science(ICETETS)*, 1-5. doi:10.1109/ICETETS.2016.7602991

Boksiner, J., Posherstnik, Y., May, B., Saltzman, M., & Kamal, S. (2013). Centrally Controlled Dynamic Spectrum Access forMANETs. *Military Communications Conference, MILCOM 2013*, 641-646. doi:10.1109/MILCOM.2013.115

Chibelushi, Eardley, & Arabo. (2013). Identity Management in the Internet of Things: The Role of MANETs for Healthcare Applications. *Computer Science and Information Technology, 1*(2), 73-81.

Choudhury, D. R., Ragha, L., & Marathe, N. (2015). Implementing and improving the performance of AODV by receive reply method and securing it from Black hole attack. *Procedia Computer Science, 45,* 564–570. doi:10.1016/j.procs.2015.03.109

Ghoreishi, S. M., Razak, S. A., Isnin, I. F., & Chizari, H. (2014). Rushing Attack Against Routing Protocols in Mobile Ad-Hoc Network. In *International Symposium on Biometrics and Security Technologies.* IEEE. doi:10.1109/ISBAST.2014.7013125

Hua, Z., Fei, G., & Wen, Q. (2011). A Password-Based Secure Communication Scheme in Battlefields for Internet of Things. *China Communications, 8*(1), 72–78.

Ikeda, M., Kulla, E., Hiyama, M., Barolli, L., Miho, R., & Takizawa, M. (2012). TCP Congestion-Control in MANETs for Multiple Traffic Considering Proactive and Reactive Routing Protocols. *15th IEEE International Conference on Network-Based Information Systems.* doi:10.1109/NBiS.2012.68

Joshi, P. (2011). *Security Issues in Routing protocols in MANETs at network layer. Procedia Computer Science, 3,* 954–960.

Kumar, Kumar, & Kumar. (2010). Improved Modified Reverse AODV Protocol. *International Journal of Computer Applications, 12*(4), 22-26.

Kumaran & Sankaranarayanan. (2010). Early detection congestion and control routing in MANET. *Seventh International Conference on Wireless and Optical Communications Networks (WOCN),* 1-5.

Li, B., Liu, Y., & Chu, G. (2010). Improved AODV routing protocol for vehicular Ad hoc networks. *Advanced Computer Theory and Engineering (ICACTE), 2010 3rd International Conference on, 4,* 337-340.

Lv, P., Wang, X., Xue, X., & Xu, M. (2015, May 1). SWIMMING: Seamless and Efficient WiFi-Based Internet Access from Moving Vehicles. *IEEE Transactions on Mobile Computing, 14*(5), 1085–1097. doi:10.1109/TMC.2014.2341652

Marcotte, R. J., & Olson, E. (2016). Adaptive forward error correction with adjustable-latency QoS for robotic networks. *2016 IEEE International Conference on Robotics and Automation (ICRA),* 5283-5288. doi:10.1109/ICRA.2016.7487739

Mi, Z., Yang, Y., & Yang, J. Y. (2015, August). Restoring Connectivity of Mobile Robotic Sensor Networks While Avoiding Obstacles. *IEEE Sensors Journal, 15*(8), 4640–4650. doi:10.1109/JSEN.2015.2426177

Mishra & Nadkarni. (2003). Security in Wireless Ad Hoc Networks. In *The Handbook of Ad Hoc Wireless Networks*. CRC Press LLC.

Qayyum, , Subhash, & Husamuddin. (2012). Security issues of Data Query Processing and Location Monitoring in MANETs. In *International Conference on Communication, Information and Computing Technology (ICCICT)*. IEEE.

Qin, Z., Denker, G., Giannelli, C., & Bellavista, P. (2014). A Software Defined Networking architecture for the Internet-of-Things. *Network Operations and Management Symposium*, 1-9.

Rajaram, A., & Palaniswami, S. (2010). The Trust-Based MAC - Layer Security Protocol for Mobile Ad Hoc Networks. *2010 6th International Conference on Wireless Communications Networking and Mobile Computing (WiCOM)*, 1-4. doi:10.1109/WICOM.2010.5600904

Rashidi, R., Jamali, M. A. J., Salmasi, A., & Tati, R. (2009). Trust routing protocol based on congestion control in MANET. *2009 International Conference on Application of Information and Communication Technologies*, 1-5. doi:10.1109/ICAICT.2009.5372623

Rath, M., Pattanayak, B. K., & Pati, B. (2015, January-March). Energy Competent Routing Protocol Design in MANET with Real time Application Provision. *International Journal of Business Data Communications and Networking*, *11*(1), 50–60. doi:10.4018/IJBDCN.2015010105

Rath, M., Pattanayak, B. K., & Pati, B. (2016, March). Energy Efficient MANET Protocol Using Cross Layer Design for Military Applications. *Defence Science Journal*, *66*(2), 146. doi:10.14429/dsj.66.9705

Semenova & Solodkov. (2015). *Network challenges in mobile group robotics: MANET approach. In 2015 Internet Technologies and Applications* (pp. 181–185). Wrexham: ITA.

Srovnal, V. Jr, Machacek, Z., & Srovnal, V. (2009). Wireless Communication for Mobile Robotics and Industrial Embedded Devices. *2009 Eighth International Conference on Networks*, 253-258. doi:10.1109/ICN.2009.46

Tardioli. (2015). *A wireless multi-hop protocol for real-time applications. Computer Communications*, 55, 4–21.

Tardioli, D. (2014). A wireless communication protocol for distributed robotics applications. *2014 IEEE International Conference on Autonomous Robot Systems and Competitions (ICARSC)*, 253-260. doi:10.1109/ICARSC.2014.6849795

Vijaya Kumar, P. D. R., & Ravichandran, T. (2013). A Real Time Multimedia Streaming in Mobile Ad Hoc Networks using Multicast Tree Structure. *Research Journal of Information Technology*, *5*(1), 24–34.

Von Mulert, J., Weich, I., & Seah, W. K. G. (2012). Security threats and solutions in MANETs: A case study using AODV and SAODV. *Journal of Network and Computer Applications, Elsevier, 35*(4), 1249–1259. doi:10.1016/j.jnca.2012.01.019

Zhu, Q. (2011). A Mobile Ad Hoc Networks Algorithm Improved AODV Protocol. *Procedia Engineering*, *23*, 229–234. doi:10.1016/j.proeng.2011.11.2494

Chapter 10
TerrorWatch:
A Prototype Mobile App to Combat Terror in Terror-Prone Nations

Solomon Sunday Oyelere
University of Eastern Finland, Finland

Olayemi Olawumi
University of Eastern Finland, Finland

Donald Douglas Atsa'am
Eastern Mediterranean University, Cyprus

Jarkko Suhonen
University of Eastern Finland, Finland

Mike Joy
University of Warwick, UK

Hope Micah Ayuba
Modibbo Adama University of Technology, Nigeria

ABSTRACT

Activities of prominent terrorist groups like Boko Haram, Al-Shabaab, Ansaru, and Ansar Dine have left thousands of people dead and properties destroyed for a number of decades in some developing nations. The high level of insecurity occasioned by operations of terror groups has impacted negatively on the socio-economic development of these nations. On the other hand, the use of mobile devices, such as cell phones, has gained prominence in developing nations over the past two decades. Putting side-by-side these two facts, namely, that the menace of terrorism among some developing nations is alarming and that the use of mobile devices is common among citizens of developing countries, this chapter develops a mobile application prototype called TerrorWatch. TerrorWatch is equipped with relevant menus, buttons, and interfaces that will guide a user on what to do when confronted with a terrorist attack or threat. The unified modeling language (UML) was deployed to design the architecture of the application, while the object-oriented paradigm served in the implementation.

DOI: 10.4018/978-1-5225-4029-8.ch010

INTRODUCTION

The level of insecurity bedeviling most developing nations is alarming (Kim and Phil, 2009). A major cause of this insecurity is terrorism. This has, no doubt, affected this category of nations socio-economically as investors tend to avoid doing business in violent-prone environments. One reassuring fact is that citizens of developing nations have embraced the use of mobile devices. Against this backdrop, the authors are poised to finding a solution to the prevailing problem of terrorism, cashing in on the impressive level of mobile device usage among citizens.

This chapter discusses the design and development of an Android mobile application prototype, called *TerrorWatch,* for developing countries. The application will help users recognize terrorist threats, organizational structures commonly used by terrorist organizations, as well as enable citizens to know when there is imminent danger of an impending terrorist attack. The application provides functionalities that serve as a reference guide to the appropriate line of action when confronted with any form of terrorist threats and/or attack. The application also allows users to warn of an escalating situation to security agents, caution other citizens to steer clear and so forth, using predefined interfaces provided by the application.

According to Whittaker (2004), the primary aim of terrorists is to intimidate the government and society through the use of violence in order to achieve some set goals. In most cases, these goals are political in nature. Terrorist organizations have been ravaging both developed and developing societies for decades. In developing countries, for instance, Boko Haram has been terrorizing Nigeria and Cameroun since 2009, while Al-Shabaab has been operating in Somalia and other East African countries for more than a decade (Wosu and Agwanwo, 2014). The activities of these and many other terrorist groups have posed serious national and regional security and economic challenges. These activities include suicide bombings, hostage-taking, sabotage, high-profile assassinations, indiscriminate and wanton destruction of public and private property, and many more. Huge budgetary allocations, that otherwise would have been channeled to economic development, are made yearly for purposes of war against insurgency. In Nigeria for instance, the year 2014 budget estimates indicated a total of N968.127 billion (nine hundred and sixty eight billion Naira, equivalent to USD 3.2 billion) was earmarked for security (Udo, 2014), and took up 20% of the entire budget for that year. By the year 2016, the budget for security purposes increased to N1.014 trillion (one trillion Naira, equivalent to USD 3.3 billion).

In another development, it is a fact that the use of mobile devices, such as cell phones, has gained prominence in developing nations over the past two decades. In Nigeria, for instance, it is almost impossible to find a household without at least one mobile phone (Oyelere, Suhonen, & Sutinen, 2016). With that in mind, this research develops an application that will incorporate security features into mobile devices to serve as a counter-measure to the menace of terrorism. Admittedly, there have been concerted efforts by various national and regional security formations to combat terrorism (Cooke, 2013). This, however, has not sufficiently quelled the menace of insurgency, and motivates the authors; to search wider for solutions through the use of mobile devices.

TerrorWatch is a tool to be used by those who require an instant and immediate guide on terrorism and terrorist threats. The application complements, but does not replace, security agents and intelligence gathering on terrorism. Rather, it is an instant solution in the absence of the Army, Police and other relevant agencies. A typical scenario of when the application could be of assistance includes sighting a bomb, firearms, or an improvised explosive device (IED) in an environment, being in a place where attack is taking place, when a terrorist is living around your neighborhood, and when terrorist groups are invading your environment, etc. The application will guide its users on the appropriate action to take in such scenarios.

Given the fact that terrorism is relatively new in most developing countries like Somalia, Nigeria, Cameroon, Mali, and the Niger Republic (McGregor, 2013), most citizens are yet to understand the practical details of this societal ill. The year 2012 saw remarkable terror incidents taking place in Africa, including the Tuareg Ansar al-Din movement that overran northern Mali (McGregor, 2013), the emergence of a new terror faction, Ansaru, from Boko Haram (Zenn, 2012), and an alliance among rebel forces that launched an offensive in the north of the Central Africa Republic (McGregor, 2013). Victims are always helpless in the event of an attack. The populace is frequently confused due to widely divergent views on how to define terrorism. Most persons do not understand the nature of terrorism and do not recognize terrorists and terrorist threats. The *TerrorWatch* application is designed specifically to address these challenges. Admittedly, several applications exist (Mukherjee, 2015; Chrisafis, 2016) for purposes of counter-terrorism. The worrisome issue is that majority of them were designed specifically for the developed world. It is not clear if such applications have options to be customized to fit the terrorism trends in developing countries (Leadbeater, 2015).

TerrorWatch is equipped with relevant menus, buttons, and Graphical User Interfaces (GUIs) that will help a user to call or message the Army, Police or other security agents, quickly, when confronted with a situation that seems to be a terrorist attack or threat. When a user is in a confused situation, as in whether such a situation has any resemblance of terrorism, the application will be useful for clarification. The functionalities of the application certainly will help to save lives and property that otherwise, would have been lost due to terrorism.

The Unified Modeling Language (UML) is deployed to design the architecture of the application (Atsa'am, 2016), while the Android Studio platform and Java served in the implementation of the application, which can be deployed on any device running the Android operating system. To achieve the design and development of this application, first the functional requirements of *TerroWatch* are analyzed. Second, the technical architecture as well as implementation details is introduced. Finally, test cases of how the application is used in real-life scenarios are shown, and a formative evaluation plan on how the application will be evaluated is introduced.

BACKGROUND

Relevance of Mobile Devices in Developing Countries

Similar to the developed world, the developing world is not left out in the use of mobile technology. This position is supported by a survey conducted by Oyelere et al (2016) in Nigeria on mobile device ownership among primary and secondary schools students. It was discovered that 54% of the respondents own mobile phones, 17% own smart phones while 10% of the respondents own tablets; 0% own a pocket PC while 1% own an e-Reader; 6% own MP3 players, and the remaining 12% own no mobile devices. This goes to show that among the study participants, 88% of primary and secondary school students in Nigeria own at least a mobile device of one form or another.

Possessing a mobile device is one thing, the use for which the mobile device is put to is another. Salim and Wangusi (2014) presented the possibility of using mobile devices to checkmate corruption in the Water Services sector of Kenya. Research conducted revealed that most Water Service Providers (WSPs) in Kenya are so dubious to the extent that they do not render to water consumers the desired services paid for. Among other integrity deficits, some WSPs are known for supplying unhygienic water to consumers, charging higher rates than the government approved rates, and zero supply for long periods. To solve this situation, Salim and Wangusi (2014) proposed a solution whereby mobile phones would be used to enable consumers provide feedback, escalate corrupt tendencies of WSPs and communicate their satisfaction or dissatisfaction through portals that are monitored by regulatory agencies. A total of 896 Kenya citizens were interviewed to find out from them their preferred method of forwarding complaints to government regarding WSPs. Among the participants, 51% opted for SMS (Short Message Service) platforms, 35% indicated preference for phone calls, while 6% chose social media as their preferred means to disseminate information on water services issues. Premised on this finding, Salim and Wangusi (2014) designed a framework that would employ use of mobile technology to ensure good governance, accountability and satisfaction within the water services sector in Kenya.

Mobile technology could also be harnessed in the area of electronic governance among developing countries. Mukonza (2013) emphasized this through a research conducted in Polokwane Municipality in South Africa. The research revealed that 78% of respondents interviewed had access to the Internet through their mobile devices in urban areas. This percentage is impressive especially coming from a developing country. The worrisome issue however arose when only 4% of the respondents indicated that they do make use of the Internet on their devices to access announcements from the government, make suggestions to government or participate in any form of governmental affairs. This is further compounded by the discovery that many municipalities in South Africa do not own a website in the first place. Even for those that own a website, their citizens are largely unaware of the existence of such. As a result, it is impossible for citizens to follow up with governmental policies and programs electronically. The research held that Polokwane Municipality in South Africa that was used as a case study has a good number of citizens with mobile devices that have access to the Internet. Therefore, it is needful for local governments to take advantage of the situation and facilitate public participation in government through mobile governance.

Oyelere et al (2016) proposed a platform for mobile learning (M-learning) in Nigeria. The research was premised on the high percentage of ownership of mobile devices among primary and secondary school students. When implemented, the students will be able to learn ICT subjects with their cell phones, tablets, and smart phones on the cloud. Teachers could post lessons and homework online for students while at the same time, interacting with students real-time. This no doubt, has the advantage of availing students the opportunity to learn at their convenience, including on the go, using their hand-held devices.

Insight on Terrorism

There is no universally acceptable definition of the term *terrorism*. Divergent views exist on the subject and as such, any definition given is strictly based on context. Whittaker (2004) views terrorism as an act of engaging in violent tendencies to cause coercion or intimidation to a government or the general citizenry. In another assertion, Gupta (2006) describes terrorism as a violent way of passing across a message by a terror group to their enemies for daring to ignore their demands. Dolnik (2007) on the other hand opines that terrorism is an action that employs threat or violence to achieve political gains, be it by a group or an individual. The definition proposed by Dolnik (2007) is adopted when referring to *terrorism* in this chapter.

In as much as the views about terrorism are divergent, they seem to converge at one thing, namely the use of violence. The overall intention of any terrorist group is to terrify the government, citizens or both in order to achieve their objectives. It is the view of Nance (2008) that some actions by individuals or group may indeed instill fear or terrify the populace but are actually not terrorism. These include incidents like vandalism, armed robbery or murder. Provided such actions are not specifically aimed at terrorizing citizens for the objective of causing a change in government policy, they do not fit the definition of terrorism.

Various methods are employed by terrorist groups to perpetrate violence. Dolnik (2007) listed these to include use of firearms, hostage taking, sabotage, bombings, and suicide bombings. Others include use of chemical, biological, radiological and nuclear agents. Nance (2008) on the other hand enumerates terrorist operations to include assassination, arson, skyjacking, bombing, and abduction.

On why some individuals engage in terrorism, Krueger (2007) at one extreme is of the opinion that marginalization from the economy as well as inability to access education make people feel resentful and consequently resort to terrorism. Nance (2008) at the other extreme holds that some groups engage in terrorism for sole reasons of gaining attention and drawing support for their platform, which may be politically or religiously inclined. Coll et al (2005) attributes the reason some individuals or group resort to acts of terrorism as simply an attempt to gain a distinct identity and for adventure. He pointed out an instance when an adherent of al-Qaeda once said he intended to move to Afghanistan to enroll in the group because of his conviction that it would be a worthwhile adventure. Irrespective of the fact that he was trained as a chef, he was convinced that he would be more fulfilled as a terrorist.

Prominent Terrorist Groups

As part of attempts to sustain the fight against terrorism, the United Nations (UN) through the UN Security Council, maintains a list of groups and entities (United Nations Security Council Subsidiary Organs, 2017) that have been proscribed as terrorists groups by the United Nations. This list, as at 9th December, 2017 is presented in Table 1 in the Appendix. Similarly, the United States through the Secretary of State occasionally designates prominent terrorist groups as Foreign Terrorist Organizations (FTOs) and have the list published (U.S. Department of State, n.d). An incomprehensive list of FTOs as at 3rd March, 2017 is presented in Table 2 in the Appendix.

It is clear from Table 1 and Table 2 that developing countries equally have their fair share of terrorism. It could be observed that a good number of terrorist organizations come from Africa and Asia where there are good numbers of developing nations.

Categories and Common Features of Terrorist Groups

Nance (2008) categorizes terrorist groups according to the geographic area of their operations. Membership of each of these categories is highly dynamic as a group could switch to any other category at any point in time.

- **Local Terrorists:** This category consists of terrorist organizations or individuals operating just within a village, town or city.
- **Regional Terrorists:** The operations of the terrorists cut across a number of cities, states or regions within the borders of a country. For example Ansaru, a breakaway faction of Boko Haram, operating within the North Eastern part of Nigeria (Zenn, 2013).
- **National Terrorists:** The operations of the terrorists encompass most of, if not all, the states or regions within the borders of a country.
- **Transnational Terrorists:** This group of terrorists carries out operations across one or more national boundaries. For example, Boko Haram carries out operations in Nigeria, Cameroon, and the Niger Republic. Another example is Al-Shabaab which operates across the borders of East African countries like Somalia and Kenya.
- **International Terrorists:** This includes those terrorist groups operating in several countries of the world. A prominent example is al-Qaeda.

Apart from the categorization by Nance (2008), Zalman (2017) advances another dimension to types of terrorism. While the former is premised on geographical location, the latter according to Zalman (2017) is based on the motive and means of attack adopted by terrorists.

- **State Terrorism:** This is carried out by a State on her citizens for purposes of achieving political goals (Zalman, 2017). The Nazi rule in Germany, as well as the sponsorship of Hizballah by Iran to actualize her foreign policy objectives have been identified by Zalman (2017) as examples of State terrorism. In same vein, the sponsorship of Nicaraguan Contras by the United States in the 1980s has been argued to be the international dimension to State terrorism (Zalman, 2017). In general, the purpose of this type of terrorism is to force citizens (Blakeley, 2012) into submitting to the dictates of elites.
- **Bioterrorism:** This refers to the premeditated release of harmful living organisms, such as viruses and bacteria, to harm humans, plants or animals with intent to advance a cause (Zalman, 2017). Once introduced into the environment, these biological agents cause fatal damage (Mahendra et al,

2017) that includes death of humans, food poisoning, destruction of plants and animals, and poisoning of oxygen.

- **Eco-Terrorism:** This form of terrorism, according to Zalman (2017), involves use of violence to achieve environmentalism. To facilitate this, extremists engage in sustained attacks on property (and lives in some cases) in order to sabotage industrial activities that cause damage to the environment (Cooke, 2013). Terrorists under this category usually feel the exploration and exploitation activities of companies harm the natural environment and therefore, must be compensated for, or discontinued.

- **Cyber-Terrorism:** This type of terrorism uses information technology to terrorize citizens for purposes of getting attention in a cause (Zalman, 2017). This is achieved, for instance, through abruptly shutting down network connections or computer servers for critical services. Other means might include hacking into public websites and control systems to disrupt or corrupt critical information (Bogdanoski, 2013).

- **Nuclear Terrorism:** Zalman (2017) defines this as the use of nuclear equipment to facilitate terror. This might be done through attack on facilities related to nuclear technology, design and development of nuclear weapons, or the use of radioactive substances to cause havoc and create panic in the society (O'Neill, 1997).

- **Narco-Terrorism:** This was coined in 1983 (Zalman, 2017) and refers to the use of violence by drug peddlers to intimidate and dissuade governments from stopping drug trafficking. Most recently, this form of terrorism is considered to mean the use of illegal drug business by terrorist organizations as a means of raising funds to finance other terror operations (Bjornehed, 2004).

Common Features of Terrorist Groups

As divergent as terrorist groups may appear, they nevertheless have some things in common. Nance (2008) presents eight common characteristics that are inherent in all terrorist organizations.

- **Violence-Prone:** All terrorist groups have a disposition to the use of violence or threat of violence to pass across their message. Different means of perpetrating violence are at their disposal, such as bombs, firearms, IEDs, etc.

- **Environment-Independent:** Terrorist groups have no specific kind of environment within which to operate. They could carry out attacks in churches, mosques, markets, schools and so on. In addition, terrorists operate both in urban or rural areas.

- **Secrecy:** Generally, terrorists operate secretly. Though in some few cases some terror groups may issue advance warnings of their planned attacks, the intention is simply to garner attention of the media and possibly inculcate fear into the populace.

- **Organized Structure:** Terrorist groups usually have an organized structure with a hierarchy that ranges from senior leadership to passive supporters. Boko Haram, for instance, has Abubakar Shekau as the supreme leader. Below him are commanders, field commanders, fighters, active supporters, and passive supporters.

- **Deliberate Action:** Terrorist actions are never random. Any act undertaken by terror groups is well planned before execution. Their attacks are well sequenced and coordinated.

- **Use of Automobiles:** Terrorist groups use means of mobility such as motorcycles and cars to get to areas of operation and back. It is very unlikely for terrorists to get to a target area by foot, unless that is the best method that could enable them get access to a gathering of people in order to execute an attack.

- **Proportionate Weaponry:** Terrorists carefully select the caliber of weapons to employ for any given operation based on need. If the purpose is to assassinate an unarmed individual, for instance, they make use of a small pistol. When a bomb is to be used, the kind of bomb selected for detonation is proportionate to the amount of havoc intended.

- **Media Attention:** Terrorist groups are constantly seeking attention of the media. They often use the media to inculcate fear into citizens and government and also as a channel to make known a cause.

Review of Existing Work on Anti-Terrorism Applications

Mobile devices have been used extensively in both developing and developed nations for communication purposes (such as emailing, text-chatting, sharing of pictures and videos, voice calls, etc), playing games, and several other uses (Mukherjee, 2015). In addition to these uses, many apps have been developed to enable mobile devices function as means to track suspected terrorists and threats. Several such apps are considered in this review.

- **TerrorView:** According to Mukherjee (2015), a company ConteGoView Inc., developed TerrorView, an app capable of synergizing with intelligence experts to gather and manipulate data from as many as 100,000 sources. Having analyzed the accumulated data, the app then alerts users of any impending terror, biological or cyber-attack within their neighborhood. This provides the user with necessary information needed to steer clear of potential danger zones.

- **FlexiSpy:** This software runs on cell phones and has the capacity to intercept an incoming or outgoing call for Android, iPhone or Blackberry (Mukherjee, 2015). FlexiSpy is able to track Global Positioning System (GPS) location which makes it possible to monitor the location of an individual. The details are compiled and presented as reports for further analysis, which could assist in counter-terrorism.
- **mSpy:** This application can run on almost all hand-held devices (Mukherjee, 2015). With mSpy, text messages on the phone of an individual can be tracked and read. Given this functionality, it is possible to uncover and escalate a plot to unleash terror attack.
- **Saip (Système d'alerte et d'information des populations):** This smartphone app was launched by the French government (Chrisafis, 2016). It is available in both English and French and has the ability to disseminate warnings to individuals; phones when shootings, bombings and other forms of attack occur around their environments. If an attack takes place near a user, the screen background turns red and displays "ALERT", in addition to a brief precautionary measure users must take to ensure their safety.
- **PowerSpy:** This technique is premised on a research finding that power consumption of a phone over time can reveal the user's location (Mukherjee, 2015). The technology is based on the reality that cellular transmissions of a smartphone consume more power as the distance from a cell mast increases, or when obstructed by things such as mountains or buildings. If the software is installed on a phone, it can locate the position of a user, real time, with very high accuracy.
- **LOCINT (Location Intelligence):** This is not actually a mobile application; however it operates in conjunction with mobile devices. If the software is installed on a system, anytime there is detection of a mobile device within a marked out territory, an alert message is sent automatically to a host system (Mukherjee, 2015). With this technology, cell phones can be tracked within a vicinity of 50 meters. Now, if a terrorist is carrying a mobile phone and their number is known, they could be tracked. It is also possible for authorities to rely on this technology to cut off communication channels among terrorists in the process of planning an attack.
- **Highster Mobile:** This software enables a cell phone to be secretly monitored. It spies on inbound and outbound text messages on the phone under scrutiny

and sends gathered information to an Online User Control Panel for prompt review (Mukherjee, 2015). It operates with GPS location tracking to monitor and update the location of a monitored phone within intervals of 10 seconds. With Highster Mobile, terror suspects can be tracked and apprehended provided their mobile numbers are known.

Curiously, all the reviewed mobile applications for counter-terrorism are largely centered on monitoring of terror suspects and tracking their movements. Attention is not given to a functionality that enables users to quickly alert other citizens to keep away from particular environments where a terror attack just occurred or is about to occur. There is no feature in any of the applications that contains images of high-profile terror suspects on the wanted list of security agents. There is equally no functionality that enables users to quickly message or call security agents in instances when a high-profile terror suspect is sighted within vicinity. These gaps need to be addressed.

ANALYSIS, DESIGN, AND IMPLEMENTATION OF *TERRORWATCH*

Analysis of Related Mobile Applications

The mobile applications earlier reviewed have good features, jointly, that are useful in counter-terrorism. Nevertheless, a number of loopholes have been identified among them which make a new application desirable. For instance, applications such as TerrorView, FlexiSpy, PowerSpy, LOCINT, and Highster Mobile presented by Mukherjee (2015) have the following shortcomings inherent in them.

- They are only concerned about tracking the movement, communication and location of terror suspects.
- It is reasonable to infer that they were implemented solely for the developed countries, using terror groups that likely have different ideologies and mode of operation from, for example, Boko Haram, Ansru, Ansar Dine, and Al-Shabaab, which operate in developing countries.
- None of these applications has functionality that a user can query to get guidance when in a confused situation that takes the semblance of terrorism.
- The apps do not have GUIs that display images of terrorists on wanted list, to enable users quickly make comparison and alert security agents if any of such terror suspects is sighted within the environment.

Another app named Saip, presented by Chrisafis (2016) has the capability to alert users and guide them on appropriate cautionary measures to take during a terror attack. However, the application is invoked only when there is a shooting or bombing within the vicinity - Saip is reactive and not proactive. Consider a scenario where a terrorist is sighted conveying IEDs, bombs, etc. Saip has no functionality that can give proper guidance to the user on what to do in such a situation. Given the various shortcomings identified in this analysis, it is imperative that a new app is needed with features that encompass the identified loopholes.

Analysis of the Proposed System

The functionalities that *TerrorWatch* must possess in order to outperform the existing applications are analyzed using Unified Modeling Language (UML). In an application development project, UML enables stakeholders to visualize, specify, document and construct artifacts of the system (Atsa'am, 2016). Several UML tools are at the disposal of developers for use in functional analysis. For purposes of this chapter, the UML use case and activity diagrams are used to analyze the functional requirements of *TerrorWatch*.

Analysis of TerrorWatch With Use Case Diagram

The use case diagrams give graphical descriptions of what functionalities a system has, which actors are involved in using those functionalities, and how those actors and functions interact (Atsa'am, 2016). A functionality of a system is called a *use case*. An *actor* could be a human person, organization or another system that has one or more roles to play in a given system. Four *actors* are identified for the *TerrorWatch* application: *User, Admin, Security Agent, GSM Service Provider. User* is any citizen that has the app installed on their mobile device. *Admin*, short for Administrator, is a user with special privileges on the application, such as the ability to update system settings. *Security Agent* refers to the Army, Police, Fire Service, or any government agency with a responsibility in counter-terrorism. The fourth actor, *GSM Service Provider (Telecommunication),* is a different system entirely; however some use cases of *TerrorWatch* must interface with it in order to function. To make calls or send messages with *TerrorWatch*, the services of a GSM provider must be invoked.

Seven use cases are identified in *TerrorWatch* as shown in Figure 1. The *Display Guide* launches the main menu of the application, while the *Select Guide* enables users to choose which menu item they desire. *Call/Message* use case consists of interfaces for users to report terror incidents to *Security Agents* or to caution other users to steer clear of certain zones. For this use case to function, a system actor

Figure 1. Use case diagram of TerrorWatch

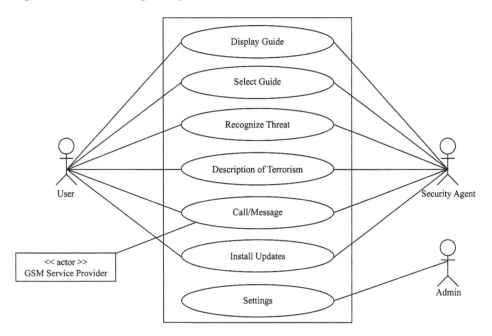

namely, *GSM Service Provider,* such as MTN, Globacom, Safaricom, Airtel, and Vodafone, must be involved. The *Recognize Threat* use case consists of pre-defined terror scenario that users can query to get clarification when they find themselves in situations that take semblance of imminent terror threat or attack. This use case also displays images of wanted terror suspects so that when users sight them within an environment, they do due diligence by way of taking proper caution not to be endangered, while at the same time alerting relevant security agents. The *Description of Terrorism* use case is necessary, especially in some developing countries where terrorism is relatively new. Terrorism-related terminologies like abduction, hostage-taking, hijack, bomb, IED, etc, are described and made easy to locate on *TerrorWatch* so users can quickly consult for clarification when the need arises. The *Install Updates* functionality enables users to update the *TerrorWatch* application when a new version, patch or fix is available. This is important because, for example, additional high profile terror suspects may be declared wanted, new terrorism-related terms and techniques may emerge with time, or higher versions of the application could come up with improved technology. The *Settings* use case is accessible to only the *Admin* for purposes of making changes to current system settings, making new versions of the application available for users, and updating system definitions.

Analysis of TerrorWatch With Activity Diagram

According to Miller (2013), UML activity diagrams focus on the flow of events that are needed to achieve some task with a system. An activity diagram is used in this section to show graphically the series of activities that take place when a user sights a wanted terror suspect, bomb, IED, etc, within the environment.

As depicted in Figure 2, when users encounter any form of terror threat within their environment, they quickly launch the mobile app on their phone and at the same time take safety precautions – generally referred to here as *take cover*. They then place a call or send a message containing the details of the threat to other users. If the recipient is the security center, security agents take measures to contain the situation and the process terminates. On the other hand, if the call or message is to civilian users, the users heed the warning and *take cover*, and the process terminates.

Design of the TerrorWatch Architecture

At this stage, the architectural design of *TerrorWatch* is presented. To achieve this, system requirements earlier specified at the analysis stage are taken into consideration. This is necessary in order to put forth a robust design that meets the objectives for which this app is intended. UML class and sequence diagrams are employed in the design of the application.

Design of TerrorWatch With Class Diagram

A class diagram shows the overview of the structure of a system in terms of its classes and the relationship between those classes (Atsa'am, 2016). Basically, *TerrorWatch*

Figure 2. Activity diagram of TerrorWatch when user sights a terror threat

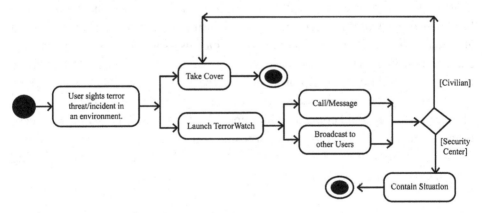

consists of five classes: *User, EscalateThreat, ThreatDetail, Call, and Message.* A class consists of three parts: class name at the top, class attributes in the middle, and the operations associated with the class at the bottom.

Three different types of relationships exist among the five classes of the app as depicted in Figure 3. An *association* relationship exists between the instances of *User* and *EscalateThreat* classes. The instance of *User* class must know about the instance of the *EscalateThreat* class in order to perform a task, and vice-versa. Clearly, this means there is dependency among the classes. The "1..*" at both ends of the association arrow is called *multiplicity*, and it means that one or many *Users* can perform one or many *EscalateThreat* tasks at a time.

A *generalization* relationship, also called inheritance, exists between the *Call* and the *Message* classes on the one hand and the *EscalateThreat* class on the other hand. The *EscalateThreat* class is a superclass in this case. The actual means by which *Threat* instances can be escalated is either through phone *Call* or *Message*, which are subclasses.

The third type of relationship depicted in Figure 3 is a *composition* relationship between the *EscalateThreat* and *ThreatDetail* classes. A *composition* relationship exists between two classes where one class is a "whole" class while the other is a "part" class. In this case, *ThreatDetail* is part of the *EscalateThreat* class, and if the latter is deleted, the former is automatically deleted.

Figure 3. Class diagram of TerrorWatch

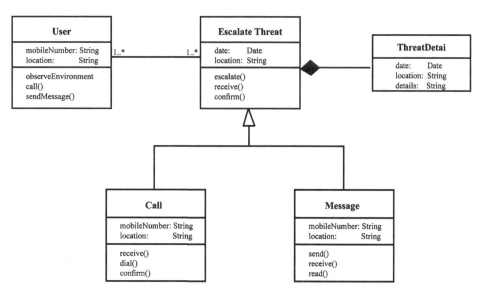

Design of TerrorWatch With Sequence Diagram

Sequence diagrams enable system designers to illustrate the interaction between users, interfaces, and objects that make up a system (Miller, 2013). With this UML tool, it is easy to show the order of sequence by which messages are passed between objects and entities of a system over time.

Basically, six objects participate in message passing in *TerrorWatch* as observed in Figure 4. The objects include: *User, App Interface, Call/Message, Security Center, Terrorism Description,* and *Terrorists Images.* Two different kinds of arrows are used in the diagram to represent particular form of communication between objects of the app. The full arrows indicate *synchronous* messages, while the dashed arrows are *reply* messages. A message is said to be *synchronous* if, upon sending the message, the sender object suspends execution while waiting for response from the receiver object. A *reply* message, as the name implies, is a feedback from an operation call.

The following sequence of events can be deduced from Figure 4.

- *User* encounters a terror threat or incident within an environment then quickly launches the application. The graphical user interface, *App Interface*, opens. *User* selects the *Call/Message* interface and dials the emergency number, or composes a text message, and sends to the emergency number. The *Security Center* receives the call or message and sends feedback to *User*.

Figure 4. Sequence diagram of TerrorWatch

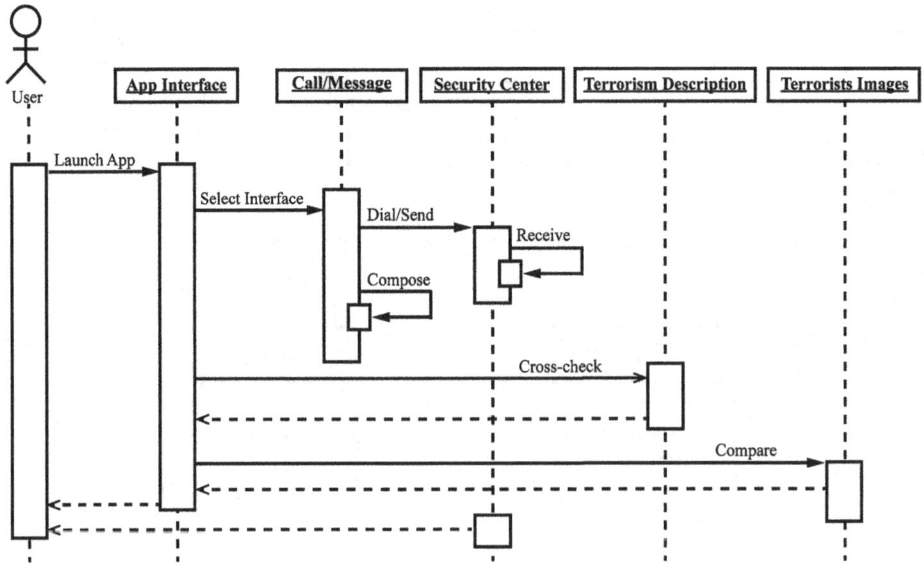

- *User* encounters a confused situation within the vicinity that seems to be a terror scenario. Among the app interfaces, *User* selects the *Terrorism Description* interface which has pre-defined terrorism terminologies and cases to cross-check against the situation at hand. If the prevailing situation fits the terrorism definition, the *App Interface* is useful next.
- *User* sights a wanted terror suspect within neighborhood. In order to be double sure, they quickly select the interface that has images of terrorists on the wanted list and compares against the person they have seen. If the comparison matches, the *App Interface* is useful next.

The architectural design is transformed into a working system in the next section, using appropriate programming tools.

Implementation

At this stage, the design carried out in the previous section is implemented and transformed into a prototype mobile application. The attributes and methods of each object are implemented and all objects are integrated such that they function as a single system. During this phase, the authors describe how the prototype application is built using object-oriented coding requirements, and also how testing is done to guarantee that it functions properly.

Development Environment

The programming methodology used in implementing *TerrorWatch* is the object-oriented paradigm (OOP). OOP is a programming style that allows a programmer to implement a program as a collection of cooperating objects (Dennis et al, 2006). A number of objects were identified and designed at the design stage. At this point, each of those objects is coded and then integrated with other objects to function as a whole system.

Testing and documentation are carried out hand-in-hand during implementation of the application. To complete program testing, the source codes are executed experimentally to make sure the desired result is achieved. To ensure the effectiveness of the program logic, the debugging feature available in the development tool is used to trace errors and fix them accordingly. Documentation has been done right from the analysis and design stage of the project by use of UML diagrams. At the implementation stage, comments are used to make short notes against source codes that may appear confusing to programmers at later times in the event of program maintenance.

TerrorWatch GUIs

Graphical User Interfaces consisting of icons, menus, buttons, texts, or other visual indicators, which enable users to interact with *TerrorWatch* via mobile devices, are implemented as shown in this section.

When a user launches the application, the main menu appears as shown in Figure 5. The main menu consists of five submenus: *Guide to Terrorism, Recognizing a Threat, Description of Terrorism, Call,* and *Message.*

Upon encountering a terror attack or threat by a user, the *Guide to Terrorism* submenu, shown in Figure 6, is available to provide guidance on the appropriate line of action to take.

Figure 7 shows the submenu a user can quickly consult to determine if an ongoing situation around the environment has any terrorism connotation.

If a user comes across a terror suspect within the neighborhood, the submenu shown in Figure 8 is quickly queried to compare the suspect against the images of terrorists populated in the application. If the comparison is in the affirmative, security agents are immediately notified. The user must, however, do so in a way that their safety is not compromised.

Figure 9 shows the interface where users can place calls to the security center or other users to escalate terror instances.

In order to send messages to the security center and to other users regarding terror incidents, the interface shown in Figure 10 suffices.

Figure 5. Main menu

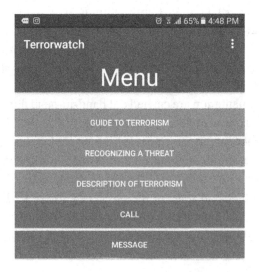

Figure 6. Guide to terrorism

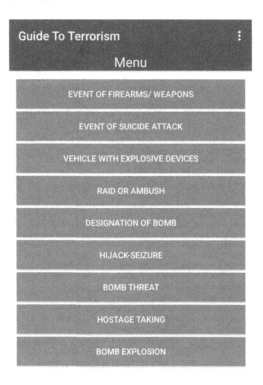

Deployment Platform

TerrorWatch is a mobile application developed to be compatible with all versions of the Android operating system. The hardware must be a tablet, smartphone, or phone of any brand, running the Android operating system. In addition, the mobile devices require a minimum of 512 MB memory of RAM. The fact that *TerrorWatch* requires GSM network to function, the mobile device must be provided with at least one functional Subscriber Identification Module (SIM) card to establish a network connection.

Deployment diagrams, according to Miller (2013), are used in modeling the physical deployment of a system to the production or test environment, detailing the hardware and software requirement. The UML deployment diagram in Figure 11 illustrates how *TerrorWatch* is to be deployed. The TerrorWatch application is sitting on the Android operating system, both of them located in a smartphone.

Figure 7. Recognizing a threat

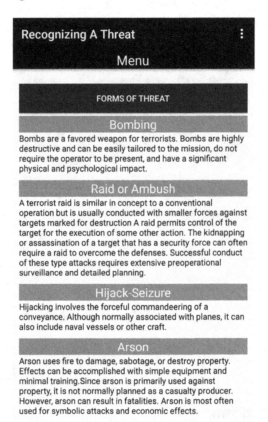

EVALUATION PLAN, EXPECTED SOLUTIONS, AND RECOMMENDATIONS

The next step in the development of the tool is to deploy and evaluate *TerrorWatch* in a real-life setting. Two locations have been identified for the deployment, and they are localities ravaged by Boko Haram in North-East Nigeria: Borno and Adamawa states.

To achieve the evaluation process, the application would be installed on the phones of select individuals, 50 in each state, for test-run. It is intended that during this procedure, the functionalities of *TerrorWatch* are utilized by 100 users, within three months, to determine how well this application meets its design goals. After the three-month duration, feedback will be collected from users to assist in corrective maintenance of the app.

Figure 8. Description of terrorism

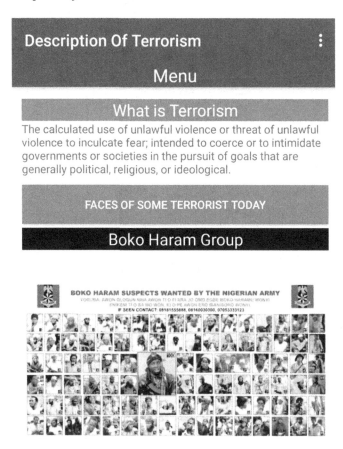

When deployed to live usage, it is envisaged that the awareness level of citizens of emerging nations on terrorism-related issues would tremendously improve. This is given the fact that *TerrorWatch* has special features dedicated specifically to enlighten users on what terrorism is all about. Users of the app will have various descriptions of terrorism on their fingertips to quickly consult when in confused situations. The application also has the capacity to curtail the menace of terrorism currently ravaging most developing nations. With the escalation feature, through message or call, potential terror attacks that would otherwise have occurred can be prevented. Even if they do occur, casualty figure would be reduced provided a user gave advance warning on sighting a threat, and other users or security agents in turn heed the warning. *TerrorWatch* is handy to give the needed guidance to citizens on what to do when they find themselves in the midst of a terror threat or attack.

Figure 9. Call interface

Figure 10. Message interface

Figure 11. Deployment diagram of TerrorWatch

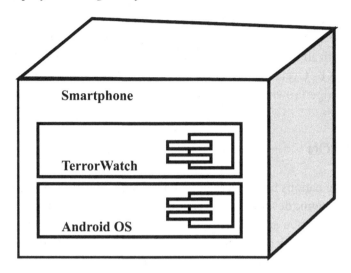

It is recommended that, as many as possible, citizens of developing nations have a fully developed version of the application installed on their mobile devices. Users should not compromise their personal safety when escalating issues with *TerrorWatch*. Cautionary measures must be taken by users attempting to report terror incidents with the application. Users should ensure that their safety is not sold out to any suspects that might be around them when escalating terror situations.

FUTURE RESEARCH DIRECTIONS

The application developed in this chapter is a prototype. Further work needs to be done in order to put forth an all-encompassing version of *TerrorWatch*. For instance, the menus, buttons and texts that users will make use of while navigating the application are implemented entirely in the English language. It turns out that English is not the only popular language among all the developing countries for which the application is intended. Other languages like French, Arabic, Swahili, Hausa, Yoruba, Ibo, Tiv, Zulu, Shona, and many others, are widely spoken across emerging nations. These have to be put into consideration in subsequent versions of the application.

Aside from the language barrier issue, *TerrorWatch* has no intelligence of its own. It has no capacity to detect bombs, IEDs and other threats automatically. The human user has to initiate an escalation cycle with the application, each time. This has to be equally researched, so that an intelligent version of the application could emerge. This is necessary due to the fact that an automated system is not erratic or prone to judgmental bias unlike humans.

It might be appropriate to consider developing a version of *TerrorWatch* that is compatible with all forms of mobile phones, not just smart phones. This is premised on the findings by Oyelere et al (2016) which revealed that only 17% of respondents in a survey in Nigeria owned smart phones; while majority owned non-smart phones.

CONCLUSION

Most emerging nations have had their own fair share of terrorism. There can be no reasonable economic development in environments that are insecure. Apart from the high rate of corruption and inadequate technology, many developing countries are backward economically as a result of insecurity associated with them. It is natural for investors to avoid doing business in countries where terrorism holds sway. The reassuring side is that emerging nations have embraced the use of mobile devices and associated technologies, which are what *TerrorWatch* needs to function. It is envisaged that with this application, terrorism will be reduced reasonably, thereby rendering the environments conducive for economic activities. Huge budgetary spending on security would equally be directed towards more productive sectors of the economy. All thanks to mobile technologies.

REFERENCES

Atsa'am, D. (2016). *A practical guide to using UML tools in system analysis and design*. Saarbrucken, Germany: Lambert Academic Publishing.

Bjornehed, E. (2004). Narco-Terrorism: The Merger of the war on drugs and the war on terror. *Global Crime*, 6(3&4), 305–324. doi:10.1080/17440570500273440

Blakeley, R. (2012). State violence as state terrorism. In M. Breen-Smyth (Ed.), *The Ashgate research companion to political violence* (pp. 63–78). Farnham, UK: Ashgate Publishing.

Bogdanoski, M. (2013). Cyber terrorism – global security threat: Contemporary macedonian defence. *International Scientific Defence, Security and Peace Journal*, *13*, 59-72.

Chrisafis, A. (2016). *France launches smartphone app to alert people to terror attacks*. Retrieved March 26, 2017, from https://www.theguardian.com/world/2016/jun/08/france-smartphone-app-alert-terror-attacks-saip

Coll, S., Fouda, Y., Stern, J., & Sageman, M. (2005). Who joins al Qaeda. In K. J. Greenberg (Ed.), *Al Qaeda now* (pp. 27–41). Cambridge, UK: Cambridge University Press. doi:10.1017/CBO9780511510489.005

Cooke, S. (2013). Animal rights and the environment. *Journal of Terrorism Research*, *4*(2), 26–36. doi:10.15664/jtr.532

Dennis, A., Wixom, B., & Roth, R. (2006). *Systems analysis and design* (3rd ed.). John Wiley & Sons, Inc.

Dolnik, A. (2007). *Understanding terrorist innovation technology, tactics and global trends*. New York, NY: Routledge. doi:10.4324/9780203088944

Gupta, D. K. (2006). *Who are the terrorists?* San Diego State University: Chelsea House Publishers.

Kim, T., & Phil, D. (2009). *The sources of insecurity in the third world: external or internal? Shinjuku-ku*. Tokyo: Waseda Institute for Advanced Study.

Krueger, A. B. (2007). *What makes a terrorist: economies and roots of terrorism*. Princeton, NJ: Princeton University Press.

Leadbeater, C. (2015). *New app could alert travellers about terror attacks*. Retrieved March 26, 2017, from http://www.telegraph.co.uk/travel/news/New-app-could-alert-travellers-about-terror-attacks/

Mahendra, P., Meron, T., Fikru, G., Hailegebrael, B., Vikram, G. & Venkataramana, K. (2017). An overview of biological weapons and bioterrorism. *American Journal of Biomedical Research, 5*(2), 24-34.

McGregor, A. (2013). Islamist groups mount joint offensive in Mali. *Terrorism Monitor, In-Depth Analysis of the War on Terror*, *XI*(1), 1–3.

Miller, R. (2003). *Practical UML: A hands-on introduction for developers*. Retrieved April 21, 2017, from http://edn.embarcadero.com/article/31863

Mukherjee, S. (2015). *Counter-terrorism in your pocket: Smartphone apps that make you feel safer (sometimes)*. Retrieved March 26, 2017, from http://www.dnaindia.com/scitech/report-now-apps-can-help-you-fight-terrorism-2149233

Mukonza, R. M. (2013). M-government in South Africa's local government: A missed opportunity to enhance public participation? In *Proceedings of the 7th International Conference on Theory and Practice of Electronic Governance* (vol. ICEGOV'13, pp. 374-375). New York: ACM. doi:10.1145/2591888.2591966

Nance, M. W. (2008). *Terrorist recognition handbook: a practitioner's manual for predicting and identifying terrorist activities* (2nd ed.). CRC Press. doi:10.1201/9781420071849

O'Neill, K. (1997). *The nuclear terrorist threat.* Retrieved December 8, 2017, from http://www.isis-online.org/publications/terrorism/threat.pdf

Oyelere, S. S., Suhonen, J., & Sutinen, E. (2016). M-learning: A new paradigm of learning ICT in Nigeria. *International Journal of Interactive Mobile Technologies, 10*(1), 35–44. doi:10.3991/ijim.v10i1.4872

Salim, A., & Wangusi, N. (2014). Mobile phone technology: An effective tool to fight corruption in Kenya. In *Proceedings of 15th Annual International Conference on Digital Government Research* (pp. 300-305). New York: ACM.

Udo, B. (2014). *Jonathan signs Nigeria's 2014 budget as defence gets 20 per cent.* Retrieved March 26, 2017, from http://www.premiumtimesng.com/business/161390-jonathan-signs-nigerias-2014-budget-defence-gets-20-per-cent.html

United Nations Security Council Subsidiary Organs. (2017). *Sanctions list materials.* Retrieved December 9, 2017, from https://scsanctions.un.org/fop/fop?xml=htdocs/resources/xml/en/consolidated.xml&xslt=htdocs/resources/xsl/en/al-qaida.xsl

U.S. Department of State. (n.d.). *Foreign terrorist organizations.* Retrieved March 3, 2017, from https://www.state.gov/j/ct/rls/other/des/123085.htm

Whittaker, J. D. (2004). *Terrorists and terrorism in the contemporary world.* London: Routledge.

Wosu, E., & Agwanwo, D. E. (2014). Boko haram insurgency and national security challenges in Nigeria: An analysis of a failed state. *Global Journal of Human-Social Science, 14*(7), 10–19.

Zalman, A. (2017). *Types of terrorism: A guide to different types of terrorism.* Retrieved December 6, 2017, from https://www.thoughtco.com/types-of-terrorism-3209376

Zenn, J. (2013). Ansaru: A profile of Nigeria's newest jihadist movement. *Terrorism Monitor, In-Depth Analysis of the War on Terror, 11*(1), 7–9.

KEY TERMS AND DEFINITIONS

Android: An operating system designed mainly to run touchscreen handheld devices such as smartphones and tablets.

Architecture: A model that conceptualizes the structure and behaviour of a system to enable an observer to have an overview of that system.

Graphical User Interface: A medium consisting of icons, menus, buttons, texts, or other visual indicators that enable users to interact with a system.

Mobile Application: Also referred to as app, is software developed to run on devices such as phones, smartphones, and tablets.

Mobile Device: Handheld computing device such as phone, smartphone, or tablet.

Terrorism: The use of violence or threat of violence against civilians or military to achieve political goals.

Unified Modeling Language: A graphical language that provides a way for conceptualizing the design of a system.

APPENDIX: LISTS OF TERRORIST ORGANIZATIONS

The lists of terrorist organizations maintained by the United Nations, on the one hand, and the United States, on the other hand, are presented. Comparison between these lists reveals that similarities exist among them.

Table 1. Terrorist entities and groups

Name	Region	Location of Operations
Abu Sayyaf Group	Asia	Philippines
Al-Itihaad Al-Islamiya / Aiai	Africa	Somalia
Egyptian Islamic Jihad	Africa	Egypt
Al-Qaida		
Al Rashid Trust	Asia	Pakistan
Armed Islamic Group	Africa	Algeria
Asbat Al-Ansar		Lebanon
Harakat Ul-Mujahidin / Hum	Asia	Pakistan
Islamic Army of Aden		Yemen
Islamic Movement of Uzbekistan		Uzbekistan
Libyan Islamic Fighting Group	Africa	Libyan Arab Jamahiriya
Makhtab Al-Khidamat	Asia	Pakistan
The Organization of Al-Qaida In The Islamic Maghreb	Africa	Algeria, Mali, Mauritania, Morocco, Niger, Tunisia
Wafa Humanitarian Organization	Asia, Middle East	Pakistan, Saudi Arabia Kuwait, United Arab Emirates
Jaish-I-Mohammed	Asia	Pakistan
Jam'yah Ta'awun Al-Islamia	Asia	Kandahar City, Afghanistan
Rabita Trust	Asia	Pakistan
Ummah Tameer E-Nau (UTN)	Asia	Afghanistan, Pakistan
Afghan Support Committee (ASC)	Asia	Pakistan, Afghanistan
Revival of Islamic Heritage Society	Asia	Pakistan, Afghanistan
Al-Haramain Islamic Foundation	Europe	Bosnia and Herzegovina
Al-Haramain Islamic Foundation (Somalia)	Africa	Somalia
Eastern Turkistan Islamic Movement (ETIM)	Asia	Turkistan
Moroccan Islamic Combatant Group	Asia, Europe	Afghanistan, United Kingdom, Morocco
Global Relief Foundation (GRF)	America	United States

continued on following page

Table 1. Continued

Name	Region	Location of Operations
Jemaah Islamiyah	Asia	Philippines, Malaysia, Indonesia
Benevolence International Foundation	Africa, Asia, America, Middle East	United States, Sudan, Bangladesh, Yemen, Gaza Strip
Lashkar Jhangvi (LJ)	Asia	Pakistan
Ansar Al-Islam	Middle East	Iraq
Islamic International Brigade (IIB)	Asia, Eurasia	Afghanistan Russia
Special Purpose Islamic Regiment (SPIR)	Eurasia	Russia
Djamat Houmat Daawa Salafia (DHDS)	Africa	Algeria
Al-Haramain Foundation	Asia	Indonesia, Pakistan
Al-Haramayn Foundation	Africa	Kenya, Tanzania
Al Furqan	Europe	Bosnia and Herzegovina
Taibah International-Bosnia Offices	Europe	Bosnia and Herzegovina
Al-Haramain & Al Masjed Al-Aqsa Charity Foundation	Europe	Bosnia and Herzegovina
Al-Haramain: Afghanistan Branch	Asia	Afghanistan
Al-Haramain: Albania Branch	Europe	Albania
Al-Haramain: Bangladesh Branch	Asia	Bangladesh
Al-Haramain: Ethiopia Branch	Africa	Ethiopia
Al-Haramain: The Netherlands Branch	Europe	Netherlands
Al-Qaida In Iraq	Middle East	Iraq, Syria
AL-Haramain Foundation (Union of the Comoros)	Africa	Comoros
Lashkar-E-Tayyiba	Asia	Pakistan
Islamic Jihad Group	Europe, Asia	Uzbekistan, Afghanistan, Germany, Pakistan
Al-Akhtar Trust International	Asia	Pakistan
Rajah solaiman movement	Asia	Philippines
Al-Qaida In The Arabian Peninsula (AQAP)	Middle East	Yemen, Saudi Arabia
Harakat-ul Jihad Islami	Asia	India, Pakistan, Afghanistan
Emarat Kavkaz	Euroasia, Europe, Asia	Russia, Sweden, Afghanistan, Pakistan
Tehrik-E Taliban Pakistan (TTP)	Asia	Pakistan, Afghanistan
Jemmah Anshorut Tauhid (JAT)	Asia	Indonesia
Mouvement Pour L'unification Et Le Jihad en Afrique De L'ouest (MUJAO)		

continued on following page

Table 1. Continued

Name	Region	Location of Operations
Ansar Eddine	Africa	Mali
Muhammad Jamal Network (MJN)	Africa	Egypt, Libya, Mali
Al-Nusrah Front for the People of the Levant	Middle East	Syrian Arab Republic, Iraq
Jama;atu Ahlis Sunna Lidda;awati Wal-Jihad (Boko Haram or Western Education Sinful)	Africa	Nigeria
Al Mouakaoune Biddam	Africa	Mali
Al Moulathamoun	Africa	Mali, Algeria, Niger
Al Mourabitoun	Africa	Mali
Ansarul Muslimina fi Biladis Sudan (Ansaru)	Africa	Nigeria
Ansar Al-Shari;a in Tunisia (AAS-T)	Africa	Tunisia
Abdallah Azzam Brigades (AAB)	Middle East	Lebanon, Syria, Arabian Peninsula
Ansar al Charia Derna	Africa	Libya, Tunisia
Ansar al Charia Benghazi	Africa	Libya, Tunisia
Hilal Ahmar Society Indonesia (HASI)	Asia	Indonesia
The Army of Emigrants and Supporters	Middle East	Syria
Harakat Sham al-Islam	Middle East	Syria
Mujahidin Indonesian Timur (MIT)	Asia	Indonesia
Jund Al-Khilafah in Algeria (JAK-A)	Africa	Algeria
Jamaat-Ul-Ahrar (JUA)	Asia	Afghanistan, Pakistan
Hanifa Money Exchange Office (BRANCH LOCATED IN Albu Kamal, Syrian Arab Republic)	Middle East	Syrian Arab Republic
Selselat Al-Thahab	Middle East	Iraq
Jaysh Khalid Ibn al Waleed	Middle East	Syria
Jund Al Aqsa	Middle East	Syrian Arab Republic

United Nations Security Council Subsidiary Organs, 2017.

Table 2. Foreign terrorist organizations

Name	Region	Location of Operations
Abu Nidal Organization (ANO)	Middle East	Palestinian Territories
Abu Sayyaf Group (ASG)	Asia	Philippines
Communist Party of the Philippines/New People's Army (CPP/NPA)	Asia	Philippines
Jemaah Islamiya organization (JI)	Asia	Indonesia
Lashkar i Jhangvi	Asia	Pakistan
Al-Qaeda Kurdish Battalions	Middle East	Iraq
Continuity Irish Republican Army (CIRA)	Europe	Ireland, United Kingdom
Islamic State of Iraq and the Levant (formerly Al-Qaeda in Iraq aka Tanzim Qa;idat al-Jihad fi Bilad al-Rafidayn (QJBR))	Worldwide	Iraq, Syria, Libya, Nigeria
Islamic Jihad Union (IJU)	Asia	Uzbekistan
Harkat-ul-Jihad al-Islami (HUJI-B)	Asia	Bangladesh
Al-Shabaab	Africa	Somalia
Jundallah (People's Resistance Movement of Iran, or PRMI) (Iran)	Asia	Iran
Army of Islam (Palestinian)	Middle East	Palestinian Territories
Indian Mujahideen (IM) (India)	Asia	India
Jamaah Ansharut Tauhid (JAT)	Asia	Indonesia
Abdullah Azzam Brigades	Middle East	Iraq
Haqqani network	Asia	Afghanistan
Ansar Dine	Africa	Mali
Boko Haram	Africa	Nigeria
Ansaru	Africa	Nigeria
al-Mulathamun Brigade	Africa	Algeria
Ansar al-Shari'a in Benghazi	Africa	Libya
Ansar al-Shari'a in Darnah	Africa	Libya
Ansar al-Shari'a in Tunisia	Africa	Tunisia
Ansar Bayt al-Maqdis	Africa, Middle East	Egypt
Al-Nusra Front	Middle East	Syria
Mujahideen Shura Council in the Environs of Jerusalem	Africa, Middle East	Egypt
Jaysh Rijal al-Tariq al Naqshabandi (JRTN)	Middle East	Iraq
ISIL Khorasan	Asia	Afghanistan
ISIL Libya	Africa	Libya
Al-Qa'ida in the Indian Subcontinent	Asia	India

U.S. Department of State, n.d.

Chapter 11

The Role of Trust in Mobile Technologies Usage in Emerging Countries

Alev Kocak Alan
Gebze Technical University, Turkey

ABSTRACT

M-commerce is supposed to be a critical issue for initiating consumer relationships due to the opportunities of m-technologies such as combining subsistent advantage of the wireless internet, mobility, and flexibility, especially in emerging nations. But consumers still perceive high risk about m-commerce. Thereby, they prefer to make online transaction with a company they trust. The purpose of the chapter is to underline the substantiality of trust in m-commerce. The chapter presents integrative review of the trust literature; a conceptual model is proposed and tested by SEM with 226 m shopping users. The relative effects of the main of antecedents (relative benefits of mobile shopping, propensity to trust, firm reputation) of trust as well as the extent which personal evaluations exert on trust in m-commerce and satisfaction of m-commerce is the key research question explored in the chapter. The result shows that a significant percentage of the variability in trust and satisfaction of m-commerce can be statistically explained.

INTRODUCTION

Nowadays, the exceeding growth in the use of mobile technologies has resulted in phenomenal growth of mobile commerce (also known as m-commerce) for satisfying consumers' needs and wants. With the increasing penetration of smart phones and tablets and development of the wireless technologies, mobile technologies proceed

DOI: 10.4018/978-1-5225-4029-8.ch011

to engrain into daily life of consumers and promote m-commerce. Stafford and Gillenson (2003, p.33) propose that m-commerce ensures "support and promotion for e-commerce transactions to roaming users". At any time, in any places and in any circumstances m-commerce provides convenience and flexibility of mobile technologies and offers easy computing and online transactions (Frauholz and Unnithan, 2004). Additionally, m-commerce can have both online transactional process by merchandising goods or services and online non-transactional process by searching goods or services (Stafford and Gillenson, 2003). Laukkanen and Lauronen (2005) suggest that the main benefits for consumer for preferring m-commerce are consumers' perceived safety, access regardless of location, convenience and usability. However, the adaptation of mobile devices is one of the significant influencer of increasing the usage rate of m-commerce (Mahatanankoon et al., 2006). Unfortunately, likewise the early times of the internet, m-commerce is run into same problems such as anxieties about security and privacy issues (Mahatanankoon et al., 2006). Furthermore, in a study about technology acceptance, Dahlberg, Mallat and Öörni (2003) interpret fears toward mobile devices as potential risk for losing privacy by reason of security system problems or software failures. Moreover some relatively negative technical aspects retain the usage of mobile devices for instance screen size, resolution, keypad, computational power, memory usage of mobile device, and battery life of mobile devices e.g. (La Polla et al., 2013). Moreover, studies about the adoption of new technology (Hsiao, 2003; Mcknight et al., 2011) show that type of fears toward technology as playing a challenging role for the new technology adoption of the individuals. Therefore, consumer' trust of mobile technology is a one of the main driver for mobile phone usage because users of mobile devices need to eliminate uncertainty and risk (Siau and Shen, 2003).

On the other hand, according to Pay-Pal Global Mobile Research (2014-2015) report, as m-commerce holds to outstrip general commerce in three countries in order of; China, UAE and Turkey which are presently possessing m-commerce. Moreover the amount of mobile devices usage in online shopping is %53 in Turkey. When the report is examined deeply, it has been shown that one of the main barriers that need to be addressed to help people shop mobile is their concern about trust about m-commerce. Frequently the reason behind postponing or refusing mobile purchase is the lack of trust (Lee and Turban, 2001). That's why in this chapter we would like to focus on one of the main drivers of mobile commerce namely, trust. Previous researches in this area are inadequate understanding of the antecedents and the outcomes of consumer' trust and understanding the role of consumer' trust in m-commerce in a holistic view. This chapter shows this need by reviewing the broad extant literature on consumer' trust with the aim of providing researchers different distances for finding out the benefits of consumer' trust in mobile technologies usage. In this way, making a comparison with past studies in the field, this chapter presents a more integrative review of the trust literature, its antecedents and consequences, its importance in m-commerce can be observed in terms of the explicit dimensions.

Additionally, in this study, as an emerging economies representative, Turkish consumers are selected. According to the five institutions, namely, Dow Jones, International Monetary Fund (IMF), Morgan Stanley Capital International (MSCI), Standard and Poor's (S&P) and Russell Investment, common emerging market list Turkey is an one of the emerging market in 2016. People in the emerging nations like Turkey are more intend to use m-commerce because of the fact of transportation problem. While education, healthcare and other quality of life components getting better, transportation problem in emerging markets are getting worse (Carvalho et al., 2010). Due to that fact; citizens of emerging markets spend a lot of time coming and going to work or school etc. in public transport (Patel, 2006). They lose too much time in the traffic and they use mobile devices for shopping to make this "waiting time" productively by shopping through their mobile devices. Moreover, due to the lack of the infrastructure for the widespread broadband connection, mobile phone operators provides easy and affordable way to access the web. That's why consumers feel more comfortable to buy mobile. In this context, while reviewing the broad extant literature on consumer' trust in mobile technologies usage, this chapter offers a conceptual model and examines consumer' trust in m-commerce in one of the emerging market setting using structural equation modeling (SEM) techniques. Also the present study provides several novel prescriptions for practicing trust in m-commerce.

BACKGROUND

The term of emerging market, is also used as a replacement for emerging economies or developing countries, signifies a business phenomenon which is totally described the countries that are reconstructing their economies in the line with market orientation and investigate in capacity of productivity (Khanna and Palepu, 2000). Emerging markets are steered away from their traditional economies, which are based on agriculture and exporting raw materials to industrializing and adopting mixed economy (Nee, 1992). Emerging markets have four main characteristics that differs them from other economies. They have a big power because of large population, resources and market (Dawar and Chattopadhyay, 2002). They play an important role in making major political, economic, and social decisions and have a big slice in the world's economic pie. They are transitive nations that they are adapting reforms in political, economic, domestically and technological (Khanna and Palepu, 2000). By undertaking open door policy, they catch sustainable economic growth that makes them world's fastest growing economies and they contributes growth of trade (Aivazian et al., 2003). Additionally, they have a critical volume for the usage of mobile technologies (Cruz et al., 2010). According to GSMA Accelerating affordable smartphone ownership in emerging markets 2016 report; in the year 2016 3.5 billion people are connecting to the internet, of which a huge amount estimated 2.5 billion are from emerging markets. In the report, it is mentioned that using mobile devices remains most popular market segment with the penetration rate of 49%. When the report is examined deeply, since 2008, the selling prices of cellphones have price reduction around 30 percent in Asia, 25 percent in Latin America and the Caribbean and 20 percent in Africa. With respect to the penetration of mobile phones in emerging markets, consumers are more comfortable while buying mobile. But regulatory guidelines regarding to privacy and consumer protection in the mobile shopping context, consumers still have problems about "trust" issue to shop mobile. However, building trust is still inconvenient and necessitate different method in mobile commerce environment (Shao and Li, 2009). In mobile commerce context, trust is operationalized as a combination of the credibility, competence, benevolence, and integrity of mobile vendors (Kim et al., 2012). Siau and Shen (2003) categorize trust in mobile context into two dimension: trust in mobile technology and trust in mobile vendors. Mobile vendors can build trust by combining these two dimensions.

The notion of trust has been studied in a huge range of disciplines from psychology to business to pharmacy in different perspectives but mainly it is conceptualized as "a state involving confident positive expectations about another's motives with respect to oneself in situations entailing risk" (Boon and Holmes, 1991). From past to present, online retailing give consequence to the construct of trust (Jarvenpaa et al., 1999; Liu et al., 2005; Ponte et al., 2015). Jarvenpaa et al. (1999) describe trust in online shopping as "a consumer's willingness to rely on the seller and take action in circumstances where such action makes the consumer vulnerable to the seller". Trust is a central perspective in plenty economic transactions and perceptual and is a subjective perception or a belief by ones regarding another (Pennington et al., 2003). According to Fishbein's (1979) reasoned action theory, consumer' trust promote the interaction between buyer and seller and can ensure consumers with high expectations of satisfying transactions. In the circumstances of uncertainty trust constitutes positive attitude interaction with online retailer, minimizing uncertainty and fulfilling anticipations for a satisfactory transaction, thereby positively affecting consumer response to transaction (Pavlou, 2003). In e-commerce there is a lot of evidence showing that trust is a main driver of consumers' intentness to make transaction with online retailers (Bhattac-herjee, 2002; Mukherjee et al., 2007; Ponte et al., 2015).

Consumer's trust can be considered a cognitive and affective state in its nature and the concept of trust has been studied in a large amount of empirical studies and focused on different aspects of trust in the specific content of m-commerce settings

(Grabner-Kräuter and Kaluscha, 2003; Fang et al., 2014). Empirical research shows that there are several factors can influence the complicated process of generating consumer' trust in m-commerce (McKnigh et al., 2002; Nica, 2015). The main antecedents of trust are perceived reputation of the online store (Jarvenpaa et al., 1999; Jarvenpaa et al., 2000; McKnight et al., 2002; Eastlick et al., 2006; Koufaris and Hampton-Sosa; 2004), perceived size of the online shopping (Jarvenpaa et al., 1999; Jarvenpaa et al., 2000; Chen and Barnes, 2007), relative benefits of m-commerce perceived ease of use of the web site (Gefen et al., 2003; Koufaris and Hampton-Sosa; 2004); visiting frequency of web site (Pavlou; 2003); disposition to trust (McKnight et al., 2002; Kim et al., 2009; Chen and Dibb, 2010). The main consequences of trust are behavioral intentions (McKnight et al., 2002), attitude (Pennington et al., 2003; Wu et al., 2010), willingness to transact (McKnight et al., 2002), satisfaction (Eastlick et al., 2006) etc. In line with past studies, in this chapter, Kim, Shin and Lee' (2009) trust review is developed and a broad consumer' trust review in m-commerce and e-commerce settings is done with the antecedents, consequences and their main contribution to the literature for m-commerce and e-commerce is given. M-commerce refers to using mobile devices like cell phones, tablets to sell and buy products and services while e-commerce refers to use computer to sell and products and services. This review is shown in Table 1.

MAIN FOCUS OF THE CHAPTER

Aim of the Study and the Proposed Model

Figure 1 presents the framework linking relative benefits of mobile shopping, propensity to trust, firm reputation to trust in mobile shopping and satisfaction of mobile shopping. The model rests upon the theory of reasoned action that concerns with individual motivational influencers as drivers of the likelihood of performing specific behaviors (Ajzen and Fishbein, 1975; Montano and Kasprzyk, 2015) and technology acceptance model which is reproduced from the theory of reasoned action by Davis (1989). Technology acceptance model suggest that relative benefits of technology like of perceived ease of use, perceived usefulness determines attitude toward accepting technology and individual's behavior tendency to use (Wu and Wang, 2005). The relative effects of the main of antecedents (relative benefits of mobile shopping, propensity to trust, firm reputation) of trust as well as the extension to which personal evaluations exert on trust in mobile shopping and satisfaction of mobile shopping is the key research question explored in the present study

Table 1. Summary of trust literature in e-commerce and m-commerce

Author	Context Research	Research	Trustor/Trustee	Antecedents of Trust	Consequences of Trust	Key Findings for Trust Literature
Ponte et al. (2015)	Online shopping for travel	Field survey	Consumer' trust in purchasing travel online	• Perceived privacy • Information quality • Security perception	• Perceived value • Purchase intention	• Perceived value and trust has effect on online purchase intention. • Perceived information quality and security perception are the key predictors of perceived trust.
Chiu et al. (2012)	Online retailing	Field survey	Consumer' trust in online retailing (for a specific popular website)	Satisfaction	Repeat purchase intention (habit as a moderator in the relationship)	The high level of habit decreases the effect of trust on re-purchase intention.
Chen and Dibb (2010)	Online retailing	Field survey	Consumer' trust in online retailing (computer as a product category)	• Website quality • Website usability • Website security and privacy concern • Website' download speed • Qualified information about product • Qualified information about service • Aesthetic view	Website approach intentions	In consumer online behavior, the web site interface is so important by effecting consumer' trust.
Kim et al. (2010)	Online retailing	Field survey	Consumer' trust on electronic commerce	• Navigation functionality • Security perception • Cost of transaction	Loyalty	The amount of perceived trust towards e-commerce website plays a role on purchase tourism products and services online.
Sparks and Browning (2010)	Online booking hotel	Experiential survey	Consumer' trust on hotel booking	• The aim of the judgments (core or interpersonal) • Overall cumulative valance set of judgments (positive or negative • Enframing of judgments (first thing come to mind: negative or positive) • Numerical rating generated by consumers	NA	Trust is key influencer on consumer evaluations in hotel context.
Wu et al. (2010)	Internet retailing	Experiential survey	Consumers' trust in online retailing	• Disposition to trust • Web site assurance • Interactivity	• Risk • Attitude toward online retailer • Attitude toward online retailer' website	Interactivity perception and web site assurance positively affect consumer' initial online trust.

continued on following page

Table 1. Continued

Author	Context Research	Research	Trustor/ Trustee	Antecedents of Trust	Consequences of Trust	Key Findings for Trust Literature
Kim et al. (2009)	M-Banking	Field survey	Consumer' trust in m-banking	• Relative benefits of mobile banking • Personal intention to trust • Structural assurances to banking in m-commerce • Firm reputation	Usage intention of mobile banking	• The relative benefits, intention to trust and structural guarantee had a important impact on trust in m-banking. • The trust perception and relative benefits of mobile banking are significant in generating personal propensity to make use of banking services.
Kim et al. (2009)	Online retailing	Field survey	Consumer' trust in online retailing	• E- retail quality • Fulfillment or • Reliability • Responsiveness • Design of website • Security or Privacy	E-loyalty	• Both consumer' online satisfaction and consumer' online trust influence development of online loyalty process. • Characteristics of e-retail quality have changing effects on online satisfaction and online trust. • Both consumer' online satisfaction and consumer' online trust are influenced online retailer fulfillment or reliability.
Beaudoin (2008)	Internet use	Field survey	The relationship between internet usage and interpersonal trust	• The internet usage tendency of social resources • The use of internet • Perceived information overload	NA	The motivations of social resource for internet usage on initial trust are mediated by both perceived information and use of internet.
Chang and Chen (2008)	Online retailing	Field survey	Consumer' trust in online retailing	• Website quality • Website brand	Purchase intention	Both the quality of web site and brand influence trust and perceived risk, and finally, purchase intention of consumer.
Martin et al. (2008)	Online shopping	Field survey	Consumer' trust in a Web site.	• Warranty • Security/ privacy policies • Service quality • Interacting experience • Design of web site	NA	Some of the features online companies like security, privacy policies, service quality, and warranty agreements have a direct impact on consumer' trust.
Chau et al. (2007)	Online retailing	Experiential survey	Consumer' trust in online retailing (mobile phone as a product category)	• Disposition to trust • Perceived ease of use • Structural assurance • Calculative based belief	NA	Customers' trust on e-vendor has significant effects on their decisions to exit from the vendor's website, and that salient trust antecedents vary in different stages of decision making process of the consumer.

continued on following page

Table 1. Continued

Author	Context Research	Research	Trustor/Trustee	Antecedents of Trust	Consequences of Trust	Key Findings for Trust Literature
Chen and Barnes (2007)	Online retailing	Field survey	Consumer initial trust in an e-bookshop website	• *Perceived technology* o Perceived usefulness o Ease of use o Perceived enjoyment • *Risks* o Security o Privacy • *Company competence* o Size o Reputation o Intentness to customize o Interaction with customers	Purchase intention	Varied levels of trust propensity moderate the relationships between consumers' online initial trust and their perceptions of a web site.
Mukherjee and Nath (2007)	Online retailing	Field survey	Consumer' trust in online retailing	• Shared values • Communication • Opportunistic behavior • Privacy • Security	• Commitment • Behavioral intentions	• The privacy and security characteristics of the website act as main antecedents of consumer' trust, and in sequence increase relationship commitment which is shown in the modified model of CTT. • Consumer' behavioral intentions are behaved as consequences of both consumer' trust and consumer commitment.
Eastlick et.al. (2006)	Online retailing	Field survey	Consumer' trust in online business to consumer retailing	Services e-retailer Reputation	Commitment toward a services e-retailer	The importance of consumer' trust and commitment in online services in B-to-C relationships is shown.
Bart et al. (2005)	Online retailing	Field survey	Consumer' trust in online retailing (in some different categories like automobile, finance, sports etc.)	• Privacy • Security • Navigation • Brand strength • Advice • Order fulfillment • Community features • Absence of errors	NA	Online trust is influenced by different drivers but brand strength and advice are the main drivers of online trust.
Liu et al. (2005)	Internet retailing	Experiential survey	Consumer' trust in book e-stores	• Privacy • Awareness of e-store • Access of e-store • E-store Choice • Security of e-store	Behavioral intention	Privacy has a main impact on initial trust.

continued on following page

241

Table 1. Continued

Author	Context Research	Research	Trustor/ Trustee	Antecedents of Trust	Consequences of Trust	Key Findings for Trust Literature
Gefen and Straub (2004)	Internet retailing	Simulation experiment	Consumer' trust in online products and online services	• Social presence • Familiarity • Propensity to trust	Purchase intentions	A explanatory models of e-trust is proposed by adding the social presence dimensions as an antecedent of trust.
Kim and Prabhakar (2004)	Internet Banking	Field survey	Consumers' initial trust in e-Channel as a banking medium	• Trustor's intention trust • WOM • Structural assurances	Adoption of Internet banking	• The disposition to trust, structural assurances, and relational content of WOM were important predictors of consumer' trust in the e-commerce. • For the adoption of internet usage, consumer trust is a necessary fact but Trust is necessary but not a adequate circumstance
Koufaris and Hampton-Sosa (2004)	Internet retailing	Experiential survey	Consumers' initial trust in online companies	• *Consumer' perceptions about the company* o Willingness to customize o Company reputation o Company size • *Perceptions about the web site* o Usefulness o Ease of use o Security control • *Trust propensity*	NA	Consumer' perception about the company and consumer' perception about the web site of the company has a significant impact on new consumers' initial trust.
Pavlou and Gefen (2004)	Online auction	Field survey	Buyer trust in the community of online auction sellers	• Institution-based trust • Feedback mechanism • Third-party escrow services • Credit card guarantees	• Perceived risk • Transaction intentions	The feedback mechanisms and the escrow services of third-party' effectiveness associated with consumer' trust in the intermediary increased consumer' trust in e-commerce.
Welzcuch and Lundgren (2004)	Internet retailing	Field survey	Consumer' trust in online retailers	• Institution based trust • Personality • Perception • Experience • Knowledge	NA	Perception based characteristics are the main determinants of consumer' trust in online retailers.
Gefen et al. (2003)	Internet retailing	Field survey	Consumer' trust in online vendors	• Calculative based trust • Institution based structural assurances • Institution based situational normality • Knowledge based familiarity • Perceived ease of use	• Perceived usefulness • Intended use	• The technological appearance of the online retailer site and consumer' trust has an impact on consumer' usage intention of e-commerce. • Consumer' trust is accreted by condition of the interaction.

continued on following page

Table 1. Continued

Author	Context Research	Research	Trustor/ Trustee	Antecedents of Trust	Consequences of Trust	Key Findings for Trust Literature
Pavlou (2003)	Internet retailing	Experiential survey	Consumer' trust in e-commerce	• Reputation • Satisfaction with past transactions • Frequency	• Perceived risk • Perceived usefulness • Perceived ease of use • Intention to transact	• Trust and perceived risk are acted direct antecedents of tendency to transaction. • Trust is also shown as an indirect antecedent of tendency to transaction through perceived risk, usefulness, and ease of use.
Pennington et al. (2003–4)	Internet retailing	Experiential survey	Consumers' perceived trust in vendors	• System trust • Perceived vendor reputation	• Attitude toward vendor • Purchase intent	• Trust mechanism and vendor guarantee have a direct impact on system trust. • System trust plays a significant role in the nomological network by directly impressing trust in online vendors and indirectly impressing attitudes and tendency to purchase in e-commerce.
Suh and Han (2003)	Internet Banking	Field survey	Consumer' trust in e-commerce	• Security control • Authentication • Nonrepudiation • Confidentiality • Privacy protection • Data integrity	• Attitude toward using • Behavioral intention to use	Trust is the mediating the relationship between consumer perception of strength for non-repudiation, online retailer' privacy concerns, data integrity and e-commerce admission.
Ba and Pavlou (2002)	Online auction	Experiential survey	Buyer trust in e-sellers	Feedback profile (online feedback mechanisms)	Price premiums	• From the consumers' point view of initial trust in online transaction is significant. • For generating price premiums, online firms develop trust in sellers' credibility.
Bhattac-herjee (2002)	E-commerce (retail, bank)	Field survey	Individual trust in online firms	Familiarity	Willingness to transact	An instrument for measuring individual trust in online firms is developed and validated.
McKnight et al. (2002)	Internet retailing	Experiential survey	Consumer' trust in web vendors	• *Disposition to trust* • *Institution based trust* o structural assurance o situational normality • *Perceived site quality*	• *Trusting intentions / willingness to depend* o Subjective probability of depending	Trust is examined as a multidimensional construct and a validated measure is developed for trust.
McKnight et al. (2002)	Legal advice web site	Experiential survey	Consumer' trust in web vendors	• Perceived vendor reputation • Perceived site quality • Structural assurance of the Web	• *Behavioral intentions* o tendency to share o personal information with web vendor o tendency to shop from a web-site	The results provide strong support for the proposed TBM.

243

Figure 1. Conceptual framework

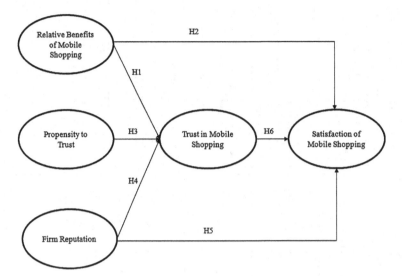

Hypotheses

Roger's (1995) theory of innovation assumes that innovative technology's characteristics impress the level of adoption and diffusion of the new technology. The innovation underlying m-shopping gives its adopters value in the way of ease of use, feedback mechanism, efficiency, flexibility, escrow services of third-party', credit card guarantees or convenience (Pavlou and Gefen, 2004). The main aim of m-shopping is to make the trading in a convenience way, perform electronic transaction and deliver value to the consumer regardless of his/her location when he/she is in the range of connection (Barnes, 2002). Comparing with the traditional shopping, m-shopping provides its adaptors some advantages, such as, consumer do not need to go to the shopping malls and they even do not need to take into consideration shop' operating hours. Relative benefits includes the individual's perception of m-shopping serve them some benefits like the ability to access any information about goods, brands or services at any time, in any places and in any circumstances and provides easy store access (Lu and Yu-Jen Su, 2009).

Kim et al. (2009) find that relative benefits increase the level of consumer' trust and attitudes. Likewise, Chau et al. (2007) and Mukherjee and Nath (2007) suggest the same positive relationship. Moreover in the technology acceptance model (TAM) Davis et al. (1989) mention that individual intend to satisfy or not satisfy an technological development to the extent he/she believe that it will support them implement his/her job performance in advance. Based on past researches, the following hypotheses are proposed;

H1: Relative benefits of mobile shopping are positively related to consumer' trust in mobile shopping.

H2: Relative benefits of mobile shopping are positively related to consumer satisfaction in mobile shopping.

Hofstede's theory of cultural values assumes that traits like individual propensity to trust is attached with individual's cultural background, personality and progressive experience (Hofstede, 2003). Lee and Turban (2001) suggest that propensity to trust is a personality characteristic and play a significant role to form trust. Mayer, Davis, and Schoorman (1995) also find that relationship and propose that the higher the level of consumer' trust propensity, the higher the affect of generating trust. Koufaris and Hampton-Sosa (2004) show that propensity to trust is positively related to consumer' trust. McKnight et al.' (2002) study on online retailer store imply that intention to trust play an important role on forming consumer' trust. Based on past researches, the following hypothesis is proposed;

H3: Propensity to trust is positively related to consumer' trust in mobile shopping.

Doney and Cannon (1997) define firm reputation as the consumer' belief that the firm is honest, fair and concerned about its consumers. A good firm reputation can be gained not only being honest or fair but also doing right things (Drumwright, 1994). Bensebaa (2004) emphasizes that firm reputation is conceived as an important equity for an e-commerce firms because of the subsistent suspense associated with online trading. If the consumer' consideration about the firm has a good reputation, this will be a signal of quality and help decision making process (De Ruyter et al., 2001). Jin, Yong and Kim (2008) suggest that firm reputation is consisting of consumer's past good online retailer experiences and in the end this experience shapes halo effect. Eventually, consumer is more in tendency of evaluating positively well-known retailer comparing with relatively unknown retailer. E-retailer's reputation has been offered as one of the key antecedent that forms consumer' trust (Eastlick et al., 2006). Johnson and Grayson (2005) assume that consumer perceptions of firm reputation are adequately included trust. Consumer assessment of the firm reputation will positively affect his/ her assessment of the trustworthiness of a retailer (Doney and Cannon, 1997).

This chapter conceptualizes the construct of e-satisfaction as general level of e-satisfaction upon the past experiences with the e-retailer (Gabarino and Johnson, 1999). Likewise firm reputation and consumer' trust relation, retailing literature affirms that e- retailer's good reputation ensures the same halo effect to cause the high level of consumer satisfaction (Jin et al., 2008). Pavlou (2003) shows that good reputation of firm builds consumer satisfaction. In another saying, regardless from firm performance, make e-shopping at a reputable e-retailer can be concluded in e-satisfaction. Therefore the following hypotheses are proposed;

H4: Firm reputation is positively related to consumer' trust in mobile shopping.
H5: Firm reputation is positively related to consumer satisfaction in mobile shopping.

As mentioned before, consumer' trust is an important antecedent of forming long term relationship between retailer and consumer (Verhoef et al., 2002). In any type of consumer and retailer relationship, consumers' trust assessment before any type of transaction is shown to have a significant direct effect on consumer's satisfaction (Singh and Sirdeshmukh, 2000). This relationship is proved in e-retailing studies where consumer' trust plays as a critical role for starting specific exchange episode (Ghane et al., (2011); Kim and Swinney, 2009). In the previous studies, consumer' trust is shown empirically as a key driver of consumer satisfaction in e-commerce (Jin and Park, (2006); Kim and Swinney, 2009). In line with the past studies, following hypothesis is proposed

H6: Consumer' trust in mobile shopping is positively related to consumer satisfaction in mobile shopping.

Sample and Data Collection

A mobile device based online questionnaire was conducted and e-mails providing information about the study were sent to registered survey. Thus, respondents who had shopping experiences in mobile context were included in the sample. The respondents were asked to participate the study if they had used their mobile devices before when they made online shopping like buying e-book, foods, booking hotel or ticket, banking, money transactions etc. A sum of 226 Turkish consumers who satisfied the sampling conditions agreed to participate in the study.

During the sampling process, non-probability convenience sampling technique was used (Krathwohl, 1997). When the population size is too large, this sampling approach is the most commonly used technique in consumer behavior and marketing research since testing the entire population or using an independent random sampling that perfectly represents the entire population.

Before data collecting, a pilot test with 20 consumers was applied to ratify the psychometric characteristics of the scales. Based on feedback from the pilot test some modifications were done and the final questionnaire comprised 15 questions. The participants were asked the survey thinking about their last mobile shopping experience. Three weeks after data collection, with a response rate of nearly 70%, 226 surveys were collected. Sample's demographic characteristics are shown in Table 2.

Table 2. Demographic characteristics of the sample (n:226)

Characteristics		N	%
Gender	Male	100	44,2%
	Female	126	55,8%
Age	Less than 20	5	25,5%
	20-30	145	47,7%
	30-40	60	14,9%
	40-50	16	7,5%
Educational level	~College	105	49,4%
	University	121	45,0%
Mobile shopping frequency	Once a year	10	32,4%
	3-4 times a year	25	23,0%
	Once a month	155	44,6%
	3-4 times a month	36	
Monthly income	Less than 500 €	4	4,8%
	500-1500 €	79	51,4%
	1500-2500 €	89	23,4%
	2500-3500 €	42	10,6%
	More than 3500 €	12	9,8%

Measures

For testing the hypotheses, multi-item scales were adapted from past studies to measure the all constructs. The survey was natively designed in English and then translated into Turkish by two researchers who are proficient in both Turkish and English and then retranslated into English by a third researcher using the parallel translation method. The three bilingual translators then jointly ensured that all expressions and wording were properly stated in both versions. Also, question items were evaluated by two faculty members in the marketing to improve content and face validity. According to the feedback from these faculty members, the question items were refined to clarify their meaning.

To make the measurement participants responded to all of the survey items using a 5-point Likert scale (from 1 = "Strongly disagree" to 5 = "Strongly agree").The relative benefits of mobile shopping, firm reputation and propensity to trust scales proposed by Kim et al. (2009) were used. Satisfaction from Oliver (1980) and trust from the suggestion of Liu et al. (2005) were adapted. The measurement items are displayed in Table 2.

Measure Assessments

In accordance with Anderson and Gerbing's (1988) two-step approach, first confirmatory factor analysis (CFA) is conducted to test relative benefits, propensity to trust, firm reputation, trust in mobile shopping and consumer satisfaction of mobile shopping using the maximum likelihood estimation technique. Table 3 also shows all factor loadings for each construct and reliability estimates for them. Sight that composite reliability (CR) scores range from 0.73 to 0.95, and the Cronbach's alpha estimates line up from 0.71 to 0.91, these estimates indicate that all measures are reliable (Fornell and Larcker, 1981; Nunnally, 1978).

Additionally, for the signal of convergent validity, all factor loadings are large and significant. Discriminant validities of the measures are evaluated by regarding average variance extracted (AVE), AVE loadings line up from 0.59 to 0.87 (Fornell and Larcker, 1981). Moreover the measurement model fits good to the observed data except χ^2 and root mean squares error approximation (χ^2: 352.10; χ^2/df: 4.63; (RMSEA): 0.08; (CFI): 0.93; (IFI): 0.93). The reason for that is their sensitivity to sample size (Fan et al., 1999).

Hypotheses Testing

Structural equation modeling (SEM) technique was performed with the software of AMOS 16 to test the above hypotheses. All of the descriptive statistics of and inter-correlation coefficients across the constructs used in the proposed model are shown in the Table 4. An evaluation of the bi-variate correlations predicates that all of the correlations are found both significant and in the line with expected direction.

Figure 2 shows Structural equation model with parameter estimated path coefficients for the hypothesized effects. The model fits the observed data very well (χ^2:437,37; χ^2/df:5.60; CFI:0.91; IFI:0.91; NFI:0.90; RMSEA:0.08). Additionally, five of the six hypothesized effects are supported, and the model clarifies a significant percentage of the variability in trust in mobile shopping (93 percent) and satisfaction of mobile shopping (79 percent) both statistically and substantively.

Concerning the hypothesized effects, H1 hypothesizes a positive effect of relative benefits on consumer' trust, and this hypothesis is supported by the statistical tests (β:0.20; t:2.88; p<0.01). This is strong evidence for mobile shopping is perceived by consumer more convenient, effective and efficient than Internet or off-line shopping and these types of relative benefits enhance consumer' trust. Moreover location free service of mobile shopping is admitted by consumers to motivate their trust. H2 offers relative benefits about mobile shopping is positively related with consumer satisfaction is supported (β:0.40; t:3.67; p<0.001). H3 hypothesizes a positive effect of propensity of trust on consumer' trust is supported by the

Table 3. Factor loadings and reliability scores

Construct	Standardized Loadings	Cronbach's Alpha	AVE	CR
Relative benefits (adapted Kim et al., 2009)		.81	.69	.90
Mobile shopping (m-shopping) has more advantages than Internet or offline shopping because services are not limited by location.	.87**			
M-shopping is more convenient than Internet or offline shopping.	.88**			
M-shopping is more efficient than Internet or offline shopping.	.84**			
M-shopping is more effective than Internet or offline shopping.	.71**			
Propensity to trust (adapted Kim et al., 2009)		.71	.59	.73
I am cautious in using new technologies to do my work.	.96**			
In a new business relationship, I have to be careful until I see the evidence of a firm's trustworthiness.	.51**			
Firm reputation (adapted Kim et al., 2009)		.90	.85	.94
The online shopping site has a good reputation.	.95 **			
The online shopping site is recognized widely.	.90**			
The online shopping site offers good services	.91**			
Trust (adapted from Liu et al., 2005)		.88	.80	.92
The policy of m-shopping stores on how it would use any personal information about me makes me feel that the shopping store is trustworthy.	.90**			
The privacy policy of m-shopping stores on the notices of personal information collection makes me feel that the shopping store is trustworthy.	.89**			
The security policy of m-shopping stores makes me feel that the shopping store is trustworthy.	.89**			
Satisfaction (adapted from Oliver, 1980)		.91	.87	.95
My choice to continue doing m-shopping is wise.	.95**			
I am satisfied with my decision to continue doing m-shopping.	.94**			
I think I did the right thing by deciding to continue doing m-shopping.	.91**			

Note: CCR: composite construct reliability. χ^2:352.10 (df:76), p<0.001; χ^2/df:4.63; Root mean squares error approximation (RMSEA): 0.08; comparative fit index (CFI):0.93; normed of fit index (NFI):0.91, Tucker Lewis index (TLI):0.90 and incremental fit index (IFI):0,93, **p<0.001.

Table 4. Descriptive statistics and correlations estimates

	Mean	Std Deviation	1	2	3	4	5
1- Relative benefits	3.98	0.55	1.00				
2- Propensity to trust	3.24	0.34	.45(**)				
3- Firm reputation	3.18	0.58	.48(**)	.44 (**)			
4- Trust	3.47	0.41	.42(**)	.41(**)	.38(**)		
5- Satisfaction	4.16	0.53	.60(**)	.50(**)	.51(**)	.45(**)	1.00

Note: **Correlation is significant at p < 0.001(2-tailed).

Figure 2. Proposed model with estimated path coefficients

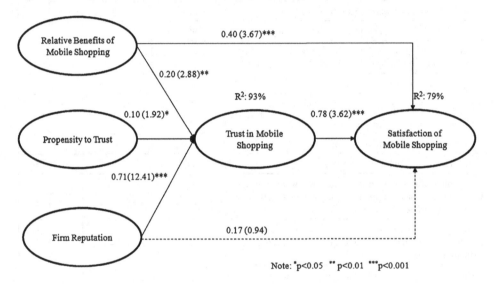

statistical tests (β:0.10; t:1.92; p<0.05). This is a proof of whenever consumer sees an evidence of a firm's trustworthiness in a new business relationship, consumer' trust can be developed. The positive relation between firm reputation and consumer' trust (H4) is supported (β: 0.71; t:12.41; p<0.001). If the mobile shopping site has a good reputation, is recognized widely and offers good services, consumer will trust this mobile shopping site. H5 assumes that mobile shopping site reputation exerts consumer satisfaction is not supported by the statistical tests. It can be due to fact that the reputation of firm is not enough to make a consumer satisfied. In fact, especially in online shopping, consumer is seeking for beneficial things such as good consumer service, fast delivery time, accurate good or service etc. (Park and Kim, 2003). H6 hypothesizes a positive effect of consumer' trust on consumer satisfaction is supported (β:0.78; t:3.62; p<0.001). In Table 5 all of the structural parameter estimates are shown.

SOLUTIONS AND RECOMMENDATIONS

Economies of developing countries are important issue for worldwide because they contribute upgrowth in the global economy. Comparing the developing countries with the developed countries' penetration rate of usage of mobile devices; it occurs that developing countries are well ahead than developed countries. Both mobile consumers, retailing practitioners, and retailing academicians have noticed that the growth of the mobile commerce is a critical issue for emerging nations. From consumer side, with the development of mobile devices and modern wireless communication technologies, m-commerce is an effective and efficient way for computing and online transactions. From retailing practitioner's side, m-commerce provides them to create a new marketing channel, leverages the traditional retailer sales and also supports to form good relationship with consumers. From retailing academician's side, m-commerce is a new research area that offers additional insights about the consumer choice. This chapter makes a contribution to this line by focusing on the consumer' trust mechanism in m-commerce and explores the importance of using m-commerce in the emerging nations. The proposed research model achieves this challenge by clarifying a significant percentage of the variability in trust in mobile shopping (93 percent) and satisfaction of mobile shopping (79 percent) both statistically and substantively with the 226 mobile shopping users. The results are a good evidence to reveal that consumer trust in mobile shopping is a critical driver for increasing consumer satisfaction in emerging nations.

Table 5. Structural parameter estimates

Hypothesized Path	Standardized Estimates	t-Value	Results
H1: Relative benefits → Consumer' trust	.20	2.88**	Accepted
H2: Relative benefits → Satisfaction	.40	3.67***	Accepted
H3: Propensity to trust → Consumer' trust	.10	1.92*	Accepted
H4: Firm reputation → Consumer' trust	.71	2.41***	Accepted
H5: Firm reputation → Satisfaction	-.17	-.94	Not Accepted
H6: Consumer' trust → Satisfaction	.78	3.62***	Accepted

Note: *p<0.05; ** p<0.01; ***p<0.001

Mainly this study has some rewarding contributions to the e-retailing literature. First it offers a more integrative and comprehensive review of the trust literature with the context, trust' antecedents and consequences and key findings of the studies for trust literature. Additionally, the determination of the methodologies that used in the past researches is given. The main obvious value of this trust literature review is showing academicians what is already researched about consumer' trust and what is the extensive knowledge about consumer' trust in online settings. Moreover, this review identifies the experts on consumer' trust and key research questions about consumer' trust in m-commerce that need farther researches. This review will be a beneficial guide for the academicians to see the big picture of the consumer' trust in m-commerce settings.

Second, proposed hypothesis is an evidence for in emerging nations, relative benefits of mobile shopping is a powerful issue by forming consumer' trust and consumer satisfaction. As growing the mobile technologies, everyday billions of people get online with the mobile devices that cause gaining a new potential consumer for firms. When the firms impress and satisfy each consumer and show them relative benefits of mobile shopping in terms of ease of use, perceived usefulness, perceived enjoyment of online technology, perceived enjoyment of online technology, perceived information overload etc., they gain new consumer. In fact, the main relative benefit of m-commerce is providing easy access to the stores. In other words, instead of driving, walking, taking public transportation to the shopping area, losing time while walking around the stores and waiting long lines for payment; consumer can only click their mobile device for shopping. Nothing is wrong to have the shopping experience of going to the shopping area, but in emerging nations like Turkey, people lose too much time in the traffic and shopping areas are so far and wide located so it is hard to find enough time to visit brick and mortar shops. So it can be recommended to m-commerce companies to underline and promote the importance of relative benefits of online shopping and use this tool for generating consumer' trust and satisfaction.

Third, the chapter further confirms that reputation of mobile shopping firm is an outstanding phenomenon for building consumer' trust. Consumer is more tend to perceive high risk level when involving online shopping then traditional shopping in the way of payment issues, delivery terms and personal information disclosure, etc., and may only prefer to make transaction with the e-retailer that he/she can trust. If the company has good reputation in consumer's perception, consumer is more disposed to do online transaction. So creating a powerful, reliable, good company reputation is a critical strategic tool for companies for sustaining long term relationship with the consumers. With the m-commerce, companies can touch billions of consumers in a month and each of them can be a new consumer. If the company manages to impress new consumer, he/she can likely encourage his/her friend to make shopping from that m-commerce company. It would be a good advantage for companies to attract new consumer. Also it is a good way for adding value to the firm's reputation.

Finally, taking these findings together, this chapter tries to underline the importance of consumer' trust in m-commerce and reveals rewarding effects of consumer' trust mechanism in m-commerce and evaluates antecedents and outcomes of this complex phenomenon.

FUTURE RESEARCH DIRECTIONS

This chapter focuses on antecedent and consequences of consumer' trust to generate long term relationship with consumers in m-shopping in the emerging nations in a holistic view. Future researches can examine individual trust in specific sectors such as mobile banking, mobile apps usage for playing games, mobile booking, mobile chatting, mobile social networks usage, mobile gambling, mobile brokerage etc.

This chapter provides evidence that in emerging nations, relative benefits of mobile shopping, consumer's propensity to trust and firm reputation are important antecedents of consumer' trust. Future researches can also focus on service quality of web site, design of web site, word-of-mouth referrals and consumer past experience about the web site and their effect on forming consumer' trust.

Moreover, this chapter only set sight on consumer' trust in emerging nations. Future researches may investigate consumer' trust both in emerging and developed nations and compare the differences of trust drivers between countries.

CONCLUSION

While attempting to explain the critical phenomenon of consumer' trust in m-commerce and to elucidate how consumers act different to m-commerce companies when they have an enough level of trust and elucidate a number of important issues in emerging nation's context, this chapter created more research topics. This type of outcomes is especially sighted when a complex area of investigation that has capacity of revealing substantial incoming information. Broadly, the subject of consumer' trust in m-commerce will be examined in great detail, and future research in this topic would make remarkable contribution to the field of e-retailing.

REFERENCES

Aivazian, V., Booth, L., & Cleary, S. (2003). Do emerging market firms follow different dividend policies from US firms? *Journal of Financial Research, 26*(3), 371–387. doi:10.1111/1475-6803.00064

Ajzen, I., & Fishbein, M. (1975). *Belief, attitude, intention and behavior: An introduction to theory and research.* Academic Press.

Ba, S., & Pavlou, P. A. (2002). Evidence of the effect of trust building technology in electronic markets: Price premiums and buyer behavior. *Management Information Systems Quarterly, 26*(3), 243–268. doi:10.2307/4132332

Barnes, S. J. (2002). The mobile commerce value chain: Analysis and future developments. *International Journal of Information Management, 22*(2), 91–108. doi:10.1016/S0268-4012(01)00047-0

Bart, Y., Shankar, V., Suştan, F., & Urban, G. L. (2005). Are the drivers and role of online trust the same for all web sites and consumers? A large-scale exploratory emprical study. *Journal of Marketing, 69*(4), 133–152. doi:10.1509/jmkg.2005.69.4.133

Beaudoin, C. E. (2008). Explaining the relationship between internet use and interpersonal trust: Taking into account motivation and information overload. *Journal of Computer-Mediated Communication, 13*(3), 550–568. doi:10.1111/j.1083-6101.2008.00410.x

Bensebaa, F. (2004). The impact of strategic actions on the reputation building of e-businesses. *International Journal of Retail & Distribution Management, 32*(6), 286–301. doi:10.1108/09590550410537999

Bhattacherjee, A. (2002). Individual trust in online firms: Scale development and initial test. *Journal of Management Information Systems, 19*(1), 211–241. doi:10.1080/07421222.2002.11045715

Carvalho, W. L., da Cruz, R. O. M., Câmara, M. T., & de Aragão, J. J. G. (2010). Rural school transportation in emerging countries: The Brazilian case. *Research in Transportation Economics, 29*(1), 401–409. doi:10.1016/j.retrec.2010.07.051

Chau, P. Y., Hu, P. J. H., Lee, B. L., & Au, A. K. (2007). Examining consumers' trust in online vendors and their dropout decisions: An empirical study. *Electronic Commerce Research and Applications, 6*(2), 171–182. doi:10.1016/j.elerap.2006.11.008

Chen, J., & Dibb, S. (2010). Consumer' trust in the online retail context: Exploring the antecedents and consequences. *Psychology and Marketing, 27*(4), 323–346. doi:10.1002/mar.20334

Chen, Y. H., & Barnes, S. (2007). Initial trust and online buyer behaviour. *Industrial Management & Data Systems, 107*(1), 21–36. doi:10.1108/02635570710719034

Chiu, C. M., Hsu, M. H., Lai, H., & Chang, C. M. (2012). Re-examining the influence of trust on online repeat purchase intention: The moderating role of habit and its antecedents. *Decision Support Systems, 53*(4), 835–845. doi:10.1016/j.dss.2012.05.021

Cruz, P., Barretto Filgueiras Neto, L., Munoz-Gallego, P., & Laukkanen, T. (2010). Mobile banking rollout in emerging markets: Evidence from Brazil. *International Journal of Bank Marketing, 28*(5), 342–371. doi:10.1108/02652321011064881

Dahlberg, T., Mallat, N., & Öörni, A. (2003). Trust enhanced technology acceptance model-consumer acceptance of mobile payment solutions: Tentative evidence. *Stockholm Mobility Roundtable, 22*, 23.

Davis, F. D. (1989). Perceived usefulness, perceived ease of use, and user acceptance of information technology. *Management Information Systems Quarterly, 13*(3), 319–340. doi:10.2307/249008

Davis, F. D., Bagozzi, R. P., & Warshaw, P. R. (1989). User acceptance of computer technology: A comparison of two theoretical models. *Management Science, 35*(8), 982–1003. doi:10.1287/mnsc.35.8.982

Dawar, N. D. N., & Chattopadhyay, A. (2002). Rethinking marketing programs for emerging markets. *Long Range Planning, 35*(5), 457–474. doi:10.1016/S0024-6301(02)00108-5

De Ruyter, K., Wetzels, M., & Kleijnen, M. (2001). Customer adoption of e-service: An experimental study. *International Journal of Service Industry Management, 12*(2), 184–207. doi:10.1108/09564230110387542

Doney, P. M., & Cannon, J. P. (1997). An examination of the nature of trust in buyer-seller relationships. *The Journal of Marketing*, 35-51.

Drumwright, M. E. (1994). Socially responsible organizational buying: Environmental concern as a noneconomic buying criterion. *Journal of Marketing, 58*(3), 1–19. doi:10.2307/1252307

Eastlick, M. A., Lotz, S. L., & Warrington, P. (2006). Understanding online B-to-C relationships: An integrated model of privacy concerns, trust, and commitment. *Journal of Business Research, 59*(8), 877–886. doi:10.1016/j.jbusres.2006.02.006

Fan, X., Thompson, B., & Wang, L. (1999). Effects of sample size, estimation methods, and model specification on structural equation modeling fit indexes. *Structural Equation Modeling, 6*(1), 56–83. doi:10.1080/10705519909540119

Fang, Y., Qureshi, I., Sun, H., McCole, P., Ramsey, E., & Lim, K. H. (2014). Trust, Satisfaction, and Online Repurchase Intention: The Moderating Role of Perceived Effectiveness of E-Commerce Institutional Mechanisms. *Management Information Systems Quarterly, 38*(2), 407–427. doi:10.25300/MISQ/2014/38.2.04

Fishbein, M. (1979). *A theory of reasoned action: some applications and implications*. Academic Press.

Fraunholz, B., & Unnithan, C. (2004). Critical success factors in mobile communications: A comparative roadmap for Germany and India. *International Journal of Mobile Communications, 2*(1), 87–101. doi:10.1504/IJMC.2004.004489

Garbarino, E., & Johnson, M. S. (1999). The different roles of satisfaction, trust, and commitment in customer relationships. *The Journal of Marketing*, 70-87.

Gefen, D. (2000). E-commerce: The role of familiarity and trust. *Omega, 28*(6), 725–737. doi:10.1016/S0305-0483(00)00021-9

Gefen, D., Karahanna, E., & Straub, D. W. (2003). Trust and TAM in online shopping: An integrated model. *Management Information Systems Quarterly, 27*(1), 51–90. doi:10.2307/30036519

Gefen, D., & Straub, D. W. (2004). Consumer' trust in B2C e-Commerce and the importance of social presence: Experiments in e-Products and e-Services. *Omega, 32*(6), 407–424. doi:10.1016/j.omega.2004.01.006

Ghane, S. O. H. E. I. L. A., Fathian, M., & Gholamian, M. R. (2011). Full relationship among e-satisfaction, e-trust, e-service quality, and e-loyalty: The case of Iran e-banking. *Journal of Theoretical and Applied Information Technology, 33*(1), 1–6.

Grabner-Kräuter, S., & Kaluscha, E. A. (2003). Empirical research in on-line trust: A review and critical assessment. *International Journal of Human-Computer Studies, 58*(6), 783–812. doi:10.1016/S1071-5819(03)00043-0

Hofstede, G. (2003). *Culture's consequences: Comparing values, behaviors, institutions and organizations across nations.* Sage Publications.

Hsiao, R. L. (2003). Technology fears: Distrust and cultural persistence in electronic marketplace adoption. *The Journal of Strategic Information Systems, 12*(3), 169–199. doi:10.1016/S0963-8687(03)00034-9

Hsin Chang, H., & Wen Chen, S. (2008). The impact of online store environment cues on purchase intention: Trust and perceived risk as a mediator. *Online Information Review, 32*(6), 818–841. doi:10.1108/14684520810923953

Jarvenpaa, S. L., Tractinsky, N., & Saarinen, L. (1999). Consumer' trust in an internet store: a cross-cultural validation. *Journal of Computer-Mediated Communication, 5*(2).

Jarvenpaa, S. L., Tractinsky, N., & Vitale, M. (2000). Consumer' trust in an internet store. *Information Technology Management, 1*(1/2), 45–71. doi:10.1023/A:1019104520776

Jin, B., Yong Park, J., & Kim, J. (2008). Cross-cultural examination of the relationships among firm reputation, e-satisfaction, e-trust, and e-loyalty. *International Marketing Review, 25*(3), 324–337. doi:10.1108/02651330810877243

Johnson, D., & Grayson, K. (2005). Cognitive and affective trust in service relationships. *Journal of Business Research, 58*(4), 500–507. doi:10.1016/S0148-2963(03)00140-1

Khanna, T., & Palepu, K. (2000). Is group affiliation profitable in emerging markets? An analysis of diversified Indian business groups. *The Journal of Finance, 55*(2), 867–891. doi:10.1111/0022-1082.00229

Kim, G., Shin, B., & Lee, H. G. (2009). Understanding dynamics between initial trust and usage intentions of mobile banking. *Information Systems Journal, 19*(3), 283–311. doi:10.1111/j.1365-2575.2007.00269.x

Kim, H. W., Xu, Y., & Gupta, S. (2012). Which is more important in Internet shopping, perceived price or trust? *Electronic Commerce Research and Applications, 11*(3), 241–252. doi:10.1016/j.elerap.2011.06.003

Kim, J., Jin, B., & Swinney, J. L. (2009). The role of e-retail quality, e-satisfaction and e-trust in online loyalty development process. *Journal of Retailing and Consumer Services, 16*(4), 239–247. doi:10.1016/j.jretconser.2008.11.019

Kim, K. K., & Prabhakar, B. (2004). Initial trust and the adoption of B2C e-commerce: The case of internet banking. *ACM SIGMIS Database, 35*(2), 50-64.

Kim, M. J., Chung, N., & Lee, C. K. (2011). The effect of perceived trust on electronic commerce: Shopping online for tourism products and services in South Korea. *Tourism Management, 32*(2), 256–265. doi:10.1016/j.tourman.2010.01.011

Koufaris, M., & Hampton-Sosa, W. (2004). The development of initial trust in an online company by new consumers. *Information & Management, 41*(3), 377–397. doi:10.1016/j.im.2003.08.004

La Polla, M., Martinelli, F., & Sgandurra, D. (2013). A survey on security for mobile devices. *IEEE Communications Surveys and Tutorials, 15*(1), 446–471. doi:10.1109/SURV.2012.013012.00028

Laukkanen, T., & Lauronen, J. (2005). Consumer value creation in mobile banking services. *International Journal of Mobile Communications, 3*(4), 325–338. doi:10.1504/IJMC.2005.007021

Lee, M. K., & Turban, E. (2001). A trust model for consumer internet shopping. *International Journal of Electronic Commerce, 6*(1), 75–91. doi:10.1080/108644 15.2001.11044227

Liu, C., Marchewka, J. T., Lu, J., & Yu, C. S. (2005). Beyond concern—a privacy-trust-behavioral intention model of electronic commerce. *Information & Management, 42*(2), 289–304. doi:10.1016/j.im.2004.01.003

Lu, H. P., & Yu-Jen Su, P. (2009). Factors affecting purchase intention on mobile shopping web sites. *Internet Research, 19*(4), 442–458. doi:10.1108/10662240910981399

Mahatanankoon, P., Wen, H. J., & Lim, B. B. (2006). Evaluating the technological characteristics and trust affecting mobile device usage. *International Journal of Mobile Communications, 4*(6), 662–681. doi:10.1504/IJMC.2006.010361

Martín, S. S., & Camarero, C. (2008). Consumer' trust to a web site: Moderating effect of attitudes toward online shopping. *Cyberpsychology and Behavior, 11*(5), 549-554.

Mayer, R. C., Davis, J. H., & Schoorman, F. D. (1995). An integrative model of organizational trust. *Academy of Management Review, 20*(3), 709–734.

Mcknight, D. H., Carter, M., Thatcher, J. B., & Clay, P. F. (2011). Trust in a specific technology: An investigation of its components and measures. *ACM Transactions on Management Information Systems, 2*(2), 12. doi:10.1145/1985347.1985353

McKnight, D. H., Choudhury, V., & Kacmar, C. (2002). Developing and validating trust measures for e-commerce: An integrative typology. *Information Systems Research, 13*(3), 334–359. doi:10.1287/isre.13.3.334.81

McKnight, D. H., Choudhury, V., & Kacmar, C. (2002). The impact of initial consumer' trust on intentions to transact with a web site: A trust building model. *The Journal of Strategic Information Systems, 11*(3), 297–323. doi:10.1016/S0963-8687(02)00020-3

Montano, D. E., & Kasprzyk, D. (2015). Theory of reasoned action, theory of planned behavior, and the integrated behavioral model. *Health behavior: Theory, research and practice.*

Mukherjee, A., & Nath, P. (2007). Role of electronic trust in online retailing: A re-examination of the commitment-trust theory. *European Journal of Marketing, 41*(9/10), 1173–1202. doi:10.1108/03090560710773390

Nee, V. (1992). Organizational dynamics of market transition: Hybrid forms, property rights, and mixed economy in China. *Administrative Science Quarterly, 37*(1), 1–27. doi:10.2307/2393531

Nica, E. (2015). Satisfaction and Trust in E-Commerce. *Psychosociological Issues in Human Resource Management, 3*(1), 107–112.

Oliver, R. L. (1980). A cognitive model of the antecedents and consequences of satisfaction decisions. *JMR, Journal of Marketing Research, 17*(4), 460–469. doi:10.2307/3150499

Park, C. H., & Kim, Y. G. (2003). Identifying key factors affecting consumer purchase behavior in an online shopping context. *International Journal of Retail & Distribution Management, 31*(1), 16–29. doi:10.1108/09590550310457818

Patel, A. (2006). Mobile Commerce in Emerging Economics. In Handbook of Research in Mobile Business: Technical, Methodological, and Social Perspectives (pp. 429-434). IGI Global. doi:10.4018/978-1-59140-817-8.ch030

Pavlou, P. A. (2003). Consumer acceptance of electronic commerce: Integrating trust and risk with the technology acceptance model. *International Journal of Electronic Commerce, 7*(3), 101–134.

Pavlou, P. A., & Gefen, D. (2004). Building effective online marketplaces with institution-based trust. *Information Systems Research, 15*(1), 37–59. doi:10.1287/isre.1040.0015

Pennington, R., Wilcox, H. D., & Grover, V. (2003). The role of system trust in business-to-consumer transactions. *Journal of Management Information Systems*, *20*(3), 197–226. doi:10.1080/07421222.2003.11045777

Ponte, E. B., Carvajal-Trujillo, E., & Escobar-Rodríguez, T. (2015). Influence of trust and perceived value on the intention to purchase travel online: Integrating the effects of assurance on trust antecedents. *Tourism Management*, *47*, 286–302. doi:10.1016/j.tourman.2014.10.009

Rogers, E. M. (1995). Diffusion of Innovations: modifications of a model for telecommunications. In *Die Diffusion von Innovationen in der Telekommunikation* (pp. 25–38). Springer Berlin Heidelberg. doi:10.1007/978-3-642-79868-9_2

Shao Yeh, Y., & Li, Y. M. (2009). Building trust in m-commerce: Contributions from quality and satisfaction. *Online Information Review*, *33*(6), 1066–1086. doi:10.1108/14684520911011016

Siau, K., & Shen, Z. (2003). Building consumer' trust in mobile commerce. *Communications of the ACM*, *46*(4), 91–94. doi:10.1145/641205.641211

Singh, J., & Sirdeshmukh, D. (2000). Agency and trust mechanisms in consumer satisfaction and loyalty judgments. *Journal of the Academy of Marketing Science*, *28*(1), 150–167. doi:10.1177/0092070300281014

Sparks, B. A., & Browning, V. (2011). The impact of online reviews on hotel booking intentions and perception of trust. *Tourism Management*, *32*(6), 1310–1323. doi:10.1016/j.tourman.2010.12.011

Stafford, T. F., & Gillenson, M. L. (2003). Mobile commerce: What it is and what it could be. *Communications of the ACM*, *46*(12), 33–34. doi:10.1145/953460.953483

Suh, B., & Han, I. (2003). The impact of consumer' trust and perception of security control on the acceptance of electronic commerce. *International Journal of Electronic Commerce*, *7*(3), 135–161.

Verhoef, P. C., Franses, P. H., & Hoekstra, J. C. (2002). The effect of relational constructs on customer referrals and number of services purchased from a multiservice provider: Does age of relationship matter? *Journal of the Academy of Marketing Science*, *30*(3), 202–216. doi:10.1177/0092070302303002

Walczuch, R., & Lundgren, H. (2004). Psychological antecedents of institution-based consumer' trust in e-retailing. *Information & Management*, *42*(1), 159–177. doi:10.1016/j.im.2003.12.009

Wu, G., Hu, X., & Wu, Y. (2010). Effects of perceived interactivity, perceived web assurance and disposition to trust on initial online trust. *Journal of Computer-Mediated Communication, 16*(1), 1–26. doi:10.1111/j.1083-6101.2010.01528.x

Wu, J. H., & Wang, S. C. (2005). What drives mobile commerce?: An empirical evaluation of the revised technology acceptance model. *Information & Management, 42*(5), 719–729. doi:10.1016/j.im.2004.07.001

Chapter 12

A SEM–Neural Network Approach for Predicting Antecedents of Factors Influencing Consumers' Intent to Install Mobile Applications

Yakup Akgül
Alanya Alaaddin Keykubat University, Turkey

ABSTRACT

This chapter explores the present gap in the literature regarding the acceptance of mobile applications by investigating the factors that affect users' behavioral intention to use apps in Turkey. First, structural equation modeling (SEM) was used to determine which variables had significant influence on intention to install. In a second phase, the neural network model was used to rank the relative influence of significant predictors obtained from SEM. The results reveal that habit, performance expectancy, trust, social influence, and hedonic motivation affect the users' behavioral intention to use apps.

INTRODUCTION

Recently, people are progressively eager to adopt new technologies in their daily lives by accepting and using modern technologies is common habit, making technology, now more than ever become a part of our usual activities (Islam, Low and Hasan, 2013). As of May 2017, Apple's App Market contained 2.2 million and Google's

DOI: 10.4018/978-1-5225-4029-8.ch012

Google Play Market contained 2.8 million apps (Statista, 2017a). Consumers have downloaded apps at a astounding percentage. As of May 2017, Apple has had 140 billion total downloads from its market since its origination in 2016 (Statista, 2017b). In the firstquarter of 2016 alone, Google had an estimated 64 billion downloads and Apple had 100 million downloads (Android Authority, 2017). Mobile applications are designed to extend the capabilities of the mobile devices for mobile device operating systems, which end-user software apps, (Purcell, 2011). Mobile applicatios are defined as software or programmes that are designed to perform specific tasks, which can usually be downloaded onto users' mobile devices (Kwon et al., 2013; Mozeik et al., 2009; Wang et al., 2015). As well, users can install different kinds of mobile applications, such as game, music, shopping, bank payment applications and so forth, which are delivered by the third-party software providers (Grotnes, 2009; Islam, Islam and Mazumder, 2010; Taylor, Voelker and Pentina, 2011). By the installation of these applications, the functions of the mobile devices are expanded. The number of mobile apps has been rising, and this rise contributed to the arising range of consumer needs that are being served by mobile apps (Kim, Yoon & Han, 2014). Because of the disadvantages of websites due to their restrictive functionality, many companies provide mobile apps to the customers (Magrath and McCormick, 2013). Compared to mobile websites, mobile applications are preferred by consumers primarily because they are perceived as more convenient, faster and easier to browse (Mobile Apps: What Consumers Really Need and Want, 2016). Many recent works that have examined the factors involved in a consumer's adoption of distinct mobile device services, such as mobile payments (Lu, Yang, Chau and Cao, 2011; Zhou, 2013), mobile banking (Chen, 2013), financial services (Chemingui and Ben Iallouna, 2013), health services (Deng, Mo and Liu, 2014), mobile learning (Callum, Jeffrey and Kinshuk, 2014), mobile data services (Al-Debei & Al-Lozi, 2014) and mobile games (Jiang, Peng and Liu, 2015). Regardless, there have not been many works that have assessed the determinants that affect the installation of mobile apps on mobile devices in Turkey context. One of the main drawbacks of conventional statistical techniques used for the prediction of users' behavior is that they usually examine only linear relations among variables. In order to overcome this issue, relative importance of significant variables will be determined using neural networks, capable to model complex non-linear relationships.

The UTAUT2 model is adjusted version of Unified Theory of Acceptance and Use of Technology (UTAUT) model. The primary model is developed by Venkatesh, Moris, Davis, and Davis (2003), which has PE, EE, SI and FC constructs. HM, PV and HT factors have been added into UTAUT2 model. According to Venkatesh et al. (2012), UTAUT2 has the applicability from the context of organizational to a consumer usage.

While mobile phones or smartphones were found in 96.9% of the houses in April of 2016, fixed phone availability was 25.6%. In the same period, 22.9% of the dwellings were desktop computers, 36.4% portable, while tablet computers were 29.6%. In 2015, 20.9% of TVs with internet connection were calculated as 24.6% in 2016 (http://www.tuik.gov.tr/PreHaberBultenleri.do?id=21779 26.05.2017).

Recently, mobile apps changed consumers' consumption behavior significantly because of having ubiquity and portability. Smartphone users enable to receive and diffuse information much more quickly and easily based on these qualities than ever before (Islam et al., 2013). As Wang et al. (2015) maintain "Today's mobile technologies are known to possess the capabilities to satisfy users' entertainment and spontaneous needs, help fulfilling one's efficiency desires, assist in making time-critical arrangements, and cater to mobility-related situational needs" (Wang, 2015: 5-6).

REVIEW OF THE LITERATURE

Hypothesis Development

The relationships between the eight independent variables (PE, EE, SI, FC, HM, PV, HT and TR) and the dependent variable (BI) are examined in the previous empirical studies.

Behavioral Intention (BI)

Behavioral Intention (BI) is defined as a person's perceived likelihood or "subjective probability that he or she will engage in a given behavior" (Homburg et al., 2005). Also, Islam et al. (2013), defined behavioural intention as an individual's intention to carry out a given act, which can foresee coinciding behaviours when an individual performs deliberately. In addition, behavioural intention is the subjective possibility of carrying out behaviour and also the cause of certain usage behaviour (Yi et al., 2006). The willingness of an individual to carry out a particular behavior can be examined by his or her BI. In this book chapter, BI is used to describe how great the individuals' appeal to adopt mobile applications. Zhang et al. (2012), indicated that BI is the most notable determinant that determines individual's existent behavior in TAM theory. Therefore, intentions show the motivational determinants that leverage behaviour and are indicators of how hard people are willing to try and the effort they put in to embark on a behaviour. Also, it was found that behavioural intention is to be the primary factor of individual mobile services usage and that usage intentions are rational indicators of future system use (Mafe et al., 2010). According to The Theory of Reasoned Action (Fishbein and Ajzen, 1975), Technology Acceptance Model (Davis, 1989) and the Theory of Planned Behavior (Ajzen, 1991) and former works have validated that a consumer's intentions are critical forecaster of a consumer's actual behavior (Kim et al., 2008; Pavlou, 2003; Shin, 2009; Taylor and Todd, 1995; Venkatesh et al., 2003; Yang, 2013). In this study, a consumer's intention to install an application is seen as a prominent predictor of actually installing the application.

Performance Expectancy (PE)

"The degree to which using a technology will provide benefits to consumers in performing certain activities" is defined as Performance Expectancy (PE) (Venkatesh et al., 2012:159). Empirical studies of AbuShanab and Pearson (2007) that customers has high PE, which has high BI to use internet banking in Jordan, which evaluated using MLR. This is further supported by Shi (2009) indicated that PE has positive influence on BI to use smart phone online application software. Sun, Cao and You (2010) remarked that PU has a positive and significant effect on BI to use m-commerce in China, which evaluated using SEM. This result aligned with Leong et al. (2013b), found that PU has a positive and significant influence on BI to use m-credit card, which was analysed using SEM. These empirical studies expose that PE as a substantial determinant to influence the BI to adopt mobile technology. On the other hand, Im, Hong and Kang (2011) asserted that PE has insignificant effect on BI to adopt MP3 and internet banking, which indifferent in U.S. and Korea. Furthermore, Lin, Zimmer and Lee (2013) found that PE has positive affect on BI to adopt podcasting, in a Northeastern United States college, which evaluated using PLS. Oliveira, Faria and Thomas (2014) carried out a study, which proved that PE positively influences BI to adopt m-banking. In addition to, a recent emprical study conducted by Slade, Williams, Dwivedi and Piercy (2014) found out that PE positively influences the behavioral intention of mobile payment, which was analysed by regression analysis. And also, the same year Martins, Oliveira, and Popovič (2014) conducted a study and revealed that PE has positive relation with BI to adoption of internet banking in a Portugal University. According to Venkatesh et al. (2012) the consumers are the users of the technology in a consumer user context rather than in an organizational user context (Venkatesh et al., 2012). This study adopts this definition of Performance Expectancy and consumers. Moreover, apps enable the users to purchase goods and services, get expert tips regarding goods and services and browse anytime at anyplace (Morris, 2016). This factor is equivalent to Perceived Usefulness (PU) in the Technology Acceptance Model (TAM) (Venkatesh et al., 2003). In previous studies, PE has been proved to significantly affect the consumer behavioral intention in the context of m-commerce (Chong, 2013b), mobile internet (Venkatesh et al., 2012). Thus, the following hypothesis is proposed:

H1: Performance expectancy affects the behavioral intention to use mobile apps.

Effort Expectancy (EE)

Effort expectancy (EE) is defined as is "the degree of ease/effort associated with consumers' use of the technology" (Venkatesh et al., 2012:159). Effort expectancy EE is the degree to which a technology is easy to use (Jambulingam, 2013). Moreover, Effort Expectancy is equal to Perceived Ease of Use in Technology Acceptance Model (TAM) (Venkatesh et al., 2003). AlAwadhi and Morris (2008) carried out a study that revealed EE and BI has a positive relationship to employ e-government services in Kuwait. On the other hand, Wu, Tao and Yang (2007) indicated that EE has insignificant effect on the BI to adopt 3G services in Taiwan. Besides, the study of Yang (2010) showed that EE insignificantly influences the attitude of US consumer to use m-shopping services, which validated using SEM. Differently, Tan, Sim, Ooi and Phusavat (2011) verified that PEU has a significant influence on the BI to adopt m-learning by using the multiple regression in Perak, Malaysia. EE has positive influence on the BI to adopt the technology, which has similar results from these empirical studies. In addition, Im, Hong, and Kang (2011) found that EE has positive influence on BI to adopt MP3 players and internet banking usage in Korea and U.S. and, which analysed by using covariance SEM. Teo and Noyes (2012) found that EE has a significant influence on the individual BI to use information technology by using SEM approach in the among Singapore trainee teachers. Chang (2013) found out that EE has positive effect on the BI to use library mobile applications in the eastern Taiwan, which analysed by SEM. The same year, Tai and Ku (2013) validated that EE has a significant positive effect on the intention of adopting for mobile stock trading for stock investors in Taiwan. Besides that, Alharbi and Drew (2014) found that EE has positive affection on the BI to employ m-learning system in Griffith University. In addition to that, a recent study conducted by Teo, Tan, Ooi, Hew and Yew (2015) provided evidence that EE has a positive influence on BI for utilization of m-payment in Malaysia. Effort expectancy has been a compulsory factor in previous studies on the technology acceptance, where the degree of the ease of use of the technology system affected significantly the behavioral intention of various technologies, such as 3G (Liao, Tsou and Huang, 2007), wireless internet (Lu, Yu, Liu and Yao, 2003), electronic commerce (Ha and Stoel, 2009) and m-commerce (Chong, 2013). Therefore, the following hypothesis is proposed:

H2: Effort expectancy affects the behavioral intention to use mobile apps.

Social Influence (SI)

Social Influence (SI) cites to "the consumers perceive that important others (e.g. family and friends) believe that they should use a particular technology" (Venkatesh et al, 2012:157-178). Lu, Yao and Yu (2005) showed that SI negatively influences the BI to use wireless internet services among university students in Texas. Akour (2009) found that the most influential factor of m-learning acceptance in tertiary education, which extrinsic effect of freshman students in Oklahoma State University. Taylor et al. (2011), found that students' adoption and usage of mobile apps is strongly effected by their friends compared to family members in U.S. Midwest universities, which tested using logistic regression models. Also, Yu (2012) emphasized that SI has positive influences to adopt m-banking in major Taipei downtown areas and, which evaluated using PLS regression. Beside this, Chong, Chan, and Ooi (2012) showed that SI was the determinant of BI to employ mobile commerce. Jaradat and Rababaa (2013) indicated that SI positively influences the users' BI on m-commerce adoption and usage in Jordan public university students. The same year, Alwahaishi and Snasel (2013) validated that SI has a positive influence on BI to use of mobile internet in Saudi Arabia. Furthermore, Leong et al. (2013a) proved that SI has a crucial function in influencing the BI to use m-entertainment. Differently, Yang (2013) found that subjective norm does not influence the intention to use mobile apps among college students in Southeast America by using multiple regression analyses. A recent study conducted by Jawad and Hassan (2015), SI has a positive relation on BI to adoption mobile learning by using regression model. Moreover, SI is equivalent to subjective norm in the Theory of Reason Action and Theory of Planned Behavior, where it is an important factor that affects the adoption of a system (Venkatesh et al., 2003). Likewise since m-shopping fashion apps are not a mandatory technology, in the sense that the consumers have the free choice to use them, social influence has the potential to affect the behavioral intention to use m-shopping fashion apps. Chong (2013) found that SI is a significant determinant of the consumers' behavioral intention to use m-commerce, and that social influence affects the consumer's intention to use mcommerce in Malaysia. Hence, the following hypothesis is proposed:

H3: Social influence affects the behavioral intention to use mobile apps.

Facilitating Conditions (FC)

Facilitating Conditions (FC) is defined as "the consumers" perceptions of the resources and support available to perform a behavior" (Venkatesh at al., 2012: 159). Wu et al. (2007) found that FC significantly effects the behavioural intention for 3G mobile telecommunication services. Zhou (2008) found that FC will positively influence BI to adopt m-commerce in China. Yang (2010) showed that FC is positively related to BI to use mobile shopping services in U.S. This result is in line with the findings Yeoh and Chan (2011), indicated that FC has positive and significant impact on BI for internet banking adoption by using MLR. Regardless, Teo et al. (2012) indicated that FC has no positive and significant effect on the BI to use technology. And also, Jambulingam (2013) found that FC has no positive and significant influence on BI to influence m-learning adoption. In addition to that, Thomas, Singh, and Gaffar (2013) also found that FC is positively related to BI to adopt m-learning in University of Guyana. Also, Chong (2013a) found that FC has positive relationship with BI to adopt m-commerce in China by using MLR. Chong (2013) applied the UTAUT model in order to investigate the mcommerce adoption, and the study found that facilitating conditions had a significant influence on the user behavior intention to use m-commerce. Facilitating conditions in the context of m-shopping fashion apps relates to online supports and helps, m-devices, internet connection, and so forth (Hew et al., 2015; Magrath and McCormick, 2013). If the consumers have the necessary support and resources, they will have the intention to use a technology (Venkatesh et al., 2012). Hence, the following hypothesis is proposed:

H4: Facilitating conditions affect the behavioral intention to use mobile apps.

Hedonic Motivation (HM)

Hedonic Motivation (HM) is defined as "the pleasure or enjoyment derived from using a new technology" (Venkatesh et al., 2012:161). HM plays a vital role in predicting the intentions for technology use (Venkatesh et al., 2012). Hedonic Motivation has been shown to be an important factor in determining the acceptance of technology in previous technology acceptance studies. HM is the fun or pleasure derived from using a technology (Brown and Venkatesh, 2005). To, Liao and Lin (2007) found that hedonic attitudes directly influences the intention to search but an indirectly influence the intention to purchase in Taiwan. Magni, Taylor and Venkatesh (2010) hedonic factors influence individual's intentions to explore a technology, but the influences differ across stages of technology adoption in U.S. The same year, Yang (2010) found that hedonic aspects are crucial factors of consumer to use of m-shopping services. Escobar-Rodríguez and Carvajal-Trujillo (2013), found that HM has a positive impact on BI to purchase online airline ticket in Spain by using questionnaires and, which analyzed by using SEM. Also, the same year Raman and Don (2013) conducted a study on undergraduates' students in University Utara Malaysia. The results indicated that HM and BI has a positive relationship to adopt Learning Management System. Nonetheless, Lewis et al. (2013) found that

HM has not positive influence the intention to use classroom technology in the United States of America. A recent study conducted by Bere (2014) has found that HM has a positive relationship with BI to employ m-learning in South Africa and which analysed multiple regression. The same year, Harsono and Suryana (2014) conducted a study on college students in Bandung. The results showed that HM has positive influence on the BI to use social media. In addition to that, Alalwan, Dwivedi and Williams (2014) studied on Jordanian banking customers. The results verified that HM has a positive impact on the consumers' intention and use of internet banking in Jordan. Moreover, if a technology creates pleasure and fun while the user is using it, users are able to gain enjoyment, which influences their behavioral intention to pursue the technology (Lee, 2009). Venkatesh et al. (2012) proved HM as a significant factor that affects the behavioral intention to use mobile internet in a consumer context. Similarly in an m-shopping service context in a study by Yang (2010) it was concluded that hedonic factors are critical determinants of the m-shopping consumer usage, and that hedonic performance expectancy is gained by the users thought the fun obtained by using various features and functions in m-shopping technology. Hence, the following hypothesis is proposed:

H5: Hedonic motivation affects the behavioral intention to use mobile apps.

Price Value (PV)

Price Value (PV) refers to "consumers" cognitive trade off between the perceived benefits of the applications and the monetary cost of using them" (Dodds et al., 1991: 307-319). Venkatesh et al. (2012) highlights that PV in consumer decision making regarding technology use is an important factor influencing BI which is tested using PLS. Moreover, Munnukka (2004) indicated that PV has an influence on consumer use of mobile services in Finland. Toh et al., (2009) showed that perceived cost negatively impacts the intention to use m-commerce among Malaysian users. Prata, Moraes and Quaresma (2012) found out that mobile apps price is the main reason to buy an app in Brazil. Nonetheless, Chong (2013b) conducted a study regarding the cost that impacts the intention to adopt m-commerce among users in China. Yang (2013) showed that PV has a positive influence on BI to adopt mobile learning of undergraduate students in China. Furthermore, Xu s' (2014) study carried out a study and the resultd verified that PV has positive impact on users' continuance intention in online gaming in China. In addition to that, Dhulla and Mathur (2014) also found that PV has positive influence on BI to adopt cloud computing in Mumbai. Apart from that, a recent study conducted by Arenas-Gaitán, Peral-Peral, and Ramón-Jerónimo (2015) also showed that PV has a positive impact on BI to accept internet banking in the south of Spain. This finding is consistent with the research done by

Unyolo (2012) found that PV has a positive impact on BI to adopt mobile money. When it comes to the consumer use setting the main difference is that consumers are the ones who bear the monetary costs of the use of a technology. Therefore, as the technology is not provided for free by the organization unlike in the organizational use context, the cost of using the technology and pricing structure have significant impact on consumers' technology use (Venkatesh et al., 2012). M-shopping fashion apps are mostly free to download as vendors of fashion products aim to attract more and more consumers to use the mobile shopping app and hence make purchases. Other costs for using mshopping fashion apps are the cost of the internet, mobile device, mobile device maintenance (Wei et al., 2009). Price value in our study is defined as the as consumers' cognitive trade-off between the perceived benefits of the mobile shopping fashion applications and the monetary cost for using them (Dodds et al., 1991; Venkatesh et al., 2012). The price value can be positive or negative; depending if the perceived benefits exceed the monetary costs of using the technology (Venkatesh et al., 2012). Hence, the following hypothesis is proposed:

H6: Price value affects the behavioral intention to use mobile apps.

Habit (HT)

Habit (HT) refers "the extent to which people tend to perform behaviors automatically because of learning" (Limayem et al., 2007:705-737). Venkatesh et al., (2012) indicated that habit has direct and indirect impacts on BI to use technology. Liao, Palvia and Lin (2006) conducted a study in Taiwan and found that habit has influence the continuance intention to use e-commerce. Liao et al., (2011b) utilised UTAUT2 research model and reported that HT was one of the determinants that has positive relationship on BI to use web portals. As well as, Pahnila, Siponen and Zheng (2011) indicated that habit has an impact on the use of Tao Bao in University of Shanghai, China. As well as, HT has been verified by Chong and Ngai (2013) found that HT has positive impact on BI to adopt location-based social media for travel planning in various mobile phone shops in China's shopping mall and, which analyzed using PLS regression. The same year, Lewis et al. (2013) HT has a positive impact on BI to use technology in higher education classrooms in the United States and which was validated using Smart-PLS. Likewise, Oechslein, Fleischmann and Hess (2014) found that HT has a positive impact on BI to accept social recommender systems at German university. According to a recent empirical study conducted by Wong et al., (2014) indiacated that HT has a positive impact on BI to adopt mobile TV in Malaysia and, which was examined using PLS.

In previous studies, habit has been defined as the extent that individuals tend to execute behaviors automatically because of learning (Venkatesh et al., 2012;

Limayem, Hirt & Cheung, 2007). In accordance with this definition we define habit, as the extent that individuals tent to use m-shopping fashion apps automatically. With increased experience in using a technology, the users start using the technology habitually (Venkatesh et al., 2012). Furthermore habit can predict one's future behavior and people are more likely to have a good intention to perform acts they have performed often in the past (Ouellette & Wood, 1998). When habit is present people tend to rely more on habit compared to other external information and choice strategies (Gefen, 2003). Moreover, Venkatesh et al., (2012) found that habit affects the behavioral intention to use technology. Also, in a study conducted by Liao, Palvia and Lin (2006), it was found that habit influences the user's intention to continue to use e-commerce. When a behavior has been done many times in the past, future behavior becomes automatic (Aarts, Verplanken & Knippenberg, 1998). Therefore, once the users have been using the app, this action becomes a routine and habit which influences the individuals to use the apps. Hence, the following hypothesis is proposed:

H7: Habit affects the behavioral intention to use mobile apps.

Trust (TR)

It has been validated that trust is a critical determinant to influence users' decisions in uncertain environments (Pavlou, 2003). Studies have also showed that trust has no positive impact on perceived risk (Hong, 2015; Kim et al., 2008; Liao, Liu, & Chen, 2011a; Pavlou, 2003). Mobile apps is a much newer technology, compared to mobile websites and ecommerce, and shopping via mobile apps for products and services are recent trend, therefore users of mobile apps are exposed to new vulnerabilities and risks (Joubert and Belle, 2013; Magrath & McComick, 2013). Moreover, because personal information is being stored on users' mobile apps in order to make the purchase of the goods and services possible, the risks of privacy and security are quite high. Asymmetric information regarding the product and services purchased by the user of the app and the vendor of the product ans service are present, because the user cannot physically try and see the goods and services (Eliasson et al., 2009). Several studies have also showed that trust has a positive relationship between the decision to repurchase from an online vendor (Hong and Cha, 2013; Hsu, Chang and Chuang, 2015; Kwahk and Park, 2012; Pavlou and Gefen, 2004; Roca et al., 2009; Shin et al., 2013). Likewise in an mobile shopping context there is lack of physical interaction between in our case the vendor of the products and services and the user of the mobile app; the user of the app has the risk regarding personal information stored and accessible by the app, therefore users need to have trust in order to have intend to use the apps (Chong et al., 2010; Vasileiadis,

2014; Wei et al., 2009). Moreover, in a study by Luarn and Lin (2005) on mobile banking acceptance, it was found that issues related to security and privacy have more significant influence than the original TAM factors of perceived usefulness and perceived ease of use of the technology system. Research done in the context of online shopping by applying TAM, for example, Gefen, Karahanna and Straub (2003) showed that consumer trust in the m-vendor affects their intentions to use mobile commerce; as trust significantly reduces the perception of risk which a consumer faces in the online commerce context. Furthermore trust in the mobile vendors was found to affect the behavioral intention to use m-shopping, as the more trust the consumer has in the m-vendors, the more it is willing to use m-shopping (Groß, 2015b). In mobile shopping studies trust most often refers to the customer and mobile vendors relationships, and is defined as the consumer's "willingness to rely on an Exchange partner in whom one has confidence" (Groß, 2015b: 220; Moorman, Deshpande and Zaltman 1993: 82), and in our case mobile vendors, "including beliefs about their ability, competence, integrity and benevolence" (Groß, 2015b: 220; Lin and Wang, 2006). In consistence with previous studies, we adopt this definition of Trust (trust in the mobile vendors). Kim and Yoon (2013) utilized TAM and the results showed that perceived information usefulness, perceived entertaining usefulness, and perceived ease of use all had significant impact on attitude toward app usage, which in turn had a significant influence on behavioral intention to use apps. Another recent study done by Hew and Lee (2015) also examined the behavioral intention to use mobile apps, utilized the Unified Theory of Acceptance and Use of Technology 2 (UTAUT2). The researchers indicated that all of the dimensions except price value and social influence were significantly related to behavioral intention to use mobile apps. Only one study, Shen (2015), examined perceived risk. Therefore, our theoretical model and related study uniquely contributes to the known body of work. Based on the above, we propose the following hypotheses (see Figure 1): The following hypothesis is proposed:

H8: Trust affects the behavioral intention to use mobile apps. Figure 1 demonstrates the proposed conceptual framework of this research.

RESEARCH METHOD

Measures of the Constructs

A survey instrument was constructed by adapting measures from prior research to ensure the content validity of the scales. The measurement of performance expectancy adapted from the scale developed by Venkatesh et al.(2012), Venkatesh et al.(2003),

Figure 1. UTAUT2 model

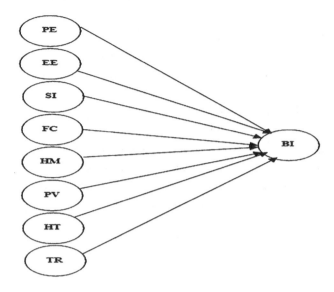

Mallat et al., 2009, Hövels 2010 and Leong et al. (2013), effort expectancy adapted from the scale developed by Venkatesh et al.(2012), Venkatesh et al.(2003) and Davis et al. (1989), Social Influence adapted from the scale developed by Venkatesh et al. (2012), Moore and Benbasat (1991) Venkatesh and Davis (1991) Leong et al. (2013) and Yang (2010), Facilitating Conditions adapted from the scale developed by Venkatesh et al. (2012) and Venkatesh et al. (2003), Hedonic Motivation adapted from the scale developed by Venkatesh et al. (2012), Yang (2013) and To et al. (2007), Price Value adapted from the scale developed by Venkatesh et al. (2012) and Prata et al. (2012), Habit adapted from the scale developed by Venkatesh et al. (2012) and Verplanken & Orbell (2003), Trust adapted from the scale developed by (Groß, 2015b), Behavioural Intention adapted from the scale developed by Venkatesh et al.(2012), Venkatesh et al. (2003), Davis (1989) and Akour (2009). Thirty questionnaires were distributed to bank customers who have experienced using internet banking in Turkey, and minor changes to the scales were made accordingly to ensure that the questions were not repetitive. Pilot test respondents were not used in the further analysis.

The descriptive statistics of the sample showed that females account for 51.1 and males 48.9 percent of respondents. The percent of 28.6 was in the age group 18-24 years, 49.8 percent of respondents were between 25-34 years of age, 19 percent of respondents were between 35-44 years of age and 2.2 percent was in the age group 45-54 years of age. In this context, younger generation prefers to use internet banking services compared to older age groups (35 years old above). In addition, majority respondents claimed that they use mobile applications for three to six years (46.1 percent), followed by more than six years (42 percent) and less than three years (11.9). The majority of respondents were bachelor degree and represented (37.5%), followed by master degree (22.7 percent), Ph.D. degree (10 percent), vocational school degree (12.6 percent), high school degree (16.4 percent) and other education level (0.7 percent). Majority respondents claimed that they use android (72.9 percent), followed IOS (23.4 percent), windows (3.3 percent) and the other (0.4 percent).

Finally, the survey instrument used in this study consisted of a total of 43 items related to the nine constructs of the research model. The items were measured using a five-point Likert-type scale for all constructs. To ensure the content validity of the instrument, all construct measures were adapted from their original source and slightly modified to fit the technology context studied. The validation of the survey instrument was done by experts from the field of information technology as well as web and application developers.

DATA COLLECTION PROCESS

To reach mobile application users, a Web-based survey was used. A snowball sampling method was applied. A total of 343 surveys were collected from the participants, of which 269 were found to be usable in the data analysis.

Method of Measurement and Structural Model Analysis

PLS, which is known as a variance-based SEM, provides tremendous advantages in marketing and consumer behavior studies (Henseler et al., 2009; Henseler, 2010; Hair et al., 2011; Henseler et al., 2012; Reinartz et al., 2009; Roldán & Sánchez-Franco, 2012; Sarstedt, 2008), and helps to understand the relations among the sets of observed variables (Hair et al., 2012; Rigdon et al., 2010). Thus, using SmartPLS software 2.0 (M3) (Chin, 1998b; Ringle, Wende, & Becker, 2014; Tenenhaus et al, 2005; Wetzels et al., 2009; Chin and Newsted 1999; Ringle et al., 2005b), the PLS algorithm, bootstrapping and blindfolding procedure were performed in this study to assess the measurement and structural model. The analysis should be carried out on the basis of the path weighting scheme (Henseler et al., 2012; Henseler et al., 2009). This study uses recent guidelines provided by Chin (2010), Gil-Garcia (2008), and others (Hair et al., 2011; Hair et al., 2012a, Hair et al., 2012b; Hair et al., 2012c; Hair et al., 2013a; Hair et al., 2013b).

According to Chin (2010), and Henseler and Chin (2010) the first step in evaluating SEM is the measurement model, and, secondly, the structural model results (the two-stage approach). The PLS path modeling algorithm presents the outer and the inner estimation stages (Hair et al., 2013; Vinzi et al., 2010). According to Ringle et al. (2010), non-parametric assessment criteria, such as construct reliability (> 0.6), outer loadings (> 0.7), indicator reliability (> 0.5), and average variance extracted (> 0.5), must satisfy the minimum requirements. For measurement assessment, construct validity is defined as "the extent to which an operationalization measures the concept it is supposed to measure" (Bagozzi and Yi, 1988; Bagozzi et al., 1991: 421). The construct validity is the extent to which a set of items in an instrument represents the construct to be measured. If the measurement model shows an acceptable level of model fit, then it is an evidence for the availability of construct validity (Hair et al., 2014). Furthermore, the structural model would assess the R^2 measures and the level and significance of the path coefficients by performing the bootstrapping procedure of 5000 resamples (Chin, 1998b; Croteau and Bergeron, 2001; Gil-Garcia, 2008; Hair et al., 2011). First, researchers should check the sign, magnitude, and significance of each path coefficient, all of which should be consistent with theory. To evaluate the predictive power of the research model, researchers should examine the explained variance (R^2) of the endogenous constructs. Using R^2 to assess the structural model is consistent with the objective of PLS to maximize variance explained in the endogenous variables. The literature suggests that R^2 values of 0.67, 0.33, and 0.19 are substantial, moderate, and weak, respectively (Chin, 1998b). The path coefficients of the PLS structural model have been measured, and bootstrap analysis was performed to assess the statistical significance of the path coefficients. The path coefficients have standardized values between -1 and +1. The estimated path coefficients which are close to +1 represent strong positive linear relationship and vice versa for negative values (Hair et al., 2013). Collectively, the R^2 in the research model is fit based on the study context, and the path coefficients (beta and significance) specify the significance level of acceptance of the research hypotheses (Chin, 1998b). Data analysis utilized a two-step approach as recommended by Anderson and Gerbing (1988). The first step involves the analysis of the measurement model, while the second step tests the structural relationships among the latent constructs. The aim of the two-step approach is to establish the reliability and validity of the measures before assessing the structural relationship of the model. Secondly, the significance of the path coefficients, thirdly, the level of the R^2 values, fourthly, f^2 effect size, and, thirdy, the predictive relevance including Q^2 and q^2 effect size were assessed. In the final step, using neural networks, we have verified the strength of the effect of independent variables on dependent variables whose significance was determined by SEM analysis. Data analysis was conducted in the Statistical Package for Social Sciences (SPSS 24) and SmartPLS software 2.0 (M3).

The internal consistency reliability was evaluated by using both Cronbach's alpha and composite reliability. According to Table 1, the internal consistency reliability

Table 1. Evaluation of the reflective measurement model

LC	Range of Factor Loadings	Number of Items	CR[a]	A[b]	AVE[c]	Inter-Construct Correlations[d]								
						BI	EE	FC	HM	Habit	PE	PV	SI	TRust
BI	0,838-0,941	5	0,95	0,94	0,81	1								
EE	0,756-0,848	5	0,91	0,87	0,66	0,53	1							
FC	0,553-0,869	5	0,87	0,80	0,57	0,55	0,66	1						
HM	0,834-0,934	3	0,92	0,88	0,80	0,59	0,60	0,60	1					
Habit	0,745-0,873	5	0,90	0,87	0,65	0,70	0,47	0,48	0,50	1				
PE	0,727-0,874	7	0,92	0,89	0,61	0,64	0,66	0,67	0,59	0,47	1			
PV	0,736-0,905	3	0,84	0,72	0,64	0,39	0,30	0,28	0,31	0,29	0,29	1		
SI	0,615-0,890	5	0,89	0,85	0,63	0,41	0,21	0,18	0,32	0,34	0,26	0,34	1	
TRust	0,827-0,894	5	0,93	0,91	0,74	0,40	0,19	0,11	0,27	0,32	0,15	0,48	0,40	1

[a]CR, composite reliability.

[b], Cronbach's alpha.

[c]AVE, average variance extracted.

[d]The square roots of the constructs' AVE values are shown in the diagonal line; non-diagonal elements are latent variable correlations.

[c]Average variance extracted (AVE)=(summation of the square of the factor loadings)/{(summation of the square of the factor loadings)+(summation of the error variances)}.

[a]Composite reliability (CR)=(square of the summation of the factor loadings)/{(square of the summation of the factor loadings)+(square of the summation of the error variances)}.

is verified because each latent construct clearly exceeds the minimum recommended level of 0.70 for composite reliability (Bagozzi and Yi, 1988) and Cronbach's alpha (Nunnally and Bernstein, 1994), respectively.

Convergent validity was estimated by using the average variance extracted (AVE). The values of each latent construct are above the suggested AVE value of 0.5, indicating a sufficient degree of convergent validity. Finally, the criterion by Fornell and Larcker (1981) is applied to evaluate discriminant validity. The square roots of all AVE scores (see diagonal elements in Table 1) are significantly larger than any other correlation coefficients among each construct, indicating good discriminant validity. Further support for discriminant validity can be derived from the fact that all of the indicator's loadings are higher than all of its cross-loadings. Hence, all relevant criteria met the requirements for testing the structure model.

Table 2. Results of hypothesis testing and predictable power

Hypotheses and Path	β Path Coef.	t-Value[a]	Effect Size[1] f^2	R^2	Effect Size[2] q^2	Q^2
H1 PE -> BI	0,310800	4,83***	0,127273	0,670	0,069915	0,533
H2 EE -> BI	-0,011392	0,18	0		0	
H3 SI -> BI	0,082181	1,96**	0,015152		0,006356	
H4 FC -> BI	0,033698	0,48	0,00303		-0,00214	
H5 HM -> BI	0,118854	1,90*	0,021212		0,012847966	
H6 PV -> BI	0,056581	1,31	0,009091		0	
H7 Habit -> BI	0,392887	7,64***	0,284848		0,164882227	
H8 TRust -> BI	0,134588	2,77***	0,036364		0,019271949	

[a]t-values for two-tailed test:
* 1.65 (sig. level 10%).
** 1.96 (sig. level=5%).
*** t-value 2.58 (sig. level = 1%) (Hair et al., 2011).
Notes: ***p<0.01, **p<0.05, *p<0.1 (two-sided).
effective size: 0 – none, 0.02 – small, 0.15 - medium, 0.35 – large (Cohen, 1988).
Effect sizes calculated using the following formulas
[1]f^2= R^2included - R^2excluded / 1- R^2included (1)
[2]q^2 = Q^2included - Q^2excluded / 1- Q^2included (2)

EVALUATION OF THE STRUCTURAL MODEL

Furthermore, the structural model would assess the R^2 measures and the level and significance of the path coefficients by performing the bootstrapping procedure of 5000 resamples (Chin, 1998b; Croteau and Bergeron, 2001; Gil-Garcia, 2008; Hair et al., 2011). First, researcher should check the sign, magnitude, and signifi- cance of each path coefficient, all of which should be consistent with theory. To evaluate the predictive power of the research model, researchers should examine the explained variance (R^2) of the endogenous constructs. Using R^2 to assess the structural model is consistent with the objective of PLS tomaximize variance explained in the endogenous variables. The literature suggests that R^2 values of 0.67, 0.33, and 0.19 are substantial, moderate, and weak, respectively (Chin, 1998b). In addition to PLS Algorithm, the bootstrapping procedure was used and we selected 269 cases, 5000 samples, and the no sign changes option to evaluate the significance of the path coefficients (Hair, Sarstedt, Ringle, & Mena, 2012). The results of the PLS-SEM analysis show, as in Table 2, the structural model estimation and the evaluation of the formulated hypotheses.

The strength of the individual path coefficients and their statistical significance are obtained by applying the bootstrap re-sampling procedure with 5000 samples. Thus, as listed in Table 2, five hypothesized paths were statistically significant. Thus, H1,

H3, H5, H7 and H8 were supported. Three of the eight hypothesized paths, from effort expectancy to behavioral intention (H2), from facilitating conditions to to behavioral intention (H4), from price value to behavioral intention (H6) were not supported by statistically significant path coefficients. Because PLS is predictive-oriented, the R^2 measure is the essential criterion for structural model assessment, which presents the amount of explained variance of the endogenous latent variable. Although no generalities exist with regard to what is a high or low level of R^2, Chin (1998) and Henseler, Ringle, and Sinkovics (2009) describe R^2 values of 0.67, 0.33 and 0.19 as substantial, moderate and weak, respectively. While the R^2 values were estimated with the bootstrapping procedure, the values of Stone–Geisser's Q2 (Geisser 1974; Stone 1974) for assessing the research model's ability to predict were calculated by using the blindfolding procedure (Tenenhaus et al. 2005). Even though Q^2 can be measured in two forms, in this study the cross-validated redundancy measures of Q^2 are used, as suggested by Hair, Ringle, and Sarstedt (2011).

As in Table 2, The R^2 values of the endogenous latent construct were also obtained using the PLS algorithm procedure. According to the guideline by Cohen (1988), the fitted multiple regression model depends on R^2, and if R^2 value lies between 0.02 and 0.12, the model is weak, 0.13 and 0.25 is moderate and 0.26 and above is good (Gaur & Gaur, 2006; Griffith, 1996). However, Hair et al. (2012) suggested that the judgement of R^2 value is high/low depends on the specific research context. To evaluate the structural models' predictive power, R squares (R^2) were calculated. R squares (R^2) indicates the amount of variance explained by the exogenous variables (Barclay et al., 1995). Using a bootstrapping technique with a re-sampling of 5000. The Stone–Geisser's Q^2 (Geisser, 1975; Stone, 1974) for the predictive sample reuse technique can be applied as a criterion for the predictive relevance besides looking at the magnitude of the R^2. According to Henseler et al. (2009), this measure is used to assess the research model's capability to predict. However, Stone–Geisser's Q^2 indicates to the interpretation that the model of our study is satisfying the predictive relevance, given that the results of R^2 versus Q^2. As the endogenous latent construct the R^2 value for behavioral intention is 0.670 with a Q^2 value of 0.533, which is relatively high. Thus, the explanatory power of performance expectancy, effort expectancy, social influence, facilitating conditions, hedonic motivation, price value, habit and trust variables explained %67 of the variance in behavioral intention is substantial. According to Hair et al. (2013), in SEM models, Q^2 values bigger than zero for a reflective endogenous construct imply the path model's predictive relevance for a particular construct (Using cross-validated redundancy is recommended). This study picked an omission distance (D)=8. By performing blindfolding procedures, Q^2 value is considerably above zero, which supports the model's (Figure 1) predictive relevance for the eight endogenous constructs. Moreover, the path model has predictive relevance for the endogenous construct because all Q^2-values are consistently larger than zero (Henseler, Ringle, and Sinkovics 2009). In addition, the f^2 effect size, which shows the impact of a specific predictor construct on an endogenous latent construct, and the q^2 effect size for the predictive relevance are presented in Table 2. Besides measuring the values of R^2 and Q^2, the literature further suggests evaluating both effect size f^2 and q^2 for the R^2-values and Q^2-values, respectively. Whereas the effect size f^2 indicates how strongly the latent endogenous variable is influenced by individual exogenous variables, the effect size q^2 evaluates the predictive relevance of the exogenous variables for a certain endogenous variable (Hair et al., 2013; Hair, Ringle, and Sarstedt, 2011). In order to judge both of these effect sizes, Chin (1998) and Henseler, Ringle, and Sinkovics (2009) define values of 0.02, 0.15 and 0.35, which indicate small, medium and large effects, respectively.

Considering the underlying research model, the exogenous variable habit has a medium effect size on behavioral intention ($f^2 = 0,285$) and PE has a small effect size on BI ($f^2 = 0,127$). Meanwhile, all other f^2-values involve a small effect size.

In terms of the prediction relevance of the individual exogenous variables, the q^2-value of 0,165 for the variable habit determines medium effect on the predictive relevance for BI. For all other q^2-values, the analysis reveals a weak contribution for the prediction relevance. Table 2 provides an overview of all relevant criteria for assessing the quality of the structure model.

We also conducted a global fit measure Goodness of fit (GoF) assessment for PLS path modelling, which is defined as geometric mean of the average communality and average R2 (for endogenous constructs; Tenenhaus et al. (2005) following the procedure used by Akter, D'Ambra and Ray (2011), Chin, 2010; Hair et al., 2012. Following the guidelines of Wetzels et al. (2009), we estimated the GoF values (see formula 1), which may serve as cut-off values for global validation of PLS models. Regarding model quality, Wetzels et al. (2009) provide a global fit (GoF) measure for PLS path modeling and derive a GoF measure with effect sizes for R2 by substituting the minimum average AVE of 0.50. The GoF measures have been suggested as baseline values for validating the PLS model globally (the cut value of $GoF_{small} = 0.1$, $GoF_{medium} = 0.25$, and $GoF_{large} = 0.36$) (Akter, D'Ambra, & Ray 2010; Tenenhaus et al., 2005; Wetzels et al. 2009). The research model obtained a GoF value of 0.68, which is greater than the cut-off value of 0.36. (see Table 3).

Table 3. Structural model

Fit Measures	Endogenous Construct	Final Model
R^2	Behavioral Intention	0,670
GoF		0,68

(1) GoF = $\sqrt{}$ Average Communality x Average R^2

NEURAL NETWORK ANALYSIS

This book chapter utilizes a multi-analytical approach by integrating SEM and neural network analysis, one of the most prominent artificial intelligence techniques. SEM and Multiple Regression Analysis (MRA) are able to ascertain only linear relationships, which may lead to oversimplification of complex decision-making processes (Chan and Chong, 2012; Sim et al., 2014; Tan et al., 2014). Partial least squares (PLS) is not suitable to be used since there are strong foundations to support the TAM because of being the TAM has been well established. Although the covariance-based SEM is suitable for theory validation, it is only capable of ascertaining linear relationships, leading to the possibilities of oversimplification of the complexities of the decision to adopt applications. To surmount this drawback, an integrated SEM-NN approach was utilized. The superiority of using this approach is that the neural network model is able to learn complex linear and non-linear relations between predictors and the adoption decision (Chan and Chong, 2012). Also, ANNs are more robust and can provide higher prediction accuracy than linear models (Tan et al., 2014) and may surmount common statistical techniques, such as MRA (Chong, 2013a; Sim et al., 2014). Although NN is able to uncover both linear and nonlinear relationships without strong theoretical foundations, it is not suitable for hypothesis testing and examining causal relationships due to its "black-box" operation (Chan and Chong, 2012). Anyhow, since neural network is able to "learn" through training processes and tolerate noisy samples, it is superior to the PLS method. Therefore, both SEM and NN methods aimed to take advantages, in this book chapter a combined SEM-NN approach utilized by first validating the TAM theory and the external variables, followed by examination of the normalized importance of the significant determinants derived from the SEM analysis. Therefore, in this book chapter, a two-stage approach is adopted (Chong, 2013b; Leong et al., 2013; Tan et al., 2014). First, SEM is used to test the overall research model and determine significant hypothesized predictors, which are then, in a second stage, used as inputs to the neural network model used to determine the relative importance of each predictor variable.

Artificial neural network (ANN) is, defined as "a massively parallel distributed processor made up of simple processing units, which have a neural propensity for storing experimental knowledge and making it available for use" (Haykin, 2001:2). ANN "resembles the human brain whereby knowledge is acquired by the network through a learning process while inter neuron connection strengths called synaptic weights, which are used to store knowledge" (SPSS, 2012). ANN comprise of neurons or nodes that are disseminated in three layers, namely input, hidden and output layers. Every input neuron is given a synaptic weight that is conveyed to the hidden layer with some hidden neurons before being transformed into an output value by an activation function. The synaptic weights of the connections will be altered via an iterative training process and the knowledge attained from the process will be kept for an upcoming predictive use. ANN's application to information system researches remains scarce although it has been engaged in various disciplines (Shmueli and Koppius).

There are many variety of neural networks, but in this book chapter one of the most common and popular – feed forward back-propagation multilayer perceptron (MLP) will be used by researcher (Chong et al., 2015; Huang, 2010; Negnevitsky, 2011). MLP neural network algorithm executes a neural network which is a constitution of several layers of artificial neurons engendered by input signals and is conveyed to the network through synapses to other neurons which are present in different layers. A common neural network constitute of discrete hierarchical layers, i.e. one input, one or more hidden and one output layer. The number of hidden layers depends of the complexity of the problem to be solved. With one hidden layer, any continuous function can be represented, while with two hidden layers even discontinuous functions can be modelled (Negnevitsky, 2011). In the technology acceptance neural network models usually only one hidden layer is used (Chong et al., 2015; Chong, 2013a; Chong, 2013b; Huang, 2010; Leong et al., 2013; Sim et al., 2014; Tan et al., 2014). Each layer constitute of neurons, which are connected with the neurons of the following layer and each connection is represented by an adaptable synaptic weight. In the feed-forward networks the signals are fed forward from the input layer, through the network, to the output layer. MLP belongs to the class of supervised learning ANNs, which means that knowledge is stored in the network by iteratively exposing it to patterns of known inputs and outputs. The error, i.e. the difference between desired (known) and actual (predicted) output, is calculated and propagated back in the opposite direction, in order to adjust synaptic weights so to minimize the estimation error.

The number of neurons in the input layer is equal to the number of inputs, i.e. predictors, while the number of neurons in the out-put layer is equal to the number of outputs, i.e. dependent variables. The number of neurons in the hidden layer affects both prediction accuracy and speed of network training. Simulation experiments indicate that to some point higher number of neurons in the hidden layer gives higher estimation accuracy (Negnevitsky, 2011);however, too many of them can dramatically increase the computational load. Another problem is over-fitting. If the number of hidden neurons is too big, the network might simply memorize all training examples and not be able to generalize, i.e. to give correct output with data not used in the training. There is no heuristic way to determine the number of hidden neurons, so usually the trial-and-error (Chan and Chong, 2012; Chong et al., 2015; Chong, 2013a, 2013b) and the rules-of-thumb are used. One of the most widely known empirically-driven rules-of-thumb is that the optimal number of hidden neurons is usually between the number of the input and number of the output neurons (Blum, 1992). Many researchers suggested other rules, in which the number of hidden neurons also depends on the number of both input and output neurons (Gnana Sheela and Deepa, 2013). Despite its importance, there is no unique rule for selecting the optimum number of hidden neurons. It should be noted that, incertain cases, all these rules-of-thumb should be tested before the final application. In most cases, the network that performs best on the testing set with the least number of hidden neurons should be selected. Also, there are many other factors that can influence selection of the number of hidden neurons, like the number of hidden layers, the sample size, the neural network architecture, the complexity of the activation function, the training algorithm, etc.(Gnana Sheela and Deepa, 2013).

The Figure 2 (Architecture of Applied Neural Network) which is given below represents artificial Perceptron neural model with 5 inputs $\{x_1, x_2, ..., x_5\}$ in which each input xi has an associated synapse wi and an output y. The Neural network model which is displayed in Figure 2 states the relationship between antecedents of application acceptance and behavioral intention. The synaptic weight shows the strength of the relationship between variables. In this book chapter, neural network is modelled in SPSS 22, with the input layer consisting of five independent significant

Figure 2. ANN model in the study

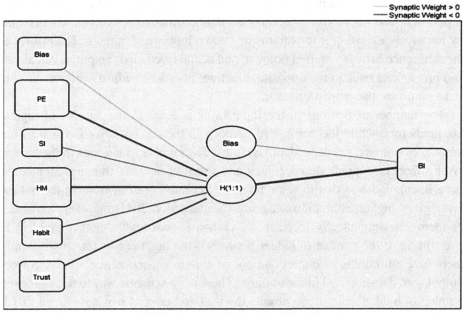

Hidden layer activation function: Sigmoid

Output layer activation function: Sigmoid

variables from SEM (i.e. of performance expectancy, social influence, hedonic motivation, habit and trust), while the output layer consists of one output variable (behavioral intention). Following the recommendations given above, the number of nodes in one hidden layer is set to 2.Sigmoid function is used as an activation function for neurons in both hidden and output layers (Chan and Chong, 2012; Leong et al., 2013). In order to increase the effectiveness of training, i.e. to provide shorter training times and better performance (Negnevitsky,2011), all inputs and outputs were normalized to the range [0, 1]. In order to avoid over-fitting, a ten-fold cross validation was performed, where by 90% of the data was used for network training and leaving the remaining 10% was used to measure the prediction accuracy of the trained network (Chong et al., 2015; Chong, 2013a; Chong, 2013b; Leong et al., 2013; Sim et al., 2014; Tan et al., 2014). As a measure of the predictive accuracy of the model, the Root Mean Square of Error (RMSE) of both training and testing data sets for all ten neural networks, as well as the averages and standard deviations for both data sets are computed and presented in Table 4. The average RMSE of the neural network model are quite small (0.1123 for training data and 0.0884 for testing data), indicating a quite accurate prediction (Leong et al., 2013; Sim et al., 2014; Tan et al., 2014). that the ANN models are quite reliable in capturing the relationships between predictors and outputs. The importance of every independent variable is a measure of how much the value predicted by the network model varies with different values of the independent variable (Chong, 2013a). The normalized importance is the ratio of the importance of each predictor to the highest importance value. In order

Table 4. RMSE of neural networks

ANN	Training	Testing
ANN1	0,1225	0,0882
ANN2	0,1212	0,0996
ANN3	0,1219	0,0819
ANN4	0,1129	0,0879
ANN5	0,1126	0,0889
ANN6	0,0897	0,112
ANN7	0,1109	0,0864
ANN8	0,1231	0,0899
ANN9	0,1102	0,1269
ANN10	0,1123	0,0791
Average	0,1123	0,0884
Standard deviation	0,0029	0,0217

to understand the relative importance of independent variables to predict adoption of mobile applications, a sensitivity analysis was performed in the neural network model. The summary of the normalized importance of independent variables is given in Table 5. The importance of an independent variable is a measure of the degree to which the network's model predicted changes in the output values with respect to the changes in values of independent variables (Chong, 2013a). On the basis of the neural network results, the most significant independent variable in predicting mobile application acceptance was HM, followed by PE, Trust, Habit and SI.

DISCUSSION

This book chapter has proposed eight hypotheses based on conducting a literature review. By statistically analyzing the collected data five of the hypothesis were supported and proved to affect the behavioral intention to use apps, and three rejected. The factors that were found to affect the behavioral intention are Performance Expectancy, social influence, Hedonic Motivation, habit and trust. All the factors that have been proven in this study to significantly affect the behavioral intention to use apps, have a positive influence on behavioral intention, which in accordance with technology acceptance theories (Ajzen et al., 1985; Davis et al., 1989; Venkatesh et al., 2003; Venkatesh al., 2012). Moreover this study has rejected three hypotheses, as the statistical analysis for Effort Expectancy, facilitating conditions and trust showed that these factors do not statistically significantly affect the behavioral intention to use apps. This was to an extent expected as this book chapter investigates the behavioral intention to use apps in Turkey, which is a context that has not been addressed before in previous research. Likewise previous technology acceptance research suggest that different cultural and technological contexts are to generate different factors that affect the acceptance of a particular technology (Gefen et al.,2003; Venkatesh et al., 2012), which means that identical factors that were identified to influence

Table 5. Normalized importance of constructs

Variables	Importance	Normalized Importance
HM	0,376	100%
PE	0,275	73,1%
TRUST	0,149	0,408%
HABİT	0,108	0,307%
Sİf	0,093	0,265%

the acceptance of m-commerce and m-shopping (Yang 2012; Wei et al., 2009), mobile internet (Venkatesh et al., 2012), in previous research do not influence the behavioral intention to use apps in Turkey.

Among all the other factors that affect behavioral intention, this study's results indicate that habit, is the factor that has the strongest influence on behavioral intention, and hence is the strongest predictor the behavioral intention to use apps. This result is similar to the studies conducted by Venkatesh et al. (2012), Liao et al. (2006). Also, Hew et al. (2015), which studied technology acceptance in the context of mobile applications, found that Habit is the most important factor, which affects the intention to use mobile applications. When the using of apps becomes frequent, habit emerges and becomes a force that increases the behavioral intention to continue using the mobile applications (Hew et al., 2015). Also, in today's Turkish society mobile devices have become a part of people's everyday life, which makes the users automatically reliant on mobile applications too. Since our results indicate that performance expectancy is the second most important factor in determining the intention to use apps, it can be inferred that, due to users prior get into the habit of use of apps, and then they find useful, users will continue to use these apps. As people continue to use the apps, this fosters unplanned use of the apps. Here behavior evolves into habit, and users find that they must use apps. Therefore, in the context of Habit plays a very important role in determining the behavioral intentions to use the app.

After habit, this study reveals that performance expectancy is the second most important factor in predicting the user behavioral intention to use apps. This induces that the more people find apps useful, the more they will have the intention to use these apps. This finding is consistent with the research done by Davis, Bagozzi and Warshaw (1989), their aim was to find the most important factors that affect people's intentions to use technology, their investigation concluded that perceived usefulness of the technology is the strongest determinant of people's intentions to use the technology. This result is in line with the findings of AbuShanab et al. (2007), Chong et al. (2013), Leong et al. (2013b), Lewis et al. (2013), Liao et al., (2011), Lin et al. (2013), Martins et al. (2014), Oliveira et al. (2014), Oechslein, Fleischmann, and Hess (2014), Shi (2009), Slade et al. (2014), Sun et al. (2010), Wong et al. (2014).

Facilitating conditions has not been proven to statistically significantly affect the behavioral intention to use apps, which is not consistent with previous work done by Chong (2013), Venkatesh et al. (2012). This implies that consumers do no find it important to have the necessary support and help while using apps, and the more support, and guidelines they have the more they are not willing to use apps. This surprisingly result is in line with the findings of Arenas-Gaitán et al. (2015), Chong (2013), Slade et al., (2014), Thomas et al. (2013), Yang (2010), Yeoh et al. (2011) and Zhou (2008).

Likewise hedonic motivation significantly affects the behavioral intention to use apps which is in alignment with Hew et al. (2015), Venkatesh et al. (2012) and Yang (2010). Therefore, from the results of this study it can be inferred that if the users of apps find the various features and functions in apps fun, the users have the intention to use these apps, and the intention to use will increase the more they find the apps entertaining. Hence, Hedonic Motivations plays a factor of importance in when it comes to determining the intention to use apps. This result is aligned with the study done by Bere (2014), Escobar-Rodríguez et al. (2013), Raman et al. (2013), Harsono et al. (2014) and Alalwan et al. (2014), which found that HM has a positive impact on BI.

In this study social influence relates to the degree to which significant others (friends and relatives) believe that the user should use apps. The results of this study indicate that social influence affect the behavioral intention to use the apps. Yang (2013) and Hew et al. (2015) investigated mobile application's acceptance and found that social influence could not affect the behavioral intention to use mobile apps, which is in not alignment with our results. Therefore users are influenced by the opinions and suggestions of family and friends who think they should or should use apps. This may be because app reviews and expert opinions are made more available online, hence users can make decisions if to use the app based on these reviews without having to consult relatives and friends. Likewise apps are a relatively new technology (Kim et al., 2014), many of the people the users perceives important, could be not even using the m-shopping fashion apps, and the user would not be influences significantly by family and friends surrounding the him/her. The result was consistent with previous empirical findings conducted by Alwahaishi et al. (2013), Chong et al. (2012), Fuksa (2013), Jaradat et al. (2013), Jawad et al. (2013), Martín and Herrero (2012) and Yu (2012).

The results of this study indicate that in Turkey the Price Value factor for apps does not influence the willingness to use these apps. This finding is supported in the study conducted by Hew et al. (2015) on the acceptance of mobile apps, in which the Price Value factor did not affect the behavioral intention to use mobile apps. On the other hand, the empirical research done by Venkatesh et al. (2012) proved the Price Value factor as significant by conducting empirical research in China. However the people contrary to Turkey could be more price sensitive in China, for instance due to lower GDP per capita than in Turkey (Data.worldbank.org, 2017). This could be an underpinning reason why this factor did not prove to be significant in the context of apps in Turkey. Moreover, users' who are willing to use apps in Turkey are not influenced by the Price Value but by other factors, that proved to be significant, such as if app is useful (Performance Expectancy), if the app is entertaining (Hedonic Motivation), the users are used to the apps (Habit), and if the app is trustworthy. Therefore as long as the app is useful, fun to use…etc., people are willing to use apps without taking into consideration the Price Value. The result was consistent with previous empirical findings conducted by Unyolo (2012), Xu (2014), Yang (2013), Dhulla et al. (2014) and Arenas-Gaitán et al. (2015), and which verified that PV has a positive influence on BI.

Effort Expectancy was found to have an insignificant effect on the user behavioral intention to use apps in Turkey, which is in contrast with prior technology acceptance studies and models (Chong, 2013; Venkatesh et al., 2012; Davis et al., 1989; Oliveira et al., 2014). However this result is consistent with the study on m-commerce acceptance of Wei et al. (2009), which concluded that there is no significant relationship between the perceived ease of use of m-commerce and consumer intention to use mcommerce.

Additionally, the results of this study show that Facilitating Conditions do not affects the behavioral intention to use apps, while Effort Expectancy does not have a significant effect. This could indicate that providing Facilitating Conditions are present, which means people have access to the resources necessary to use the apps, (there are satisfactory online and offline support made available), than the difficulty level of using the apps, is not a hindrance in the intention to use the apps. Hence Effort Expectancy does not affect the behavioral intention to use apps. Moreover, most of our respondents are relatively young, aged between 25 and 24, and therefore are used to technology and capable of learning how apps work. It can be inferred that people in Turkey are experienced with technology and have a good foundation of knowledge on how to use the technology and mobile apps. Hence, they find it relatively easy to learn how to use apps. Therefore the difficulty level of using the apps is not a significant predictor of the behavioral intention to use apps in Turkey. This is not consistent with the past studies conducted by AlAwadhi et al. (2008), Im et al. (2011), Chang (2013), Tai et al. (2013), Alharbi et al. (2014) and Teo et al. (2015), which endorsed that EE has a positive impact on BI.

An expected finding in our study is that Trust resulted to have a significant effect on the behavioral intention to use apps in Turkey. However this result is not coherent with the study conducted by Tang and Chi (2016), who found that consumer's trust did not influence significantly the consumers' intention to use an online store. On the contrary, trust in our study was defined as the willingness to rely on the apps vendors in whom the individual has confidence (Groß, 2015a; Moorman et al.,1993). One reason underpinning these finding could be that the trust in the apps vendor influence the intention to use apps because the individuals in Turkey have already gained trust in the online vendors from establishing a good relationship from previous experience with them. This was obtained first through practicing with the vendors via the computer platform (e-commerce), then through m-websites and finally with apps. In other words, people in Turkey are used to shopping online, have experience with online vendors from e-commerce and therefore they have overcome the trust concerns regarding relying on application vendors.

"Adopter categories are classifications of the members of a social system on the basis of innovativeness, the degree to which an individual or other unit of adoption is relatively earlier in adopting new ideas than other members of a system" (Rogers, 2003: 22). The relatively earlier adopters of innovativeness in a social system also differ from later adopters as they are characterized by a greater ability to cope with uncertainty and risk (Rogers, 1995), which can be an additional explanation why trust does not play an important role in predicting the willingness to use m-shopping fashion apps. Furthermore, Groß (2015b) empirically verified that the trust in the m-vendor affects the intention to use m-shopping in Germany.

MANAGERIAL IMPLICATIONS

An innovative methodology that is based on the combined application of structural equation modeling and neural networks provides special originality to the paper. In this sense, after checking the validity of the model and testing the effect of independent variables on the dependent variable within the SEM analysis, neural networks were used in the research as well, thus enabling additional verification of the results provided by the SEM analysis. The paper provides useful theoretical implications to academic researchers and scholars, as well as managerial implications to mobile application providers. The managerial practical implications from this research are that managers and marketers should pay special attention to Habit, Performance Expectancy, social influence, Hedonic Motivation and trust factors, and should ensure that these factors are met, in order to increase the acceptance and usage apps. Since habit is the most significant factor and performance Expectancy is the second most significant factor in affecting the intention to use apps it is important that marketers and retailers when designing their app focus on features that will make apps useful for the users, provide them with quality information about apps. Because the better the apps will support the users' activities the more will these apps be attractive. Managers should make sure the apps add value to their users by ensuring that they help them increase their performance. Furthermore Habit is an important factor therefore managers when designing apps could refer to the similar design of prevalent computer software, and popular websites, as the more people are used to using a certain technology, it becomes quickly a routine and habit. Likewise, when it comes to Hedonic Motivation managers could enforce functions on the apps that would create enjoyable and entertaining experience. For instance, Hedonic Motivation can increase by adding animated features, fun content, and interaction to the apps.

DISCUSSION OF METHOD

The proposed research model is reliable which was proved though statistical analysis. However not all the independent factors of the proposed research model were found to have a significant linear relationship with the independent variable, and three hypothesis were rejected. Therefore the findings of this research do not fully correspond to the original UTAUT 2 model, which was expected till an extent as this study investigated the behavioral intention factor for a different context (mobile applications), that was not addressed previously by studies.

Due to the time constrain the authors prioritized getting sufficient number of respondents to be able to carry out statistics analysis, and hence the convenience sampling method was used. Moreover, if the survey contained less questions the number of respondents could have been increased. However it was not possible to delete some of the survey questions, as they had their own factor they corresponded to, and were taken from previous research. In these previous research, these survey questions had been proved to be significant for their given factor. Thus, deleting some questions would result in lower reliability and validity of the collected data. Moreover, the majority of the respondents are of relatively young age, however this study did not pursue the investigation on the effect that the moderating variables (such as age, gender, etc.) have on the behavioral intention to use apps, as a larger sample and more time was required to be able to efficiently conduct such a research.

STRENGTH AND WEAKNESS OF THE RESEARCH

This research work contributes to a theoretical understanding of the factors that drive the intention to use of mobile applications. Therefore the purpose of this study has been fulfilled. Some of the strengths of this study are that, the multiple linear regression analysis showed that 67% (adjusted $R^2=0,670$) of the total variability in the behavioral intention to use apps is explained by the independent factors in the research model. This indicates that the model of this study is useful, and has good predictive value for the behavioral intention to use the apps from a consumer's perspective. Therefore the model of this study can be applied for further studies on apps. Also other mobile applications studies could make use of this research's model for future research.

Moreover this study identified five factors that affect the behavioral intention to use apps in Turkey. And the results indicate that habit is the factor that has the strongest influence on the behavioral intention to use apps. Likewise the study was conducted by applying the UTAUT 2 model developed by Venkatesh et al. (2012) as a base for the proposed research model, while previous technology acceptance studies applied older technology acceptance models. Moreover this research provides implications for management, and future research. However, there are also some weaknesses present in the study. The study used nonprobability sampling, which is an inferior method compared to probability sampling. This method however was perceived as necessary for the authors due to the population of the study being unknown, and a limited time frame that the primary data collection had to be gathered. This method enabled the authors to conduct the study on apps and collect the necessary sample size. The collection of the questionnaire was extremely challenging because to access the users of apps in Turkey took a lot of time. Even though 269 surveys have been collected, if more surveys were collected the credibility of the findings could have been increased further. Furthermore, the results of the study are limited due to the differences in the demographic variables (e.g. age, gender etc.) of the respondents. Moreover the predictability of the research model could have been increased if more independent factors have been proposed in our research model to affect the behavioral intention to use m-shopping fashion apps. However, more factors would make the questionnaire longer and made the respondents less willing to answer the questionnaire making the primary data collection less manageable.

SUGGESTION FOR FURTHER RESEARCH

Apart from the managerial implications, this study provides some implications for scholars too. This study proposed a model for measuring the behavioral intention to use apps based on the UTAUT 2. By conducing reliability analysis, testing the proposed research model empirically, it has been proved that the model is valid and reliable for apps. This study shed light upon the factors that affect the behavioral intention to use apps in Turkey, hence it is recommended to explore the proposed research model and results in other cultural contexts. Furthermore, researchers could study the acceptance of same technology in different countries to explain the role that the factor of national culture plays in the acceptance of technology. Future research could address how factors that affect the behavioral intention to use apps differ for different age, gender and experience groups. Likewise it would be interesting to address the investigation of how the acceptance of technology differs among users and non-users of a certain technology.

Likewise, future studies should strive to optimize the UTAUT 2 model by expanding it with additional variables that either directly or indirectly impact the behavioral intention to use a technology or are moderating variables. More factors that affect the acceptance of apps should be developed, and tested. It would be useful that future studies would interview the users of apps, to develop additional factors that affect their acceptance, as there is a gap in the literature when it comes to apps and mobile applications in general. Lastly, future researchers should use the longitudinal approach to predict adoption intention over time. As such, the model should be validated at different points in time. For example, future studies should study adoption intention in stages, such as pre-adoption and post-adoption of mobile apps.

CONCLUSION

The purpose of this book chapter was to identify the factors that affect the behavioral intention to use apps in Turkey. Based on the previous technology acceptance studies and the UTAUT 2 model, this study developed the proposed research model (see Figure 1) and hypothesized eight factors that affect the users' behavioral intention to use apps. Quantitative analyses were implemented to test the eight hypotheses, and provide the source for answering research question and of this study. The tested research model is depicted in Figure 1, and Table 2 summarizes the factors that were proved to be significant.

The results of the hypotheses testing show that performance expectancy, social influence, hedonic motivation, habit and trust directly affect and are determinants of the behavioral intention to use apps in Turkey. Moreover, results indicate that habit of mobile apps has the strongest influence on the user's behavioral intention to use apps. The second strongest factor that affects the behavioral intention to use apps is performance expectancy. Consequently, the third most influential factor is trust, and lastly, social influence. Furthermore, results also showed that habit, performance expectancy and hedonic motivation all affect positively the behavioral intention to use apps, which is in consistence with previous technology acceptance theories and trust and social influence affect positively the behavioral intention to use apps, which is in not consistence with previous technology acceptance theories. The other three independent factors of the proposed research model, effort expectancy, facilitating conditions and price value were rejected to statistically significantly, affect the behavioral intention to use apps in Turkey.

REFERENCES

Aarts, H., Verplanken, B., & van Knippenberg, A. (1998). Predicting behavior from actions in the past: Repeated decision making or a matter of habit? *Journal of Applied Social Psychology*, *28*(15), 1355–1374. doi:10.1111/j.1559-1816.1998.tb01681.x

AbuShanab, E., & Pearson, J. M. (2007). Internet banking in Jordan: The unified theory of acceptance and use of technology (UTAUT) perspective. *Journal of Systems and Information Technology*, *9*(1), 78–97. doi:10.1108/13287260710817700

Ajzen, I. (1985). *From intentions to actions: A theory of planned behavior*. Springer Berlin Heidelberg.

Ajzen, I. (1991). The theory of planned behavior. *Organizational Behavior and Human Decision Processes*, 179–211.

Akour, H. (2009). Determinants of mobile learning acceptance: An empirical investigation in higher education (Order No. 3408682, Oklahoma State University). Retrieved from ProQuest Dissertations and Theses, 379.

Akter, S., D'Ambra, J., & Ray, P. (2011). Trustworthiness in mHealth information services: An assessment of a hierarchical model with mediating and moderating effects using partial least squares (PLS). *Journal of the American Society for Information Science and Technology*, *62*(1), 100–116. doi:10.1002/asi.21442

Al-Debei, M., & Al-Lozi, E. (2014). Explaining and predicting the adoption intention of mobile data services: A value-based approach. *Computers in Human Behavior*, *35*, 326–338. doi:10.1016/j.chb.2014.03.011

Alalwan, A., Dwivedi, Y., & Williams, M. (2014). Examining Factors Affecting Customer Intention And Adoption Of Internet Banking In Jordan. *UK Academy for Information Systems Conference Proceedings 2014*.

AlAwadhi, S., & Morris, A. (2008). The use of the UTAUT model in the adoption of E-government services in Kuwait. *Proceedings of the 41st Hawaii International Conference on System Sciences*, 1-11. doi:10.1109/HICSS.2008.452

Alharbi, S., & Drew, S. (2014). Mobile learning-system usage: Scale development and empirical tests. *International Journal of Advanced Research in Artificial Intelligence*, *3*(11), 31–47. doi:10.14569/IJARAI.2014.031105

Alwahaishi, S., & Snasel, V. (2013). Consumers' acceptance and use of information and communications technology: A UTAUT and Flow Based Theoretical Model. *Journal of Technology Management & Innovation*, *8*(2), 102–112. doi:10.4067/S0718-27242013000200005

Anderson, J. C., & Gerbing, D. (1988). Structural equation modeling in practice: A review and recommended two-step approach. *Psychological Bulletin*, *103*(3), 411–423. doi:10.1037/0033-2909.103.3.411

Android Authority. (2017). Retrieved from http://www.androidauthority.com/google-play-store-vs-the-apple-app-store-601836/

Apps, M. (2016). *What Consumers Really Need and Want. A Global Study of Consumers' Expectations and Experiences of Mobile Applications.* Available at: https://info.dynatrace.com/rs/compuware/images/Mobile_App_Survey_Report.pdf

Arenas-Gaitán, J., Peral-Peral, B., & Ramón-Jerónimo, M. A. (2015). Elderly and Internet Banking: An Application of UTAUT2. *Journal of Internet Banking and Commerce, 20*(1).

Bagozzi, R. P., & Yi, Y. (1988). On the Evaluation of Structural Equation Models. *Journal of the Academy of Marketing Science, 16*(1), 74–94. doi:10.1007/BF02723327

Bagozzi, R. P., Yi, Y., & Phillips, L. W. (1991). Assessing construct validity in organiza¬tional research. *Administrative Science Quarterly, 36*(3), 421–458. doi:10.2307/2393203

Barclay, D., Higgins, C., & Thompson, R. (1995). The partial least squares (PLS) approach to causal modeling: Personal computer adoption and use as an illustration. *Technology Studies, 2*(2), 285–309.

Bere, A. (2014, April). *Exploring determinants for mobile learning user acceptance and use: An application of UTAUT.* Paper presented at the 11th International Conference on Information Technology: New Generarions, Las Vegas, NV. doi:10.1109/ITNG.2014.114

Blum, A. (1992). *Neural Networks.* New York: Wiley.

Brown, S. A., & Venkatesh, V. (2005). A model of adoption of technology in the household: A baseline model test and extension incorporating household life cycle. *Management Information Systems Quarterly, 29*(4), 399–426. doi:10.2307/25148690

Callum, K., & Jeffrey, L. (2014). Comparing the role of ICT literacy andanxiety in the adoption of mobile learning. *Computers in Human Behavior, 39*, 8–19. doi:10.1016/j.chb.2014.05.024

Chan, F. T. S., & Chong, A. Y.-L. (2012). A SEM-neural network approach forunderstanding determinants of interorganizational system standard adoptionand performances. *Decision Support Systems, 54*(1), 621–630. doi:10.1016/j.dss.2012.08.009

Chang, C. C. (2013). Library mobile appication university libraries. *Library Hi Tech, 31*(3), 478–492. doi:10.1108/LHT-03-2013-0024

Chemingui, H., & Ben lallouna, H. (2013). Resistance, motivations, trust and intention to use mobile financial services. *International Journal of Bank Marketing, 31*(7), 574–592. doi:10.1108/IJBM-12-2012-0124

Chen, C. (2013). Perceived risk, usage frequency of mobile banking services. *Managing Service Quality, 23*(5), 410–436. doi:10.1108/MSQ-10-2012-0137

Chin, W. W. (1998b). The partial least squares approach for structural equation modeling. In G. A. Marcoulides (Ed.), *Modern Methods for Business Research* (pp. 295–336). Lawarence Erlbaum Associates.

Chin, W. W. (2010). How to write up and report PLS analyses. In *Handbook of Partial Least Squares* (pp. 655–690). Berlin: Springer. doi:10.1007/978-3-540-32827-8_29

Chin, W. W., & Newsted, P. R. (1999). Structural equation modeling analysis with small samples using partial least squares. *Statistical Strategies for Small Sample Research, 2*, 307-342.

Chong, A. (2013b). A two-staged SEM-neural network approach for understanding and predicting the determinants of m-commerce adoption. *Expert Systems with Applications, 40*(4), 1240–1247. doi:10.1016/j.eswa.2012.08.067

Chong, A. Y. L. (2013a). Predicting m-commerce adoption determinants: A neural network approach. *Expert Systems with Applications, 40*(1), 523–530. doi:10.1016/j.eswa.2012.07.068

Chong, A. Y. L., Chan, F. Y. L., & Ooi, K. B. (2014). Predicting consumer decisions to adopt mobile commerce: Cross country empirical examination between China and Malaysia. *Decision Support Systems, 53*(1), 34–43. doi:10.1016/j.dss.2011.12.001

Chong, A. Y. L., Darmawan, N., Ooi, K. B., & Lin, B. (2010). Adoption of 3G services among Malaysian consumers: An empirical analysis. *International Journal of Mobile Communications, 8*(2), 129–149. doi:10.1504/IJMC.2010.031444

Chong, A. Y.-L., Liu, M. J., Luo, J., & Ooi, K.-B. (2015). Predicting RFID adoption in healthcare supply chain from the perspective of users. *International Journal of Production Economics, 159*, 66–75. doi:10.1016/j.ijpe.2014.09.034

Chong, A. Y. L., & Ngai, E. T. W. (2013). What Influences Travellers' Adoption of a Location-based Social Media Service for Their Travel Planning? *PACIS 2013 Proceedings*, 210.

Cohen, J. (1988). *Statistical Power Analysis for the Behavioral Sciences*. Hillsdale, NJ: Lawrence Erlbaum.

Croteau, A. M., & Bergeron, F. (2001). An information technology trilogy: Business strategy, technological deployment and organizational performance. *The Journal of Strategic Information Systems*, *10*(2), 77–99. doi:10.1016/S0963-8687(01)00044-0

Davis, F. (1989). Perceived usefulness, perceived ease of use, and user acceptanceof information technology. *Management Information Systems Quarterly*, *13*(3), 319–340. doi:10.2307/249008

Davis, F. D., Bagozzi, R. P., & Warshaw, P. R. (1989). User acceptance of computer technology: A comparison of two theoretical models. *Management Science*, *35*(8), 982–1003. doi:10.1287/mnsc.35.8.982

Deng, Z., Mo, X., & Liu, S. (2014). Comparison of the middle-aged and older users' adoption of mobile health services in China. *International Journal of Medical Informatics*, *83*(3), 210–224. doi:10.1016/j.ijmedinf.2013.12.002 PMID:24388129

Dhulla, T. V., & Mathur, S. K. (2014). Adoption of Cloud Computing by Tertiary Level Students – A Study. *Journal of Exclusive Management Science*, *3*(3).

Dodds, W. B., Monroe, K. B., & Grewal, D. (1991). Effects of Price, Brand, and Store Information on Buyers. *JMR, Journal of Marketing Research*, *28*(3), 307–319. doi:10.2307/3172866

Eliasson, M., Holkko-Lafourcade, J., & Smajovic, S. (2009). *E-commerce: A study of women's online purchasing behavior.* Thesis within Business Administration. Jonkoping.

Escobar-Rodriguez, T., & Carvajal-Trujillo, E. (2014). Online purchasing tickets for low cost barriers: An application of the unified theory of acceptance and use of technology (UTAUT) model. *Tourism Management*, *43*(1), 70–88. doi:10.1016/j.tourman.2014.01.017

Falk, R. F., & Miller, N. B. (1992). *A primer for soft modeling.* University of Akron Press.

Fishbein, M., & Ajzen, I. (1975). *Belief, attitude, intention, and behavior: anintroduction to theory and research.* Addison-Wesley.

Fornell, C., & Larcker, D. F. (1981). Evaluation Structural Equation Models with Unobservable Variables and Measurement Error. *JMR, Journal of Marketing Research*, *18*(1), 39–50. doi:10.2307/3151312

Fuksa, M. (2013). Mobile technologies and services development impact on mobile Internet usage in Latvia. *Procedia Computer Science, 26*(1), 41–50. doi:10.1016/j.procs.2013.12.006

Gaur, A. S., & Gaur, S. S. (2006). Statistical methods for practice and research: A guide to data analysis using SPSS. *Sage (Atlanta, Ga.)*.

Gefen, D. (2003). TAM or just plain habit: A look at experienced online shoppers. *Journal of End User Computing, 15*(3), 1–13. doi:10.4018/joeuc.2003070101

Gefen, D., Karahanna, E., & Straub, D. W. (2003). Trust and TAM in online shopping: An integrated model. *Management Information Systems Quarterly, 27*(1), 51–90. doi:10.2307/30036519

Geisser, S. (1974). A Predictive Approach to the Random Effect Model. *Biometrika, 61*(1), 101–107. doi:10.1093/biomet/61.1.101

Geisser, S. (1975). The predictive sample reuse method with applications. *Journal of the American Statistical Association, 70*(350), 320–328. doi:10.1080/01621459.1975.10479865

Gil-Garcia, J. R. (2008). Using partial least squares in digital government research. Handbook of research on public information technology, 239-253. doi:10.4018/978-1-59904-857-4.ch023

Gnana Sheela, K., & Deepa, S. N. (2013). Review on methods to fix number of hidden neurons in neural networks. *Mathematical Problems in Engineering*.

Griffith, D. A. (1996). *Some guidelines for specifying the geographic weights matrix contained in spatial statistical models*. Practical Handbook of Spatial Statistics.

Groß, M. (2015a). Mobile shopping: A classification framework and literature review. *International Journal of Retail & Distribution Management, 43*(3), 221–241. doi:10.1108/IJRDM-06-2013-0119

Groß, M. (2015b). Exploring the acceptance of technology for mobile shopping: An empirical investigation among Smartphone users. *International Review of Retail, Distribution and Consumer Research, 25*(3), 215–235. doi:10.1080/09593969.2014.988280

Grøtnes, E. (2009). Standardization as open innovation: Two cases from the mobile industry. *Information Technology & People, 22*(4), 367–381. doi:10.1108/09593840911002469

Ha, S., & Stoel, L. (2009). Consumer e-shopping acceptance: Antecedents in a technology acceptance model. *Journal of Business Research, 62*(5), 565–571. doi:10.1016/j.jbusres.2008.06.016

Hair, J., Hult, T. M., Ringle, C. M., & Sarstedt, M. (2014). *A primer on partial least squares structural equation modelling (PLS-SEM)*. Thousand Oaks, CA: Sage.

Hair, J. F., Hult, G. T. M., Ringle, C. M., & Sarstedt, M. (2013). *A Primer on Partial Least Squares Structural Equation Modeling (PLS-SEM)* (1st ed.). Thousand Oaks, CA: Sage.

Hair, J. F., Ringle, C. M., & Sarstedt, M. (2011). PLS-SEM: Indeed a Silver Bullet. *Journal of Marketing Theory and Practice, 18*(2), 139–152. doi:10.2753/MTP1069-6679190202

Hair, J. F., Sarstedt, M., Ringle, C. M., & Mena, J. A. (2012). An assessment of the use of partial least squares structural equation modeling in marketing research. *Journal of the Academy of Marketing Science, 40*(3), 414–433. doi:10.1007/s11747-011-0261-6

Harsono, I. L. D., & Suryana, L. A. (August, 2014). Factors Affecting the Use Behavior of Social Media Using UTAUT 2 Model. *Proceedings of the First Asia-Pacific Conference on Global Business, Economic, Finance and Social Science.*

Haykin, S. (2001). *Neural networks: A comprehensive foundation*. Upper Saddle River, NJ: Prentice Hall.

Henseler, J., & Chin, W. W. (2010). A comparison of approaches for the analysis of interaction effects between latent variables using partial least squares path modeling. *Structural Equation Modeling, 17*(1), 82–109. doi:10.1080/10705510903439003

Henseler, J., Ringle, C. M., & Sarstedt, M. (2012). Using partial least squares path modeling in international advertising research: Basic concepts and recent issues. In S. Okazaki (Ed.), *Handbook of Research in International Advertising* (pp. 252–276). Cheltenham, UK: Edward Elgar Publishing. doi:10.4337/9781781001042.00023

Henseler, J., Ringle, C. M., & Sinkovics, R. R. (2009). The Use of Partial Least Squares Path Modeling in International Marketing. In R. R. Sinkovics & P. N. Ghauri (Eds.), *Advances in International Marketing* (Vol. 20, pp. 277–320). Bingley, UK: Emerald. doi:10.1108/S1474-7979(2009)0000020014

Herrero, Á., & San Martín, H. (2012). Developing and testing a global model to explain the adoption of websites by users in rural tourism accommodations. *International Journal of Hospitality Management, 31*(4), 1178–1186. doi:10.1016/j.ijhm.2012.02.005

Hew, J., Lee, V., Ooi, K.-B., & Wei, J. (2015). What catalyses mobile apps usage intention: An empirical analysis. *Industrial Management & Data, 115*(7), 1269–1291. doi:10.1108/IMDS-01-2015-0028

Homburg, C., Hoyer, W. D., & Koschate, N. (2005). *Customers' Reactions to Price Increases: Do Customer Satisfaction and Perceived Motive Fairness Matter?* Academy of Marketing.

Hong, I. (2015). Understanding the consumer's online merchant selection process: The roles of product involvement, perceived risk, and trust expectation. *International Journal of Information Management, 35*(3), 322–336. doi:10.1016/j.ijinfomgt.2015.01.003

Hong, I., & Cha, H. (2013). The mediating role of consumer trust in an online merchant in predicting purchase intention. *International Journal of Information Management, 33*(6), 927–939. doi:10.1016/j.ijinfomgt.2013.08.007

Hövels, V. (2010). *Drivers and inhibitors of the behavioral intention to use branded mobile applications in a retail environment* (Master's thesis). Available from the University of Amsterdam"s dissertations and theses database.

Hsu, M., Chang, C., & Chuang, L. (2015). Understanding the determinants of online repeat purchase intention and moderating role of habit: The case of online group-buying in Taiwan. *International Journal of Information Management, 35*.

Huang, J.-C. (2010). Remote health monitoring adoption model based on artificial neural networks. *Expert Systems with Applications, 37*(1), 307–314. doi:10.1016/j.eswa.2009.05.063

Im, I., Hong, S., & Kang, M. S. (2011). An international comparison of technology adoption: Testing the UTAUT model. *Information & Management, 48*(1), 1–8. doi:10.1016/j.im.2010.09.001

Islam, M. Z., Low, P. K. C., & Hasan, I. (2013). Intention to use advanced mobile phone service (AMPS). *Management Decision, 51*(4), 824–838. doi:10.1108/00251741311326590

Islam, R., Islam, R., & Mazumder, T. (2010). Mobile application and its global impact. *IACSIT International Journal of Engineering and Technology, 10*(6), 72–78.

Jambulingam, M. (2013). Behavioural intention to adopt mobile technology among tertiary students. *World Applied Sciences Journal, 22*(9), 1262–1271.

Jaradat, M. R. M., & Rababaa, M. S. (2013). Assessing key factor that influence on the acceptance of mobile commerce based on modified UTAUT. *International Journal of Business and Management, 8*(23), 102–112.

Jawad, H. H. M., & Hassan, Z. B. (2015). Applying UTAUT to evaluate the acceptance of mobile learning in higher education in Iraq. *International Journal of Science and Research, 4*(5), 952–954.

Jiang, G., Peng, L., & Liu, R. (2015). Research on the factors influencing mobile gameadoption in China. *Proceedings of 4th international conference on logistics,informatics and service science, 5*, 1297–1302.

Joubert, J., & Van, J. (2013). The role of trust and risk in mobile commerce adoption within South Africa. *International Journal of Business Human Technology, 3*(2), 27–38.

Kim, D., Ferrin, D., & Rao, R. (2008). A trust-based consumer decision-makingmodel in electronic commerce: The role of trust, perceived risk, and theirantecedents. *Decision Support Systems, 44*(2), 544–564. doi:10.1016/j.dss.2007.07.001

Kim, S., & Yoon, D. (2013). Antecedents of mobile app usage among smartphone users. In *American Academy of Advertising Conference Proceedings* (pp. 72–83). Academic Press.

Kim, S. C., Yoon, D., & Han, E. K. (2014). Antecedents of mobile app usage among smartphone users. *Journal of Marketing Communications*, 1–18.

Kwahk, K., & Park, J. (2012). Investigating the determinants of purchase intentionin C2C e-commerce. *World Academy of Science, Engineering and Technology, 6*(9), 487–491.

Kwon, J. M., Bae, J.-i., & Blum, S. C. (2013). Mobile applications in the hospitality industry. *Journal of Hospitality and Tourism Technology, 4*(1), 81–92. doi:10.1108/17579881311302365

Lee, M. C. (2009). Understanding the behavioral intention to play online games: An extension of the theory of planned behaviour. *Online Information Review, 33*(5), 849–872. doi:10.1108/14684520911001873

Leong, L. Y., Hew, T. S., Tan, G. W. H., & Ooi, K. B. (2013b). Predicting the determinants of the NFC-enabled mobile credit card acceptance: A neural networks approach. *Expert Systems with Applications*, *40*(14), 5604–5620. doi:10.1016/j. eswa.2013.04.018

Leong, L. Y., Ooi, K. B., Chong, A. Y. L., & Lin, B. (2013a). Modelling the stimulators of the behavioral intention to use mobile entertainment: Does gender really matter? *Computers in Human Behavior*, *29*(5), 2109–2121. doi:10.1016/j.chb.2013.04.004

Lewis, C. C., Fretwell, C. E., Ryan, J., & Parham, J. B. (2013). Faculty Use of Established and Emerging Technologies in Higher Education: A Unified Theory of Acceptance and Use of Technology Perspective. *International Journal of Higher Education*, *2*(2). doi:10.5430/ijhe.v2n2p22

Liao, C., Liu, C., & Chen, K. (2011a). Examining the impact of privacy: trust and riskperceptions beyond monetary transactions: an integrated model. *Electronic Commerce Research and Applications*, *10*(6), 702–715. doi:10.1016/j. elerap.2011.07.003

Liao, C., Palvia, P., & Lin, H. (2006). The roles of habit and web site quality in e-commerce. *International Journal of Information Management*, *26*(6), 469–483. doi:10.1016/j.ijinfomgt.2006.09.001

Liao, C., To, P.-L., Liu, C.-C., Kuo, P.-Y., & Chuang, S.-H. (2011b). Factors influencing the intended use of web portals. *Online Information Review*, *35*(2), 237–254. doi:10.1108/14684521111128023

Liao, C., Tsou, C., & Huang, M. (2007). Factors influencing the usage of 3G mobile services in Taiwan. *Online Information Review*, *31*(6), 759–774. doi:10.1108/14684520710841757

Limayem, M., Hirt, S. G., & Cheung, C. M. K. (2007). How Habit Limits the Predictive Power of Intentions. The Case of IS Continuance. *Management Information Systems Quarterly*, *31*(4), 705–737. doi:10.2307/25148817

Lin, H. H., & Wang, Y. S. (2005). Predicting consumer intention to use mobile commerce in Taiwan. *Mobile Business, International Conference*, 406-412.

Lin, S. J., Zimmer, J. C., & Lee, V. (2013). Podcasting acceptance on campus: The differing perspectives of teachers and students. *Computers & Education*, *68*(1), 416–428. doi:10.1016/j.compedu.2013.06.003

Lu, J., Yao, J., & Yu, C. (2005). Personal innovativeness, social influences and adoption of wireless Internet services via mobile technology. *The Journal of Strategic Information Systems, 14*(3), 245–268. doi:10.1016/j.jsis.2005.07.003

Lu, Y., Yang, S., Chau, P., & Cao, Y. (2011). Dynamics between the trust transfer process and intention to use mobile payment services: A cross-environment perspective. *Information & Management, 48*(8), 393–403. doi:10.1016/j.im.2011.09.006

Luarn, P., & Lin, H. H. (2005). Toward an understanding of the behavioral intention to use mobile banking. *Computers in Human Behavior, 21*(6), 873–891. doi:10.1016/j.chb.2004.03.003

Mafe, C. R., Blas, S. S., & Tavera-Mesias, J. F. (2010). A comparative study of mobile messaging services acceptance to participate in television programmes. *Journal of Service Management, 21*(1), 69–102. doi:10.1108/09564231011025128

Magni, M., Taylor, M. S., & Venkatesh, V. (2010). 'To play or not to play': A cross-temporal investigation using hedonic and instrumental perspectives to explain user intentions to explore a technology. *International Journal of Human-Computer Studies, 68*(9), 572–588. doi:10.1016/j.ijhcs.2010.03.004

Magrath, V., & McCormick, H. (2013). Marketing design elements of mobile fashion retail apps. *Journal of Fashion Marketing and Management: An International Journal, 17*(1), 115–134. doi:10.1108/13612021311305173

Mallat, N., Rossi, M., Tuunainen, V. K., & Öörni, A. (2009). The impact of use context on mobile services acceptance: The case of mobile ticketing. *Information & Management, 46*(3), 190–195. doi:10.1016/j.im.2008.11.008

Martins, C., Oliveira, T., & Popovic, A. (2014). Understanding the internet banking adoption: A unified theory of acceptance and the use of technology and perceived risk application. *International Journal of Information Management, 34*(1), 1–13. doi:10.1016/j.ijinfomgt.2013.06.002

Moore, G. C., & Benbasat, I. (1991). Development of an instrument to measure the perceptions of adopting an information technology innovation. *Information Systems Research, 2*(3), 192–222. doi:10.1287/isre.2.3.192

Moorman, C., Deshpande, R., & Zaltman, G. (1993). Factors Affecting Trust in Market Research Relationships. *Journal of Marketing, 57*(1), 81. doi:10.2307/1252059

Mozeik, C. K., Beldona, S., Cobanoglu, C., & Poorani, A. (2009). The adoption of restaurant-based e-services. *Journal of Foodservice Business Research, 12*(3), 247–265. doi:10.1080/15378020903158525

Munnukka, J. T. (2004). *Perception-based pricing strategies for mobile services in customer marketing context* (Order No. C820658, Jyvaskylan Yliopisto). Retrieved from ProQuest Dissertations and Theses.

Negnevitsky, M. (2011). *Artificial intelligence: A guide to intelligent systems* (3rd ed.). Pearson Education.

Nunnally, J. C., & Bernstein, I. H. (1994). *Psychometric Theory* (3rd ed.). New York: McGraw-Hill.

Oechslein, O., Fleischmann, M., & Hess, T. (2014). *An Application of UTAUT2 on Social Recommender Systems: Incorporating Social Information for Performance Expectancy.* Paper presented at the 47th Hawaii International Conference on System Science. doi:10.1109/HICSS.2014.409

Oliveira, T., Faria, M., Thomas, M. A., & Popovič, A. (2014). International journal of information management. Extending the understanding of mobile banking adoption: When UTAUT meets TTF and ITM. *International Journal of Information Management, 34*(1), 689–703. doi:10.1016/j.ijinfomgt.2014.06.004

Ouellette, J. A., & Wood, W. (1998). Habit and intention in everyday life: The multiple processes by which past behavior predicts future behavior. *Psychological Bulletin, 124*(1), 54–74. doi:10.1037/0033-2909.124.1.54

Pahnila, S., Siponen, M., & Zheng, X. (2011). Integrating habit into UTAUT: The Chinese eBay case. *Pacific Asia Journal of the Association for Information Systems, 3*(2), 1–30.

Pavlou, P. (2003). Consumer acceptance of electronic commerce: Integrating trust and risk with the technology acceptance model. *International Journal of Electronic Commerce, 7*(3), 69–103.

Pavlou, P., & Gefen, D. (2004). Building effective online marketplaces with institution-based trust. *Information Systems Research, 15*(1), 37–59. doi:10.1287/isre.1040.0015

Prata, W., Moraes, A. D., & Quaresma, M. (2012). User's demography and expectation regarding search, purchase and evaluation in mobile application store. *Work (Reading, Mass.), 41*(1), 1124–1311. PMID:22316870

Purcell, K. (2011). *Half of adult cell phone owners have apps on their phones.* Retrieved August 20, 2013, from http://pewinternet.org/~/media/Files/Reports/2011/PIP_Apps-Update-2011.pdf

Raman, A., & Don, Y. (2013). Preservice Teachers' Acceptance of Learning Management Software: An Application of the UTAUT2 Model. *International Education Studies*, 6(7), 157–164. doi:10.5539/ies.v6n7p157

Reinartz, W. J., Haenlein, M., & Henseler, J. (2009). An empirical comparison of the efficacy of covariance-based and variance-based SEM. *International Journal of Research in Marketing*, 26(4), 332–344. doi:10.1016/j.ijresmar.2009.08.001

Rigdon, E. E., Ringle, C. M., & Sarstedt, M. (2010). Structural Modeling of Heterogeneous Data with Partial Least Squares. In N. K. Malhotra (Ed.), *Review of Marketing Research* (pp. 255–296). Armonk: Sharpe. doi:10.1108/S1548-6435(2010)0000007011

Ringle, C. M., Sarstedt, M., & Schlittgen, R. (2010). Finite Mixture and Genetic Algorithm Segmentation in Partial Least Squares Path Modeling: Identification of Multiple Segments in a Complex Path Model. In A. Fink, B. Lausen, W. Seidel, & A. Ultsch (Eds.), *Advances in Data Analysis, Data Handling and Business Intelligence* (pp. 167–176). Berlin: Springer.

Ringle, C. M., Wende, S., & Becker, J.-M. (2014). *SmartPLS 3. Hamburg: SmartPLS*. Available from http://www.smartpls.com

Ringle, C. M., Wende, S., & Will, A. (2005). *SmartPLS 2.0 (M3) Beta*. Retrieved from http://www.smartpls.de

Ringle, C. M., Wende, S., & Will, A. (2005b). *SmartPLS 2.0*. Retrieved from www.smartpls.de

Roca, J., Garcia, J., & de la Vega, J. (2009). The importance of perceived trust, security and privacy in online trading systems. *Information Management & Computer Security*, 17(2), 96–113. doi:10.1108/09685220910963983

Rogers, E. (1995). *Diffusion of innovations* (4th ed.). New York: Free Press.

Rogers, E. (2003). *Diffusion of innovations* (5th ed.). New York: Free Press.

Roldán, J. L., & Sánchez-Franco, M. J. (2012). Variance-based structural equation modeling: guidelines for using partial least squares in information systems research. In M. Mora, O. Gelman, A. Steenkamp, & M. Raisinghani (Eds.), Research methodologies in engineering of software systems and information systems: Philosophies, methods, and innovations (pp. 193–221). Hershey, PA: Information Science Reference. doi:10.4018/978-1-4666-0179-6.ch010

Sarstedt, M. (2008). A review of recent approaches for capturing heterogeneity in partial least squares path modeling. *Journal of Modelling in Management, 3*(2), 140–161. doi:10.1108/17465660810890126

Shen, G. (2015). Users' adoption of mobile applications: Product type and message framing's moderating effect. *Journal of Business Research, 68*(11), 2317–2321. doi:10.1016/j.jbusres.2015.06.018

Shi, W. W. (2009). *An Empirical Research on Users' Acceptance of Smart Phone Online Application Software.* Paper presented at the International Conference on Electronic Commerce and Business Intelligence. doi:10.1109/ECBI.2009.102

Shin, D. (2009). Towards an understanding of the consumer acceptance of mobile wallet. *Computers in Human Behavior, 25*(6), 1343–1354. doi:10.1016/j.chb.2009.06.001

Shin, J., Chung, K., Oh, J., & Lee, C. (2013). The effect of site quality on repurchaseintention in internet shopping through mediating variables: The case ofuniversity students in South Korea. *International Journal of Information Management, 33*(3), 453–463. doi:10.1016/j.ijinfomgt.2013.02.003

Shmueli, G., & Koppius, O. R. (2011). Predictive analytics in information systems research. *Management Information Systems Quarterly, 35*(3), 553–572. doi:10.2307/23042796

Sim, J. J., Tan, G. W.-H., Wong, J. C. J., Ooi, K.-B., & Hew, T.-S. (2014). Understandingand predicting the motivators of mobile music acceptance – A multi stageMRA-Artificial neural network approach. *Telematics and Informatics, 31*(4), 569–584. doi:10.1016/j.tele.2013.11.005

Slade, E., Williams, M., Dwivedi, Y., & Piercy, N. (2014). Exploring consumer adoption of proximity mobile payments. *Journal of Strategic Marketing, 1*(1), 1–15.

SPSS. (2012). *IBM SPSS neural networks 21.* IBM Corporation.

Statista. (2017a). Retrieved from http://www.statista.com/statistics/276623/number-of-apps-available-in-leading-app-stores/

Statista. (2017b). Retrieved from http://www.statista.com/statistics/263794/number-of-downloads-from-the-apple-app-store/

Stone, M. (1974). Cross-Validatory Choice and Assessment of Statistical Predictions. *Journal of the Royal Statistical Society. Series A (General), 36*(2), 111–147.

Sun, Q., Cao, H., & You, J. (2010, May). Factors influencing the adoption of mobile service in China: An integration of TAM. *Journal of Computers*, *5*(5), 799–806. doi:10.4304/jcp.5.5.799-806

Tai, Y. M., & Ku, Y. C. (2013). Will stock investors use mobile stock trading? A benefit-risk assessment based on a modified UTAUT model. *Journal of Electronic Commerce Research*, *14*(1), 67–84.

Tan, G. W.-H., Ooi, K.-B., Leong, L.-Y., & Lin, B. (2014). Predicting the drivers ofbehavioral intention to use mobile learning: A hybrid SEM-Neural Networksapproach. *Computers in Human Behavior*, *36*, 198–213. doi:10.1016/j. chb.2014.03.052

Tan, G. W. H., Sim, J. J., Ooi, K. B., & Phusavat, K. (2012). Determinants of mobile learning adoption: An empirical analysis. *Journal of Computer Information Systems*, 82–91.

Tang, T., & Chi, W. (2016). *The Role of Trust in Customer Online Shopping Behavior: Perspective of Technology Acceptance Model*. Available at: http://onemvweb.com/ sources/sources/role_trust_online_shopping.pdf

Taylor, D., Voelker, T., & Pentina, I. (2011). Mobile application adoption by young adults: A social network perspective. *International Journal of Mobile Marketing*, *6*(2), 60–70.

Taylor, S., & Todd, P. (1995). Understanding information technology usage: A test ofcompeting models. *Information Systems Research*, *6*(2), 144–176. doi:10.1287/ isre.6.2.144

Tenenhaus, M., Esposito Vinzi, V., Chatelin, Y.-M., & Lauro, C. (2005). PLS Path Modeling. *Computational Statistics & Data Analysis*, *48*(1), 159–205. doi:10.1016/j. csda.2004.03.005

Teo, A. C., Tan, G. W. H., Ooi, K. B., Hew, T. S., & Yew, K. T. (2015). The effect of convenience and speed in m-payment. *Industrial Management & Data Systems*, *115*(2), 311–331. doi:10.1108/IMDS-08-2014-0231

Teo, T., & Noyes, J. (2012). Explaining the intention to use technology among pre-service teachers: A multi-group analysis of the Unified Theory of Acceptance and Use of Technology. *Interactive Learning Environments*, *2*(1), 51–66.

Teo, T., & Noyes, J. (2012). Explaining the intention to use technology among pre-service teachers: A multi-group analysis of the Unified Theory of Acceptance and Use of Technology. *Interactive Learning Environments*, *2*(1), 51–66.

Thomas, T. D., Singh, L., & Gaffar, K. (2013). The utility of the UTAUT model in explaining mobile learning adoption in higher education in Guyana. *International Journal of Education and Development Using Information and Communication Technology*, *9*(3), 71–85.

To, P. L., Liao, C., & Lin, T. H. (2007). Shopping motiviation on Internet: A study based on utilitarian and hedonic value. *Technovation*, *27*(12), 774–787. doi:10.1016/j.technovation.2007.01.001

Unyolo, T. (2012). *Building Consumer mobile money adoption and trust in conditions where infrastructure are unreliable* (Unpublished MBA Thesis). Gordon Institute of Business Science, University of Pretoria.

Vasileiadis, A. (2014). Security Concerns and Trust in the Adoption of M-Commerce. *Social Technologies*, *4*(1), 179–191. doi:10.13165/ST-14-4-1-12

Venkatesh, V., Morris, M. G., Davis, G. B., & Davis, F. D. (2003). User Acceptance of Information Technology: Toward a Unified View. *Management Information Systems Quarterly*, *27*(3), 425–478. doi:10.2307/30036540

Venkatesh, V., Thong, J. Y. L., & Xu, X. (2012). Consumer acceptance and use of information technology: Extending the Unified Theory of Acceptance and use of technology. *Management Information Systems Quarterly*, *36*(1), 157–178.

Verplanken, B., & Orbell, S. (2003). Reflections of past behavior: A self-report index of habit strenght. *Journal of Applied Social Psychology*, *33*(6), 1313–1330. doi:10.1111/j.1559-1816.2003.tb01951.x

Vinzi, V. E., Trinchera, L., & Amato, S. (2010). *PLS path modeling: From foundations to recent developments and open issues for model assessment and improvement. In Handbook of Partial Least Squares* (pp. 47–82). Springer.

Wang, D., Zheng, X., Law, R., & Tang, P. K. (2015). Accessing hotel-related smartphone apps using online reviews. *Journal of Hospitality Marketing & Management*.

Wei, T. T., Marthandan, G., Chong, A. Y. L., Ooi, K. B., & Arumugam, S. (2009). What drives Malaysian M-commerce adoption? An empirical analysis. *Industrial Management & Data Systems*, *109*(3), 370–388. doi:10.1108/02635570910939399

Wetzels, M., Odekerken-Schroder, G., & Oppen, C. V. (2009). Using PLS path modeling for assessing hierarchical construct models: Guidelines and empirical illustration. *Management Information Systems Quarterly*, *33*(1), 177–195. doi:10.2307/20650284

Wong, C. H., Tan, G. W. H., Loke, S. P., & Ooi, K. B. (2014). Mobile TV: A new form of entertainment? *Industrial Management & Data Systems, 114*(7), 1050–1067. doi:10.1108/IMDS-05-2014-0146

Wu, Y. L., Tao, Y. H., & Yang, P. C. (2007, December). *Using UTAUT to explore the behaviour of 3G mobile communication users.* Paper presented at the Industrial Engineering and Engineering Management (IEEE, 2007) International Conference, Singapore.

Xu, X. (2014). *Understanding Users' Continued Use of Online Games: An Application of UTAUT2 in Social Network Games.* Paper presented at the Sixth International Conferences on Advances in Multimedia.

Yang, H. (2013). Bon appétit for apps: Young American consumers' acceptance of mobile applications. *Journal of Computer Information Systems, 53*(3), 85–96. doi :10.1080/08874417.2013.11645635

Yang, K. (2010). Determinants of US consumer mobile shopping services adoption: Implications for designing mobile shopping services. *Journal of Consumer Marketing, 27*(3), 262–270. doi:10.1108/07363761011038338

Yang, K. (2012). Consumer technology traits in determining mobile shopping adoption: An application of the extended theory of planned behavior. *Journal of Retailing and Consumer Services, 19*(5), 484–491. doi:10.1016/j.jretconser.2012.06.003

Yang, S. (2013). Understanding Undergraduate Students' Adoption of Mobile Learning Model: A Perspective of the Extended UTAUT2. *Journal of Convergence Information Technology, 8*(10).

Yeoh, S. K., & Chan, B. Y. F. (2011). Internet Banking Adoption in Kuala Lumpur: An Application of UTAUT Model. *International Journal of Business and Management, 6*(4), 161–167.

Yi, M., Jackson, J., Park, J., & Probst, J. (2006). Understanding information technology acceptance by individual professionals: Toward an integrative view. *Information & Management, 43*(3), 350–363. doi:10.1016/j.im.2005.08.006

Yu, C. S. (2012). Factors affecting individuals to adopt mobile banking: Empirical evidence from the UTUAT model. *Journal of Electronic Commerce Research, 13*(2), 104–121.

Zhang, L., Zhu, J., & Liu, Q. (2012). A meta-analysis of mobile commerce adoption and the moderating effect of culture. *Computers in Human Behavior, 28*(5), 1902–1911. doi:10.1016/j.chb.2012.05.008

Zhou, T. (2008, August). *Exploring mobile user acceptance based on UTAUT and contextual offering.* Paper presented at the International Symposium on Electronic Commerce and Security, Guangzhou City. doi:10.1109/ISECS.2008.10

Compilation of References

Aarts, H., Verplanken, B., & van Knippenberg, A. (1998). Predicting behavior from actions in the past: Repeated decision making or a matter of habit? *Journal of Applied Social Psychology*, *28*(15), 1355–1374. doi:10.1111/j.1559-1816.1998.tb01681.x

AbuShanab, E., & Pearson, J. M. (2007). Internet banking in Jordan: The unified theory of acceptance and use of technology (UTAUT) perspective. *Journal of Systems and Information Technology*, *9*(1), 78–97. doi:10.1108/13287260710817700

ACCA. (2009). ACCA's 12 tenets of tax. Retrieved from http://www.accaglobal.com/content/dam/acca/global/pdf/tech-tp-ttt.pdf

Adepetun, A. (2017, January 1). How communication service tax will cripple ICT sector. The Guardian.

Adepetun, A. (2017, May 11). ITU launches 'Ebola-Info-Sharing' mobile application. *T.guardian. ng*. Retrieved from https://t.guardian.ng/business-services/business/itu-launches-ebola-info-sharing-mobile-application/

Adjei, J.K. & Odei-Appiah, S. (2008, May 14). Interview of Victor Dostov, Paycash. Personal communication () .

Adomi, E. E., & Kpangban, E. (2010). Application of ICTs in Nigerian secondary schools. *Library Philosophy and Practice*, 345.

Aivazian, V., Booth, L., & Cleary, S. (2003). Do emerging market firms follow different dividend policies from US firms? *Journal of Financial Research*, *26*(3), 371–387. doi:10.1111/1475-6803.00064

Ajzen, I. (1985). *From intentions to actions: A theory of planned behavior*. Springer Berlin Heidelberg.

Ajzen, I. (1991). The theory of planned behavior. *Organizational Behavior and Human Decision Processes*, 179–211.

Ajzen, I., & Fishbein, M. (1975). *Belief, attitude, intention and behavior: An introduction to theory and research*. Academic Press.

Akintoye, A. (2017, May 10). *The mobile app that detects ebola presence in an area and helps prevents Ebola Virus Disease.* Retrieved from TheNigerianVoice.com: https://www.thenigerianvoice.com/news/157520/1/the-mobile-app-that-detects-ebola-presence-in-an-area-and-helps-prevents-ebola-virus-disease.html

Akour, H. (2009). Determinants of mobile learning acceptance: An empirical investigation in higher education (Order No. 3408682, Oklahoma State University). Retrieved from ProQuest Dissertations and Theses, 379.

Akter, S., D'Ambra, J., & Ray, P. (2011). Trustworthiness in mHealth information services: An assessment of a hierarchical model with mediating and moderating effects using partial least squares (PLS). *Journal of the American Society for Information Science and Technology, 62*(1), 100–116. doi:10.1002/asi.21442

Alalwan, A., Dwivedi, Y., & Williams, M. (2014). Examining Factors Affecting Customer Intention And Adoption Of Internet Banking In Jordan. *UK Academy for Information Systems Conference Proceedings 2014.*

Alao, A. A., & Sorinola, O. O. (2015). Cashless policy and customers' satisfaction: A study of commercial banks in Ogun State, Nigeria. *Research Journal of Finance and Accounting, 6*(2), 37–47.

AlAwadhi, S., & Morris, A. (2008). The Use of the UTAUT Model in the Adoption of E-government Services in Kuwait. In *Proceeding of 41st Hawaii International Conference on System Sciences,* Hawaii (pp. 219-219). doi:10.1109/HICSS.2008.452

Al-Debei, M., & Al-Lozi, E. (2014). Explaining and predicting the adoption intention of mobile data services: A value-based approach. *Computers in Human Behavior, 35,* 326–338. doi:10.1016/j.chb.2014.03.011

Alexander, A. (2004). Going Nomadic: Mobile learning in higher education. *EDUCAUSE Review, 39*(5), 29–35.

Alharbi, S., & Drew, S. (2014). Mobile learning-system usage: Scale development and empirical tests. *International Journal of Advanced Research in Artificial Intelligence, 3*(11), 31–47. doi:10.14569/IJARAI.2014.031105

Allen, F., Demirgue-Kunt, A., Klapper, L., Soledad, M., & Peria, M. (2012). The foundations of financial inclusion: Understanding ownership and use of formal accounts. *World Bank Policy Research Working Paper.*

Alwahaishi, S., & Snasel, V. (2013). Consumers' acceptance and use of information and communications technology: A UTAUT and Flow Based Theoretical Model. *Journal of Technology Management & Innovation, 8*(2), 102–112. doi:10.4067/S0718-27242013000200005

Anderson, J. C., & Gerbing, D. (1988). Structural equation modeling in practice: A review and recommended two-step approach. *Psychological Bulletin, 103*(3), 411–423. doi:10.1037/0033-2909.103.3.411

Android Authority. (2017). Retrieved from http://www.androidauthority.com/google-play-store-vs-the-apple-app-store-601836/

Annan, N. K., Ofori-Dwumfuo, G. O., & Falch, M. (2014). Mobile Learning Platform: a case study of introducing m-learning in Tertiary Education. *GSTF Journal on Computing, 2*(1).

Apps, M. (2016). *What Consumers Really Need and Want. A Global Study of Consumers' Expectations and Experiences of Mobile Applications.* Available at: https://info.dynatrace.com/rs/compuware/images/Mobile_App_Survey_Report.pdf

Appsagainstebola. (2017, May 30). *Apps against Ebola.* Retrieved from appsagainstebola.org: www.appsagainstebola.org

Araujo, Santos, & Rocha. (2014). Implementation of a routing protocol for ad hoc networks in search and rescue robotics. *2014 IFIP Wireless Days (WD)*, 1-7.

Arenas-Gaitán, J., Peral-Peral, B., & Ramón-Jerónimo, M. A. (2015). Elderly and Internet Banking: An Application of UTAUT2. *Journal of Internet Banking and Commerce, 20*(1).

Arnold, M. (2003). On the phenomenology of technology: The "Janus-faces" of mobile phones. *Information and Organization, 13*(4), 231–256. doi:10.1016/S1471-7727(03)00013-7

Asabere, N. Y. (2013). Benefits and Challenges of Mobile Learning Implementation: Story of Developing Nations. *International Journal of Computers and Applications, 73*(1).

Ashraf, N., Aycinena, C., Martinez, A., & Yang, D. (2010). Female empower: Further evidence from a commitment savings product in the Philippines. *World Development, 28*(3), 333–344. doi:10.1016/j.worlddev.2009.05.010

Asongu, S. (2015). The impact of mobile phone penetration on African inequality. *International Journal of Social Economics, 42*(8), 706–716. doi:10.1108/IJSE-11-2012-0228

Atsa'am, D. (2016). *A practical guide to using UML tools in system analysis and design.* Saarbrucken, Germany: Lambert Academic Publishing.

Avram, D. O., & Kühne, S. (2008). Implementing responsible business behavior from a strategic management perspective: Developing a framework for Austrian SMEs. *Journal of Business Ethics, 82*(2), 463–475. doi:10.1007/s10551-008-9897-7

Awad, N. F., & Krishnan, M. S. (2006). The personalization privacy paradox: An empirical evaluation of information transparency and the willingness to be profiled online for personalization. *Management Information Systems Quarterly, 30*(1), 13–28. doi:10.2307/25148715

B. C. G. (2011). *The Boston Consulting Group.* The Socio-Economic Impact of Mobile.

Babu, S. C., Glendenning, C. J., Asenso-Okyere, K., & Govindarajan, S. K. (2011). Farmers' Information Needs and Search Behaviors: Case Study in Tamil Nadu, India. International Food Policy Research Institute. Retrieved May 12, 2017 from http://ageconsearch.umn.edu/bitstream/126226/2/Farmers%20information%20needs%20and%20search%20behaviour%2case%20study%20in%20Tamil%20Nadu%20India.pdf

Bachhav, N. B. (2012). Information Needs of the Rural Farmers: A Study from Maharashtra, India: A Survey. *Library Philosophy and Practice*. Retrieved from http://digitalcommons.unl.edu/libphilprac/866

Baden, L. R., Kanapathipillai, R., Campion, E. W., Morrissey, S., Rubin, E. J., & Drazen, J. M. (2014). 10). Ebola — An Ongoing Crisis. *The New England Journal of Medicine*, *371*(15), 1458–1459. doi:10.1056/NEJMe1411378 PMID:25237780

Bagga, M. (2010). vKVK - A Way to Empower Krishi Vigyan Kendra. *Information Technology in Developing Countries*, *20*(3), 18–21.

Bagozzi, R. P., & Yi, Y. (1988). On the Evaluation of Structural Equation Models. *Journal of the Academy of Marketing Science*, *16*(1), 74–94. doi:10.1007/BF02723327

Bagozzi, R. P., Yi, Y., & Phillips, L. W. (1991). Assessing construct validity in organiza¬tional research. *Administrative Science Quarterly*, *36*(3), 421–458. doi:10.2307/2393203

Balasubramanian & Drake. (2015). Service Quality, Inventory and Competition among Mobile Money Agents (manuscript no. MSOM-15-289). Manufacturing & Service Operations Management.

Balasubramanian, S., Peterson, R. A., & Jarvenpaa, S. L. (2002). Exploring the implications of m-commerce for markets and marketing. *Journal of the Academy of Marketing Science*, *30*(4), 348–361. doi:10.1177/009207002236910

Bandura, A. (1977). Self-efficacy: Toward a unifying theory of behavioral change. *Psychological Review*, *84*(2), 191–215. doi:10.1037/0033-295X.84.2.191 PMID:847061

Bandura, A. (2001). Social Cognitive Theory: An Agentic Perspective. *Annual Review of Psychology*, *52*(1), 1–26. doi:10.1146/annurev.psych.52.1.1 PMID:11148297

Bank of Ghana. (2017). *Impact of Mobile Money on the Payment System in Ghana: An Econometric Analysis*. Payment Systems Department.

Barclay, D., Higgins, C., & Thompson, R. (1995). The partial least squares (PLS) approach to causal modeling: Personal computer adoption and use as an illustration. *Technology Studies*, *2*(2), 285–309.

Barki, H., & Hartwick, J. (1994). Measuring user participation, user involvement, and user attitude. *Management Information Systems Quarterly*, *18*(1), 59–82. doi:10.2307/249610

Barnes, S. J. (2002). The mobile commerce value chain: Analysis and future developments. *International Journal of Information Management, 22*(2), 91–108. doi:10.1016/S0268-4012(01)00047-0

Barros, C. P., & Caporale, G. M. (2012). Banking consolidation in Nigeria, 2000–2010. *Journal of African Business, 13*(3), 244–252. doi:10.1080/15228916.2012.727756

Bart, Y., Shankar, V., Suştan, F., & Urban, G. L. (2005). Are the drivers and role of online trust the same for all web sites and consumers? A large-scale exploratory emprical study. *Journal of Marketing, 69*(4), 133–152. doi:10.1509/jmkg.2005.69.4.133

Ba, S., & Pavlou, P. A. (2002). Evidence of the effect of trust building technology in electronic markets: Price premiums and buyer behavior. *Management Information Systems Quarterly, 26*(3), 243–268. doi:10.2307/4132332

Bass-Fimmons, E., & Kinuthia, W. (2015). Mobile Learning in Ghana: A Content Analysis of YouTube Videos promoting Teacher Development Opportunities within Higher Education. Retrieved from http://transform2015.net/live/Resources/Papers/Mobile%20Learning.pdf

Bastable, C. F. (1917). *Public finance*. London: Macmillan and Company Limited.

Bayero, M. A. (2015). Effects of Cashless Economy Policy on financial inclusion in Nigeria: An exploratory study. *Procedia: Social and Behavioral Sciences, 172*, 49–56. doi:10.1016/j.sbspro.2015.01.334

Beaudoin, C. E. (2008). Explaining the relationship between internet use and interpersonal trust: Taking into account motivation and information overload. *Journal of Computer-Mediated Communication, 13*(3), 550–568. doi:10.1111/j.1083-6101.2008.00410.x

Beck, T., Demirgue-Kunt, A., Martinez, A., & Peria, M. (2007). Reaching out: Access to and use of banking services across countries. *Journal of Financial Economics, 85*(1), 234–266. doi:10.1016/j.jfineco.2006.07.002

Beeching, N. J., Fenech, M., & Houlihan, C. F. (2014). Ebola virus disease. *BMJ (Clinical Research Ed.), 349*, g7348. PMID:25497512

Bensebaa, F. (2004). The impact of strategic actions on the reputation building of e-businesses. *International Journal of Retail & Distribution Management, 32*(6), 286–301. doi:10.1108/09590550410537999

Beratarrechea, A., Lee, A. G., Willner, J. M., Jahangir, E., Ciapponi, A., & Rubinstein, A. (2014). The impact of mobile health interventions on chronic disease outcomes in developing countries: A systematic review. *Telemedicine Journal and e-Health, 20*(1), 75–82. doi:10.1089/tmj.2012.0328 PMID:24205809

Bere, A. (2014, April). *Exploring determinants for mobile learning user acceptance and use: An application of UTAUT*. Paper presented at the 11th International Conference on Information Technology: New Generarions, Las Vegas, NV. doi:10.1109/ITNG.2014.114

Betjeman, T. J., Soghoian, S. E., & Foran, M. P. (2013). mHealth in Sub-Saharan Africa. *International Journal of Telemedicine and Applications*, (6): 482324. PMID:24369460

Bhargavi, V. S., Seetha, M., & Viswanadharaju, S. (2016). A hybrid secure routing scheme for MANETS. *2016 International Conference on Emerging Trends in Engineering, Technology and Science(ICETETS)*, 1-5. doi:10.1109/ICETETS.2016.7602991

Bhattacharya, K. (2015). From Giant Robots to Mobile Money Platforms: The Rise of ICT Services in Developing Countries. *IEEE Internet Computing*, *19*(5), 82–85. doi:10.1109/MIC.2015.99

Bhattacherjee, A. (2009, February 12). An empirical analysis of the antecedents of electronic commerce DFID. Douglas Alexander sets out how branchless banking can help the poorest people. Retrieved September 26, 2009, from http://www.dfid.gov.uk/Media-Room/Speeches-andarticles/2009/Douglas-Alexander-sets-out-how-branchless-banking-can-help-the-poorest-people/

Bhattacherjee, A., & Sanford, C. (2004). Persuasion strategies for information technology usage: An elaboration likelihood model. Retrieved from http://mis.temple.edu/research/documents/BhattacherjeeITUsage.pdf

Bhattacherjee, A. (2001a). Understanding Information Systems Continuance: An Expectation-Confirmation Model. *Management Information Systems Quarterly*, *25*(3), 351–370. doi:10.2307/3250921

Bhattacherjee, A. (2002). Individual trust in online firms: Scale development and initial test. *Journal of Management Information Systems*, *19*(1), 211–241. doi:10.1080/07421222.2002.11045715

Bholah, L. A., & Beharee, K. (2016). Mobile health applications for Mauritius and Africa. In *Proceedings of the IEEE International Conference on Emerging Technologies and Innovative Business Practices for the Transformation of Societies (EmergiTech)*, Balaclava, Mauritius (pp. 300-302). IEEE.

Bird, B. H., Spengler, J. R., Chakrabarti, A. K., Khristova, M. L., Sealy, T. K., Coleman-McCray, J. D., ... Spiropoulou, C. F. (2016). Humanized mouse model of ebola virus disease mimics the immune responses in human disease. *The Journal of Infectious Diseases*, *213*(5), 703–711. doi:10.1093/infdis/jiv538 PMID:26582961

Bjornehed, E. (2004). Narco-Terrorism: The Merger of the war on drugs and the war on terror. *Global Crime*, *6*(3&4), 305–324. doi:10.1080/17440570500273440

Blakeley, R. (2012). State violence as state terrorism. In M. Breen-Smyth (Ed.), *The Ashgate research companion to political violence* (pp. 63–78). Farnham, UK: Ashgate Publishing.

Bloomfield, L., & Regan, A. (2015). EbolaTracks: An automated SMS system for monitoring persons potentially exposed to Ebola virus disease. *Eurosurveillance*, *20*(1), 20999. PMID:25613652

Blum, A. (1992). *Neural Networks*. New York: Wiley.

Blumenstock, J. E., Callen, M., Ghani, T., & Koepke, L. (2015, May). Promises and pitfalls of mobile money in Afghanistan: evidence from a randomized control trial. In *Proceedings of the Seventh International Conference on Information and Communication Technologies and Development* (p. 15). ACM. doi:10.1145/2737856.2738031

Bogdanoski, M. (2013). Cyber terrorism – global security threat: Contemporary macedonian defence. *International Scientific Defence, Security and Peace Journal, 13*, 59-72.

Boksiner, J., Posherstnik, Y., May, B., Saltzman, M., & Kamal, S. (2013). Centrally Controlled Dynamic Spectrum Access forMANETs. *Military Communications Conference, MILCOM 2013*, 641-646. doi:10.1109/MILCOM.2013.115

Booker, E. (2017, May 30). Magpi Mobile Data Tool Aids Ebola Fight. *InformationWeek*. Retrieved from http://www.informationweek.com/healthcare/mobile-and-wireless/magpi-mobile-data-tool-aids-ebola-fight/d/d-id/1317577

Boone, L.E. and Kurtz, D.L. (2006). Contemporary business. Boulevard: Thomson South-Western.

Brookings Institution. (2013). Retrieved 20 February 2017 from https://www.youtube.com/watch?v=yE-jFQnu5Jg

Brown, S. A., Massey, A. P., Montoya-Weiss, M. M., & Burkman, J. R. (2002). Do I really have to? User acceptance of mandated technology. *European Journal of Information Systems, 11*(4), 283–295. doi:10.1057/palgrave.ejis.3000438

Brown, S. A., & Venkatesh, V. (2005). A model of adoption of technology in the household: A baseline model test and extension incorporating household life cycle. *Management Information Systems Quarterly, 29*(4), 399–426. doi:10.2307/25148690

Brown, S. H., & Coney, R. D. (1994). Changes in physicians' computer anxiety and attitudes related to clinical information system use. *Journal of the American Medical Informatics Association, 1*(5), 381–394. doi:10.1136/jamia.1994.95153426 PMID:7850562

Bryant, T. (2006). Social software in academia. *EDUCAUSE Quarterly, 29*(2), 61.

Byomire, G., & Maiga, G. (2015). A model for mobile phone adoption in maternal healthcare. In Proceedings of the *IST-Africa Conference '15*. IEEE. doi:10.1109/ISTAFRICA.2015.7190562

Callum, K., & Jeffrey, L. (2014). Comparing the role of ICT literacy andanxiety in the adoption of mobile learning. *Computers in Human Behavior, 39*, 8–19. doi:10.1016/j.chb.2014.05.024

Carlos Roca, J., José García, J., & José de la Vega, J. (2009). The importance of perceived trust, security and privacy in online trading systems. *Information Management & Computer Security, 17*(2), 96–113. doi:10.1108/09685220910963983

Carlson, P. J., Kahn, B. K., & Rowe, F. (1999). Organizational impacts of new communication technology: A comparison of cellular phone adoption in France and the United States. *Journal of Global Information Management, 7*(3), 19–29. doi:10.4018/jgim.1999070102

Carlsson, C., Carlsson, J., Hyvonen, K., Puhakainen, J., & Walden, P. (2006, January). Adoption of mobile devices/services—searching for answers with the UTAUT. In *Proceedings of the 39th Annual Hawaii International Conference* on *System Sciences HICSS '06* (Vol. 6, p. 132a). IEEE.

Carvalho, W. L., da Cruz, R. O. M., Câmara, M. T., & de Aragão, J. J. G. (2010). Rural school transportation in emerging countries: The Brazilian case. *Research in Transportation Economics*, *29*(1), 401–409. doi:10.1016/j.retrec.2010.07.051

Cenciarelli, O., Pietropaoli, S., Malizia, A., Carestia, M., D'Amico, F., Sassolini, A., ... Gaudio, P. (2015). Ebola Virus Disease 2013-2014 Outbreak in West Africa: An Analysis of the Epidemic Spread and Response. *International Journal of Microbiology*, *2015*, 1–12. doi:10.1155/2015/769121 PMID:25852754

Chand, S. (2016). Canons of taxation and equity in taxation explained. Retrieved from https://www.yourarticlelibrary.com/tax/canons-of-taxation-and-equity-in-taxation-explained/26284/

Chandran, R. (2014). Pros and cons of Mobile banking. *International Journal of Scientific and Research Publications*, *4*(10).

Chan, F. T. S., & Chong, A. Y.-L. (2012). A SEM-neural network approach forunderstanding determinants of interorganizational system standard adoptionand performances. *Decision Support Systems*, *54*(1), 621–630. doi:10.1016/j.dss.2012.08.009

Chang, C. C. (2013). Library mobile appication university libraries. *Library Hi Tech*, *31*(3), 478–492. doi:10.1108/LHT-03-2013-0024

Chatterjee, P., & Rose, R. L. (2012). Do payment mechanisms change the way consumers perceive products? *The Journal of Consumer Research*, *38*(6), 1129–1139. doi:10.1086/661730

Chauhan, S. (2015). Acceptance of mobile money by poor citizens of India: Integrating trust into the technology acceptance model. *Info*, *17*(3), 58–68. doi:10.1108/info-02-2015-0018

Chau, P. Y., Hu, P. J. H., Lee, B. L., & Au, A. K. (2007). Examining consumers' trust in online vendors and their dropout decisions: An empirical study. *Electronic Commerce Research and Applications*, *6*(2), 171–182. doi:10.1016/j.elerap.2006.11.008

Chemingui, H., & Ben lallouna, H. (2013). Resistance, motivations, trust andintention to use mobile financial services. *International Journal of Bank Marketing*, *31*(7), 574–592. doi:10.1108/IJBM-12-2012-0124

Chen, C. (2013). Perceived risk, usage frequency of mobile banking services. *Managing Service Quality*, *23*(5), 410–436. doi:10.1108/MSQ-10-2012-0137

Cheney, J. S. (2008). An Examination of Mobile Banking and Mobile Payments: Building Adoption as Experience Goods? Retrieved December 10, 2017 from https://philadelphiafed.org/-/media/consumer-finance-institute/payment-cards-center/publications/discussion-papers/2008/D2008MobileBanking.pdf

Chen-Hsiun, C. (2013). Instructional design models of mobile learning. *EXCEL International Journal of Multidisciplinary Management Studies*, *3*, 4.

Chen, J. V., Yen, D. C., & Chen, K. (2009). The acceptance and diffusion of the innovative smart phone use: A case study of a delivery service company in logistics. *Information & Management*, *46*(4), 241–248. doi:10.1016/j.im.2009.03.001

Chen, J., & Dibb, S. (2010). Consumer' trust in the online retail context: Exploring the antecedents and consequences. *Psychology and Marketing*, *27*(4), 323–346. doi:10.1002/mar.20334

Chen, Y. H., & Barnes, S. (2007). Initial trust and online buyer behaviour. *Industrial Management & Data Systems*, *107*(1), 21–36. doi:10.1108/02635570710719034

Chibelushi, Eardley, & Arabo. (2013). Identity Management in the Internet of Things: The Role of MANETs for Healthcare Applications. *Computer Science and Information Technology, 1*(2), 73-81.

Chin, W. W., & Newsted, P. R. (1999). Structural equation modeling analysis with small samples using partial least squares. *Statistical Strategies for Small Sample Research*, *2*, 307-342.

Chin, W. W. (1998b). The partial least squares approach for structural equation modeling. In G. A. Marcoulides (Ed.), *Modern Methods for Business Research* (pp. 295–336). Lawarence Erlbaum Associates.

Chin, W. W. (2010). How to write up and report PLS analyses. In *Handbook of Partial Least Squares* (pp. 655–690). Berlin: Springer. doi:10.1007/978-3-540-32827-8_29

Chiu, C. M., Hsu, M. H., Lai, H., & Chang, C. M. (2012). Re-examining the influence of trust on online repeat purchase intention: The moderating role of habit and its antecedents. *Decision Support Systems*, *53*(4), 835–845. doi:10.1016/j.dss.2012.05.021

Chong, A. Y. L., & Ngai, E. T. W. (2013). What Influences Travellers' Adoption of a Location-based Social Media Service for Their Travel Planning? *PACIS 2013 Proceedings*, 210.

Chong, A. (2013b). A two-staged SEM-neural network approach for understanding and predicting the determinants of m-commerce adoption. *Expert Systems with Applications*, *40*(4), 1240–1247. doi:10.1016/j.eswa.2012.08.067

Chong, A. Y. L. (2013a). Predicting m-commerce adoption determinants: A neural network approach. *Expert Systems with Applications*, *40*(1), 523–530. doi:10.1016/j.eswa.2012.07.068

Chong, A. Y. L., Chan, F. Y. L., & Ooi, K. B. (2014). Predicting consumer decisions to adopt mobile commerce: Cross country empirical examination between China and Malaysia. *Decision Support Systems*, *53*(1), 34–43. doi:10.1016/j.dss.2011.12.001

Chong, A. Y. L., Darmawan, N., Ooi, K. B., & Lin, B. (2010). Adoption of 3G services among Malaysian consumers: An empirical analysis. *International Journal of Mobile Communications*, *8*(2), 129–149. doi:10.1504/IJMC.2010.031444

Chong, A. Y.-L., Liu, M. J., Luo, J., & Ooi, K.-B. (2015). Predicting RFID adoption inhealthcare supply chain from the perspective of users. *International Journal of Production Economics, 159,* 66–75. doi:10.1016/j.ijpe.2014.09.034

Choudhury, D. R., Ragha, L., & Marathe, N. (2015). Implementing and improving the performance of AODV by receive reply method and securing it from Black hole attack. *Procedia Computer Science, 45,* 564–570. doi:10.1016/j.procs.2015.03.109

Chrisafis, A. (2016). *France launches smartphone app to alert people to terror attacks.* Retrieved March 26, 2017, from https://www.theguardian.com/world/2016/jun/08/france-smartphone-app-alert-terror-attacks-saip

Churchill, C. (2014). "Microinsurance: Much progress, but challenges remain" (available at http://www.ilo.org/global/about-the-ilo/newsroom/comment-analysis/WCMS_237793/lang--en/index.htm) Last visited 12-1-15.

CNBC Africa. (2016). Africa Rising Smartphone Penetration Hits 30% in Nigeria. Retrieved November 6, 2017 from https://www.cnbcafrica.com/news/western-africa/2016/07/13/africa-rising_smartphone-penetration-hits-30-in-nigeria/

Cobcroft, R. S., Towers, S. J., Smith, J. E., & Bruns, A. (2006). Mobile learning in review: Opportunities and challenges for learners, teachers, and institutions.

Cobla, G.M., Assibey, E.O. & Asante, Y. (2015). Mobile Money Technology and Spending Behaviour of Students at the University of Ghana.

Cohen, J. (1988). *Statistical Power Analysis for the Behavioral Sciences.* Hillsdale, NJ: Lawrence Erlbaum.

Coll, S., Fouda, Y., Stern, J., & Sageman, M. (2005). Who joins al Qaeda. In K. J. Greenberg (Ed.), *Al Qaeda now* (pp. 27–41). Cambridge, UK: Cambridge University Press. doi:10.1017/CBO9780511510489.005

Compeau, D. R., & Higgins, C. A. (1995). Computer self-efficacy: Development of a measure and initial test. *Management Information Systems Quarterly, 19*(2), 189–211. doi:10.2307/249688

Conole, G., Latt, M. d., Dillion, T., & Darby, J. (2006). JISC LXP Student experiences of technologies. *Draft final report.*

Consumer Financial Protection Bureau (CFPB). (2015). *Mobile financial services; A summary of comments from the public on opportunities, challenges, and risks for the underserved.*

Cooke, S. (2013). Animal rights and the environment. *Journal of Terrorism Research, 4*(2), 26–36. doi:10.15664/jtr.532

Croteau, A. M., & Bergeron, F. (2001). An information technology trilogy: Business strategy, technological deployment and organizational performance. *The Journal of Strategic Information Systems, 10*(2), 77–99. doi:10.1016/S0963-8687(01)00044-0

Cruz, P., Barretto Filgueiras Neto, L., Munoz-Gallego, P., & Laukkanen, T. (2010). Mobile banking rollout in emerging markets: Evidence from Brazil. *International Journal of Bank Marketing*, *28*(5), 342–371. doi:10.1108/02652321011064881

Dahiya, N., & Kakkar, A. K. (2016). Mobile health: Applications in tackling the Ebola challenge. *Journal of Family Medicine and Primary Care*, *5*(1), 192. doi:10.4103/2249-4863.184667 PMID:27453876

Dahlberg, T., Mallat, N., & Öörni, A. (2003). Trust enhanced technology acceptance model-consumer acceptance of mobile payment solutions: Tentative evidence. *Stockholm Mobility Roundtable, 22*, 23.

Darling-Hammond, L., Zielezinski, M. B., & Goldman, S. (2014). *Using technology to support at-risk students' learning*. Stanford Center for Opportunity Policy in Education.

Davidson, N., & McCarty, M. Y. (2011). "Driving Customer Usage of Mobile Money for the Unbanked.

Davis, F. D. (1989). Perceived usefulness, perceived ease of use, and user acceptance of information technology. *Management Information Systems Quarterly*, *13*(3), 319–340. doi:10.2307/249008

Davis, F. D., Bagozzi, R. P., & Warshaw, P. R. (1989). User acceptance of computer technology: A comparison of two theoretical models. *Management Science*, *35*(8), 982–1003. doi:10.1287/mnsc.35.8.982

Davis, H. L., Hoch, S. J., & Ragsdale, E. E. (1986). An anchoring and adjustment model of spousal predictions. *The Journal of Consumer Research*, *13*(1), 25–37. doi:10.1086/209045

Dawar, N. D. N., & Chattopadhyay, A. (2002). Rethinking marketing programs for emerging markets. *Long Range Planning*, *35*(5), 457–474. doi:10.1016/S0024-6301(02)00108-5

De Ruyter, K., Wetzels, M., & Kleijnen, M. (2001). Customer adoption of e-service: An experimental study. *International Journal of Service Industry Management*, *12*(2), 184–207. doi:10.1108/09564230110387542

De Weerdt, J., & Dercon, S. (2006). Risk-sharing networks and insurance against illness. *Journal of Development Economics*, *81*(2), 337–357. doi:10.1016/j.jdeveco.2005.06.009

Deb, A., & Kubzansky, M. (2012). *Bridging the Gap: The Business Case for Financial Capability*. A report commissioned and funded by the Citi Foundation. Cambridge, MA: Monitor, March.

Demombynes, G. & Thegeya, A. (2012). "Kenya's Mobile Revolution and the Promise of Mobile Savings." The World Bank Africa Region Poverty Reduction and Economic Management Unit March 2012

Deng, Z., Mo, X., & Liu, S. (2014). Comparison of the middle-aged and older users' adoption of mobile health services in China. *International Journal of Medical Informatics*, *83*(3), 210–224. doi:10.1016/j.ijmedinf.2013.12.002 PMID:24388129

Dennis, A., Wixom, B., & Roth, R. (2006). *Systems analysis and design* (3rd ed.). John Wiley & Sons, Inc.

Dhama, K., Malik, Y. S., Malik, S. V., & Singh, R. K. (2015). Ebola from emergence to epidemic: The virus and the disease, global preparedness and perspectives. *Journal of Infection in Developing Countries*, *9*(5), 44–445. doi:10.3855/jidc.6197 PMID:25989163

Dhulla, T. V., & Mathur, S. K. (2014). Adoption of Cloud Computing by Tertiary Level Students – A Study. *Journal of Exclusive Management Science*, *3*(3).

di Castri, S. (2013). *Mobile Money: Enabling Regulatory Solutions*. London, United Kingdom: GSMA.

Diekmann, F., Loibl, C., & Batte, M. T. (2009). The Economics of Agricultural Information: Factors Affecting Commercial Farmers' Information Strategies in Ohio. *Review of Agricultural Economics*, *31*(4), 853–872. doi:10.1111/j.1467-9353.2009.01470.x

Diniz, E. H., de Albuquerque, J. P., & Cernev, A. K. (2011). Mobile Money and Payment: a literature review based on academic and practitioner-oriented publications (2001-2011).

Dodds, W. B., Monroe, K. B., & Grewal, D. (1991). Effects of Price, Brand, and Store Information on Buyers. *JMR, Journal of Marketing Research*, *28*(3), 307–319. doi:10.2307/3172866

Dolnik, A. (2007). *Understanding terrorist innovation technology, tactics and global trends*. New York, NY: Routledge. doi:10.4324/9780203088944

Doney, P. M., & Cannon, J. P. (1997). An examination of the nature of trust in buyer-seller relationships. *The Journal of Marketing*, 35-51.

Donovan, K. (2012). Mobile money for financial inclusion. In T. Kelly & C. Rossotto (Eds.), *Information and Communication for Development* (pp. 61–74). Washington, DC: World Bank.

Dovi, E. (2008). Boosting Domestic Savings in Africa.

Drumwright, M. E. (1994). Socially responsible organizational buying: Environmental concern as a noneconomic buying criterion. *Journal of Marketing*, *58*(3), 1–19. doi:10.2307/1252307

Eastlick, M. A., Lotz, S. L., & Warrington, P. (2006). Understanding online B-to-C relationships: An integrated model of privacy concerns, trust, and commitment. *Journal of Business Research*, *59*(8), 877–886. doi:10.1016/j.jbusres.2006.02.006

Economides, N., & Jeziorski, P. (2015). Mobile money in Tanzania.

eHealthAfrica. (2017, May 18). eHealth Africa Transforms Disease Surveillance and Response in Sierra Leone. Retrieved from https://www.ehealthafrica.org/latest/2017/3/30/ehealth-africa-transforms-disease-surveillance-and-response-in-sierra-leone

Elfeky, A. I. M., & Masadeh, T. S. Y. (2016). The Effect of Mobile Learning on Students' Achievement and Conversational Skills. *International Journal of Higher Education*, *5*(3), 20. doi:10.5430/ijhe.v5n3p20

Eliasson, M., Holkko-Lafourcade, J., & Smajovic, S. (2009). *E-commerce: A study of women's online purchasing behavior.* Thesis within Business Administration. Jonkoping.

Elly, T., & Silayo, E. E. (2013). Agricultural Information Needs and Sources of the Rural Farmers in Tanzania: A Case of Iringa Rural District. *Library Review, 62*(8&9), 547–566. doi:10.1108/LR-01-2013-0009

Embuka, A. (2015, March 30). Taxation: The swivel of the economy. DailySun.

Entner, R. (2012). The wireless industry: The essential engine of us economic growth. *Recon Analytics, 30*, 33.

Escobar-Rodriguez, T., & Carvajal-Trujillo, E. (2014). Online purchasing tickets for low cost barriers: An application of the unified theory of acceptance and use of technology (UTAUT) model. *Tourism Management, 43*(1), 70–88. doi:10.1016/j.tourman.2014.01.017

Evans, C. (2008). The effectiveness of m-learning in the form of podcast revision lectures in higher education. *Computers & Education, 50*(2), 491–498. doi:10.1016/j.compedu.2007.09.016

Ewart, C. K. (1991). Social action theory for a public health psychology. *The American Psychologist, 46*(9), 931–946. doi:10.1037/0003-066X.46.9.931 PMID:1958012

EYGM. (2014). Mobile money – the next wave of growth. Optimizing operator approaches in a fast-changing landscape. Retrieved 21 February 2017 from http://www.ey.com/Publication/vwLUAssets/EY_-_Mobile_money_-_the_next_wave_of_growth_in_telecoms/$FILE/EY-mobile-money-the-next-wave.pdf

Fähnrich, C., Denecke, K., Adeoye, O. O., Benzler, J., Claus, H., Kirchner, G., ... Krause, G. (2015). Surveillance and Outbreak Response Management System (SORMAS) to support the control of the Ebola virus disease outbreak in West Africa. *Eurosurveillance, 20*(12), 21071. doi:10.2807/1560-7917.ES2015.20.12.21071 PMID:25846493

Fain, D., & Roberts, M. L. (1997). Technology vs consumer behavior: The battle for the financial services customer. *Journal of Direct Marketing, 11*(1), 44–54. doi:10.1002/(SICI)1522-7138(199724)11:1<44::AID-DIR5>3.0.CO;2-Z

Falk, R. F., & Miller, N. B. (1992). *A primer for soft modeling.* University of Akron Press.

Fang, Y., Qureshi, I., Sun, H., McCole, P., Ramsey, E., & Lim, K. H. (2014). Trust, Satisfaction, and Online Repurchase Intention: The Moderating Role of Perceived Effectiveness of E-Commerce Institutional Mechanisms. *Management Information Systems Quarterly, 38*(2), 407–427. doi:10.25300/MISQ/2014/38.2.04

Fan, X., Thompson, B., & Wang, L. (1999). Effects of sample size, estimation methods, and model specification on structural equation modeling fit indexes. *Structural Equation Modeling, 6*(1), 56–83. doi:10.1080/10705519909540119

Fasina, F. O., Shittu, A., Lazarus, D., Tomori, O., Simonsen, L., Viboud, C., & Chowell, G. (2014). Transmission dynamics and control of Ebola virus disease outbreak in Nigeria, July to September 2014. *Eurosurveillance, 19*(40), 20920. doi:10.2807/1560-7917.ES2014.19.40.20920 PMID:25323076

Feldmann, H., & Geisbert, T. W. (2011). Ebola haemorrhagic fever. *Lancet, 377*(9768), 849–862. doi:10.1016/S0140-6736(10)60667-8 PMID:21084112

Fishbein, M. (1979). *A theory of reasoned action: some applications and implications.* Academic Press.

Fishbein, M., & Ajzen, I. (1975). Belief, attitude, intention and behavior: An introduction to theory and research.

Fishbein, M., & Ajzen, I. (1975). *Belief, attitude, intention, and behavior: anintroduction to theory and research.* Addison-Wesley.

Fogel, J., & Nehmad, E. (2009). Internet social network communities: Risk taking, trust, and privacy concerns. *Computers in Human Behavior, 25*(1), 153–160. doi:10.1016/j.chb.2008.08.006

Foon, Y. S., & Fah, B. C. Y. (2011). Internet banking adoption in Kuala Lumpur: An application of UTAUT model. *International Journal of Business and Management, 6*(4), 161–167.

Fornell, C., & Larcker, D. F. (1981). Evaluation Structural Equation Models with Unobservable Variables and Measurement Error. *JMR, Journal of Marketing Research, 18*(1), 39–50. doi:10.2307/3151312

Fraunholz, B., & Unnithan, C. (2004). Critical success factors in mobile communications: A comparative roadmap for Germany and India. *International Journal of Mobile Communications, 2*(1), 87–101. doi:10.1504/IJMC.2004.004489

Fuksa, M. (2013). Mobile technologies and services development impact on mobile Internet usage in Latvia. *Procedia Computer Science, 26*(1), 41–50. doi:10.1016/j.procs.2013.12.006

Furukawa, M. F., Ketcham, J. D., & Rimsza, M. E. (2007). Physician practice revenues and use of information technology in patient care. *Medical Care, 45*(2), 168–176. doi:10.1097/01.mlr.0000241089.98461.e5 PMID:17224780

G. S. M. A. (2013). Global Mobile Money Deployment Tracker." Retrieved from http://www.wirelessintelligence.com/mobile-money

Gallego, M. D., Luna, P., & Bueno, S. (2008). User acceptance model of open source software. *Computers in Human Behavior, 24*(5), 2199–2216. doi:10.1016/j.chb.2007.10.006

Garbarino, E., & Johnson, M. S. (1999). The different roles of satisfaction, trust, and commitment in customer relationships. *The Journal of Marketing*, 70-87.

Gaur, A. S., & Gaur, S. S. (2006). Statistical methods for practice and research: A guide to data analysis using SPSS. *Sage (Atlanta, Ga.).*

Gefen, D. (2000). E-commerce: The role of familiarity and trust. *Omega, 28*(6), 725–737. doi:10.1016/S0305-0483(00)00021-9

Gefen, D. (2003). TAM or just plain habit: A look at experienced online shoppers. *Journal of End User Computing, 15*(3), 1–13. doi:10.4018/joeuc.2003070101

Gefen, D., Karahanna, E., & Straub, D. W. (2003). Trust and TAM in online shopping: An integrated model. *Management Information Systems Quarterly, 27*(1), 51–90. doi:10.2307/30036519

Gefen, D., & Straub, D. W. (2004). Consumer' trust in B2C e-Commerce and the importance of social presence: Experiments in e-Products and e-Services. *Omega, 32*(6), 407–424. doi:10.1016/j.omega.2004.01.006

Geisser, S. (1974). A Predictive Approach to the Random Effect Model. *Biometrika, 61*(1), 101–107. doi:10.1093/biomet/61.1.101

Geisser, S. (1975). The predictive sample reuse method with applications. *Journal of the American Statistical Association, 70*(350), 320–328. doi:10.1080/01621459.1975.10479865

Gencer, M. (2011). *The Mobile Money Movement: Catalyst to Jumpstart Emerging Markets.* Innovations Publication Winter.

Ghane, S. O. H. E. I. L. A., Fathian, M., & Gholamian, M. R. (2011). Full relationship among e-satisfaction, e-trust, e-service quality, and e-loyalty: The case of Iran e-banking. *Journal of Theoretical and Applied Information Technology, 33*(1), 1–6.

Ghoreishi, S. M., Razak, S. A., Isnin, I. F., & Chizari, H. (2014). Rushing Attack Against Routing Protocols in Mobile Ad-Hoc Network. In *International Symposium on Biometrics and Security Technologies.* IEEE. doi:10.1109/ISBAST.2014.7013125

Giginyu, I. B. (2015). CBN Grants Licenses to 21 Mobile Money Operators. Retrieved 6 November, 2017 from https://www.dailytrust.com.ng/news/business/cbn-grants-licences-to-21-mobile-money-operators/121506.html

Gikas, J., & Grant, M. M. (2013). Mobile computing devices in higher education: Student perspectives on learning with cellphones, smartphones & social media. *The Internet and Higher Education, 19*, 18–26. doi:10.1016/j.iheduc.2013.06.002

Gil-Garcia, J. R. (2008). Using partial least squares in digital government research. Handbook of research on public information technology, 239-253. doi:10.4018/978-1-59904-857-4.ch023

Gnana Sheela, K., & Deepa, S. N. (2013). Review on methods to fix number of hidden neurons in neural networks. *Mathematical Problems in Engineering.*

Grabner-Kräuter, S., & Kaluscha, E. A. (2003). Empirical research in on-line trust: A review and critical assessment. *International Journal of Human-Computer Studies, 58*(6), 783–812. doi:10.1016/S1071-5819(03)00043-0

Greenacre, J. (2013). The rise of mobile money: Regulatory issues for Australia. *JASSA,* (1), 24.

Griffith, D. A. (1996). *Some guidelines for specifying the geographic weights matrix contained in spatial statistical models*. Practical Handbook of Spatial Statistics.

Grimus, M., & Ebner, M. (2014). Learning and Teaching with Mobile Devices an Approach in Secondary Education in Ghana. *In proceedings of International Conference on Mobile Learning 2014, 10*. Madrid-Spain.

Grimus, M., Ebner, M., & Holzinger, A. (2012). Mobile Learning as a Chance to Enhance Education in Developing Countries-on the Example of Ghana. *In mLearn 2012 Conference Proceedings*, 340-345.

Grimus, M., & Ebner, M. (2016). *Mobile Learning and STEM First Experiences in a Senior High School in Ghana: Case Studies in Practice* (H. T. Crompton, Ed.). Routledge.

Groß, M. (2015a). Mobile shopping: A classification framework and literature review. *International Journal of Retail & Distribution Management, 43*(3), 221–241. doi:10.1108/IJRDM-06-2013-0119

Groß, M. (2015b). Exploring the acceptance of technology for mobile shopping: An empirical investigation among Smartphone users. *International Review of Retail, Distribution and Consumer Research, 25*(3), 215–235. doi:10.1080/09593969.2014.988280

Grøtnes, E. (2009). Standardization as open innovation: Two cases from the mobile industry. *Information Technology & People, 22*(4), 367–381. doi:10.1108/09593840911002469

Groupe Speciale Mobile Association (GSMA). (2015). *The Mobile Economy 2015*.

Groupe Speciale Mobile Association (GSMA). (2016). *The Mobile Economy 2016*. Retrieved December 10th, 2017, from https://www.gsma.com/mobileeconomy/archive/GSMA_ME_2016.pdf

Groupe Speciale Mobile Association (GSMA). (2016). The Mobile Economy 2016.https://www.gsma.com/mobileeconomy/archive/GSMA_ME_2015.pdf

GSMA. (2012). Taxation and the growth of mobile services in subSaharan Africa.

GSMA. (n.d.). Services for the Unbanked (tech. rep.). Retrieved from http://www.gsma.com/mobilefordevelopment/wp-content/uploads/2015/03/SOTIR_2014.pdf

Gupta, D. K. (2006). *Who are the terrorists?* San Diego State University: Chelsea House Publishers.

Gupta, S. (2013). Te Mobile Banking and Payment Revolution. *European Finance Review, 3*, 3–6.

Hackbarth, G., Grover, V., & Mun, Y. Y. (2003). Computer playfulness and anxiety: Positive and negative mediators of the system experience effect on perceived ease of use. *Information & Management, 40*(3), 221–232. doi:10.1016/S0378-7206(02)00006-X

Hair, J. F., Hult, G. T. M., Ringle, C. M., & Sarstedt, M. (2013). *A Primer on Partial Least Squares Structural Equation Modeling (PLS-SEM)* (1st ed.). Thousand Oaks, CA: Sage.

Hair, J. F., Ringle, C. M., & Sarstedt, M. (2011). PLS-SEM: Indeed a Silver Bullet. *Journal of Marketing Theory and Practice*, *18*(2), 139–152. doi:10.2753/MTP1069-6679190202

Hair, J. F., Sarstedt, M., Ringle, C. M., & Mena, J. A. (2012). An assessment of the use of partial least squares structural equation modeling in marketing research. *Journal of the Academy of Marketing Science*, *40*(3), 414–433. doi:10.1007/s11747-011-0261-6

Hair, J., Hult, T. M., Ringle, C. M., & Sarstedt, M. (2014). *A primer on partial least squares structural equation modelling (PLS-SEM)*. Thousand Oaks, CA: Sage.

Hall, B. H., & Khan, B. (2003). *Adoption of new technology*. National Bureau of Economic Research. doi:10.3386/w9730

Harsono, I. L. D., & Suryana, L. A. (August, 2014). Factors Affecting the Use Behavior of Social Media Using UTAUT 2 Model. *Proceedings of the First Asia-Pacific Conference on Global Business, Economic, Finance and Social Science*.

Ha, S., & Stoel, L. (2009). Consumer e-shopping acceptance: Antecedents in a technology acceptance model. *Journal of Business Research*, *62*(5), 565–571. doi:10.1016/j.jbusres.2008.06.016

Hayashi, F. (2012). *Mobile Payments: What's in It for Consumers?* Federal Reserve Bank of Kansas City.

Haykin, S. (2001). *Neural networks: A comprehensive foundation*. Upper Saddle River, NJ: Prentice Hall.

Heerden, A. v., Tomlinson, M., & Swartz, L. (2012). Bulletin of the World Health Organization. *Point of care in your pocket: a research agenda for the field of m-health, 90*(5), 393-394.

Henry, M., James, B. Q., & Sumantra, G. (1998). *The strategy process* (pp. 76–78). Hertfordshire, UK: Prentice Hall Europe.

Henseler, J., & Chin, W. W. (2010). A comparison of approaches for the analysis of interaction effects between latent variables using partial least squares path modeling. *Structural Equation Modeling*, *17*(1), 82–109. doi:10.1080/10705510903439003

Henseler, J., Ringle, C. M., & Sarstedt, M. (2012). Using partial least squares path modeling in international advertising research: Basic concepts and recent issues. In S. Okazaki (Ed.), *Handbook of Research in International Advertising* (pp. 252–276). Cheltenham, UK: Edward Elgar Publishing. doi:10.4337/9781781001042.00023

Henseler, J., Ringle, C. M., & Sinkovics, R. R. (2009). The Use of Partial Least Squares Path Modeling in International Marketing. In R. R. Sinkovics & P. N. Ghauri (Eds.), *Advances in International Marketing* (Vol. 20, pp. 277–320). Bingley, UK: Emerald. doi:10.1108/S1474-7979(2009)0000020014

Hernández, B., Jiménez, J., & Martín, M. J. (2009). Key website factors in e-business strategy. *International Journal of Information Management*, *29*(5), 362–371. doi:10.1016/j.ijinfomgt.2008.12.006

Herrero, Á., & San Martín, H. (2012). Developing and testing a global model to explain the adoption of websites by users in rural tourism accommodations. *International Journal of Hospitality Management, 31*(4), 1178–1186. doi:10.1016/j.ijhm.2012.02.005

Hew, J., Lee, V., Ooi, K.-B., & Wei, J. (2015). What catalyses mobile apps usage intention: An empiricalanalysis. *Industrial Management & Data, 115*(7), 1269–1291. doi:10.1108/IMDS-01-2015-0028

Hinson, R. E. (2011). Banking the poor: The role of mobiles. *Journal of Financial Services, 15*(4), 320–333. doi:10.1057/fsm.2010.29

Hofstede, G. (2003). *Culture's consequences: Comparing values, behaviors, institutions and organizations across nations.* Sage Publications.

Homburg, C., Hoyer, W. D., & Koschate, N. (2005). *Customers' Reactions to Price Increases: Do Customer Satisfaction and Perceived Motive Fairness Matter?* Academy of Marketing.

Hong, I. (2015). Understanding the consumer's online merchant selection process: The roles of product involvement, perceived risk, and trust expectation. *International Journal of Information Management, 35*(3), 322–336. doi:10.1016/j.ijinfomgt.2015.01.003

Hong, I., & Cha, H. (2013). The mediating role of consumer trust in an onlinemerchant in predicting purchase intention. *International Journal of Information Management, 33*(6), 927–939. doi:10.1016/j.ijinfomgt.2013.08.007

Hövels, V. (2010). *Drivers and inhibitors of the behavioral intention to use branded mobile applications in a retail environment* (Master's thesis). Available from the University of Amsterdam"s dissertations and theses database.

Hsiao, R. L. (2003). Technology fears: Distrust and cultural persistence in electronic marketplace adoption. *The Journal of Strategic Information Systems, 12*(3), 169–199. doi:10.1016/S0963-8687(03)00034-9

Hsieh, J., & Wang, W. (2007). Explaining employees' Extended Use of complex information systems. *European Journal of Information Systems, 16*(3), 216–227. Retrieved from http://www.ifc.org/wps/wcm/connect/93fdb8004a1b4f46909bfddd29332b51/Tool+4.7e.+. doi:10.1057/palgrave.ejis.3000663

Hsin Chang, H., & Wen Chen, S. (2008). The impact of online store environment cues on purchase intention: Trust and perceived risk as a mediator. *Online Information Review, 32*(6), 818–841. doi:10.1108/14684520810923953

Hsu, M., Chang, C., & Chuang, L. (2015). Understanding the determinants of onlinerepeat purchase intention and moderating role of habit: The case of onlinegroup-buying in Taiwan. *International Journal of Information Management, 35.*

Huang, J.-C. (2010). Remote health monitoring adoption model based on artificialneural networks. *Expert Systems with Applications, 37*(1), 307–314. doi:10.1016/j.eswa.2009.05.063

Hua, Z., Fei, G., & Wen, Q. (2011). A Password-Based Secure Communication Scheme in Battlefields for Internet of Things. *China Communications*, *8*(1), 72–78.

IFC (International Finance Corporation). (2011). Mobile Money Study 2011. Retrieved from http://www.ifc.org/ifcext/globalfm.nsf/ Content/Mobile+Money+Study+2011

Igbaria, M., Zinatelli, N., Cragg, P., & Cavaye, A. L. (1997). Personal computing acceptance factors in small firms: A structural equation model. *Management Information Systems Quarterly*, *21*(3), 279–305. doi:10.2307/249498

Ikeda, M., Kulla, E., Hiyama, M., Barolli, L., Miho, R., & Takizawa, M. (2012). TCP Congestion-Control in MANETs for Multiple Traffic Considering Proactive and Reactive Routing Protocols. *15th IEEE International Conference on Network-Based Information Systems*. doi:10.1109/NBiS.2012.68

Im, I., Hong, S., & Kang, M. S. (2011). An international comparison of technology adoption: Testing the UTAUT model. *Information & Management*, *48*(1), 1–8. doi:10.1016/j.im.2010.09.001

IntraHealth. (2017, May 11). IntraHealth Receives Grand Challenge Award for Ebola Response. Retrieved from https://www.intrahealth.org/news/intrahealth-receives-grand-challenge-award-for-ebola-response

Irungu, K. R. G., Mbugua, D., & Muia, J. (2015). Information and Communication Technologies (ICTs) Attract Youth into Profitable Agriculture in Kenya. *East African Agricultural and Forestry*, *81*(1), 24–33.

Isaacs, S. (2012). Turning on Mobile Learning in Africa and the Middle East, Illustrative Initiatives and Policy Implications, by the United Nations Educational, Scientific and Cultural Organization 7. UNESCO 2012, France: Place de Fontenoy, 75352 Paris 07 SP.

ISACA. (2011). Mobile Payments. Retrieved 21-1-15 from http://www.isaca.org/Groups/Professional-English/pci-compliance/GroupDocuments/MobilePaymentsWP.pdf

Islam, M. Z., Low, P. K. C., & Hasan, I. (2013). Intention to use advanced mobile phone service (AMPS). *Management Decision*, *51*(4), 824–838. doi:10.1108/00251741311326590

Islam, R., Islam, R., & Mazumder, T. (2010). Mobile application and its global impact. *IACSIT International Journal of Engineering and Technology*, *10*(6), 72–78.

Istepanian, R. S., Laxminarayan, S., & Pattichis, C. S. (2006). M-Health: Emerging Mobile Health Systems. (R. S. Istepanian, S. Laxminarayan, & C. S. Pattichis, Eds.) NY: Springer Science+Business Media, Incorporated. doi:10.1007/b137697

Jack, W., & Suri, T. (2011). *Mobile money: The economics of M-PESA (No. w16721)*. National Bureau of Economic Research. doi:10.3386/w16721

Jambulingam, M. (2013). Behavioural intention to adopt mobile technology among tertiary students. *World Applied Sciences Journal*, *22*(9), 1262–1271.

Jaradat, M. R. M., & Rababaa, M. S. (2013). Assessing key factor that influence on the acceptance of mobile commerce based on modified UTAUT. *International Journal of Business and Management, 8*(23), 102–112.

Jarvenpaa, S. L., Tractinsky, N., & Saarinen, L. (1999). Consumer' trust in an internet store: a cross-cultural validation. *Journal of Computer-Mediated Communication, 5*(2).

Jarvenpaa, S. L., & Lang, K. R. (2005). Managing the Paradoxes of Mobile Technology. *Information Systems Management, 22*.

Jarvenpaa, S. L., Tractinsky, N., & Vitale, M. (2000). Consumer' trust in an internet store. *Information Technology Management, 1*(1/2), 45–71. doi:10.1023/A:1019104520776

Jasperson, J. S., Carter, P. E., & Zmud, R. W. (2005). A comprehensive conceptualization of post-adoption behaviors associated with information technology enabled work systems. *Management Information Systems Quarterly, 29*(3), 525–558. doi:10.2307/25148694

Jawad, H. H. M., & Hassan, Z. B. (2015). Applying UTAUT to evaluate the acceptance of mobile learning in higher education in Iraq. *International Journal of Science and Research, 4*(5), 952–954.

Jenkins, B. (2008). *Developing Mobile Money Ecosystems*. Washington, DC: IFC and the Harvard Kennedy School.

Jiang, G., Peng, L., & Liu, R. (2015). Research on the factors influencing mobile gameadoption in China. *Proceedings of 4th international conference on logistics, informatics and service science, 5*, 1297–1302.

Jin, B., Yong Park, J., & Kim, J. (2008). Cross-cultural examination of the relationships among firm reputation, e-satisfaction, e-trust, and e-loyalty. *International Marketing Review, 25*(3), 324–337. doi:10.1108/02651330810877243

Jin, N. P., Lee, S., & Lee, H. (2015). The effect of experience quality on perceived value, satisfaction, image and behavioral intention of water park patrons: New versus repeat visitors. *International Journal of Tourism Research, 17*(1), 82–95. doi:10.1002/jtr.1968

Johnson, D., & Grayson, K. (2005). Cognitive and affective trust in service relationships. *Journal of Business Research, 58*(4), 500–507. doi:10.1016/S0148-2963(03)00140-1

Joshi, P. (2011). *Security Issues in Routing protocols in MANETs at network layer. Procedia Computer Science, 3*, 954–960.

Joubert, J., & Van, J. (2013). The role of trust and risk in mobile commerce adoption within South Africa. *International Journal of Business Human Technology, 3*(2), 27–38.

Kanowitz, S. (2014, August 11). Tracking Ebola with CDC's app. *GCN Technology*. Retrieved from https://gcn.com/articles/2014/08/11/ebola-virus-tracking-app.aspx?m=1

Karahanna, E., Straub, D. W., & Chervany, N. L. (1999). Information technology adoption across time: A cross-sectional comparison of pre-adoption and post-adoption beliefs. *Management Information Systems Quarterly*, *23*(2), 183–213. doi:10.2307/249751

Karaiskos, D. C., Drossos, D. A., Tsiaousis, A. S., Giaglis, G. M., & Fouskas, K. G. (2012). Affective and social determinants of mobile data services adoption. *Behaviour & Information Technology*, *31*(3), 209–219. doi:10.1080/0144929X.2011.563792

Karimuribo, E. D., Sayalel, K., Beda, E., Short, N., Wambura, P., Mboera, L. G., ... Rweyemamu, M. M. (2012). Towards One Health disease surveillance: The Southern African Centre for Infectious Disease Surveillance approach. *The Onderstepoort Journal of Veterinary Research*, *79*(2), 1–7. doi:10.4102/ojvr.v79i2.454 PMID:23327374

Katakam, A. (2014). "The State of Mobile Credit and Savings – how has mobile technology expanded credit and savings services?" GSMA Retrieved 15-1-15 from http://www.gsma.com/mobilefordevelopment/the-state-of-mobile-credit-and-savings-how-has-mobile-technology-expanded-credit-and-savings-services

Katzell, R. A., & Thompson, D. E. (1990). Work motivation: Theory and practice. *The American Psychologist*, *45*(2), 144–153. doi:10.1037/0003-066X.45.2.144

Kay, M., Santos, J., & Takane, M. (2011). mHealth: New horizons for health through mobile technologies. *World Health Organization*, (3), 66-71.

Keegan, D. (2005). The incorporation of mobile learning into mainstream education and training. In *World Conference on Mobile Learning* (p. p. 11). Cape Town.

Keengwe, J., & Bhargava, M. (2014). Mobile learning and Integration of mobile technologies in education. *Education and Information Technologies*, *19*(4), 737–746. doi:10.1007/s10639-013-9250-3

Kelman, H. C. (1958). Compliance, identification, and internalization: Three processes of attitude change. *The Journal of Conflict Resolution*, *2*(1), 51–60. doi:10.1177/002200275800200106

Khanna, T., & Palepu, K. (2000). Is group affiliation profitable in emerging markets? An analysis of diversified Indian business groups. *The Journal of Finance*, *55*(2), 867–891. doi:10.1111/0022-1082.00229

Kiable, B. D., & Nwankwo, N. G. (2009). *Curbing tax evasion and avoidance in personal income.* Owerri: Springfield Publishers.

Kijsanayotin, B., Pannarunothai, S., & Speedie, S. M. (2009). Factors influencing health information technology adoption in Thailand's community health centers: Applying the UTAUT model. *International Journal of Medical Informatics*, *78*(6), 404–416. doi:10.1016/j.ijmedinf.2008.12.005 PMID:19196548

Kikulwe, E. M., Fischer, E., & Qaim, M. (2014). Mobile money, smallholder farmers, and household welfare in Kenya. *PLoS One*, *9*(10), e109804. doi:10.1371/journal.pone.0109804 PMID:25286032

Kim, K. K., & Prabhakar, B. (2004). Initial trust and the adoption of B2C e-commerce: The case of internet banking. *ACM SIGMIS Database, 35*(2), 50-64.

Kim, S. S., & Malhotra, N. K. (2005). A longitudinal model of continued IS use: An integrative view of four mechanisms underlying postadoption phenomena. *Management science, 51*(5), 741-755. doi:10.1287/mnsc.1040.0326

Kim, S., & Yoon, D. (2013). Antecedents of mobile app usage among smartphone users. In *American Academy of Advertising Conference Proceedings* (pp. 72–83). Academic Press.

Kim, D., Ferrin, D., & Rao, R. (2008). A trust-based consumer decision-making model in electronic commerce: The role of trust, perceived risk, and their antecedents. *Decision Support Systems, 44*(2), 544–564. doi:10.1016/j.dss.2007.07.001

Kim, G., Shin, B., & Lee, H. G. (2009). Understanding dynamics between initial trust and usage intentions of mobile banking. *Information Systems Journal, 19*(3), 283–311. doi:10.1111/j.1365-2575.2007.00269.x

Kim, H. W., Xu, Y., & Gupta, S. (2012). Which is more important in Internet shopping, perceived price or trust? *Electronic Commerce Research and Applications, 11*(3), 241–252. doi:10.1016/j.elerap.2011.06.003

Kim, J., Jin, B., & Swinney, J. L. (2009). The role of e-retail quality, e-satisfaction and e-trust in online loyalty development process. *Journal of Retailing and Consumer Services, 16*(4), 239–247. doi:10.1016/j.jretconser.2008.11.019

Kim, M. J., Chung, N., & Lee, C. K. (2011). The effect of perceived trust on electronic commerce: Shopping online for tourism products and services in South Korea. *Tourism Management, 32*(2), 256–265. doi:10.1016/j.tourman.2010.01.011

Kim, S. C., Yoon, D., & Han, E. K. (2014). Antecedents of mobile app usage among smartphone users. *Journal of Marketing Communications*, 1–18.

Kim, S. H. (2008). Moderating effects of job relevance and experience on mobile wireless technology acceptance: Adoption of a smartphone by individuals. *Information & Management, 45*(6), 387–393. doi:10.1016/j.im.2008.05.002

Kim, T. G., Lee, J. H., & Law, R. (2008). An empirical examination of the acceptance behaviour of hotel front office systems: An extended technology acceptance model. *Tourism Management, 29*(3), 500–513. doi:10.1016/j.tourman.2007.05.016

Kim, T., & Phil, D. (2009). *The sources of insecurity in the third world: external or internal? Shinjuku-ku*. Tokyo: Waseda Institute for Advanced Study.

Kiriş, C. Ş.-H. K., & Kiriş, P. T.-H. M. 2008. Can SMEs in developing countries resist crisis? An analysis on Turkish and Albanian cases. In *Proceedings of the First International Conference on Balkans Studies (ICBS 2008)* (p. 208).

Kirui, O. K., Okello, J. J., & Nyikal, R. A. (2012). Awareness of Mobile Phone-Based Money Transfer Services in Agriculture by Smallholder Farmers in Kenya. *International Journal of ICT Research and Development in Africa*, *3*(1), 1–13. doi:10.4018/jictrda.2012010101

Kolog, E. A. (2017). Contextualising the Application of Human Language Technologies for Counselling. PhD Dissertation in Forestry and Natural sciences, University of Eastern Finland publication. Vol. 218.

Kolog, E. A., & Montero, C. S. (2017). Towards automated e-counselling system based on counsellors emotion perception. *Education and Information Technologies*, 1-23. doi:10.1007/s10639-017-9643-9

Kolog, E. A., Montero, S. C., & Sutinen, E. (2016). Annotation Agreement of Emotions in Text: The Influence of Counselors' Emotional State on their Emotion Perception. In *Proceeding of International Conference on Advanced Learning Technologies (ICALT)* (pp. 357-359). IEEE. doi:10.1109/ICALT.2016.21

Kolog, E. A., Sutinen, E., & Vanhalakka-Ruoho, M. (2014). E-counselling implementation: Students' Life stories and counselling technologies in perspective. *International Journal of Education and Development Using Information and Communication Technology*, *10*(3), 32–48.

Kolog, E. A., Sutinen, E., Vanhalakka-Ruoho, M., Sohunen, J., & Anohah, E. (2015). Using Unified Theory of Acceptance and Use of Technology Model to Predict Students' Behavioral Intention to Adopt and Use E - Counseling in Ghana. *International Journal of Modern Education and Computer Science*, *7*(11), 1–11. doi:10.5815/ijmecs.2015.11.01

Koole, M. L. (2009). A model for framing mobile learning. *Mobile learning: Transforming the delivery of education and training, 1*(2), 25-47.

Korucu, A. T., & Alkan, A. (2011). Differences between m-learning (mobile learning) and e-learning, basic terminology and usage of m-learning in education. *Procedia: Social and Behavioral Sciences*, *15*, 1925–1930. doi:10.1016/j.sbspro.2011.04.029

Koufaris, M., & Hampton-Sosa, W. (2004). The development of initial trust in an online company by new consumers. *Information & Management*, *41*(3), 377–397. doi:10.1016/j.im.2003.08.004

Krause, P. R., Bryant, P. R., Clark, T., Dempsey, W., Henchal, E., Michael, N. L., . . . Gruber, M. F. (2015). Immunology of protection from Ebola virus infection. *Science translational medicine, 7*(286).

Krueger, A. B. (2007). *What makes a terrorist: economies and roots of terrorism*. Princeton, NJ: Princeton University Press.

Kuhn, J. H., Becker, S., Ebihara, H., Geisbert, T. W., Johnson, K. M., Kawaoka, Y., . . . Jahrling, P. B. (2010). Proposal for a revised taxonomy of the family Filoviridae: classification, names of taxa and viruses, and virus abbreviations. *Archives of virology, 155(12)*, 2083-2103.

Kuisma, T., Laukkanen, T., & Hiltunen, M. (2007). Mapping the reasons for resistance to internet banking: A means-end approach. *International Journal of Information Management, 27*(2), 75–85. doi:10.1016/j.ijinfomgt.2006.08.006

Kukulska-Hulme, A. (2007). Mobile usability in educational contexts: What have we learnt? *The International Review of Research in Open and Distributed Learning, 8*(2). doi:10.19173/irrodl.v8i2.356

Kumar, K., McKay, C., & Rotman, S. (2010). Microfinance and mobile banking: The story so far.

Kumar, Kumar, & Kumar. (2010). Improved Modified Reverse AODV Protocol. *International Journal of Computer Applications, 12*(4), 22-26.

Kumaran & Sankaranarayanan. (2010). Early detection congestion and control routing in MANET. *Seventh International Conference on Wireless and Optical Communications Networks (WOCN)*, 1-5.

Kurkela, L. J. (2011). Systemic approach to learning paradigms and the use of social media in higher education. *IJET, 6*, 14–20.

Kusimba, S. B., Yang, Y., & Chawla, N. V. (2015). Family networks of mobile money in Kenya. *Information Technologies & International Development, 11*(3).

Kwahk, K., & Park, J. (2012). Investigating the determinants of purchase intentionin C2C e-commerce. *World Academy of Science, Engineering and Technology, 6*(9), 487–491.

Kwon, H. S., & Chidambaram, L. 2000. A test of the technology acceptance model: The case of cellular telephone adoption. In Proceedings of the 33rd Annual Hawaii International Conference on System Sciences. IEEE.

Kwon, J. M., Bae, J.-i., & Blum, S. C. (2013). Mobile applications in the hospitality industry. *Journal of Hospitality and Tourism Technology, 4*(1), 81–92. doi:10.1108/17579881311302365

La Polla, M., Martinelli, F., & Sgandurra, D. (2013). A survey on security for mobile devices. *IEEE Communications Surveys and Tutorials, 15*(1), 446–471. doi:10.1109/SURV.2012.013012.00028

Lal, R., & Sachdev, I. (2015). *Mobile Money Services-Design and Development for Financial Inclusion (Vol. 83)*. Working Paper 15.

Lan, Y.-F., & Huang, S.-M. (2012). Using mobile learning to improve the reflection: A case study of traffic violation. *Journal of Educational Technology & Society, 15*(2), 179–193.

Laouris, Y., & Eteokleous, N. (2005). We need an educationally relevant definition of mobile learning. In *Proceedings of the 4th World Conference on Mobile Learning* (pp. 290-294).

Laukkanen, T., & Kiviniemi, V. (2010). The role of information in mobile banking resistance. *International Journal of Bank Marketing, 28*(5), 372–388. doi:10.1108/02652321011064890

Laukkanen, T., & Lauronen, J. (2005). Consumer value creation in mobile banking services. *International Journal of Mobile Communications, 3*(4), 325–338. doi:10.1504/IJMC.2005.007021

Laukkanen, T., Sinkkonen, S., Kivijärvi, M., & Laukkanen, P. (2007). Innovation resistance among mature consumers. *Journal of Consumer Marketing*, *24*(7), 419–427. doi:10.1108/07363760710834834

Lawack, V. A. (2012). Mobile money, financial inclusion and financial integrity: The South African case. *Wash. JL Tech. & Arts*, *8*, 317.

Law, E. L. C. (2011, June). The measurability and predictability of user experience. In *Proceedings of the 3rd ACM SIGCHI symposium on Engineering interactive computing systems* (pp. 1-10). ACM. doi:10.1145/1996461.1996485

Lawrence, C. S., & Kinder, P. D. (1987). *Law and business*. New Jersey: McGraw-Hill Publishing.

Leach, J. (2011). M-Insurance: The Next Wave of Mobile Financial Services? Retrieved 11-1-15 from http://www.microensure.com/news.asp?id=47&start=5

Leadbeater, C. (2015). *New app could alert travellers about terror attacks*. Retrieved March 26, 2017, from http://www.telegraph.co.uk/travel/news/New-app-could-alert-travellers-about-terror-attacks/

J. Ledgerwood, J. Earne, & C. Nelson (Eds.). (2013). *The new microfinance handbook: A financial market system perspective*. World Bank Publications. doi:10.1596/978-0-8213-8927-0

Leea, W.J., Kimb, T.U., Chungc, J.-Y. (2002). User acceptance of the mobile Internet.

Lee, H. Y., Lee, Y.-K., & Kwon, D. (2005). The intention to use computerized reservation systems: The moderating effects of organizational support and supplier incentive. *Journal of Business Research*, *58*(11), 1552–1561. doi:10.1016/j.jbusres.2004.07.008

Lee, K. C., & Chung, N. (2009). Understanding factors affecting trust in and satisfaction with mobile banking in Korea: A modified DeLone and McLean's model perspective. *Interacting with Computers*, *21*(5), 385–392. doi:10.1016/j.intcom.2009.06.004

Lee, M. C. (2009). Understanding the behavioral intention to play online games: An extension of the theory of planned behaviour. *Online Information Review*, *33*(5), 849–872. doi:10.1108/14684520911001873

Lee, M. K., & Turban, E. (2001). A trust model for consumer internet shopping. *International Journal of Electronic Commerce*, *6*(1), 75–91. doi:10.1080/10864415.2001.11044227

Leong, L. Y., Hew, T. S., Tan, G. W. H., & Ooi, K. B. (2013b). Predicting the determinants of the NFC-enabled mobile credit card acceptance: A neural networks approach. *Expert Systems with Applications*, *40*(14), 5604–5620. doi:10.1016/j.eswa.2013.04.018

Leong, L. Y., Ooi, K. B., Chong, A. Y. L., & Lin, B. (2013a). Modelling the stimulators of the behavioral intention to use mobile entertainment: Does gender really matter? *Computers in Human Behavior*, *29*(5), 2109–2121. doi:10.1016/j.chb.2013.04.004

Leon, N., Schneider, H., & Daviaud, E. (2012). Applying a framework for assessing the health system challenges to scaling up mHealth in South Africa. *BMC Medical Informatics and Decision Making*, *12*(1), 123. doi:10.1186/1472-6947-12-123 PMID:23126370

Lewis, C. C., Fretwell, C. E., Ryan, J., & Parham, J. B. (2013). Faculty Use of Established and Emerging Technologies in Higher Education: A Unified Theory of Acceptance and Use of Technology Perspective. *International Journal of Higher Education*, *2*(2). doi:10.5430/ijhe.v2n2p22

Li, B., Liu, Y., & Chu, G. (2010). Improved AODV routing protocol for vehicular Ad hoc networks. *Advanced Computer Theory and Engineering (ICACTE), 2010 3rd International Conference on*, *4*, 337-340.

Liao, C., Liu, C., & Chen, K. (2011a). Examining the impact of privacy: trust and risk perceptions beyond monetary transactions: an integrated model. *Electronic Commerce Research and Applications*, *10*(6), 702–715. doi:10.1016/j.elerap.2011.07.003

Liao, C., Palvia, P., & Lin, H. (2006). The roles of habit and web site quality in e-commerce. *International Journal of Information Management*, *26*(6), 469–483. doi:10.1016/j.ijinfomgt.2006.09.001

Liao, C., To, P.-L., Liu, C.-C., Kuo, P.-Y., & Chuang, S.-H. (2011b). Factors influencing the intended use of web portals. *Online Information Review*, *35*(2), 237–254. doi:10.1108/14684521111128023

Liao, C., Tsou, C., & Huang, M. (2007). Factors influencing the usage of 3G mobile services in Taiwan. *Online Information Review*, *31*(6), 759–774. doi:10.1108/14684520710841757

Limayem, M., Hirt, S. G., & Cheung, C. M. K. (2007). How habit limits the predictive power of intention: the case of information systems continuance. *Management Information Systems Quarterly*, *31*(4), 705–737. doi:10.2307/25148817

Lindsay, R., Jackson, T. W., & Cooke, L. (2011). Adapted technology acceptance model for mobile policing. *Journal of Systems and Information Technology*, *13*(4), 389–407. doi:10.1108/13287261111183988

Lin, H. H., & Wang, Y. S. (2005). Predicting consumer intention to use mobile commerce in Taiwan. *Mobile Business, International Conference*, 406-412.

Lin, S. J., Zimmer, J. C., & Lee, V. (2013). Podcasting acceptance on campus: The differing perspectives of teachers and students. *Computers & Education*, *68*(1), 416–428. doi:10.1016/j.compedu.2013.06.003

Liu, C., Marchewka, J. T., Lu, J., & Yu, C. S. (2005). Beyond concern—a privacy-trust-behavioral intention model of electronic commerce. *Information & Management*, *42*(2), 289–304. doi:10.1016/j.im.2004.01.003

López-Nicolás, C., Molina-Castillo, F. J., & Bouwman, H. (2008). An assessment of advanced mobile services acceptance: Contributions from TAM and diffusion theory models. *Information & Management*, *45*(6), 359–364. doi:10.1016/j.im.2008.05.001

Luarn, P., & Lin, H. H. (2005). Toward an understanding of the behavioral intention to use mobile banking. *Computers in Human Behavior, 21*(6), 873–891. doi:10.1016/j.chb.2004.03.003

Lu, H. P., & Yu-Jen Su, P. (2009). Factors affecting purchase intention on mobile shopping web sites. *Internet Research, 19*(4), 442–458. doi:10.1108/10662240910981399

Lu, I. R., Kwan, E., Thomas, D. R., & Cedzynski, M. (2011). Two new methods for estimating structural equation models: An illustration and a comparison with two established methods. *International Journal of Research in Marketing, 28*(3), 258–268. doi:10.1016/j.ijresmar.2011.03.006

Lu, J., Yao, J., & Yu, C. (2005). Personal innovativeness, social influences and adoption of wireless Internet services via mobile technology. *The Journal of Strategic Information Systems, 14*(3), 245–268. doi:10.1016/j.jsis.2005.07.003

Luo, X., Li, H., Zhang, J., & Shim, J. P. (2010). Examining multi-dimensional trust and multi-faceted risk in initial acceptance of emerging technologies: An empirical study of mobile banking services. *Decision Support Systems, 49*(2), 222–234. doi:10.1016/j.dss.2010.02.008

Lu, Y., Yang, S., Chau, P., & Cao, Y. (2011). Dynamics between the trust transfer process and intention to use mobile payment services: A cross-environment perspective. *Information & Management, 48*(8), 393–403. doi:10.1016/j.im.2011.09.006

Lv, P., Wang, X., Xue, X., & Xu, M. (2015, May 1). SWIMMING: Seamless and Efficient WiFi-Based Internet Access from Moving Vehicles. *IEEE Transactions on Mobile Computing, 14*(5), 1085–1097. doi:10.1109/TMC.2014.2341652

Lyman, T. R., Mark, P., & Porteous, D. (2008). Regulating Transformational Branchless Banking: Mobile Phones and Other Technology to Increase Access to Finance." CGAP Focus Note No. 43. Washington, DC: CGAP. Retrieved June 18, 2008 from http://www.cgap.org/p/site/c/template.rc/1.9.2583

MacNeil, A., Farnon, E. C., Morgan, O. W., Gould, P., Boehmer, T. K., Blaney, D. D., . . . Rollin, P. E. (2011). Filovirus Outbreak Detection and Surveillance: Lessons From Bundibugyo. *J. Infect. Dis., 204*(Suppl. 3), S761-S767.

Mafe, C. R., Blas, S. S., & Tavera-Mesias, J. F. (2010). A comparative study of mobile messaging services acceptance to participate in television programmes. *Journal of Service Management, 21*(1), 69–102. doi:10.1108/09564231011025128

Magid, L. (2014, October 30). An Android App That Could Help Fight Ebola. *Forbes*. Retrieved from https://www.forbes.com/sites/larrymagid/2014/10/30/an-android-app-that-could-help-fight-ebola/#3fedfa6c7fc4

Magni, M., Taylor, M. S., & Venkatesh, V. (2010). 'To play or not to play': A cross-temporal investigation using hedonic and instrumental perspectives to explain user intentions to explore a technology. *International Journal of Human-Computer Studies, 68*(9), 572–588. doi:10.1016/j.ijhcs.2010.03.004

Magrath, V., & McCormick, H. (2013). Marketing design elements of mobile fashion retail apps. *Journal of Fashion Marketing and Management: An International Journal, 17*(1), 115–134. doi:10.1108/13612021311305173

Mahatanankoon, P., Wen, H. J., & Lim, B. B. (2006). Evaluating the technological characteristics and trust affecting mobile device usage. *International Journal of Mobile Communications, 4*(6), 662–681. doi:10.1504/IJMC.2006.010361

Mahendra, P., Meron, T., Fikru, G., Hailegebrael, B., Vikram, G. & Venkataramana, K. (2017). An overview of biological weapons and bioterrorism. *American Journal of Biomedical Research, 5*(2), 24-34.

Mahmood, M. A., Burn, J. M., Gemoets, L. A., & Jacquez, C. (2000). Variables affecting information technology end-user satisfaction: A meta-analysis of the empirical literature. *International Journal of Human-Computer Studies, 52*(4), 751–771. doi:10.1006/ijhc.1999.0353

Malaquias, R. F., & Hwang, Y. (2016). An empirical study on trust in mobile banking: A developing country perspective. *Computers in Human Behavior, 54*, 453–461. doi:10.1016/j.chb.2015.08.039

Mallat, N., Rossi, M., Tuunainen, V. K., & Öörni, A. (2009). The impact of use context on mobile services acceptance: The case of mobile ticketing. *Information & Management, 46*(3), 190–195. doi:10.1016/j.im.2008.11.008

Marcotte, R. J., & Olson, E. (2016). Adaptive forward error correction with adjustable-latency QoS for robotic networks. *2016 IEEE International Conference on Robotics and Automation (ICRA)*, 5283-5288. doi:10.1109/ICRA.2016.7487739

Maree, J., Piontak, R., Omwansa, T., Shinyekwa, I., & Njenga, K. (2013). Developmental uses of mobile phones in Kenya and Uganda.

Marinagi, C., Belsis, P., & Skourlas, C. (2013). New directions for pervasive computing in logistics. *Procedia: Social and Behavioral Sciences, 73*, 495–502. doi:10.1016/j.sbspro.2013.02.082

Martín, S. S., & Camarero, C. (2008). Consumer' trust to a web site: Moderating effect of attitudes toward online shopping. *Cyberpsychology and Behavior, 11*(5), 549-554.

Martins, C., Oliveira, T., & Popovic, A. (2014). Understanding the internet banking adoption: A unified theory of acceptance and the use of technology and perceived risk application. *International Journal of Information Management, 34*(1), 1–13. doi:10.1016/j.ijinfomgt.2013.06.002

Mas, I. (2011). Enabling different paths to the development of Mobile Money ecosystems. Mobile Money for the Unbanked, Annual Report 2011. Retrieved 17-1-15 from http://ssrn.com/abstract=1843623

Mashenene, R. (2015). The Dynamics of Mobile Phone Technologies and the Performance of Micro and Small Enterprises in Tanzania.

Mawona, A., & Mpogole, H. (2013). ICT and Financial Inclusion: Adoption of Mobile Phone Banking Among Small Business Owners in Iringa, Tanzania.

Mayer, R. C., Davis, J. H., & Schoorman, F. D. (1995). An integrative model of organizational trust. *Academy of Management Review*, *20*(3), 709–734.

McGregor, A. (2013). Islamist groups mount joint offensive in Mali. *Terrorism Monitor, In-Depth Analysis of the War on Terror*, *XI*(1), 1–3.

McKay, C., & Pickens, M. (2010). *Branchless Banking 2010: Who's Served? At What Price? What's Next?* Washington, DC: Consultative Group to Assist the Poor.

Mcknight, D. H., Carter, M., Thatcher, J. B., & Clay, P. F. (2011). Trust in a specific technology: An investigation of its components and measures. *ACM Transactions on Management Information Systems*, *2*(2), 12. doi:10.1145/1985347.1985353

McKnight, D. H., Choudhury, V., & Kacmar, C. (2002). Developing and validating trust measures for e-commerce: An integrative typology. *Information Systems Research*, *13*(3), 334–359. doi:10.1287/isre.13.3.334.81

McKnight, D. H., Choudhury, V., & Kacmar, C. (2002). The impact of initial consumer' trust on intentions to transact with a web site: A trust building model. *The Journal of Strategic Information Systems*, *11*(3), 297–323. doi:10.1016/S0963-8687(02)00020-3

Mereku, D. K., Yidana, I., Hordzi, W., Tete-Mensah, I., Tete-Mensah, W., & Williams, J. B. (2009). *Pan African Research Agenda on the Pedagogical Integration of ICTs: Ghana Report*. Retrieved 5th Otober, 2017, from http://www.ernwaca.org/panaf/pdf/phase-1/Ghana-PanAf_Report.pdf

Merritt, C. (2010). Mobile money transfer services: The next phase in the evolution of person-to-person payments. *Journal*, *5*(2), 143–160.

Migiro, S.O. (2006). Diffusion of ICTs and E-commerce adoption in manufacturing SMEs in Kenya : research article.

Miller, R. (2003). *Practical UML: A hands-on introduction for developers*. Retrieved April 21, 2017, from http://edn.embarcadero.com/article/31863

Minges, M. (2015). Exploring the relationship between broadband and economic growth. Background paper prepared for the World Development Report 2016: Digital Dividends. Retrieved from https://www.pubdocs.worlbank.org.en/391452529895999/WDR16-BP-Exploring-the-Relationship-between-Broadband-and-Economic-Growth-minges.pdf

Ministry of Education. (2008). *ICT in education policy" Republic of Ghana*. Retrieved 23 April, 2017, from http://www.moe.gov.gh/assets/media/docs/ICTinEducationpolicy_NOV2008.pdf

Min, Q., Ji, S., & Qu, G. (2008). Mobile commerce user acceptance study in China: A revised UTAUT model. *Tsinghua Science and Technology*, *13*(3), 257–264. doi:10.1016/S1007-0214(08)70042-7

Mirzoyants, A. (2013). *Mobile Money in Tanzania: Use, Barriers and Opportunities*. Intermedia Financial Inclusion Tracker Surveys Project, February.

Mishra & Nadkarni. (2003). Security in Wireless Ad Hoc Networks. In *The Handbook of Ad Hoc Wireless Networks*. CRC Press LLC.

Mittal, S., & Mehar, M. (2012). How Mobile Phones Contribute to Growth of Small Farmers? Evidence from India. *Zeitschrift für Ausländische Landwirtschaft, 51*(3), 227–244.

Mi, Z., Yang, Y., & Yang, J. Y. (2015, August). Restoring Connectivity of Mobile Robotic Sensor Networks While Avoiding Obstacles. *IEEE Sensors Journal, 15*(8), 4640–4650. doi:10.1109/JSEN.2015.2426177

Montano, D. E., & Kasprzyk, D. (2015). Theory of reasoned action, theory of planned behavior, and the integrated behavioral model. *Health behavior: Theory, research and practice.*

Moore, G. C., & Benbasat, I. (1991a). Development of an instrument to measure the perceptions of adopting an information technology innovation. *Information Systems Research, 2*(3), 192–222. doi:10.1287/isre.2.3.192

Moorman, C., Deshpande, R., & Zaltman, G. (1993). Factors Affecting Trust in Market Research Relationships. *Journal of Marketing, 57*(1), 81. doi:10.2307/1252059

Morawczynski, O. (2009). Exploring the usage and impact of "transformational" mobile financial services: The case of M-PESA in Kenya. *Journal of Eastern African Studies: the Journal of the British Institute in Eastern Africa, 3*(3), 509–525. doi:10.1080/17531050903273768

Mostakhdemin-Hosseini, A., & Tuimala, J. (2005). Mobile learning framework. In *Proceedings IADIS International Conference Mobile Learning 2005*, (pp. 203-207).

Mozeik, C. K., Beldona, S., Cobanoglu, C., & Poorani, A. (2009). The adoption of restaurant-based e-services. *Journal of Foodservice Business Research, 12*(3), 247–265. doi:10.1080/15378020903158525

Mukherjee, S. (2015). *Counter-terrorism in your pocket: Smartphone apps that make you feel safer (sometimes).* Retrieved March 26, 2017, from http://www.dnaindia.com/scitech/report-now-apps-can-help-you-fight-terrorism-2149233

Mukherjee, A., & Nath, P. (2007). Role of electronic trust in online retailing: A re-examination of the commitment-trust theory. *European Journal of Marketing, 41*(9/10), 1173–1202. doi:10.1108/03090560710773390

Mukonza, R. M. (2013). M-government in South Africa's local government: A missed opportunity to enhance public participation? In *Proceedings of the 7th International Conference on Theory and Practice of Electronic Governance* (vol. ICEGOV'13, pp. 374-375). New York: ACM. doi:10.1145/2591888.2591966

Munnukka, J. T. (2004). *Perception-based pricing strategies for mobile services in customer marketing context* (Order No. C820658, Jyvaskylan Yliopisto). Retrieved from ProQuest Dissertations and Theses.

Muntaka, M. N. (2014). *Exploring mobile phone usage and potentials for enhancing higher education Ghana, West Africa*. Retrieved from https://etda.libraries.psu.edu/files/final_submissions/9560

Munyegera, G. K., & Matsumoto, T. (2016). Mobile money, remittances, and household welfare: Panel evidence from rural Uganda. *World Development, 79*, 127–137. doi:10.1016/j.worlddev.2015.11.006

Mutula, M. S., & Van Brakel, P. P. (2006). E-readiness of SMEs in the ICT sector in Botswana with respect to information access. *The Electronic Library, 24*(3), 402–417. doi:10.1108/02640470610671240

Muyinda, P. B. (2007). MLearning: Pedagogical, technical and organisational hypes and realities. *Campus-Wide Information Systems, 24*(2), 97–104. doi:10.1108/10650740710742709

Nance, M. W. (2008). *Terrorist recognition handbook: a practitioner's manual for predicting and identifying terrorist activities* (2nd ed.). CRC Press. doi:10.1201/9781420071849

Nandhi, M. A. (2012). *Effects of mobile banking on the savings practices of low income users–The Indian experience* (working paper 7). Institute for money technology and financial inclusion.

Nee, V. (1992). Organizational dynamics of market transition: Hybrid forms, property rights, and mixed economy in China. *Administrative Science Quarterly, 37*(1), 1–27. doi:10.2307/2393531

Negnevitsky, M. (2011). *Artificial intelligence: A guide to intelligent systems* (3rd ed.). Pearson Education.

NERIC. (2007). *Education Reform 2007 at a glance*. Retrieved 23 May 2017 from http://planipolis. iiep.unesco.org/upload/Ghana/Ghana_education_reform_2007.pdf

Ng-Kruelle, G., Swatman, P. A., Rebne, D. S., & Hampe, J. F. (2002). The price of convenience: Privacy and mobile commerce. *Quarterly Journal of Electronic Commerce, 3*, 273–286.

Nica, E. (2015). Satisfaction and Trust in E-Commerce. *Psychosociological Issues in Human Resource Management, 3*(1), 107–112.

Nunnally, J. C., & Bernstein, I. H. (1994). *Psychometric Theory* (3rd ed.). New York: McGraw-Hill.

Nwakaegho, T. (2016). Why Nigerians oppose proposed communication service tax bill. *Leadership*, (September).

O'Neill, K. (1997). *The nuclear terrorist threat*. Retrieved December 8, 2017, from http://www. isis-online.org/publications/terrorism/threat.pdf

O'Neill, E. C. O., & Lewis, D. (2013). Situation-based testing for pervasive computing environments. *Pervasive and Mobile Computing, 9*(1), 76–97. doi:10.1016/j.pmcj.2011.12.002

OECD. (2004). Measuring the information economy.

Oechslein, O., Fleischmann, M., & Hess, T. (2014). *An Application of UTAUT2 on Social Recommender Systems: Incorporating Social Information for Performance Expectancy.* Paper presented at the 47th Hawaii International Conference on System Science. doi:10.1109/HICSS.2014.409

Ohadike, J. (2016, September 8). Much ado about the proposed CST bill. ThisDay.

Olaleye, S. A., Sanusi, I. T., & Oyelere, S. S. (2017, September). Users Experience of Mobile Money in Nigeria. In *Proceedings of the 13th AFRICON Conference in AFRICON '17*, Cape Town. IEEE. doi:10.1109/AFRCON.2017.8095606

Oliveira, T., Faria, M., Thomas, M. A., & Popovič, A. (2014). Extending the understanding of mobile banking adoption: When UTAUT meets TTF and ITM. *International Journal of Information Management, 34*(5), 689–703. doi:10.1016/j.ijinfomgt.2014.06.004

Oliver, R. L. (1980). A cognitive model of the antecedents and consequences of satisfaction decisions. *JMR, Journal of Marketing Research, 17*(4), 460–469. doi:10.2307/3150499

Ondiege, P. (2010). Mobile Banking in Africa: Taking the Bank to the People. *AfDB Africa Economic Brief, 1*(8).

Ondiege, P. (2015). Regulatory Impact on Mobile Money and Financial Inclusion in African Countries-Kenya, Nigeria, Tanzania and Uganda. Center for Global Development (CGD).

Osazevbaru, H. O., & Yomere, G. O. (2015). Benefits and Challenges of Nigeria's Cash-Less Policy. *Kuwait Chapter of the Arabian Journal of Business and Management Review, 4*(9), 1–10. doi:10.12816/0018986

Osei-Assibey, E. (2015). What drives behavioral intention of mobile money adoption? The case of ancient susu saving operations in Ghana. *International Journal of Social Economics, 42*(11), 962–979. doi:10.1108/IJSE-09-2013-0198

Osuagwu, P. (2016). All about new telecom service tax law. Retrieved from http://www.vanguardngr.com/2016/08/new-telecom-service-tax-law

Ouellette, J. A., & Wood, W. (1998). Habit and intention in everyday life: The multiple processes by which past behavior predicts future behavior. *Psychological Bulletin, 124*(1), 54–74. doi:10.1037/0033-2909.124.1.54

Oyebode, A. (2014). M-Pesa and Beyod – Why Mobile Money Worked in Kenya and Struggles in other Markets. Retrieved 27 May 2017 from https://vc4a.com/blog/2014/01/15/m-pesa-and-beyond-why-mobile-money-worked-in-kenya-and-struggles-in-other-markets/

Oyelere, S. S., Paliktzoglou, V., & Suhonen, J. (2016). M-learning in Nigerian higher education: an experimental study with Edmodo. *International Journal of social media and interactive learning environments, 4*(1), 43-62.

Oyelere, S. S., Suhonen, J., & Sutinen, E. (2016). M-learning: A new paradigm of learning ICT in Nigeria. *International Journal of Interactive Mobile Technologies*, *10*(1), 35–44. doi:10.3991/ijim.v10i1.4872

Oye, N. D., Iahad, N. A., & Rabin, Z. A. (2011). A model of ICT acceptance and use for teachers in higher education institutions. *International Journal of Computer Science & Communication Networks*, *1*(1), 22–40.

Paessler, S., & Walker, D. H. (2012). Pathogenesis of the Viral Hemorrhagic Fevers. *Annual Review of Pathology: Mechanisms of Disease*, *8*(1), 411–440. doi:10.1146/annurev-pathol-020712-164041 PMID:23121052

Pahnila, S., Siponen, M., & Zheng, X. (2011). Integrating habit into UTAUT: The Chinese eBay case. *Pacific Asia Journal of the Association for Information Systems*, *3*(2), 1–30.

Pantano, E., & Priporas, C. V. (2016). The effect of mobile retailing on consumers' purchasing experiences: A dynamic perspective. *Computers in Human Behavior*, *61*, 548–555. doi:10.1016/j.chb.2016.03.071

Park, C. H., & Kim, Y. G. (2003). Identifying key factors affecting consumer purchase behavior in an online shopping context. *International Journal of Retail & Distribution Management*, *31*(1), 16–29. doi:10.1108/09590550310457818

Patel, A. (2006). Mobile Commerce in Emerging Economics. In Handbook of Research in Mobile Business: Technical, Methodological, and Social Perspectives (pp. 429-434). IGI Global. doi:10.4018/978-1-59140-817-8.ch030

Pavlou, P. (2003). Consumer acceptance of electronic commerce: Integrating trustand risk with the technology acceptance model. *International Journal of Electronic Commerce*, *7*(3), 69–103.

Pavlou, P. A. (2003). Consumer acceptance of electronic commerce: Integrating trust and risk with the technology acceptance model. *International Journal of Electronic Commerce*, *7*(3), 101–134.

Pavlou, P. A., & Gefen, D. (2004). Building effective online marketplaces with institution-based trust. *Information Systems Research*, *15*(1), 37–59. doi:10.1287/isre.1040.0015

Peachy, Dc. (2008). Wholesale & Prudential Policy Division, Financial Services Authority. In *Presentation at GSMA Mobile Money Summit*, Cairo, May 15.

Pedersen, P. E. (2005). Adoption of mobile Internet services: An exploratory study of mobile commerce early adopters. *Journal of Organizational Computing and Electronic Commerce*, *15*(3), 203–222. doi:10.1207/s15327744joce1503_2

Pegueros, V. (2012). *Security of mobile banking and payments*. SANS Institute Info Sec Reading Room.

Peng, R., Xiong, L., & Yang, Z. (2012). Exploring Tourist Adoption of Tourism Mobile Payment: An Empirical Analysis.

Pénicaud, C., & Katakam, A. (2013). State of the industry 2013: mobile financial services for the unbanked. GSMA. Retrieved from http://www.gsma.com/mobilefordevelopment/wp-content/uploads/2014/02/SOTIR_2013.pdf

Pennington, R., Wilcox, H. D., & Grover, V. (2003). The role of system trust in business-to-consumer transactions. *Journal of Management Information Systems*, 20(3), 197–226. doi:10.1080/07421222.2003.11045777

Petter, S., DeLone, W., & McLean, E. R. (2013). Information systems success: The quest for the independent variables. *Journal of Management Information Systems*, 29(4), 7–62. doi:10.2753/MIS0742-1222290401

Ponte, E. B., Carvajal-Trujillo, E., & Escobar-Rodríguez, T. (2015). Influence of trust and perceived value on the intention to purchase travel online: Integrating the effects of assurance on trust antecedents. *Tourism Management*, 47, 286–302. doi:10.1016/j.tourman.2014.10.009

Popper, B. (2015). *Can Mobile Banking Revolutionize the lives of the Poor?* Retrieved March 12th, 2017, from www.theverge.com/2015/2/4/.../bill-gates-future-of-banking-and-mobile-money

Prata, W., Moraes, A. D., & Quaresma, M. (2012). User's demography and expectation regarding search, purchase and evaluation in mobile application store. *Work (Reading, Mass.)*, 41(1), 1124–1311. PMID:22316870

Prgomet, M., Georgiou, A., & Westbrook, J. I. (2009). The impact of mobile handheld technology on hospital physicians' work practices and patient care: A systematic review. *Journal of the American Medical Informatics Association*, 16(6), 792–801. doi:10.1197/jamia.M3215 PMID:19717793

Prieto, J. C. S., Miguéláñez, S. O., & García-Peñalvo, F. J. (2015). Mobile acceptance among pre-service teachers: a descriptive study using a TAM-based model. In *Proceedings of the 3rd International Conference on Technological Ecosystems for Enhancing Multiculturality* (pp. 131–137). ACM. doi:10.1145/2808580.2808601

Purcell, K. (2011). *Half of adult cell phone owners have apps on their phones*. Retrieved August 20, 2013, from http://pewinternet.org/~/media/Files/Reports/2011/PIP_Apps-Update-2011.pdf

Qayyum, , Subhash, & Husamuddin. (2012). Security issues of Data Query Processing and Location Monitoring in MANETs. In *International Conference on Communication, Information and Computing Technology (ICCICT)*. IEEE.

Qin, Z., Denker, G., Giannelli, C., & Bellavista, P. (2014). A Software Defined Networking architecture for the Internet-of-Things. *Network Operations and Management Symposium*, 1-9.

Raghubir, P., & Srivastava, J. (2008). Monopoly money: The effect of payment coupling and form on spending behavior. *Journal of Experimental Psychology. Applied*, 14(3), 213–225. doi:10.1037/1076-898X.14.3.213 PMID:18808275

Raghubir, P., & Srivastava, J. (2009). The denomination effect. *The Journal of Consumer Research*, 36(4), 701–713. doi:10.1086/599222

Rai, A., Brown, P., & Tang, X. (2009). Organizational Assimilation of Electronic Procurement Innovations. *Journal of Management Information Systems*, *26*(1), 257–296. doi:10.2753/MIS0742-1222260110

Rajaram, A., & Palaniswami, S. (2010). The Trust-Based MAC - Layer Security Protocol for Mobile Ad Hoc Networks. *2010 6th International Conference on Wireless Communications Networking and Mobile Computing (WiCOM)*, 1-4. doi:10.1109/WICOM.2010.5600904

Raman, A., & Don, Y. (2013). Preservice Teachers' Acceptance of Learning Management Software: An Application of the UTAUT2 Model. *International Education Studies*, *6*(7), 157–164. doi:10.5539/ies.v6n7p157

Rashidi, R., Jamali, M. A. J., Salmasi, A., & Tati, R. (2009). Trust routing protocol based on congestion control in MANET. *2009 International Conference on Application of Information and Communication Technologies*, 1-5. doi:10.1109/ICAICT.2009.5372623

Rath, M., Pattanayak, B. K., & Pati, B. (2015, January-March). Energy Competent Routing Protocol Design in MANET with Real time Application Provision. *International Journal of Business Data Communications and Networking*, *11*(1), 50–60. doi:10.4018/IJBDCN.2015010105

Rath, M., Pattanayak, B. K., & Pati, B. (2016, March). Energy Efficient MANET Protocol Using Cross Layer Design for Military Applications. *Defence Science Journal*, *66*(2), 146. doi:10.14429/dsj.66.9705

Reinartz, W. J., Haenlein, M., & Henseler, J. (2009). An empirical comparison of the efficacy of covariance-based and variance-based SEM. *International Journal of Research in Marketing*, *26*(4), 332–344. doi:10.1016/j.ijresmar.2009.08.001

Rigdon, E. E., Ringle, C. M., & Sarstedt, M. (2010). Structural Modeling of Heterogeneous Data with Partial Least Squares. In N. K. Malhotra (Ed.), *Review of Marketing Research* (pp. 255–296). Armonk: Sharpe. doi:10.1108/S1548-6435(2010)0000007011

Ringle, C. M., Wende, S., & Becker, J.-M. (2014). *SmartPLS 3. Hamburg: SmartPLS*. Available from http://www.smartpls.com

Ringle, C. M., Wende, S., & Will, A. (2005). *SmartPLS 2.0 (M3) Beta*. Retrieved from http://www.smartpls.de

Ringle, C. M., Wende, S., & Will, A. (2005b). *SmartPLS 2.0*. Retrieved from www.smartpls.de

Ringle, C. M., Sarstedt, M., & Schlittgen, R. (2010). Finite Mixture and Genetic Algorithm Segmentation in Partial Least Squares Path Modeling: Identification of Multiple Segments in a Complex Path Model. In A. Fink, B. Lausen, W. Seidel, & A. Ultsch (Eds.), *Advances in Data Analysis, Data Handling and Business Intelligence* (pp. 167–176). Berlin: Springer.

Ringle, C. M., Sarstedt, M., & Straub, D. (2012). A critical look at the use of PLS-SEM in MIS Quarterly. *Management Information Systems Quarterly*, *36*(1), iii–xiv.

Rizk, N. (2004). E-readiness assessment of small and medium enterprises in Egypt: A micro study.

Roca, A., Afolabi, M. O., Saidu, Y., & Kampmann, B. (2015). Ebola: A holistic approach is required to achieve effective management and control. *The Journal of Allergy and Clinical Immunology, 135*(4), 856–867. doi:10.1016/j.jaci.2015.02.015 PMID:25843598

Rodrigo, R. (2011). Mobile teaching versus mobile learning. *EDUCAUSE Quarterly 101 Magazine, 34*(2).

Rogers, E. (1995). *Diffusion of innovations* (4th ed.). New York: Free Press.

Rogers, E. M. (1995). Diffusion of Innovations: modifications of a model for telecommunications. In *Die Diffusion von Innovationen in der Telekommunikation* (pp. 25–38). Springer Berlin Heidelberg. doi:10.1007/978-3-642-79868-9_2

Roldán, J. L., & Sánchez-Franco, M. J. (2012). Variance-based structural equation modeling: guidelines for using partial least squares in information systems research. In M. Mora, O. Gelman, A. Steenkamp, & M. Raisinghani (Eds.), Research methodologies in engineering of software systems and information systems: Philosophies, methods, and innovations (pp. 193–221). Hershey, PA: Information Science Reference. doi:10.4018/978-1-4666-0179-6.ch010

Rossing, J., Miller, W., Cecil, A., & Stamper, S. (2012). ILearning: The future of higher education? Student's perceptions on learning with mobile tablets. *The Journal of Scholarship of Teaching and Learning, 12*(2), 1–26. Retrieved 2 April 2017 from http://josotl.indiana.edu/article/view/2023/1985

Rozin, P., & Royzman, E. B. (2001). Negativity bias, negativity dominance, and contagion. *Personality and Social Psychology Review, 5*(4), 296–320. doi:10.1207/S15327957PSPR0504_2

Rumanyika, J. D. (2015). Obstacles towards adoption of mobile banking in Tanzania. *RE:view*.

Runde, D. (2015). M-Pesa and the rise of the global mobile money market. *Forbes*, (August), 12.

Ruuska-Kalliokulju, S., Schneider-Hufschmidt, M., Väänänen-Vainio-Mattila, K., & Von Noman, B. (2001). Shaping the Future of Mobile Devices. *SIGCHI Bulletin, 33*, 16–21.

Sacks, J. A., Zehe, E., Redick, C., Bah, A., Cowger, K., Camara, M., ... Liu, A. (2015). Introduction of mobile health tools to support Ebola surveillance and contact tracing in Guinea. *Global Health, Science and Practice, 3*(4), 646–659. doi:10.9745/GHSP-D-15-00207 PMID:26681710

Salim, A., & Wangusi, N. (2014). Mobile phone technology: An effective tool to fight corruption in Kenya. In *Proceedings of 15th Annual International Conference on Digital Government Research* (pp. 300-305). New York: ACM.

Sammadar, A. (2006). Traditional and Post-Traditional: A Study of Agricultural Rituals in Relation to Technological Complexity among Rice Producers in Two Zones of West Bengal, India. *Journal of Culture and Agriculture., 28*(2), 108–121. doi:10.1525/cag.2006.28.2.108

Sangaré, M., & Guérin, I. (2013). *Mobile money and financial inclusion in Mali: what has been the impact on saving practices?*

Saravan, R, & Raja, P. & Tayeng Sheela. (2009). Information Input Pattern and Information Need of Tribal Farmers in Arnuchal Pradesh. *Indian Journal of Extension Education*, *45*(1&2), 51–54.

Sarker, S., & Wells, J. D. (2003). Understanding mobile handheld device use and adoption. *Communications of the ACM*, *46*(12), 35–40. doi:10.1145/953460.953484

Sarstedt, M. (2008). A review of recent approaches for capturing heterogeneity in partial least squares path modeling. *Journal of Modelling in Management*, *3*(2), 140–161. doi:10.1108/17465660810890126

Sayid, O., Heights, D., Echchabi, A., Pusu, J. S., Sciences, M., & Pusu, J. S. (2012). Investigating service continuance. *Decision Support Systems*, *32*(2), 201–214.

Scharwatt, C., Katakam, A., Frydrych, J., Murphy, A., & Naghavi, N. (2014). *State of the Industry: Mobile Financial Services for the Unbanked*. Retrieved March 12th, 2016, from www.gsma.com/mobilefordevelopment/wp-content/uploads/2015/.../SOTIR_2014.pdf

Semenova & Solodkov. (2015). *Network challenges in mobile group robotics: MANET approach. In 2015 Internet Technologies and Applications* (pp. 181–185). Wrexham: ITA.

Shaikh, A. A., & Karjaluoto, H. (2015). Making the most of information technology & systems usage: A literature review, framework and future research agenda. *Computers in Human Behavior*, *49*, 541–566. doi:10.1016/j.chb.2015.03.059

Shaikh, A. A., & Karjaluoto, H. (2015). Mobile banking adoption: A literature review. *Telematics and Informatics*, *32*(1), 129–142. doi:10.1016/j.tele.2014.05.003

Shao Yeh, Y., & Li, Y. M. (2009). Building trust in m-commerce: Contributions from quality and satisfaction. *Online Information Review*, *33*(6), 1066–1086. doi:10.1108/14684520911011016

Sharehu, A. L., & Achor, E. E. (2015). Readiness of Teachers and Pupils for Use of Mobile Devices as Support for Effective Pedagogy in Nigeria: Could Location be a Major Determinant? *Online Journal òf Distance Learning Administration*, *XVIII*(3).

Sharples, M. (2000). The design of personal mobile technologies for lifelong learning. *Computers & Education*, *34*(3-4), 177–193. doi:10.1016/S0360-1315(99)00044-5

Shen, G. (2015). Users' adoption of mobile applications: Product type and message framing's moderating effect. *Journal of Business Research*, *68*(11), 2317–2321. doi:10.1016/j.jbusres.2015.06.018

Sheng, H., Nah, F. F.-H., & Siau, K. (2005). Strategic implications of mobile technology: A case study using value-focused thinking. *The Journal of Strategic Information Systems*, *14*(3), 269–290. doi:10.1016/j.jsis.2005.07.004

Shi, W. W. (2009). *An Empirical Research on Users' Acceptance of Smart Phone Online Application Software*. Paper presented at the International Conference on Electronic Commerce and Business Intelligence. doi:10.1109/ECBI.2009.102

Shin, D. (2009). Towards an understanding of the consumer acceptance of mobile wallet. *Computers in Human Behavior*, 25(6), 1343–1354. doi:10.1016/j.chb.2009.06.001

Shin, J., Chung, K., Oh, J., & Lee, C. (2013). The effect of site quality on repurchase intention in internet shopping through mediating variables: The case of university students in South Korea. *International Journal of Information Management*, 33(3), 453–463. doi:10.1016/j.ijinfomgt.2013.02.003

Shmueli, G., & Koppius, O. R. (2011). Predictive analytics in information systems research. *Management Information Systems Quarterly*, 35(3), 553–572. doi:10.2307/23042796

Shuib, L., Shamshirband, S., & Ismail, M. H. (2015). A review of mobile pervasive learning: Applications and issues. *Computers in Human Behavior*, 46, 239–244. doi:10.1016/j.chb.2015.01.002

Siau, K., & Shen, Z. (2003). Building consumer' trust in mobile commerce. *Communications of the ACM*, 46(4), 91–94. doi:10.1145/641205.641211

SIDO. (2002). Small industries development organisation in Tanzania.

Sierra, L. (2017, May 10). New smartphone app would track spread of Ebola. *Rochester.edu NewsCenter*. Retrieved from http://www.rochester.edu/newscenter/rochester-researchers-receive-nsf-grant-for-pilot-study-of-smartphone-technology-for-monitoring-of-ebola-103622/

Sim, J. J., Tan, G. W.-H., Wong, J. C. J., Ooi, K.-B., & Hew, T.-S. (2014). Understanding and predicting the motivators of mobile music acceptance – A multi stage MRA-Artificial neural network approach. *Telematics and Informatics*, 31(4), 569–584. doi:10.1016/j.tele.2013.11.005

Singh, J., & Sirdeshmukh, D. (2000). Agency and trust mechanisms in consumer satisfaction and loyalty judgments. *Journal of the Academy of Marketing Science*, 28(1), 150–167. doi:10.1177/0092070300281014

Slade, E., Williams, M., Dwivedi, Y., & Piercy, N. (2014). Exploring consumer adoption of proximity mobile payments. *Journal of Strategic Marketing*, 1(1), 1–15.

Smadi, Z. M., & Al-Jawazneh, B. E. (2011). The consumer decision-making styles of mobile phones among the University Level students in Jordan. *International Bulleting of Business Administration*.

SME Policy. (2013). Tanzania SMEs Policy Review After 10 years.

Sparks, B. A., & Browning, V. (2011). The impact of online reviews on hotel booking intentions and perception of trust. *Tourism Management*, 32(6), 1310–1323. doi:10.1016/j.tourman.2010.12.011

SPSS. (2012). *IBM SPSS neural networks 21*. IBM Corporation.

Squire, K. D., & Jan, M. (2007). Mad City Mystery: Developing scientific argumentation skills with a place-based augmented reality game on handheld computers. *Journal of Science Education and Technology*, 16(1), 5–29. doi:10.1007/s10956-006-9037-z

Sripalawat, J., Thongmak, M., & Ngramyarn, A. (2011). M-banking in metropolitan Bangkok and a comparison with other countries. *Journal of Computer Information Systems, 51*(3), 67–76.

Srovnal, V. Jr, Machacek, Z., & Srovnal, V. (2009). Wireless Communication for Mobile Robotics and Industrial Embedded Devices. *2009 Eighth International Conference on Networks,* 253-258. doi:10.1109/ICN.2009.46

Stafford, T. F., & Gillenson, M. L. (2003). Mobile commerce: What it is and what it could be. *Communications of the ACM, 46*(12), 33–34. doi:10.1145/953460.953483

Statista. (2017a). Retrieved from http://www.statista.com/statistics/276623/number-of-apps-available-in-leading-app-stores/

Statista. (2017b). Retrieved from http://www.statista.com/statistics/263794/number-of-downloads-from-the-apple-app-store/

Stone, M. (1974). Cross-Validatory Choice and Assessment of Statistical Predictions. *Journal of the Royal Statistical Society. Series A (General), 36*(2), 111–147.

Suárez, S. L. (2016). Poor people's money: The politics of mobile money in Mexico and Kenya. *Telecommunications Policy, 40*(10), 945–955. doi:10.1016/j.telpol.2016.03.001

Subia, M. P., & Nicole, M. (2014). *Mobile Money Services: "A Bank in Your Pocket" Overview and Opportunities.* ACP Observatory on Migration. Retrieved from http://publications.iom.int/system/files/pdf/mobile_money.pdf

Suh, B., & Han, I. (2003). The impact of consumer' trust and perception of security control on the acceptance of electronic commerce. *International Journal of Electronic Commerce, 7*(3), 135–161.

Sundaram, A. (2016). A Painstaking Exploration on the Influence of Perceived Benefits towards Training on Training and Development in Indian IT/ITES Industry. *Journal of Internet Banking and Commerce, 21*(2), 1.

Sunday, E., Nelson, C., Oyebade, W., & Jeremiah, K. (2017, January 1). Tax proliferation as an albatross. The Guardian.

Sung, Y. T., Chang, K. E., & Liu, T. C. (2016). The effects of integrating mobile devices with teaching and learning on students' learning performance: A meta-analysis and research synthesis. *Computers & Education, 94*, 252–275. doi:10.1016/j.compedu.2015.11.008

Sun, Q., Cao, H., & You, J. (2010, May). Factors influencing the adoption of mobile service in China: An integration of TAM. *Journal of Computers, 5*(5), 799–806. doi:10.4304/jcp.5.5.799-806

Tai, Y. M., & Ku, Y. C. (2013). Will stock investors use mobile stock trading? A benefit-risk assessment based on a modified UTAUT model. *Journal of Electronic Commerce Research, 14*(1), 67–84.

Tang, T., & Chi, W. (2016). *The Role of Trust in Customer Online Shopping Behavior: Perspective of Technology Acceptance Model.* Available at: http://onemvweb.com/sources/sources/role_trust_online_shopping.pdf

Tan, G. W. H., Sim, J. J., Ooi, K. B., & Phusavat, K. (2012). Determinants of mobile learning adoption: An empirical analysis. *Journal of Computer Information Systems*, 82–91.

Tan, G. W.-H., Ooi, K.-B., Leong, L.-Y., & Lin, B. (2014). Predicting the drivers of behavioral intention to use mobile learning: A hybrid SEM-Neural Networks approach. *Computers in Human Behavior*, *36*, 198–213. doi:10.1016/j.chb.2014.03.052

Tardioli. (2015). *A wireless multi-hop protocol for real-time applications. Computer Communications*, 55, 4–21.

Tardioli, D. (2014). A wireless communication protocol for distributed robotics applications. *2014 IEEE International Conference on Autonomous Robot Systems and Competitions (ICARSC)*, 253-260. doi:10.1109/ICARSC.2014.6849795

Tassabehji, R., Wallace, J., & Srivastava, A. (2008). Corporate Acceptance of M-Technology in the Service Sector: A Case Study. Proceedings of AMCIS 2008.

Tatem, A. J., Huang, Z., Narib, C., Kumar, U., Kandula, D., Pindolia, D. K., ... Lourenço, C. (2014). Integrating rapid risk mapping and mobile phone call record data for strategic malaria elimination planning. *Malaria Journal*, *13*(1), 52. doi:10.1186/1475-2875-13-52 PMID:24512144

Taylor, D., Voelker, T., & Pentina, I. (2011). Mobile application adoption by young adults: A social network perspective. *International Journal of Mobile Marketing*, *6*(2), 60–70.

Taylor, R., Kotian, P., Warren, T., Panchal, R., Bavari, S., Julander, J., ... Sheridan, W. P. (2016). BCX4430 — A broad-spectrum antiviral adenosine nucleoside analog under development for the treatment of Ebola virus disease. *Journal of Infection and Public Health*, *9*(3), 220–226. doi:10.1016/j.jiph.2016.04.002 PMID:27095300

Taylor, S., & Todd, P. (1995). Understanding information technology usage: A test of competing models. *Information Systems Research*, *6*(2), 144–176. doi:10.1287/isre.6.2.144

Tellez, C. (2012). Emerging Practices in Mobile Microinsurance.

Tenenhaus, M., Esposito Vinzi, V., Chatelin, Y.-M., & Lauro, C. (2005). PLS Path Modeling. *Computational Statistics & Data Analysis*, *48*(1), 159–205. doi:10.1016/j.csda.2004.03.005

Tennant, V. (2014). Understanding Changes in Post-adoption Use of Information Systems (IS): A generalized Darwinism Perspective [Thesis Doctor of Philosophy]. Accounting and Information Systems in the University of Canterbury.

Teo, A. C., Tan, G. W. H., Ooi, K. B., Hew, T. S., & Yew, K. T. (2015). The effect of convenience and speed in m-payment. *Industrial Management & Data Systems*, *115*(2), 311–331. doi:10.1108/IMDS-08-2014-0231

Teo, T., & Noyes, J. (2012). Explaining the intention to use technology among pre-service teachers: A multi-group analysis of the Unified Theory of Acceptance and Use of Technology. *Interactive Learning Environments*, 2(1), 51–66.

The Federal Reserve Board. (2013). Consumers and Mobile Financial Services.

Thomas, T. D., Singh, L., & Gaffar, K. (2013). The utility of the UTAUT model in explaining mobile learning adoption in higher education in Guyana. *International Journal of Education and Development Using Information and Communication Technology*, 9(3), 71–85.

Tina, S. (2009). Basic principles of taxation. Retrieved from http:// www.conveyline. com/a/ canon-of-Taxation/

Tiwari, R., & Buse, S. (2007). *The Mobile Commerce Prospects: A Strategic Analysis of Opportunities in the Banking Sector.* Hamburg, Germany: Hamburg University Press.

Tobbin, P. (2011). Understanding Mobile Money Ecosystem: Roles, Structure and Strategies. In *Proceedings of the 2011 Tenth International Conference on Mobile Business (ICMB)* (pp. 185-194). IEEE. doi:10.1109/ICMB.2011.19

Tobbin, P. E. (2010). Modeling Adoption of Mobile Money Transfer: A Consumer Behaviour Analysis. In *Proceedings of the 2nd International conference on M4D Mobile Communication Technology for Development M4D 2010* (pp. 280–293).

Tobbin, P. E. (2013). Examining the Adoption and Use of Mobile Data Services: A Consumer Behavior Analysis [Thesis Doctor of Philosophy]

Tologbonse, D., Fashola, O., & Obadiah, M. (2008). Policy Issues in Meeting Rice Farmers Agricultural Information Needs in Niger State. *Journal of Agricultural Extension*, 12(2), 84–94.

Tom-Aba, D., Olaleye, A., Olayinka, A. T., Nguku, P., Waziri, N., Adewuyi, P., ... Shuaib, F. (2015). Innovative technological approach to ebola virus disease outbreak response in Nigeria Using the open data kit and form hub technology. *PLoS One*, 10(6), e0131000. doi:10.1371/journal.pone.0131000 PMID:26115402

To, P. L., Liao, C., & Lin, T. H. (2007). Shopping motiviation on Internet: A study based on utilitarian and hedonic value. *Technovation*, 27(12), 774–787. doi:10.1016/j.technovation.2007.01.001

Torgan, C. (2009). *The mHealth Summit: Local & Global Converge - Kinetics.* Washington, D.C: Foundation for the National Institutes of Health.

Traxler, J. (2007). Discussing and evaluating mobile learning: the moving finger writes and having write. *The international Review of research in open and distance learning Defining, 8(2).*

U.S. Department of State. (n.d.). *Foreign terrorist organizations.* Retrieved March 3, 2017, from https://www.state.gov/j/ct/rls/other/des/123085.htm

Udo, B. (2014). *Jonathan signs Nigeria's 2014 budget as defence gets 20 per cent.* Retrieved March 26, 2017, from http://www.premiumtimesng.com/business/161390-jonathan-signs-nigerias-2014-budget-defence-gets-20-per-cent.html

UN.org. (n.d.). To invest more, countries must tap assets now outside the banks. Retrieved from www.un.org/ecosocdev/geninfo/afrec

United Nations Security Council Subsidiary Organs. (2017). *Sanctions list materials.* Retrieved December 9, 2017, from https://scsanctions.un.org/fop/fop?xml=htdocs/resources/xml/en/consolidated.xml&xslt=htdocs/resources/xsl/en/al-qaida.xsl

Unyolo, T. (2012). *Building Consumer mobile money adoption and trust in conditions where infrastructure are unreliable* (Unpublished MBA Thesis). Gordon Institute of Business Science, University of Pretoria.

URT. (2013). *Tanzania SME Development Policy 2003: "ten years after.* Implementation Review.

Utting, P. (2001). Regulatory business via multistakeholder initiatives: A preliminary assessment paper prepared under the United Nations Research Institute for Social Development (UNRISD) research project "Promoting Corporate Environmental and Social Responsibility in Developing Countries: The Potential and Limits of Voluntary Initiatives.

Vallacher, R.R., & Kaufman, J. (1996). Dynamics of action identification: Volatility and structure in the mental representation of behavior.

Van Biljon, J., & Renaud, K. (2008). Predicting technology acceptance and adoption by the elderly : a qualitative study.

van Biljon, J., & Kotzé, P. (2007). Modelling the Factors That Influence Mobile Phone Adoption, In *Proceedings of the 2007 Annual Research Conference of the South African Institute of Computer Scientists and Information Technologists on IT Research in Developing Countries, SAICSIT '07* (pp. 152-161). New York, NY: ACM. doi:10.1145/1292491.1292509

Van de Ven, A. H., & Delbecq, A. L. (1974). A task contingent model of work-unit structure. *Administrative Science Quarterly, 19*(2), 183–197. doi:10.2307/2393888

Vandoros, S. (2013). My five pounds are not as good as yours, so I will spend them. *Experimental Economics, 16*(4), 546–559. doi:10.1007/s10683-013-9351-2

Vasileiadis, A. (2014). Security Concerns and Trust in the Adoption of M-Commerce. *Social Technologies, 4*(1), 179–191. doi:10.13165/ST-14-4-1-12

Venkatakrishnan, V. (2014). Mobile phones and micro and small enterprises (mse) performance and transformation in Dodoma, Tanzania. In *Proceedings of the REPOA's 19th Annual Research Workshop.* Retrieved 3.14.16 from www.repoa.or.tz/documents/S1G2014.doc

Venkatesh, V. (2000). Determinants of perceived ease of use: Integrating control, intrinsic motivation, and emotion into the technology figure acceptance model. *Information Systems Research, 11*(4), 342–365. doi:10.1287/isre.11.4.342.11872

Venkatesh, V., & Davis, F. D. (2000). A theoretical extension of the technology acceptance model: Four longitudinal field studies. *Management Science*, *46*(2), 186–204. doi:10.1287/mnsc.46.2.186.11926

Venkatesh, V., Morris, M. G., Davis, G. B., & Davis, F. D. (2003). User acceptance of information technology: Toward a unified view. *Management Information Systems Quarterly*, *27*(3), 425–478. doi:10.2307/30036540

Venkatesh, V., Thong, J. Y. L., & Xu, X. (2012). Consumer acceptance and use of information technology: Extending the Unified Theory of Acceptance and use of technology. *Management Information Systems Quarterly*, *36*(1), 157–178.

Venkatesh, V., Thong, J. Y., & Xu, X. (2012). Consumer acceptance and use of information technology: Extending the unified theory of acceptance and use of technology. *Management Information Systems Quarterly*, *36*(1), 157–178.

Venkatesh, V., & Zhang, X. (2010). Unified theory of acceptance and use of technology: US vs. China. *Journal of Global Information Technology Management*, *13*(1), 5–27. doi:10.1080/1097198X.2010.10856507

Verhoef, P. C., Franses, P. H., & Hoekstra, J. C. (2002). The effect of relational constructs on customer referrals and number of services purchased from a multiservice provider: Does age of relationship matter? *Journal of the Academy of Marketing Science*, *30*(3), 202–216. doi:10.1177/0092070302303002

Verplanken, B., & Orbell, S. (2003). Reflections of past behavior: A self-report index of habit strenght. *Journal of Applied Social Psychology*, *33*(6), 1313–1330. doi:10.1111/j.1559-1816.2003.tb01951.x

Vijaya Kumar, P. D. R., & Ravichandran, T. (2013). A Real Time Multimedia Streaming in Mobile Ad Hoc Networks using Multicast Tree Structure. *Research Journal of Information Technology*, *5*(1), 24–34.

Vinzi, V. E., Trinchera, L., & Amato, S. (2010). *PLS path modeling: From foundations to recent developments and open issues for model assessment and improvement. In Handbook of Partial Least Squares* (pp. 47–82). Springer.

Von Mulert, J., Weich, I., & Seah, W. K. G. (2012). Security threats and solutions in MANETs: A case study using AODV and SAODV. *Journal of Network and Computer Applications, Elsevier*, *35*(4), 1249–1259. doi:10.1016/j.jnca.2012.01.019

Walczuch, R., & Lundgren, H. (2004). Psychological antecedents of institution-based consumer' trust in e-retailing. *Information & Management*, *42*(1), 159–177. doi:10.1016/j.im.2003.12.009

Walsh, S. P., White, K. M., Cox, S., & Young, R. M. (2011). Keeping in constant touch: The predictors of young Australians' mobile phone involvement. *Computers in Human Behavior*, *27*(1), 333–342. doi:10.1016/j.chb.2010.08.011

Wamuyu, P. K. (2016). Promoting savings among low income earners in Kenya through mobile money. In IST-Africa Week Conference.

Wang, D., Zheng, X., Law, R., & Tang, P. K. (2015). Accessing hotel-related smartphone apps using online reviews. *Journal of Hospitality Marketing & Management.*

Wang, Y.-M., Wang, Y.-S., & Yang, Y.-F. (2010). Understanding the determinants of RFID adoption in the manufacturing industry. *Technological Forecasting and Social Change, 77*(5), 803–815. doi:10.1016/j.techfore.2010.03.006

Warshaw, P. R. (1980). A new model for predicting behavioral intentions: An alternative to Fishbein. *JMR, Journal of Marketing Research, 17*(2), 153–172. doi:10.2307/3150927

Webster, J., & Martocchio, J. J. (1992). Microcomputer playfulness: Development of a measure with workplace implications. *Management Information Systems Quarterly, 16*(2), 201–226. doi:10.2307/249576

Wei, T. T., Marthandan, G., Chong, A. Y. L., Ooi, K. B., & Arumugam, S. (2009). What drives Malaysian M-commerce adoption? An empirical analysis. *Industrial Management & Data Systems, 109*(3), 370–388. doi:10.1108/02635570910939399

Welvu. (2017, May 30). *Ebola Provider and Patient Education App – Free Download.* Retrieved from http://www.welvu.com/

Wemakor, J. K. (2014, December 19). *The Impact of Mobile Financial Services on Ghana's Economy. How relevant?* Joy Business. Retrieved March 29th, 2017, from http://m.myjoyonline.com/marticles/business/the-impact-of-mobile-financial-services-on-ghanas-economy-how-relevant

Wesolowski, A., Buckee, C. O., Bengtsson, L., Wetter, E., Lu, X., & Tatem, A. J. (2014). Commentary: Containing the Ebola outbreak–the potential and challenge of mobile network data. *PLOS currents outbreaks.*

West, D. M. (2013). Improving health care through mobile medical devices and sensors. *Brookings Institution Policy Report, 10*, 1–13.

West, D. M. (2015). *Using mobile technology to improve maternal health and fight Ebola: A case study of mobile innovation in Nigeria.* CFTI.

Wetzels, M., Odekerken-Schroder, G., & Oppen, C. V. (2009). Using PLS path modeling for assessing hierarchical construct models: Guidelines and empirical illustration. *Management Information Systems Quarterly, 33*(1), 177–195. doi:10.2307/20650284

Wheeler, S. (2000). The Role of the Teacher in the use of ICT. In *Proceedings of National Czech Teachers Conference.* Czech Republic: University of Western Bohemia.

Whittaker, J. D. (2004). *Terrorists and terrorism in the contemporary world.* London: Routledge.

Williams, H. J. (2007). *Introduction to business.* New York: Harper Collins Publishers.

Wolfe, C. M., Hamblion, E. L., Schulte, J., Williams, P., Koryon, A., Enders, J., ... Fallah, M. (2017). Ebola virus disease contact tracing activities, lessons learned and best practices during the Duport Road outbreak in Monrovia, Liberia, November 2015. *PLoS Neglected Tropical Diseases*, *11*(6), e0005597. doi:10.1371/journal.pntd.0005597 PMID:28575034

Wong, C. H., Tan, G. W. H., Loke, S. P., & Ooi, K. B. (2014). Mobile TV: A new form of entertainment? *Industrial Management & Data Systems*, *114*(7), 1050–1067. doi:10.1108/IMDS-05-2014-0146

Wong, G., & Kobinger, G. P. (2015). Backs against the Wall: Novel and Existing Strategies Used during the 2014-2015 Ebola Virus Outbreak. *Clinical Microbiology Reviews*, *28*(3), 593–601. doi:10.1128/CMR.00014-15 PMID:25972518

World Bank. (2015). World Bank and IMF launch joint initiatives to support developing countries in strengthening tax systems. Retrieved from http://www.worldbank.org/en/news/press-release/2015/07/10/world-bank-and-the-imf-lauch-joint-initiative-to-support-developing-countries-in-strengthening-tax-systems

World Health Organization Regional Office for Africa Brazzaville. (2014a). *Contact tracing during an outbreak of Ebola virus disease.*

World Health Organization. (2014). *Case definition recommendations for Ebola or Marburg Virus Diseases.*

Wosu, E., & Agwanwo, D. E. (2014). Boko haram insurgency and national security challenges in Nigeria: An analysis of a failed state. *Global Journal of Human-Social Science*, *14*(7), 10–19.

Wu, Y. L., Tao, Y. H., & Yang, P. C. (2007, December). *Using UTAUT to explore the behaviour of 3G mobile communication users.* Paper presented at the Industrial Engineering and Engineering Management (IEEE, 2007) International Conference, Singapore.

Wu, G., Hu, X., & Wu, Y. (2010). Effects of perceived interactivity, perceived web assurance and disposition to trust on initial online trust. *Journal of Computer-Mediated Communication*, *16*(1), 1–26. doi:10.1111/j.1083-6101.2010.01528.x

Wu, J. H., & Wang, S. C. (2005). What drives mobile commerce?: An empirical evaluation of the revised technology acceptance model. *Information & Management*, *42*(5), 719–729. doi:10.1016/j.im.2004.07.001

Wu, W. W. (2011). Developing an explorative model for SaaS adoption. *Expert Systems with Applications*, *38*(2), 15057–15064. doi:10.1016/j.eswa.2011.05.039

Xu, X. (2014). *Understanding Users' Continued Use of Online Games: An Application of UTAUT2 in Social Network Games.* Paper presented at the Sixth International Conferences on Advances in Multimedia.

Yakub, J. O., Bello, H. T., & Adenuga, I. A. (2013). Mobile money services in Nigeria: An inquiry of existing models. *International Journal of Economics and Management Sciences*, *2*(9), 94–105.

Yakub, J. O., Bello, H. T., & Adenuga, I. A. (2013). Mobile Money Services in Nigeria: An inquiry of existing Models. *International Journal of Economics and Management Sciences, 2*(9), 94–105.

Yang, H. (2013). Bon appétit for apps: Young American consumers' acceptance of mobile applications. *Journal of Computer Information Systems, 53*(3), 85–96. doi:10.1080/08874417.2013.11645635

Yang, K. (2010). Determinants of US consumer mobile shopping services adoption: Implications for designing mobile shopping services. *Journal of Consumer Marketing, 27*(3), 262–270. doi:10.1108/07363761011038338

Yang, K. (2012). Consumer technology traits in determining mobile shopping adoption: An application of the extended theory of planned behavior. *Journal of Retailing and Consumer Services, 19*(5), 484–491. doi:10.1016/j.jretconser.2012.06.003

Yang, S. (2013). Understanding Undergraduate Students' Adoption of Mobile Learning Model: A Perspective of the Extended UTAUT2. *Journal of Convergence Information Technology, 8*(10).

Ye, J., Dobson, S., & McKeever, S. (2012). Situation identification techniques in pervasive computing: A review. *Pervasive and Mobile Computing, 8*(1), 36–66. doi:10.1016/j.pmcj.2011.01.004

Yeoh, S. K., & Chan, B. Y. F. (2011). Internet Banking Adoption in Kuala Lumpur: An Application of UTAUT Model. *International Journal of Business and Management, 6*(4), 161–167.

Yi, M., Jackson, J., Park, J., & Probst, J. (2006). Understanding information technology acceptance by individual professionals: Toward an integrative view. *Information & Management, 43*(3), 350–363. doi:10.1016/j.im.2005.08.006

Yoon, C., & Kim, S. (2007). Convenience and TAM in a ubiquitous computing environment: The case of wireless LAN. *Electronic Commerce Research and Applications, 6*(1), 102–112. doi:10.1016/j.elerap.2006.06.009

Yu, C. S. (2012). Factors affecting individuals to adopt mobile banking: Empirical evidence from the UTAUT model. *Journal of Electronic Commerce Research, 13*(2), 104.

Yu, C. S. (2012). Factors affecting individuals to adopt mobile banking: Empirical evidence from the UTUAT model. *Journal of Electronic Commerce Research, 13*(2), 104–121.

Yueh, H.-P., Lu, M.-H., & Lin, W. (2015). Employees' acceptance of mobile technology in a workplace: An empirical study using SEM and fsQCA. *Journal of Business Research.*

Yunus, F. M., Khan, S., Tasnuba, T., Husain, P. A., & Misiti, A. J. (2016). Are we ready to adopt mobile money in non-profit sector? *Journal of Innovation and Entrepreneurship, 5*(1), 32. doi:10.1186/s13731-016-0060-x

Zalman, A. (2017). *Types of terrorism: A guide to different types of terrorism.* Retrieved December 6, 2017, from https://www.thoughtco.com/types-of-terrorism-3209376

Zenn, J. (2013). Ansaru: A profile of Nigeria's newest jihadist movement. *Terrorism Monitor, In-Depth Analysis of the War on Terror, 11*(1), 7–9.

Zhang, L., Zhu, J., & Liu, Q. (2012). A meta-analysis of mobile commerce adoption and the moderating effect of culture. *Computers in Human Behavior, 28*(5), 1902–1911. doi:10.1016/j. chb.2012.05.008

Zhou, T. (2008, August). *Exploring mobile user acceptance based on UTAUT and contextual offering.* Paper presented at the International Symposium on Electronic Commerce and Security, Guangzhou City. doi:10.1109/ISECS.2008.10

Zhou, T., Lu, Y., & Wang, B. (2010). Integrating TTF and UTAUT to explain mobile banking user adoption. *Computers in Human Behavior, 26*(4), 760–767. doi:10.1016/j.chb.2010.01.013

Zhu, F., Carpenter, S., & Kulkarni, A. (2012). Understanding identity exposure in pervasive computing (Marinagi, Belsis, & Skourlas, 2013) environments. *Pervasive and Mobile Computing, 8*(5), 777–794. doi:10.1016/j.pmcj.2011.06.007

Zhu, Q. (2011). A Mobile Ad Hoc Networks Algorithm Improved AODV Protocol. *Procedia Engineering, 23*, 229–234. doi:10.1016/j.proeng.2011.11.2494

About the Contributors

Fredrick Mtenzi's research interests include designing secure mobile micropayment transactions in low-end mobile devices, design of robust protocols for gathering online evidence and investigations, cyber security, security auditing, techniques for improving predictive protection in cyber security, and security metrics development. Recently he has been working on developing de-identification strategies which will increase the utility and privacy of sensitive information in the era of big data. Specifically, these de-identification strategies are used in increasing the sharing of electronic healthcare records.

George S. Oreku is an associate research Professor of Applied E-commerce Security and Information Systems. Oreku's research interests include Information Security, Sensor Networks Security, cybercrime, Cyber Security, risks assessment of technology-enabled information, Mobile Banking, electronic and mobile commerce (emC), applied information systems and its integrations to R&D. He is also interested in development of culturally sensitive educational models (South Africa, Ireland, China and Tanzania). He serves as a Chairman of review committee National Council for Technical Education (NACTE), Tanzania, International Board Member of Advisory to African Institute of Policy (API) Kenya and Affiliated Professor with University of Eastern Finland (UEF). He is a team member of the Ubiquitous Computing Research Group (UCRG) at the School of Computing, Dublin Institute of Technology, Al-Zaytoonah University, Amman Jordan and North West University South Africa. He has worked as a lecturer and supervised a number of PhD and Masters Students in several Universities nationally and internationally. Professor Oreku has organized and chaired peer-reviewed international conferences and workshops in Computer Security. He is a reviewer in many International Journals and Conferences as well and a professional member of Association for Computing Machinery (ACM), IEEE, IEEE Technical Committee and Information Systems Security Association (ISSA), SANORD, ERB and WASET.

Dennis Lupiana has chaired and been a member of a number of technical committees for organizing international academic conferences. He has been a reviewer and an editor of a number of international journals and conferences. He has been involved as a Lecturer and an internal examiner by local and international higher learning institutions. Dennis Lupiana received his PhD (2015) in Context-Aware Systems from Dublin Institute of Technology, Ireland. In 2008, he received MSc in Computing (Knowledge Management) from Dublin Institute of Technology, Ireland with first class. He holds Advanced Diploma in Information Technology (2005) from the Institute of Finance Management. He also holds Full Technician Certificate (FTC) in Electronics and Telecommunications Engineering (2002) from the Dar es Salaam Institute of Technology.

* * *

Joseph K. Adjei is a Senior Lecturer and the Dean of School of Technology, Ghana Institute of Management and Public Administration (GIMPA). Joseph holds a PhD in Information Systems from Aalborg University, Denmark, and MSc in Advanced Information Technology from LSBU, UK. He is a fellow of Association of Chartered Certified Accountants. His research focuses on the development of better frameworks for implementation of Trusted Digital Identity Management Systems, Mobile Financial Services and the use of Social Media and Cloud Computing. His previous research activities have been published in reputable journals and conference proceedings.

Anthony K. Adusei is a young committed lecturer with over 9 years of experience from two of the leading Private Universities in Ghana, teaching students from various social and cultural backgrounds. Possessing excellent administrative, verbal communication and written skills along with constructive and effective teaching methods that promote a stimulating learning environment. He has the ability to work effectively as a team member or independently and has a proven ability to successfully work to tight schedules and deadlines. Anthony is also an entrepreneur with the aim of establishing a business of my own in the future to contribute to the general development of my community and to help reduce unemployment, He is currently working on a mobile project called siesiemame.com. Adusei completed his master degree with Lulea Technology University, Sweden and undergraduate degree from Wisconsin International University College. His research interest is into computer criminology, Knowledge Management, policy design and implementation and cyber law and security.

Yakup Akgül was born on March 22, 1977. He studied Department of Information Management at the university of Hacettepe, Ankara (Turkey), from which he graduated in 2001. He received Masters (2010) and Ph.D. (2015) in Business Administration at Süleyman Demirel University, Isparta, Turkey. He works as an Assistant Professor at the Alanya Alaaddin Keykubat University, Alanya/Antalya, Turkey.

Benjamin Enahoro Assay teaches mass communication at Delta State Polytechnic, Ogwashi-Uku, Nigeria. He holds BA and MA degrees in mass communication from Delta State University, Abraka and University of Nigeria, Nsukka respectively. Assay is on the verge of being awarded a doctorate degree in mass communication by the Benue State University, Makurdi, Nigeria. He has published articles in scholarly journals and contributed chapters in several books locally and internationally. His research interests cover areas such as information and communication technology and national development; international communication and comparative media studies, media, democracy and good governance, population and health communication, and public relations and advertising. He is a member of several professional bodies, including African Council for Communication Education (ACCE) Nigeria chapter, Advertising Practitioners Council of Nigeria (APCON), Association of Communication Scholars and Professionals of Nigeria (ACSPN), Nigeria Institute of Public Relations (NIPR), Association for Promoting Nigerian Languages and Culture (APNILAC), National Association for Research Development (NARD), among others.

Donald Atsa'am is a Computer Science lecturer with the University of Agriculture, Makurdi, Nigeria. He holds a B.Tech (Hons) and an M.Sc in Computer Science. Donald is currently running a Ph.D programme in Applied Mathematics and Computer Science at the Eastern Mediterranean University, Famagusta, North Cyprus. His research interests are in Data Mining, Machine Learning, and Multi Agent Systems. Donald is happily married to Doose and blessed with a son, Torbem.

Hope Ayuba holds a B.Tech. degree in Computer Science from Modibbo Adama University of Technology, Yola. His main research interests are related to Information System design and Mobile applications.

Gordian Bwemelo joined the College of Business Education in 2009 as an Assistant Lecturer in Marketing after earning a Master Degree in Business Administration from the University of Dar es Salaam. While teaching marketing related courses at certificate, diploma and bachelor degree levels, he has been conducting research and consulting services in various business enterprises. Bwemelo has managed to publish some academic papers and would like to further his interest in sharing his knowledge through publications and consultancy.

Kwetishe Joro Danjuma is a PhD Candidate and holds a Lecturing position in Computer Science at the Modibbo Adama University of Technology, Yola, Nigeria. His research interest focuses on data mining and machine learning in healthcare. His other research interests include data science, and information and communication technology for development (ICT4D).

Samuel Nii Odoi Devine works at the Faculty of Science and Technology in Presbyterian University College, Ghana. He holds a B.Sc. degree in ICT and M.Sc. degree in IT. He is a researcher, writer and avid speaker with a strong affinity for computers, and has been involved in several software projects as a consultant in the integration of information systems into the operations of a number of organizations. His research areas include Big Data, Machine Learning, Natural Language Processing, Knowledge Management and Information Security.

Alev Kocak Alan, Ph.D., is an assistant professor in Department of Business Administration at Gebze Tchnical University since 2009. She received her PhD degree at GIT. Her studies focus on consumer behavioural, retail marketing and experiential marketing. Her researches has been published in several scholarly journals including in Service Business, The Service Industries, and in numerous Turkish-language scholarly journals.

Emmanuel Awuni Kolog received his PhD in Computer science from the University of Eastern Finland. Emmanuel also holds a Master degree in Business Administration (MBA) from the Lapland University of Applied sciences in Finland where he specialized in the International business management. After he graduated from his PhD, he has since been affiliated to the School of computing of the University of Eastern Finland. Emmanuel's research interest is multidisciplinary which is basically centered in the fields of Computer science and Business management. Specifically, his research interests span the areas of Natural language processing, Computational linguistics, Machine learning applications, Educational technology, ICT4D and Mobile learning. His other research areas include Business intelligence, Knowledge and innovation management and International business strategies.

Teemu H. Laine received a PhD in Computer Science from the University of Eastern Finland in 2012. His current research as an Associate Professor at the Luleå University of Technology focuses on context-aware games for education and well-being. His other research interests include educational technology, context-aware system architectures, context modeling and inference, and ICT for development.

Renatus Mushi is a lecturer in the Department of Computer Science at the Institute of Finance Management (IFM), Tanzania. Currently, he is a PhD student at Dublin Institute of Technology (DIT), Ireland. His area of expertise is technology acceptance, focusing on the best use of mobile phone technology in the SMEs.

Sunday Adewale Olaleye had a Master of Science in Information Systems from the Abo Akademi University, Turku, Finland, MBA, International Business Management, Lapland University of Applied Sciences, Tornio, Finland and Nordic Master School in Innovative ICT (NMS iICT Certificate), University of Turku, School of Economics, Finland. Currently doing his doctoral studies at the Department of Marketing, Oulu Business School, Finland. He has presented papers at conferences and published in academic journals. His research interests are Emerging Mobile Technologies, Mobile Commerce and Mobile Apps.

Olayemi Olawumi received a PhD in Computer Science from the University of Eastern Finland. He currently works in Technology Risk and Compliance at ICON Clinical Research Limited in Dublin. Recently he has been working on secure data transmission technique on wireless interfaces using steganography and cryptography. His primary research interests include Computer Networks & Security, Wireless Security, Smart Homes, Data Loss Prevention and Computational Intelligence.

Elisha Sunday Oyelere is a medical doctor with over 13 years experience in clinical practice in Nigeria, West Africa and has been involved in management of common tropical and infectious diseases and their complications. He is currently a PhD candidate at the Obafemi Awolowo University, Ile-Ife, Nigeria while holding a lecturer position at the department of pharmacology, University of Medical Sciences, Ondo, Nigeria.

Solomon Sunday Oyelere holds an early stage researcher position and PhD candidate at University of Eastern Finland. His research interests are in the fields of mobile and interactive computing, computer science education and mobile robots. He has several years of experience as a Lecturer in Computer Science at Modibbo Adama University of Technology, Yola-Nigeria and Dorben Polytechnic Abuja-Nigeria.

Chandan Kumar Panda is a young academician and researcher in the subject area of extension education and allied disciplines. Presently, he is an Assistant Professor (Extension Education) in Bihar Agricultural University, Sabour. He has six years of teaching, research and extension experiences. Dr. Panda had published one book. He had published 25 research papers in national and international peer reviewed journals and also contributed 12 book chapters in edited volume. He had attended 15 national and 4 international seminars/conferences etc. in his credit. He has successfully guided one Post Graduate Student as Major Advisor and three Post Graduate Students as Co-Advisor. He had successfully completed one national research project as Principal Investigator(PI) and continuing two research projects as PI. Dr. Panda is also recipient of Young Scientist Award. His areas of interest are HRM in agriculture, ICT in Agricultural Extension, Developing Indicators for Monitoring and Evaluation of Social Science Research.

Mamata Rath is currently Assistant Professor at Dept. of Information Technology, C.V. Raman College of Engineering, Bhubaneswar, India. Her research interests include Wireless Networks, Internet of Things (IoT), Computer Security, Smart Applications, Real Time Systems, E-commerce & ERP. She has around 30 number of good quality research publications in the area of Mobile Ad-hoc networks, Real time Applications, Smart Applications for Smart City and Internet of Things in good journals with high impact and internationally reputed conferences. She has been part of few good international conferences and acted as reviewer in few selected international journals.

Ismaila Temitayo Sanusi is a PhD student at the Philosophical Faculty, University of Eastern Finland. His research interest is in Mobile Technologies, ICT in Education, Entrepreneurship and TVET. He has presented papers at conferences and published in academic journals.

Jarkko Suhonen holds a research manager position at the School of Computing, University of Eastern Finland. He received his MSc from University of Joensuu, Finland in 2000 and his PhD from University of Joensuu in 2005. Dr. Suhonen has published over 80 peer-reviewed articles in scientific journals, conferences, workshops and chapters of books. His research interests include online and blended learning, design in educational technology and computing education. Dr. Suhonen is a coordinator of the IMPDET-LE, online doctoral programme at University of Eastern Finland. He serves on committees for international conferences and special issues of journals, and acts as a reviewer in several scientific journals.

Samuel Tweneboah holds a BSc degree in science education from the University of Education, Winneba and an MSc degree in Photonics from the University of Eastern Finland. His primary research is in the area of technology enhanced teaching and learning, especially in developing countries. He is currently doing an MSc in learning and education technology at the University of Oulu, Finland. He is always looking out for new ways of improving classroom teaching and learning via the use of digital technology.

Dandison C. Ukpabi is a Doctoral Student in the Digital Marketing and Communication Research Group of the University of Jyväskylä, Finland. He has presented papers in the Bled eConference and the European Marketing Academy Conference (EMAC). His research interest focuses on e-tourism, digital marketing and social media, relationship marketing and marketing strategy.

Index

U

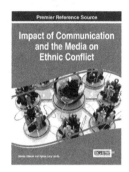

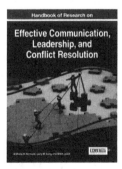

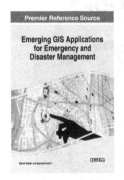
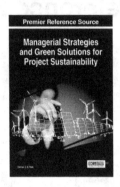

Information Resources Management Association

Advancing the Concepts & Practices of Information Resources Management in Modern Organizations

EST. 1987

Become an IRMA Member

Members of the **Information Resources Management Association (IRMA)** understand the importance of community within their field of study. The Information Resources Management Association is an ideal venue through which professionals, students, and academicians can convene and share the latest industry innovations and scholarly research that is changing the field of information science and technology. Become a member today and enjoy the benefits of membership as well as the opportunity to collaborate and network with fellow experts in the field.

IRMA Membership Benefits:

- **One FREE Journal Subscription**
- **30% Off Additional Journal Subscriptions**
- **20% Off Book Purchases**
- Updates on the latest events and research on Information Resources Management through the IRMA-L listserv.
- Updates on new open access and downloadable content added to Research IRM.
- A copy of the Information Technology Management Newsletter twice a year.
- A certificate of membership.

IRMA Membership $195

Scan code or visit **irma-international.org** and begin by selecting your free journal subscription.

Membership is good for one full year.